UNIVERSITY OF NORTH CAROLINA AT CHAPEL HILL
DEPARTMENT OF ROMANCE LANGUAGES

NORTH CAROLINA STUDIES
IN THE ROMANCE LANGUAGES AND LITERATURES

Founder: URBAN TIGNER HOLMES
Editor: FRANK A. DOMÍNGUEZ

Distributed by:

UNIVERSITY OF NORTH CAROLINA PRESS

CHAPEL HILL
North Carolina 27515-2288
U.S.A.

NORTH CAROLINA STUDIES IN THE
ROMANCE LANGUAGES AND LITERATURES
Number 285

JACQUES ROUBAUD
AND THE INVENTION OF MEMORY

JACQUES ROUBAUD
AND THE
INVENTION OF MEMORY

BY
JEAN-JACQUES F. POUCEL

CHAPEL HILL

NORTH CAROLINA STUDIES IN THE ROMANCE
LANGUAGES AND LITERATURES
U.N.C. DEPARTMENT OF ROMANCE LANGUAGES

2006

Library of Congress Cataloging-in-Publication Data

Poucel, Jean-Jacques.
    Jacques Roubaud and the invention of memory / by Jean-Jacques F. Poucel.
    p. cm. – (North Carolina studies in the Romance languages and literatures ; no. 285).
    Based on the author's thesis (Ph. D. – University of Colorado at Boulder, 1998) presented under the title: Memory, tradition and innovation in the work of Jacques Roubaud.
    Includes bibliographical references and index.
    ISBN 978-0-8078-9289-3
    1. Roubaud, Jacques–Criticism and interpretation. I. Title.

PQ2678.O77Z78 2006
843'.914–dc22   2006048334

Cover design: Heidi Perov

© 2006. Department of Romance Languages. The University of North Carolina at Chapel Hill.

DEPÓSITO LEGAL: V. 4.949 - 2006

ARTES GRÁFICAS SOLER, S. L. - LA OLIVERETA, 28 - 46018 VALENCIA
www.graficas-soler.com

CONTENTS

	Page
ACKNOWLEDGEMENTS	9
PREFACE	11
ABBREVIATIONS	19
CHAPTER ONE: A TROUBALDIAN POETICS	21
Trobar	23
Nostalgia, Volitional Archaism, and Resistance	25
Unity of the Grand Chant	31
Abstract Rhythm Theory	34
Fin'amors	37
Axioms	38
Le Néant, Memory and the Trobar Clus: Entrebescar	42
Estribot	51
CHAPTER TWO: CRISTAL DU TROBAR: "TOMBEAUX DE PÉTRARQUE"	56
The Extreme Contemporary: *Quenines* and "Tombeaux de Pétrarque"	60
Quenines	63
"Tombeaux de Pétrarque"	65
Rime sparse	68
CHAPTER THREE: $\in$: SONNET OF SONNETS, AN OPEN SET	91
CHAPTER FOUR: CONSTRAINT AND READING IN *TRENTE ET UN AU CUBE*	118
Ou vivions nous?	137

	Page
CHAPTER FIVE: THE WRITING OF LIFESTYLE: *AUTOBIOGRAPHIE, CHAPITRE DIX*	148
CHAPTER SIX: DEATH, MOURNING, ELEGY: *QUELQUE CHOSE NOIR*	174
CHAPTER SEVEN: METAFICTIONAL PLAY IN *LA BELLE HORTENSE*	199
CHAPTER EIGHT: MEMORY, DESTRUCTION, AND PRESENCE: RE-CREATION IN '*LE GRAND INCENDIE DE LONDRES*'	219
BIBLIOGRAPHY	253
TOMBEAUX DE PÉTRARQUE	277
INDEX	281

ACKNOWLEDGEMENTS

OVER the course of the years it took for this book to arrive I have benefited from the kind help of many people, each of whom I hereby publicly thank: Pierre Wassef, for handing me *Quelque Chose Noir*; Jacques Jouet, for providing rare documents in the early stages of research; Chris Braider, Andy Cowell, Ned Duval, Sydney Lévy, Chuck Porter, and an anonymous reader for their attentive and critical remarks at different stages of the writing process; Daniel Levin Becker, Cyndy Brown, and Karen Gangel for their care in helping prepare the manuscript for publication; Frank Domínguez and the staff of UNCSRLL, for their professionalism. Some expenses related to the publication of this book have been defrayed by The Frederick W. Hilles Publication Fund awarded by the Yale Whitney Humanities Center Council of Fellows; for this I am also grateful.

Certain personal conversations have played an especially important role in the development of my thinking during this project. In particular, I appreciate the generous remarks of my colleagues Ann Smock, Monika Laskowski-Caujolle and Peter Consenstein, as well as the encouragement I received from Marcel Bénabou, Denise and Pierre Getzler, Jacques Jouet, and Jacques Roubaud; for me, these conversations remain among the most enlightening and exhilarating. I am thankful, too, for the support, inspiration and insight provided to me by a small host of dear friends, each of whom has shared and deepened my appreciation for poetry: Richard Deming, Nancy Kuhl, Abigail Lang, Warren Motte, and Cole Swensen. I am especially indebted to Warren Motte who, before serving as my doctoral thesis advisor, played a pivotal role in helping me discover French literature as an undergraduate student.

Finally, and above all, I would like to thank my parents, to whom I dedicate this book, and Marita Kheim, whose companionship and love have sustained and improved me.

PREFACE

SINCE 1967, Jacques Roubaud has been methodically transforming the landscape of French literature. A poet, novelist, translator, playwright, essayist, and editor, Roubaud is an active member of the Oulipo or *Ouvroir de Littérature Potentielle* (The Workshop for Potential Literature). An expert in both mathematics and literature, Roubaud has systematically elaborated a poetics of experiment sharply focused on inventing new forms of literary expression.

Though varied in subject matter and form, each of his numerous compositions participates in a comprehensive literary master plan he calls the *Projet*. Initially conceiving this ambitious program in 1961, Roubaud has now invested more than forty-four years of his life in the invention, clarification, and transformation of a poetics rooted in mathematics and poetry. That Roubaud has imagined, elaborated, and then consistently worked toward completing this extended literary project stands as an invitation to consider his work as a coherent oeuvre, one that recalls–not without some irony–the great works of the nineteenth century.

In an age that postulates the end of literature and the beginning of *écriture*, it may appear anachronistic to consider the unifying poetics of a single author. Twentieth-century literary studies have deemphasized the value of the oeuvre as product in order to celebrate the process of literature as a collaborative creative act. This shift in emphasis grounds the self-reflexive concerns of aesthetics in the concrete material of art–which, for literature, means language. In French literature, explicitly since Mallarmé, the play between literary process and totality is articulated in the question of the Book, and its relation to the world. The invention of a unifying poetic process, such as the one implicitly inscribed in Roubaud's *Projet*, further interrogates the tension between process and completion, between *l'écriture* and *l'oeuvre*.

What is a Roubaldian poetics? Plainly stated, it is a strategy by which a methodical memory of tradition becomes the basis of literary innovation. Two imperatives ground Roubaud's overall poetics. The first, borrowed from Raymond Queneau and François Le Lionnais, the co-founders of the Oulipo, is the decision to comport oneself toward language as if it could be mathematized. Largely modeled after a transposition of Bourbakian axiomatic method as a means of thinking about and composing literature, various modes of counting subtend Roubaud's critical and creative methodology. That is, Roubaud approaches language as a series of numbers, as families of forms, whose connectivity becomes the architecture of his memory and his innovative techniques. The second precept underlying his poetics, purportedly borrowed from Octavio Paz, is the imperative to adopt an attitude of homage and profanation toward literary tradition. Revising, recollecting and rewriting tradition–all fundaments of extending innovation–requires both a respect for and battle with literary tradition. Although different in nature, these two approaches to literature have fueled Roubaud's poetic project for more than forty years; they are axiomatic to his poetics. As will become clear with the more complex definition of Roubaud's *Projet*, his is a poetics based on a systematic reading and rewriting of literary history, in particular, the history of the lyric as form, and as formal memory of language.

The conceptual theory uniting his poetics begins with this definition of literature: "*Poetry is the memory of language*" (M9 23). By imagining and articulating a continuous and transformative reciprocity between literature and language, this hypothesis funds an investigation of the dialogic relationship among language, personal memory, collective memory, and history. Several remarks are pertinent here. First, like the Russian Formalists whose work he is furthering, Roubaud aspires to an inclusive theory of literature, one that might be applied to all languages and forms: Roubaldian poetics postulates, at least in theory, the possibility of totality–and that totality would be subsumed under the double aegis of mathematics and poetry. Second, echoing the reciprocity between Saussure's "parole" and "langue," Roubaud's definition of literature as memory of language is diachronically transformational: Roubaldian poetics postulates and investigates continuity and change in literary form; be they poems, novels or works of criticism, Roubaud's writings initiate changes in experimental method. Third, the proposition that all literature is memory of language–which, for Roubaud, means all languages, as well as "the languageness of languages"–sets forth an agenda of research based on modes of abstraction and codification. That is, for Roubaud, as for Roman Jakobson, literary language can always be read as both referential and self-reflexive, so that, in answering the question What is literature?, Roubaud finds that in addition to being form-based, literature always speaks of language, or, citing John Thomson, that "whatever else I may be talking about, I am talking also about language itself" (M9 23). These liminal answers led Roubaud and his friend Pierre Lusson to develop a "Théorie du rythme abstrait" (Abstract Rhythm Theory, or ART). Which has become the basis for Roubaud's study of rhythm and its role in a poetics of memory.

Over the years, Roubaud has cultivated a sustained interest in the mnemonic aspects of poetry, specifically identifying rhythm as a central element of memory arts. In his view, poetic rhythm functions as a deep structure to language, and as such it is profoundly linked to the survival of cultural traditions and the evolution of languages and the literatures that sustain them. Memory, in his work, is a sixth sense, a living human faculty whose privileged domain is language, in the broadest possible concept of that word.

In an attempt to chart various landscapes that support literature's memory of language, Roubaud and his collaborators have pursued the following hypothesis: "Rhythm is the hierarchized, sequential combinatory of discrete events considered solely in terms of the same and the different" (M9 23). Relying on this hypothesis, Roubaud has elaborated and tested ART as a quantitative method for analyzing rhythmic developments in literary history, most prominently in his sustained study of changes in fixed form poems and verse metrics. If Roubaud's methods of rhythmic analysis are limited to formal qualities, their mathematical foundations make his approach amenable to both a generative understanding of, and a speculative incursion into, the evolution of poetic forms.

My analysis of Roubaud's work suggests that his research on rhythm helps construct the landscape of his poetic memory; it is the blueprint by which he invents and records his own literary memory. In virtually all of Roubaud's writing, the elaboration of

ART *implies* a poetics of memory based on order and unity; yet, one of the most salient features of Roubaud's work is its insistent affirmation of the impossibility of completion. Given the preference of process over product, my discussion of the *Projet* describes how his speculative approach to literary form imagines and designates new spaces where he may innovate memory through form.

Because rhythm is a primary element in poetry's mnemonic function, memorization, along with its necessary counterpart, forgetting (or destruction), is a privileged activity in Roubaud's works. His art of memory powerfully presents and reconfigures a collective and personal tradition; his work postulates that there is continuity and change in literary and linguistic developments, and that they may be traced along an interconnected and motivated chain of written occurrences. If all literature is the memory of language, and if its memory is transmitted through rhythm, then conscious literary invention depends on an understanding and strategic interruption of the chain of events embedded in the current state of language. For Roubaud, to approach the historicity of poetry with an attitude of homage and profanation is simultaneously to respect, remember, mock and reconstruct his own literary tradition, to renew and play with language as a medium of memory.

Writing under constraint–the Oulipian writing strategy deployed by Roubaud–can be read as a game that directs experimentation with the explicit goals of the invention, recollection, and transformation of tradition. In adopting particular formal constraints as techniques for composition, Roubaud consciously engages in a sustained research agenda, making his own memory of tradition the central object of study. According to this method, Oulipian constraints serve a double purpose: they lay bare key elements of form and they demonstrate how those structures may be further elaborated to create new codes of expressions. By optimizing the combinatorial elegance of his chosen forms, by demonstrating the potential diversification in the formal properties of literature, Roubaud deepens and differentiates his memory of the particular tradition in which he is working at that moment.

In fact, we might imagine his collected works as a conglomerate sphere of memory, an organic simulacrum of memory whose form is constantly shifting and whose meaning is transient and essential. That is, his work serves as a model of memory itself, sustained by the elaboration of certain tendencies and techniques: the intricate interweaving of *entrebescar*, the interdisciplinary hybridization of forms, the indefatigable drive toward differentiation and exhaustion of poetic forms. Even if this model provides the basis for a general theory of change, Roubaud's favorite poetic moments, his most concentrated areas of memory, remain fairly consistent throughout, as do his principle forms of predilection (the sonnet and the sestina). In my analysis of his works, I demonstrate how Oulipian constraints contribute to a refashioning of literary invention.

Each chapter of this book performs a close reading of one text, or a cluster of texts. Throughout, I trace the evolution of Roubaud's poetics and textual practices, including some analysis of his chosen traditions and his choice of constraint, or combination of constraints. In studying these primary works, I describe the vital coherence that inhabits Roubaud's oeuvre and show how the organizing principles of the *Projet* evolve over time. Change in Roubaud's work encourages changes in its reception. Indeed, like many of the best Oulipian works, Roubaldian writing applies pressure to the boundaries of interpretation and it forces us to imagine new modes of reading, new uses of literature.

Given the formal properties of Oulipian writing, I approach each work and the collected works as ludic enterprises. The very premise of Roubaud's work is to engage his reader's participation. In my view, the most promising horizons for innovative literature are those where reading and writing are openly cast in the terms of language games, as an oriented semiosis and a ludic epistemology. For, under the best circumstances, experimentation constructs the activity of literature as an imaginative philosophical dialogue. Such are the conditions one encounters upon opening, for example, *Trente et un au cube*, where the first fragments of the first line–"JE DETIENS MILLION de / syllabes comptées pour toi..." (*31* 9)–introduce an enduring collaboration and symbolic intercourse between author and reader.

In effect, a wide variety of language games abound in the Roubaldian corpus. For example, the game of Go provides an underlying substructure to his first major sonnet cycle, ϵ (*signe d'appartenance*) (1967); *Autobiographie, chapitre dix* designates a programmed treasure hunt through Surrealist free verse; *La belle Hortense* (1986) playfully recasts problems of detection in a poetically enriched setting; and '*le grand incendie de Londres*' (1989-present)–Roubaud's magisterial self-portrait and autoanalysis–simultaneously unveils and blurs the enigma of the *Projet*. In each case, writing presents one or more possible worlds, all of them rigorously obeying the laws Roubaud assigns and each implicitly related to the other by virtue of overlapping within the work itself.

Because gaming is an integral part of all Roubaldian texts and a fundamental condition of his overreaching *Projet*, my analysis accentuates the interactive principles at work in his poetics, without attempting to reduce or explicate. My aim is to provide a critical introduction to Roubaud's poetics, poetry, and prose, not an explanation or a set of answers for the problems they present. Many Roubaldian works offer readers multilayered constructs that are puzzles, enigmatic objects whose mysteries are both of personal import and emblazoned into the work's formal meaning. I do not offer solutions to these puzzles; rather, I describe the techniques relevant to their composition and reception.

As other readers have noted, Roubaud's work invites its audience to participate, and generously provides amusement as well as instruction at every turn. As a collected work, the *Projet* and its ruins challenge us to imagine how all of Roubaud's writing fits together, the shape it would have taken had the *Projet* not been abandoned, the numerical figure it would have designated. Even in *'le grand incendie de Londres,'* his self-analyzing prose work, where he describes the *Projet* as an ambitious, melancholic, and mathematically informed fantasy, Roubaud generously provides readers multiple ports of entry into his imaginative universe; this plurality of structures helps us marvel at and participate in the emergence and disappearance of a vertiginously self-aware meditation on memory in literature. Along the way, I have not felt obliged to understand all that is recollected in Roubaud's work. Rather, my selection of texts has been guided by my pleasure in reading Roubaud and by the imperatives that my readings have imparted.

Given that the invention of new forms is Roubaud's most powerful critical activity, I read his work as indirect criticism of contemporary poetry. In some cases, this angle is explicitly inscribed in the text; in others, it is the contract that Roubaud forges with his reader that most clearly challenges conventional practices of reading and writing. One of the problems I address in considering each work is the status of its "user's manuals," the *modes d'emploi* that are often integrated into Oulipian works. Oulipian work tends to conflate theory and literature in useful and challenging ways, often foreseeing, disarming, and over-determining the critic's gaze. This metaliterary function is an integral part of Roubaud's major works and it informs his principal critical writings, *La fleur inverse, La vieillesse d'Alexandre*, and *Poésie, etcetera: ménage*. Each of these essays integrates creative gestures, either by recounting the life of forms as a *récit formel* or by defending the merits of poetry in a Socratic dialogue. I consider Roubaud's irony toward theory–including those he espouses from the Oulipo–an important strategy in writing through the literary belatedness of his time. His self-conscious and self-effacing attention to his readers compensates for what he perceives to be the excesses of theory.

Roubaud's *Projet* necessarily inscribes the conditions of its own historicity, both in terms of its engagement with, or disengagement from, contemporary literary practices and in terms of prefiguring possible readings in years to come. Speculation on the future is a salient aspect of Roubaud's most recent prose writings, where the failure of the *Projet* is cast in a future anterior tense and where the conditions of composition simultaneously posit the impossibility of completion while prefiguring its inevitable arrival–the *Projet* very much addresses its own intentional ruin. In his constantly renewed and shifting appraisals of the *Projet*–the process of the Book as monument, as game, as autocritique, and as self-portrait–Roubaud proposes a series of endgames in which the most consistent objective is to subvert or postpone, through shifting frames of reference and multiple solutions, the inevitability of closure.

Constantly heightening the vertiginous interrelationships between his works does not prevent Roubaud from inscribing consistent imperatives into his house of mirrors. Throughout his work, he traces the decay and rebirth, the long lives and possible ends of many literary forms; he defines, theorizes, and explores human memory as literature's most important transformative faculty; and he indefatigably invents and writes new types of poems, thereby ensuring the survival, the evolution, and the diversification of the traditions he devours, adopts and condenses. The diverse stratagems that Roubaud deploys in pursuing these goals simultaneously invite and challenge readers to account for the integrity and the potential status of his *Projet*. I hope my investigation of those problems will elucidate some of the questions facing literature today, and provide a context for understanding how Roubaud invents memory as tradition, poetics as memory, and poetry as history.

ABBREVIATIONS

All citations and abbreviations refer to the bibliography. Works by Jacques Roubaud are listed by date of publication and title. Works by all other authors may be located by name and an abbreviated title. Full publication date is given in the bibliography.

∈	∈ *(signe d'appartenance)* (1967)
M	*Mono no aware* (1970)
31	*Trente et un au cube* (1973)
A	*Autobiographie, chapitre dix* (1977)
M9	*Mezura no 9: Description du Project* (1980)
T	*Les troubadours* (1980)
D	*Dors*, précédé de *Dire la poésie* (1981)
BH	*La belle Hortense* (1985)
QN	*Quelque chose noir* (1986)
FI	*La fleur inverse* (1986)
EH	*L'enlèvement d'Hortense* (1987)
GI	*'le grand incendie de Londres'* (1989)
XH	*L'exil d'Hortense* (1990)
B	*La boucle* (1992)
LP	*L'invention du fils de Léoprepes* (1993)
PM	*Poésie, etcetera: ménage* (1995)
M:	*Mathématique: (récit)* (1997)
P:	*Poésie: (récit)* (2000)
BW	*La bibliothèque de Warburg* (2003)

Also referred to in abbreviated form are the following publications:

BC	*Batôns, chiffres et lettres* (1965) Raymond Queneau
LP	*La littérature potentielle* (1973) Oulipo
ALP	*Atlas de la littérature potentielle* (1981) Oulipo
BO	*Bibliothèque Oulipienne* I, II, III Oulipo

CHAPTER ONE

A TROUBALDIAN POETICS

IN *La fleur inverse* (1986, 1994), Jacques Roubaud treats his readers to a delightful discovery of early Provençal poetry. An original and evocative study of the art of troubadour poetry, the essay complements the earlier bilingual anthology of Provençal poems, *Les troubadours* (1971), which included a critical introduction and translations by Roubaud. In addition to providing a sophisticated formal and thematic analysis of this literary model, *La fleur inverse* lays the foundations of Roubaud's personal poetics.

In order to map critical elements of that poetics, I shall outline Roubaud's reading methodology and highlight the experimental drives he prioritizes in early Occitan poetry. My intentions here are not to assess the validity of his claims, nor to account for the diverse ways troubadour poetry has influenced Roubaud's work. Rather, I am interested in showing how the *trobar* works as an important intertext for reading Roubaud. Throughout, my approach is intended to describe maneuvers that will be revisited, developed, and subsequently amplified later in this book—as in my Chapter 2, where I analyze the poem "Tombeaux de Pétrarque." At times, I address what Roubaud most admires in troubadour poetry. Elsewhere, I question how Roubaud's medieval scholarship relates to contemporary poetics, how it posits and pursues a critique of poetry today. In short, I read *La fleur inverse* as an oblique poetic manifesto, as a coded confession, and as a blueprint for Roubaud's creative agenda.

There are many approaches to describing Roubaud's poetics. As a writer, Roubaud deploys a variety of compositional strategies, frequently combining several strategies in a single work. He internalizes distant forms and foreign styles, which he then recombines or rewrites in surprisingly original ways. In his poetry, Roubaud almost exclusively works from external material used to enrich or filter his personal affect. Categorically allergic to confessional modes of lyricism, Roubaud consciously constructs voice through the use of models, many of which are intradiscursive (like those provided by Provençal, Japanese, and American poetries) and some of which are extradiscursive, taken from outside the field of literature (models adopted from mathematics and philosophy, for example). Consequently, rarely are his poems strictly personal. Instead, they nearly always address more than one topic, often directly expounding on poetic method while casting emotional freight at a slant, encoding pathos deep within self-reflexive forms. Put otherwise, in his poetry, Roubaud speaks the personal obliquely while engaging the widest conceivable variety of other topics, most often privileging literary topics and formal languages. A careful reading of both his critical and creative works must therefore account for different levels of meaning and attempt to measure the interplay between them.

To enter Roubaud's poetics by way of his criticism presents a diversity of options. One might, for example, begin with his essays on contemporary poetics, either by situating the way Surrealist free verse had flattened the postwar rhythmic landscape (*La vieillesse d'Alexandre*; 1988) or by describing how the cultural conditions of corporate-funded globalization threaten the well-being of national languages and, by extension, their contemporary poetries (*Poésie, etcetera: ménage*; 1995). Or, alternatively, one might consider Roubaud's long-standing interest in the arts of memory (*L'invention du fils de Leoprepes*; 1993) and subsequently test his use of mnemonic techniques in writing prose and poetry. Or, adopting the line he most frequently takes to present his work, one might approach Roubaud's poetics as pure Oulipian theory, an approach that would investigate how writing under constraint stimulates literary potential. In effect, all these paths are possible and indeed necessary, for each plays an important role in Roubaud's general program of reading, memorizing, and writing poetry.

However, what is at stake in Roubaud's celebration of the troubadours is what I take to be most fundamental in his entire creative project: an imperative to imagine and extend the unity of the modern poetic tradition. For Roubaud, the modern tradition begins with the troubadours and their penchant for formal innovation, and it stretches right up to the most contemporary writing, including moments of continuity and discontinuity. It is in the very manner that Roubaud reads the rise and fall of the *trobar*, in the way that he characterizes its confrontation with nothingness and its ability to overcome the threats of oblivion, that I read his most revealing statements about poetry. It is specifically that aspect of his reading that I characterize as a "tRoubaldian poetics."

TROBAR

The troubadours are perhaps most widely lauded for their invention of love, or *fin'amors*. Classically, that conception of love is loosely modeled on feudal service. It stages the lover-singer-poet pledging devotion and obedience to his beloved, his *dona*, who–often a married woman, if not the wife of the singer's lord–would not be accessible to the advances of the singer-songwriter. The implied distance and complex social circumstances surrounding this statement of love from afar–"l'amour de loin"–are the key ingredients to the flourishing of a competitive and amorous discourse in Provence.

Trobar, an Occitan word meaning "to invent" or "to find," casts the very existence of love poetry as a question, as a quest of ever renewing discovery and affirmation. Predating by seven centuries the Modernists' call to "Make it new!" the troubadours embarked on defining and realizing the ideals of a pure love, a fin'amors, through the techniques of art, through the act of trobar, or innovation. The troubadour is thus not only a *jongleur*, but also a researcher and a competitor in the game of love and love poetry. As such, trobar, in Roubaud's use of the term, refers to invention within a general discourse, within *le grand chant courtois*, the historic moment that he celebrates from afar as well as from within; trobar is as much a discourse about love and desire as it is one about poetry, about the regenerative relationship between love and language.

Until the nineteenth century the importance of the Provençal lyric was often omitted from French literary histories. Citing its marginalization for linguistic and cultural differences, Roubaud claims that for a long time the trobar teetered on the abyss of oblivion. Thanks to the work of poets like Ezra Pound (who translated and celebrated the Provençal lyric) and to critics like Paul Zumthor, in the twentieth century, troubadour poetry has enjoyed a renewed ascendancy.

In France, the revalorization of troubadour poetry was also related to new perspectives in reading. For example, scholars like Pierre Bec recast its importance among other medieval poetries by stressing its formal sophistication and its eloquent treatment of burlesque topics.[1] Like the poets of the thirteenth and fourteenth centuries, the troubadours are now renowned for giving us poems rife with polysemic wordplay, songs that are rich in puns that cross-reference erotic and the poetic exploits.[2] As a discourse on love, a theory of fin'amors, the trobar is a signifying game heightened by its social circumstance and its hermeneutic specificities. These specificities make it well suited to the heuristic techniques of structuralist semiotics; consequently, it has become a unique case study for those interested in poetic ludics, the dynamics of intertextuality, and their sociohistorical context.

In his exposition of the trobar, Roubaud eschews a sociological approach. Instead he examines how le grand chant developed its own formal art and emphasizes the aesthetic character of debates of the period. His approach stresses the importance of stylistic and poetic innovations within the trobar as discourse, focusing precisely on the inextricable relations between questions of form and the dilemmas confronting a discourse based on innovation. In *La fleur inverse*, the word trobar therefore takes on the allure of a critical term, for it designates a chimerical horizon of expectation. We might even say that trobar restates to the Oulipian pursuit of potentiality through the elaboration of traditional forms. If, in Roubaud's reading, trobar recounts a story about the life of a discourse, its plot is animated by an ethic of discovery; trobar names the challenges facing an art whose existence depends on the constant renewal of its material resources. In *La fleur inverse*, the tale of that renewal is recounted through the *life of forms*.

The most prominent form invented by the troubadours is the *canso* (song). Because Italian Renaissance poets like Cavalcanti, Dante, and Petrarch nurtured it, and because it heavily influenced developments in the European lyric, in Roubaud's reading, the can-

---

[1] See Bec, *Burlesque et obscenité*.
[2] See Kendrick, *Game of Love*.

so takes on heroic status. It is the form that both succumbs to and triumphs against the forces of erasure. Despite its historical ends, the trobar was preserved and transmitted to the present, first in the "crystallized" form of the sestina, then through the widespread proliferation of a fragmented poetic form based on the canso's strophe: the sonnet. Both particularly potential loci for experiment and innovation, these fixed forms and their histories are key sites for reading Roubaud's work. Indeed, the sonnet spans the totality of Roubaud's writing, from ϵ (*signe d'appartenance*) (1967) to *Churchill 40* (2004), and the structure of the sestina is present in much of his writing (from individual works like "Tombeaux de Pétrarque" and the *Hortense* novels to the *Projet* and how its genesis is recounted in '*le grand incendie de Londres*'). As in much of his criticism, in *La fleur inverse* Roubaud grounds his *politique de résistance* in form itself, all the while delineating his personal genealogy of poetics and elaborating an archaeology of poetic principles.

NOSTALGIA, VOLITIONAL ARCHAISM, AND RESISTANCE

For Roubaud, the trobar is a specter haunting Modernism, a presence and absence in contemporary poetry. He designates this distant presence in several ways. The trobar has an almost immediate currency for readers who come upon the opening lines to the inaugural poem of Guillaume IX:

> *Ab la dolchor del temps novel . foillo li bosc e li aucel . chanton chascun en lor lati . segon lo vers del novel chant* (T 64).

The words are recognizable, and the poetry is accessible. Yet, the marginalization of troubadour poetry–its temporal distance, its linguistic difference, and the erasure of its social circumstances–necessarily situates the trobar as other, as a distant and strange cousin.

The centuries of intervening poetic production separating "la première poésie moderne en Europe" and contemporary innovation make for a rather formidable interval, a test case for a memory of poetry, a test of poetry as memory. The challenge of distance is implied in Roubaud's choice, for he purposefully situates the trobar and the contemporary context at opposite poles of his lyrical tradition; he designates them as the extremities of his poetic lineage.

One of Roubaud's tasks in *La fleur inverse* is to articulate this proximity and distance in order to show how one pole informs the other, how in poetry the past is always present.

As "amateur du trobar," Roubaud confesses to nursing a deep nostalgia for Provençal poetry: "Certains, dont je suis, sont devant le *trobar* comme devant un âge d'or, une Arcadie, l'Italie de Keats et Shelley, la Grèce des philosophes et de Hölderlin, la Grèce encore des mathématiciens" (*FI* 345). If that nostalgia takes root in a specific "recherche du temps perdu" or an investigation of *la dolchor del temps novel*, it also represents his idealizing that moment as the lost childhood of the modern lyric. This enthusiasm leads Roubaud to stake some polemical claims about the *novel chant*. For example, eschewing the notion that they invented the concept of love, he prefers to believe that the troubadours were the first to inextricably link love and poetry: "Les troubadours ont inventé qu'il est un lien indissoluble: celui qui unit l'amour à la poésie" (*FI* 10); and, moreover, that in doing so they virtually created rhyme: "La rime en poésie n'existe pas, ou existe pauvrement, avant les troubadours" (*FI* 10). These praises are furthered when he states that "tout ce qui en suit est chute," casting the trobar as a fiction, as a prelapsarian moment of literary history, "un *instant idéal*" (*FI* 11, 131). Yet, though the expression of this nostalgia is explicit, it is motivated by Roubaud's argument regarding innovation and renewal.

The notion of a primal poetic moment is problematic, for all poetic research presupposes a historical context. As "la notion de sonnet unique est semblable à celle de la licorne" (*M9* 14), so too is the notion of a first, ideal poetic period for the lyric. In effect, the question boils down to a discourse on origins, none of which is pure, in the final analysis, and each of which relies to some extent on difference for identity. What purpose does it serve then for Roubaud to propose the primacy of the trobar, even if under such personal terms? If nostalgia is a form of memory, a longing for an idyllic period, what makes Roubaud's longing idiosyncratic?

Although Roubaud touts their poetry as model, he deprives the troubadours of a golden age: "Les troubadours n'ont pas d'Arcadie" (*FI* 134). He thus denies the trobar an explicit field of memory.[3] Viewed polemically, this void in troubadour poetic memory

---

[3] For an evocative counterargument, see Warren, "The Troubadour *Canso*," 469-87.

situates the trobar as simultaneously timeless and grounded in the twelfth century. This eternal and historical temporality is enhanced in that le grand chant has its own characteristic season, an eternal season of love, springtime (*FI* 141). In this respect, the irony behind Roubaud's nostalgia is that his elected model, the period he chooses to imitate, lacks an external poetic history. Consequently, his fanciful depiction of the trobar makes of it a literary movement whose identity depends on the confirmation of convention and counter-conventional invention.

From a twentieth-century literary perspective, wherein the possibilities for innovation may appear diminished by the exhaustion of canonical forms and the immanence of an impeding poetic memory, the strategy of Roubaud's volitional archaism makes sense. If modern French poetry suffers from a sense of exhaustion, then bringing medieval poetic techniques into the twentieth century is a means of revitalizing contemporary poetry, and what precedes it, a means of guarding against atrophy and eventual erasure. In these terms Roubaud justifies his celebration of the trobar: "La poésie la plus contemporaine, pour survivre, doit se défendre de l'effacement, de l'oubli, de la dérision par le choix d'un archaïsme: l'archaïsme du *trobar* est le mien" (*FI* 17). Thus, dissimulated in his nostalgia for this model is an attempt to rescue both troubadour poetry and, indirectly, contemporary poetry from the potential oblivion of cultural neglect. This choice, as manifestly polemical as Roubaud makes it, is also explicitly personal and theoretical in nature.

Part of the motivation for this choice is autobiographical. Here and elsewhere, Roubaud links his love of the troubadours to his childhood in Provence. Invoking an imperative to preserve his regional and linguistic heritage, his patrimony, Roubaud relates his commitment to Provençal directly to his family, calling it his "pseudo-paternal language" in that it was the language his father spoke during his youth.[4] However, this cultural fidelity is distinguished from a sense of nationalistic pride, or patriotism, for Provençal has not been directly identified with a centralized nation-state, as have other modern languages: "La langue des Troubadours, l'oc, l'occitan, le provençal est une langue romane singulière: à la différence

---

[4] Roubaud (1988), "Poésie, contemporaine extrême," 180; hereafter cited as *EX*.

du français, de l'italien, du catalan même (qui est le plus proche) elle n'a jamais depuis le XIIIe siècle précisément, été associée à une unité politique ou territoriale quelconque" (*FI* 9). The independence of *la langue d'Oc* mediates the politics of resistance at stake in Roubaud's volitional archaism. Roubaud first identified Occitan as a language of resistance during World War II, at about the same time that he developed a childhood love of poetry; Provencal was the language Roubaud heard his parents and their friends speak while plotting against the Nazi occupation and the Vichy collaboration. In Carcasonne, where Roubaud's family spent the war years, it was the lingua franca of the *résistants*.

Deepening this historic sense of resistance, Roubaud also accentuates the staying power of Provençal as the life spring of the modern lyric. As a regional language and a cultural idiom, Provençal has successfully managed to remain intact over centuries of possible extinction. Although this struggle for permanence continues in a variety of media today, Roubaud contributes to the endurance of Provençal by anthologizing, translating and critically studying early poems written in langue d'Oc. The explicit intention of this strategy is to recall the integrity of the discourse, and to recover it from its first and nearly fatal erasure. Along the way, Roubaud cunningly links that remembrance to innovative drives in the present.

"Une sorte de bombe atomique est tombée sur le 'grand chant'" (*FI* 339), explains Roubaud, referring in part to the Albigensian crusade, the French invasion and the Inquisition, which nearly annihilated troubadour culture during the thirteenth century. After these political events eliminated key intellectuals of the period and quashed the openly discursive and competitive atmosphere of the grand chant, the trobar fell into a decline that marks the end of its golden age. This figure of a poetic catastrophe has a two-fold function in the setting of *La fleur inverse*, and arguably in Roubaud's work more generally, where disaster is always deeply coded.

First, the incorporation of this event into the essay demonstrates Roubaud's use of explicit narrative devices in his study. In *La fleur inverse*, Roubaud recounts the life of the trobar form, the canso; he sketches the rise of le grand chant and traces its decline. This narrative is animated by a host of key troubadours whose inventions advance a plot based on developments in the formal sophistication of poetic language. In Roubaldian practice, literary forms lead lives similar to those of characters in novels and consequently, by virtue of their placement in time and their gift of memory, they entertain a privileged relationship to history. The cataclysmic moment that Roubaud alludes to, the bombe atomique, juxtaposes poetic and political history; memory is under fire in both.

Secondly, after World War II, the implications of the atomic bomb are not to be understated. Dropped at the end of this "instant idéal" in poetic history, this figurative bomb links the dissolution of the trobar to a systematic cleansing based on theological intolerances. The historical reference for the Langue d'Oc region is the extermination of Cathars under the Inquisition led by Pope Innocent III. Not all Troubadours maintained vexed relations with the Catholic Church, and those that did were not necessarily Cathars. Still, with its titillating conflations of carnal and spiritual love, the trobar was an affront to stricter church doctrine. For example, the tenor of Guillaume IX's refusal to forsake a mistress exemplifies his distaste for church teachings. Summoned by the Evêque d'Angoulême, the poet prince reportedly pledged to renounce his love for a countess, nicknamed "La Dangereuse," but only once prayer had successfully brought hair back to the holy man's balding head (*FI* 37).

This bombe atomique, however, also occasions a recontextualization of poetics in the present. In resisting the disappearance of the trobar's active, competitive, and free-thinking forum of expression, Roubaud warns against the dissolution of modern poetics, the end of poetry as a support to memory. Adopting the trobar as model bespeaks a personal means of articulating resistance through poetics; yet, this argument is buried under the surface of *La fleur inverse* as an encoded subtext. That is, Roubaud does not discuss the present-day threats to poetry–media-encouraged illiteracy, to cite one commonplace example–in this book, as he does in a later essay, *Poésie, etcetera: ménage* (1995). Rather, the political significance of individual troubadours, as well as the import of contemporary poetics, is muted, carefully posited at the beginning and end of his analysis.

In the postface of the second edition of *La fleur inverse* (1992), for example, Roubaud ironically takes note of how commercial economies influence the realities of poetic communities. Giving a modern-day example of how the survival of poetry and knowledge of its art depend on the availability of books as a commodity, he recalls the "disappearance" of Ramsay Publishing and the consequent pulverization of the remaining stock of the first edition of *La fleur inverse*: "Ce qui restait de l'édition de 1986 a été pilonné; le papier imprimé des volumes a été rendu à l'état de papier pour de nouveaux et plus heureux usages, dans le meilleur des cas" (*FI* 349). Subjected to the profit-driven laws of economics, the concrete commodification of poetics plays an important role in Roubaud's theory of poetry as a form of life, and in his literary history tracing the life of forms.

In short, Roubaud's volitional archaism is personally and socially motivated, and the biographical references he provides tie the Provençal language to forms of cultural and political resistance. Although the nostalgia inherent in Roubaud's experience of le grand chant echoes early childhood memories, the rhetorical force behind his formal analyses of the canso explicitly links the trobar to contemporary problems. His nostalgia for, and memory of, this golden past is not cast in the spirit of regret or in longing for what's lost. Rather, it forges a means of thinking about the coherence of tradition and the way tradition is transmitted via the trobar's most enduring legacy, its poetic forms and invention of fin'amors. Indeed, if Roubaud's love of the trobar is colored nostalgic, the research produced by the theses in *La fleur inverse* far outstrips any tendency to idealize the period. "Si l'on admet que les thèses soutenues ici ne sont pas invraisemblables, que la poésie a affaire à l'amour de la langue et en même temps à l'amour, que la forme de la poésie d'amour la plus tenace, prodigieuse et durable, est celle du sonnet, que la forme sonnet est celle à travers laquelle le 'grand chant' est venu jusqu'à nous, on reconnaîtra que la présence et absence de la poésie des troubadours est une question qui dépasse la nostalgie" (*FI* 345). For Roubaud, to publish troubadour poetry and to celebrate the trobar in all its formal complexity is not solely a manifestation of regional pride; rather, it belongs to a complete literary program aimed at ensuring the survival of poetry itself, or rather, Roubaud's personal memory of poetry.

Roubaud's poetic agenda, as informed by the troubadours, is marked by two primary drives: first, a profound sense of unity that knits together the lives of poets and the language of their poetry; second, a universal model for the continuous renewal of a poetic praxis through invention. In both cases, it is memory that plays the operative role of building and destroying continuity.

Unity of the Grand Chant

There are many ways to depict the unity of the grand chant, all of which make of troubadour poetry a rich archaeological find for literary formalists. One can unify the grand chant as a poetic discourse, situated in a specific place (citing Piere Vidal, Roubaud calls it "*le rectangle pur* entre le Rhône et Vence, entre la mer et la Durance" [*FI* 8]), at a particular time (approximately 1100-1250 AD), in a particular language (Langue d'Oc, Occitan, Provençal), in the name of a single principle (love, fin'amors). Or, if a more concrete, linguistic approach is preferred, the grand chant can be unified as a collection of manuscripts (approximately two thousand) presently archived in national libraries, selections of which circulate in anthologies. Or, if one seeks to penetrate "le comment du *trobar*" (*FI* 15), like a scientist intent on unveiling its enigmas, one might observe the diachronic evolution in the formal attributes of the grand chant, the way geneticists study mutations in drosophila.

In *La fleur inverse*, Roubaud approaches the trobar as a single interwoven poem, as a meta-canso, animated by resolutely singular voices. Focusing on the intersection between fin'amors and poetic craft, Roubaud postulates the thematic and formal coherence of the trobar. This coherence provides the basis that links the trobar to subsequent lyrical moments. For him, the heritage of the troubadours is directly transmitted through form, and the memory embedded in form is bidirectional; the moment of the trobar prefigures, even determines, however slightly, the early poetics of the French language, via the Italian Renaissance (Cavalcanti, Dante, and Petrarch). Conversely, he also argues that the *canzone*, the sonnet, and the sestina, in all their varieties, recollect the moment(s) of their invention, the transformative process by which they are present in contemporary writing. Since the poetic techniques and thematic concerns of the trobar are inscribed in literary history, the unity of the trobar guards against its dissolution.

Any analysis of troubadour poetics, however, must confront issues of incompleteness. Having been reproduced in the fourteenth and fifteenth centuries, manuscripts of troubadour poems often vary in form. Faced with this type of variety, medieval scholarship has developed critical concepts regarding texts of that period. Recent approaches to the early literary developments in Europe have helped revise contemporary views on literary production as noncentralized. Granted the dynamics of poetic creation and transmission, the notion of a stable canon of works has become increasingly untenable.

One of the fertile theoretical concepts to emerge from recent critical readings is Paul Zumthor's idea of *mouvance*. Relating to a larger body of medieval writing, mouvance describes the concretization of "quasi-abstract" literary works, one that enacts the progressive inscription and subsequent transformation of both the language and literature in question.[5] Like Zumthor's approach, Roubaud's reading renders explicit concrete elements of the trobar by retracing development in the formal aspects of intertextuality. Roubaud's poetic analysis is not, however, extensively concerned with the complex sociohistorical relationship between orality and textuality, as is Zumthor's. Instead, working from the manuscripts themselves and related scholarship, he focuses exclusively on formal aspects of the poems. That is, though deeply concerned with thematic issues that unite the trobar (its discourse on love and its encounters with nothingness or senselessness), Roubaud also emphasizes the mnemonic techniques embedded in the poetry, primarily through an analysis of rhyme.

Hence, by circumscribing a field that is uniquely textual, Roubaud foregoes interpreting troubadour poetics from an explicitly political point of view: "Je ne suis pas en train de tenter une explication sociologique ou idéologique du *trobar*" (FI, 11). Still, he necessarily accounts for certain sociological influences in the trobar. It would be impossible, for example, to address the grand chant without accounting for its obvious development in competitive and dialogic circumstances, as intertext. In this respect, a fundamental difference exists between Zumthor's and Roubaud's approaches: whereas Zumthor analyzes the social and literary forces that influenced the emergence of medieval texts (including the troubadours and their northern counterparts, the trouvères), Roubaud limits his analysis to the trobar of the grand chant, isolating only the formal elements of their poetic

---

[5] Paul Zumthor defines *mouvance* in the following manner: "le caractère de l'oeuvre qui, comme telle, avant l'âge du livre, ressort d'une quasi-abstraction, les textes concrets qui la réalisent présentent, par le jeu des variantes et remaniments, comme une incessante vibration et une instabilité fondamentale" (*Essai de poétique médiévale*, 507).

praxis, one that may be abstracted and applied in other poetic eras. Or, more simply, Zumthor theorizes the sociohistorical development of the medieval lyric, whereas Roubaud theorizes the troubadour lyric as a model for poetic practice in general.

Unlike other scholars, whose work on troubadour poetry constitutes parts of a secondary discourse, or a body of criticism exterior to the trobar, Roubaud claims to write *within* the tradition: "Cet essai tente une monstration de l'intérieur" (*FI*, 15). This initiative of working within the discourse entails several interesting strategic consequences. First, writing from within the trobar suggests that Roubaud's work is in some measure a performance of the grand chant, a rehearsal of its poetic principles. This repetition is problematic in that *La fleur inverse* does not read like a poem–though this distinction is hardly of great importance when one considers how radically Roubaud's works question the boundaries of genre, particularly prose and poetry. Second, to write from "inside" this tradition presupposes that Roubaud's essay contributes to and possibly furthers the grand chant. Finally, claiming to write as a troubadour centuries after the trobar strains conventional notions of time and literary history. Each of these consequences is manifest in *La fleur inverse* and may be taken into account when situating its contribution to modern scholarship on Provençal poetry.

Consequently, Roubaud's tRoubaldian voice must be read as a rhetorical appropriation. In my view, more than the critical exposition of his essays, Roubaud's poetic compositions in the vein of troubadour poetics secure his claim to this heritage. The duplicity of Roubaud's troubadour voice may therefore place him in an ideal position to approach the grand chant intratextually as one long, unified meta-canso.

In order to characterize a formal unity in the trobar, Roubaud focuses on the lexical, thematic, and prosodic elements that unite the tradition. For Roubaud, these formal links provide the trobar's vital connection to subsequent poetic developments. "Traitant l'heritage des troubadours, les traces écrites dont nous disposons, les 'chansonniers,' comme une grande canso, la *chanson du grand chant*, [cet essai] s'efforce de *raconter* le lien de l'invention dans le trobar, les mots, les sons et les rimes, l'amour, le chant, la poésie" (*FI* 15). In some respects, Roubaud's analysis concentrates on the tangible aspect of the poetic tradition, while in others he is proposing a theory of the trobar that postulates the necessary interrelation of more abstract categories: "L'amour, le chant, la poésie." For Roubaud these categories are interwoven. I shall consider them separately, alternating between his reading technique–Abstract Rhythm Theory–and his depiction of fin'amors.

ABSTRACT RHYTHM THEORY

In addition to declaring troubadour poetry the cornerstone of Roubaud's own poetics, *La fleur inverse* simultaneously demonstrates the use of Abstract Rhythm Theory (ART), a method of reading that organizes poetic value according to systematic and quantifiable rhythm.[6] In *La fleur inverse*, like in Roubaud's early work on rhythm, ART is consistently presented as a method that is still in its nascent stages and thus strictly confined to an experimental practice. Also, given its abstract nature, ART may provide an analytic perspective by which the rhythmical structures of any poetic tradition can be rendered explicit, in the way topographical maps represent relief in a landscape.

One strength of Roubaud's rhythm-based reading of troubadour poetry consists in its consideration of the entire moment. As opposed to his sustained cataloguing of the French sonnet or his account of Surrealist free verse, Roubaud's approach to the trobar benefits from the fact that the trobar may be defined as confined to a clear set of texts. This wholeness, however, also has its limit in that many cansos have been separated from the musical scores. They are bereft of their melodies. Plus, the songs that have persisted in manuscript form surely represent a mere fragment of the trobar as moment. These lacunae prevent any exhaustive rhythmic reading. He makes readers aware of these limitations, proposing his theory in a potential light: "Je vais seulement indiquer ce qu'on pourrait faire" (*FI* 211).

---

[6] Abstract Rhythm Theory is a reading technique devised and developed by Pierre Lusson and Jacques Roubaud. Roubaud's most influential statement on modern poetics, *La vieillesse d'Alexandre*, discussed in chapter 5, analyzes alexandrine verse form with the aid of this reading technique. Likewise, his sustained cataloguing of the French sonnet draws on this method. See also Lusson, Le Vot, and Roubaud (1979), "La chanson de l'amour," 3-92; and (1980), "La sextine d'Arnaut Daniel," 123-57. The most rigorous, explicit, and up-to-date application of this method of reading is found in Beaudouin's *Rythme et mètre du vers classique*.

If ART is proposed under such tentative conditions, it is clear that Roubaud understands the difficulties and potential benefits of elaborating a reliable theory of rhythm, one that addresses the divergent species of poetries that have taken up residence in the French language. Yet, considering rhythm from a purely quantitative position provides for a kind of rigor that is indispensable to a theory of rhythm, regardless of whether that theory is applied to classic verse forms, as is Roubaud's dominant practice, or to other forms of writing.

For some, the notion of hierarchically organizing poetic value according to purely mathematical criteria is a rather dubious enterprise. Sensitive to the fact that poetry is sacred to the French, Roubaud toys with the shock value of his approach. Anticipating a general reader's reaction, he mocks the absurdity of his own method: "Il est clair tout d'abord qu'on a l'air de faire quelque chose d'absurde; on additionne des pommes et des poires, pis, des parapluies et des machines à coudre" (*FI* 122). And yet, in this example, where the encounter of an umbrella and a dissecting table is anything but haphazard, where the subtext targets the incommensurate juxtapositions frequently found in Surrealist work, we are reminded that counting, regardless of how playfully it is done, is a means of establishing order.

Perhaps the absurdity of Roubaud's reading technique lies in its reduction. In presenting his methodology, Roubaud begins, in a sense, like a child, adopting an attitude of naïveté. He then proceeds through various performative expositions: "Je vais le faire, en quelque sorte, 'naïvement,' sans avoir 'fondé' la théorie, ses suppositions... je procéderai par affirmation arbitraire; je montrerai comment cela se fait" (*FI* 111). The notion of naïveté is explicit in the Oulipian "mathematization of language," as proposed by Queneau and Le Lionnais, and, I would argue, it participates in the sense of engrossed play found more broadly in Oulipian work. Along with *artisanale* and *amusant*, the word *naïve* is one of the first Queneau used to characterize Oulipian research. In "La littérature potentielle" (1964), he associates the word with an intuitive process of assembling elements. Queneau's exposition of the word is nearly directly echoed in the way Roubaud orients his use of ART: "Je prends le mot naïf dans son sens périmathématique, comme on dit la théorie naïve des ensembles. Nous allons de l'avant sans trop raffiner. Nous essayons de prouver le mouvement en marchant" (*BC*

317). Method, in other words, is proposed as process first and foremost, one that is susceptible to constant transformation.

Two critical trajectories of Oulipian thinking are at stake here. First, in *La fleur inverse*, Roubaud's use of Abstract Rhythm Theory begins with examples and progresses toward generalization. Second, the process of generalization is animated by forms of intelligent play or by toying with elements in such a way that the consistency of the matter under analysis affects method. The process is very hands-on, and it invites a shifting dialogue between working principles, or axioms, and the practice of reading, which, in this case, attempts to imagine the rhythmic skeleton of individual as well as abstract, or model, cansos.

In his reading, Roubaud counts a weight for each concrete force; he models the notions of rhythm on the occurrence of certain well-defined classes of events within the body of work. Comparing each poem to the entirety of the trobar, Roubaud considers and marks the following attributes: number of syllables, lines, strophes, rhyme patterns, syntactic patterns, the appearance of binary groupings, and the lexical field in the grand chant (he decomposes the lexical field into its morphological elements, granting nouns and verbs, for example, more rhythmic importance than prepositions and articles). Working from the givens of the grand chant, Roubaud conceptualizes a rhythmic map of the canso; he plots each poem on that map, as if on a graph representing the trobar as a unified abstract model. This reading postulates a model canso—la grande dame du chant courtois—that represents the norm of the grand chant, it generates the idea of a generic canso (*FI* 235). It also helps identify and define exceptional cansos, poems that assert their singularity in the trobar. Furthermore, it is with these tools that Roubaud imagines the unity of the trobar as a meta-canso.

This method leads to interesting problems of application. How does the quantification of the grand chant confront the values implicit in the tradition? Does this approach privilege certain aesthetic principles, granting the ensemble of troubadour texts an implicit structure, one that is determined a priori?

In practice, these questions are negotiated through the enumeration of subjective choices. For example, marking the appearance of key words from the grand chant courtois accounts for the intertextual and hermeneutic aspects operative within the tradition; marking the binary oppositions within poems accounts for the canso's remarkable flirtation with paradox and love's encounters with the possibility of nothingness. Isolating these elements is not the product of arbitrary choices. Roubaud's choices are gleaned from close readings of the poems, and they attempt to isolate the salient features that unite the grand chant, while representing them in an objective, quantifiable light.

Fin'amors

Fin'amors is the central theme, the heart of le grand chant courtois. For Roubaud, as well as the troubadours, *amors* is the primary motivation for writing poetry. Undertaken in a competitive spirit of investigation, the trobar elaborates a "theory of love," not to be confused with an adherence to a code of courtly love. The critical difference between these two conceptions of love rests on their discourses of origin, the trobar and the Arthurian romances, respectively. For Roubaud, a theory of love is in constant process, alive, proven and lived through the poetic word (not unlike his application of ART), whereas a code of conduct represents a fixed set of principles, like a code of law, and is recounted, recalled, remembered, narrated, enforced.

Trobar, as poetic research, elaborates the love of a language as much as the expression of an individual poet's adoration of a beloved. Song is consequently the manifestation of a love of language and a love of the other, invariably figured as the *dona*, a figure that includes both the song and its addressee. Roubaud's tripartite genitive construction postulates the interdependence of these three principles, "l'amour, la poésie, le chant: l'amour du chant de la poésie, la poésie du chant de l'amour," including all six possible permutations of these elements (*FI* 139-40). The competition implicit in this discourse contributes to and elaborates "la gloire et mémoire de la langue."

> Se disant en rimes, se disant en vers où souvent surgit la concaténation inoubliable d'axiomes, de vérités d'amour, il apparaît que l'amour, s'il est amour d'un amoureux pour une dame, dissimulant dans l'universel l'amour de tel amoureux réel pour telle dame peut-être, est aussi, en même temps, sans qu'il soit possible de séparer l'un de l'autre, *amour de la langue*. L'amoureux le plus

> parfait est celui qui aime le mieux; qui aime le mieux parce qu'il chante le mieux, qui chante le mieux parce qu'il aime le mieux; et d'aimer mieux il grandit la gloire de celle qu'il aime, son *pretz*, son *prix*, grandit la *gloire de la langue*. Là est une fonction essentielle, la première fois dite en poésie par la poésie, de la poésie même: la gloire et mémoire de la langue. (*FI* 12)

Roubaud's conflation of "la théorie de l'amour" and "la théorie de la poésie" is explicit here. The glory of language, which has become the glory of the beloved, describes, in an axiomatic manner, the fundamentally dialogic game of one-upmanship at stake in the pursuit of *pretz*, or renown, for the dona as well as for the songs that laud her.

Two important characteristics of poetry are apparent here. First, all poetry depends on dialogues between poets and their audiences, dialogues animated by the memory of an intertext: "La poésie [est] gloire et mémoire de la langue." Second, in its function as textual innovation, Roubaud articulates the notion of pretz as the elaboration of new or refined formulae. While there are strong elements of competition between troubadours (especially if they love the same person), innovation, the prize of novelty, challenges not other individuals, but rather the forms by which the discourse itself is constituted and transformed.

Axioms

Adopting Bourbakian set theory, Roubaud uses the word *axiom* to articulate self-evident principles organizing changes in the Provençal lyric. Loosely clarifying the principles of innovation, Roubaud describes innovation in the trobar according to three unifying axioms: those of love, of unicity, and of pretz. Roubaud argues that the axiomatic character of the trobar is implicit in its wealth of maxims, aphorisms, and proverbs. An example like "*e chanz si d'amors non es faig. no vai plus que ses dona amar*" (le chant si d'amour il n'est fait ne vaut plus que d'aimer sans dame; *FI* 155) is axiomatic in that it becomes its own evidence by virtue of being forged in verse: "Le vers est lui-même axiome et donne sa vérité à l'axiome d'amour" (*FI* 155). There is, in a performative sense, a fundamental relation between the truth-value of a statement on love and its versification; verse illustrates the axiom.

The first axiom in the proposed chain is that of love. For Roubaud, it is given that "la poésie ne se peut pas sans amour" (*FI* 10) and "que l'amour soit commencement de tout implique qu'il soit axiome de lui même et du chant" (*FI* 153). And yet, Roubaud also organizes the generative forces of the trobar as a meta-canso according to two additional axioms, the "axiome de renouvellement, ou d'unicité" and the "axiome de pretz, ou d'unisonance" (*FI* 210-11). The principle expressed by these two is the requirement that love, and hence the trobar, always be new, renewed: "Toute canso doit avoir quelque chose de *novel*" (*FI* 209). The axiom of renewal affirms that each canso must be singular. The axiom of unisonance simply states that there is a measure of value assigned to cansos whose form is most imitated by other cansos.

The consequences of these axioms are significant. The axiom of love gives poetry its zero degree of being, its raison d'être, and helps guard against the abyss of meaninglessness that threatens the existence of poetry. The axiom of renewal incites a frenetic exploration of possible formulae, granting the trobar an almost unparalleled wealth of rhyme schemes: to date, 900 rhyme schemes have been identified in the 2600 preserved texts. Roubaud explicitly celebrates this multiplicity, for variety is proof of exploratory research and individuation. The axiom of pretz permits one to identify "les grandes dames de la forme-canso" within these 900 extant rhyme schemes; they are the quasi-canonical forms that have been the most imitated and refined. Because of their repetition, they are like rhymes in the meta-canso of the trobar, for they reinforce the unity of the discourse.

Using Istvan Frank's *Répertoire métrique des troubadours*, Roubaud statistically organizes troubadour poetry according to rhyme schemes, isolating the least and the most frequently used formulae. Roubaud then imagines a conceptual map, figured as a virtual graph where he plots out the formal elements of the canso as a combinatory field. This method permits him to demonstrate and analyze the specific results of the axioms of renewal and unisonority.

In Roubaud's reading of the trobar, ART provides the methodological tool enabling the intratext of the trobar to illustrate its own rules: as with the axiom of love, the truth-value of the generative axioms is intrinsically accounted for by the available poems (and, to a large extent, he simply asks readers to trust his calculations). The method "proves" the actual existence of the formal variety of the trobar, as well as its drive toward novelty.

From a theoretical perspective then, an account of all rhyme schemes intrinsic to the trobar establishes the coherence of the corpus as a literary moment, as a case study in innovation. Further analysis of particular rhyme schemes demonstrates how thoroughly this coherence permeates every level of the metatext. His analysis considers both the macro- and microeconomies of the trobar, demonstrating coherence in the collection of poems, in individual poems, as well as in the parts that constitute each canso: the *cobla* (stanza), its two distinctive parts, or *frons* (the *pedes* and the *cauda* separated by *deisis*), and each verse of the respective *volte*, including feet and syllables.

In considering a grande dame du grand chant, the most common formula (ABBA/CCDD, labeled P for Provençal), it becomes clear that coherence depends on formal embedding. Roubaud praises the pedes of this cobla (ABBA, labeled T for troubadour) for its palindromic symmetry. When compared to its next most frequent counterpart (ABAB, labeled F for français), where there is simple alternance, T is seen as more valuable, for "sa symétrie est plus forte," and when reversed, it is identical to itself (*FI* 217).

Roubaud also prefers pedes formula T over F because of the greater interval separating the A rhymes. This distance marks suspense in the return of a rhyme, positing an elementary mnemonic challenge, for rhyme establishes the unity of the frons. Other formulae, for example abab/cbcb, maintain unity throughout the cobla; here simple intrication connects the two halves of the strophe. This type of linking technique is even more apparent where coblas echo each other.

Many techniques are used to link the coblas in the canso, commonly the repetition of the same rhyme and melodic patterns from cobla to cobla (known as *coblas unisonans*). Among other possible combinations, Roubaud prefers those that entail *rime estramp*, a rhyme that tranverses the strophic barrier established in one cobla and answered or resolved in the following one(s). Distance, once again, is a valued measure for memory.

The tightest stitch between strophes occurs in *coblas capcaudadas*, in which the last rhyme of one strophe is repeated as the first line of the subsequent one. From this perspective, cansos that offer the most challenging internal unity are *coblas estramps*, in which every rhyme is suspended until the subsequent strophe. Rhymes separated by distance, as in formula T (ABBA), or in *rime estramp*, are valued because unlike *laisses*, or rhyming couplets, they demand more attention to the canso as a whole. In a sestina, like Arnaut Daniel's "Lo ferm voler q'el cor m'intra," in which each rhyme is suspended until the subsequent strophe and the intrication pattern is very complex, a more active memory is required to recall and recite the poem. Or, stated differently, memorizing that poem requires learning the entire text by heart without relying on the repetition in rhymes and rhythm that normally supports memorization. Plus, in the case of the sestina, recitation also requires singing a different melody for each strophe, for, presumably, there is no repetition in phrasing from stanza to stanza.

Rhyme is a fundamental mnemonic aspect of poetry: the easier the rhyme, the easier the poem is to remember. Roubaud's statistical analysis of rhyme schemes leads him to this evaluation: "Le résultat, comme dans le cas des trouvères, est remarquablement cohérent" (*FI* 222). Comparing the poetry of the troubadour and the trouvères, Roubaud affirms their respective unity but also argues that Provençal poetics is more sophisticated. He claims that troubadour poetry boasts broader combinations, as well as more pronounced tendencies toward difficult-to-remember rhythmic formulae.

Accordingly, the wealth of the grand chant lies in its ability as a discourse to sustain extremely complex sequences without losing track of its first axiomatic principle, fin'amors. In fact, it is the plurality of voices, the variety of forms and the complexity of poetic inter-reference in the trobar that Roubaud most celebrates. Having accounted for the rhythmical landscape of the trobar as a whole, Roubaud emphasizes its most creative forces, its most eccentric poets. To this end *La fleur inverse* explores the stylistic debate rooted in the grand chant, the opposition between the *trobar leu* (a clear, open style) and the *trobar clus* (a complex, closed style).

To explain the oppositional dynamics of these two conceptions of love and poetry, one must first examine the challenges facing fin'amors. The trobar develops according to the axioms of renewal and unity. But novelty is also required in the discovery, the praise, and the evolution of love: "L'amour doit être nouveau toujours, neuf, *novel*. Toute canso doit avoir quelque chose de *novel*" (*FI* 209). But novelty for novelty's sake threatens, in Roubaud's model, the probity of the trobar, the integrity of its axiomatic principles. If love means nothing, or is sung to no one, then singing too means nothing and novelty in song and love is of no value. This is a great danger facing the trobar: "Si l'amour ne s'adresse qu'à une image inerte, qu'à une dame inanimée, qu'au vide, le chant encore n'est rien, qui nomme l'amour, puisque l'amour n'est alors 'aucune chose'" (*FI* 52). A confrontation with nothingness unveils a fundamental dilemma facing the trobar and its "amour de la langue." In an intermittent reading of the "tenson de non re" between Aimeric de Peguilhan and Albert Sisteron, the intertext of which begins and enriches his entire essay, Roubaud considers the role of poems on nothing, as well as *estribot* poems, or enigma poems, whose register is to ask what they do or how they exist as poems at all. Roubaud's analysis of these *aporia* poems helps him articulate the dilemma of novelty that underlies each canso's occasion:

> Tel est le dilemme: ou bien le néant de n'être que nomination; ou bien celui de ne nommer que le néant.
> Ou bien l'eau bougeante mais immobile.
> Ou bien la roue qui pérpetuellement mout le vide. (*FI* 52)

This dilemma concerns the very representation of love, with which each new canso must come to terms: "*Néant de l'amour de n'être pas nommable, néant de l'amour de n'être que nomination*" (FI 327). For Roubaud this paradox permeates the entire grand chant. The two styles, the trobar *leu* and the trobar *clus* offer different responses to the threat of nothingness. The trobar, unlike its counterpart, the *roman*, never resolves this dilemma, and in this suspension of closure, in this fragility, Roubaud reads the grand chant's greatest form of unity and its clearest trajectory of continuation. Again, viewing these two styles as the opposite poles to a single poetic axis, Roubaud claims that "l'unité du *trobar* est sa réponse à la menace du néant" (*FI* 286).

Le Néant, Memory and the Trobar Clus: Entrebescar

Although ART takes into account the entirety of the grand chant, the close readings offered in *La fleur inverse* emphasize what may be considered the most esoteric aspects of this tradition, poems representing the trobar clus. Beginning with the "tenson de non re," whose allusive intertext includes Guillaume IX's "vers de dreit nien" and Jaufre Rudel's canso on "l'amor de loing," Roubaud leads readers through a selection of cansos and *vidas* that strongly privileges the more hermetic aspect of the trobar, culminating in a brief reading of Arnaut Daniel's sestina "Lo ferm voler q'el cor m'intra." In these poems Roubaud identifies "l'envers noir de l'amour" as a manifestation of the "éros mélancholique" understood by troubadours as a pathology that can, when not tempered by *mezura* (both an amorous and poetic good measure), lead to madness or death. Although never extending to the overly melancholic "gloire noire" of Romantic poetry, the trobar clus offers what some have called the inverse of the trobar leu, its countertext. For Roubaud, the opposition between these two styles does not divide the grand chant, but rather unifies its diverse affirmations of love against the threat of nothingness. That is, these two styles lead to opposing poetic trajectories that are nonetheless complementary in their proliferation of a theory of love. It is the trobar clus, the more difficult and compact one, that Roubaud adopts as his primary model and that he justifies as the poet's poetry.

Roubaud's thesis statement about the two styles is succinct. Maintaining the continuity between love, poetry and song, the opposition leu/clus results in love's paradox:

> L'hypothèse sera défendue ici d'un lien intrinsèque entre cette tension (qui ne peut pas être résolue sinon par dénégation) interne de l'amour et la coexistence antagoniste tout au long de l'histoire du trobar entre deux voies poétiques qui portent les noms de *trobar clus* (secret, fermé) et de *trobar leu* (léger, clair). L'opposition de deux styles va bien au-delà d'un problème d'obscurité ou compréhension (polémique interne de la poésie pour tous et de la poésie difficile que les troubadours ont connue et expérimentée en des termes qui n'ont guère été améliorés depuis), c'est une opposition dont la racine est dans l'amour même, dans le paradoxe de l'amour s'obstinant à l'affirmation réitérée du lien amoureux que la mélancolie sans cesse présente comme impossible. (*FI* 14-15)

The debate between an easy (open) and difficult (closed) style is intrinsic to all poetry, and the dilemma of an obstinate affirmation of love presents itself whenever *amor* is submitted to a question of verbal representation. Reducing the two styles to functions within the discourse, as if in a mathematical equation, Roubaud phrases their role in the trobar as different answers to the same question, the question of nothingness:

> L[eu] et C[lus] ne s'opposent pas seulement comme mouvement de chant, de poésie; ils apportent deux réponses antagonistes à N[éant]:
> –La réponse du L est réponse d'apparence positive: il y l'amour; il y a le *joi*; et c'est bien; l'amour existe Le printemps "est évident." Le chant est vrai.
> –La stratégie du C est très différente. Et pour la désigner mieux, j'aurai recours à Nicolas de Cuse, un des représentants moyens de la *via negativa*. (*FI* 328)

The style leu is thus recognized as the dominant function in the discourse of the grand chant, affirming the possibility and actuality of love, and the style clus is associated with this strain of 15th century theology.

It may be misleading to call the first, more common style of the trobar simple, for its poetry is complex and highly reflexive. Leu primarily refers to an aesthetic valued by the poets who propagate the currency of this style. It is an aesthetic that values clarity in naming and distinction, symmetry in oppositions and the perpetual affirmation of the poetic "I" (*ieu*) as an active and worthy servant of love. "Le mouvement L[eu] est un mouvement de désignation, de nomination, de multiplication des distinctions claires, prémonitoires, tranchés: affirmer. Affirmer dans les termes les plus lumineux, les plus doux, les plus harmonieux possibles, toutes les théories de l'amour telle qu'elle se découvre avec ses couples d'antonymes inséparés: joi e dolors, folie et sens. Mais aussi, et dans le même mouvement, canso et sirventes, poésie et prose" (*FI* 326). Although this description emphasizes multiplication in distinctions, both in terms of formal attributes and subject matter, these distinctions never become confused. The trobar leu defends the purity of love and the canso (the discourse's double dona). It seeks to distill this purity through the art of opposition. In his canso "Non es mervalha s'eu chan," for example, Bernart de Ventadour, considered a master of the trobar leu and acclaimed by his audiences, both medieval and modern, employs the principle of distinction to identify a true love and true lover: "*Ai Deus se fosson trian. d'entr-ls faus li fin amador* Ah Dieu si on pouvait trier d'entre les faux les vrais amants"; *T* 116-17) and, as the following cobla demonstrates, he balances the opposing forces of joy and suffering, good and bad:

> *Aquest'amors me fer tan gen. al cor d'una dosa sabor. cen vetz mor lo jorn de dolor. e reviu de joi autre cen. ben es mos mal de bel semblan. que mais val mos mals qu'autre bes. e pois mos mals aitan bosm'es. bos er los bes apres l'afan.*
> Cet amour me blesse noblement   au coeur de sa douce saveur
>   cent fois le jour je meurs de douleur   et je revis de joie encore cent   mon mal est d'un si beau visage   qu'il vaut mieux mon mal qu'autre bien   et puisque mon mal m'est si bon
>   bon est le bien après le mal. (*T* 116-17)

Among the qualities he appreciates in Bernart de Ventadour's poems, Jacques Roubaud notes the transparency of his language, which affirms the benefits of suffering despite adversity. This language is not only easy to understand, but also pleasant to hear, composed of gentle sounds (*mots peignés*). Clarity is a function of accessibility and luminosity that opposes and contrasts binaries such as *dolor/joi* and *mal/bes*. Although the polarities proliferated by the trobar leu are complex and multifarious, Roubaud explicitly emphasizes that they remain "practicable," or feasible, for they clearly demarcate difference, often hierarchically, in a dialectical affirmation of love's truths.

The trobar clus values an entirely different set of aesthetic principles. Unlike the trobar leu, poems of the trobar clus propose oppositions that are not applicable to love but that nevertheless generate important reflexive continuity within the elaboration of fin'-amors. He explains thus: "Le mouvement C[lus], *au contraire*, tente de rendre impraticable, impossible à soutenir les distinctions de L[eu], mais *sans les effacer*. Il affirme, lui, l'indissolubilité du chant de la poésie et de l'amour; mais qu'en même temps tout le *joi* est douleur, que toute canso est sirventes, le printemps hiver, le chant des oiseaux silence, que les mots les plus hirsutes peuvent donner la douceur au coeur; il affirme que tout tient ensemble en opposant tout, intérieurement, aux vers, aux axiomes d'amour. Il dit que tout est *mezura*. Que le gel est fleur" (*FI* 326). The impossibility of the oppositions maintained by the style clus must be figured as antithetical to the viable oppositions affirmed in the style leu–that is, as Lynne Lawner suggests (1968), the trobar clus can be productively read as a countertext, or *countra-clau*, to the trobar leu, as its poetic inversion. It questions, from within the axiomatic conventions, the clarity of distinctions and difference proposed as fin'amors. In this respect, this second style both reacts to and enriches the first, more popular style of the grand chant: although it exploits a methodology that is opposite to the trobar leu, obscuring the clarity of its distinctions, the trobar clus affirms the principle of measure intrinsic to the practice of "amour, chant, poésie."

Whereas the trobar leu appeals more generally to broader, less engaged audiences, Roubaud represents the trobar clus as corresponding to a philosopher-poet's style. Clearly Roubaud's preference reveals his position within polemical debates on the value of difficult poetry. Yet his praise of the trobar clus also unveils how this style effectively renews its own poetic tradition. Sometimes called *trobar ric*—a term discarded by Roubaud because it confuses the use of rare words (common in both styles) with a strategy defined by formal complexity and stylistic extremes—the trobar clus problematizes the language of love itself. Both styles are highly reflexive in their incorporation of intertextual allusion, but their approaches to allusion differ in that the clear style continues to affirm the validity of conventions. Whereas the style leu aspires to a clear exposition of love and its terminology, the style clus attempts to turn conventions in upon themselves, blurring distinctions and challenging the praxis of song. The style clus therefore poses more difficulty in comprehension, for it assumes knowledge of convention of the sort possessed by troubadour poets.

Setting aside the sequential binary oppositions intrinsic to the style leu, Roubaud claims that "le concept clef de la manière 'clus' est l'*entrebescar*" (319). Imperfectly translated as "interlacing" or "intertwining," this poetic method entails thematic and formal interweaving. Presented as a definition of poetry in Bernart Marti's canso "Bel m'es lai latz fontana," entrebescar simultaneously describes the kiss and the song of love. In the *tornada*, or coda of this poem, Bernart Marti—whose mentor, Marcabru, is known as the initiator of this style clus—describes the relief of undoing a false love, thereby purifying the language and acts of love:[7]

---

[7] Roubaud identifies at least two branches of the trobar clus, the first of which lacks luster because of its theologically motivated deviance from the principles of amors: "Le 'trobar clus' de Marcabru est un hermétisme polémique d'inspiration principalement religieuse, catholique, contre les conceptions de l'amors telles que le trobar est en train (on est à la seconde ou troisième génération des troubadours) de

*En breu m'es com fils de lana. lo fortz fres e la capsana. qui que-s
greu. so-us autrei. tota-l rengua ab correi. c'aisi vauc entrebescant.
los motz e-l so afinant. lengu'entrebescada. es en la baizada.*
En un instant comme fil de laine   je brise le frein et le licou
    même si cela déplaît   je vous l'assure   et la bride et la
    courroie   ainsi je vais enlaçant   les mots et rendant purs les
    sons   comme la langue s'enlance   à la langue dans le baiser.
(T 106-7)

The double-entendre of "entrebescar" in this translation, "enlaçant" (enlacing) and "s'enlance" (to throw oneself around, toward), reveals two principles of the trobar in the style clus. First the "enweaving" of words purifies song, and therefore love as well. Second, the intertwining of tongues evokes both the act of kissing and the act of poetry. The physicality of this latter image is in itself memorable. That this formulation should occur in the *envoi* of the canso, as a call to other poets and future loves, implies that entrebescar figures a more general intertextual practice of the trobar. Having stated his views on love as law, on fidelity and servitude to "Na Desirada," the emblematic beloved, Marti sends his poem into a dialogue whose game is to formulate a theory on *amors*. Entrebescar, in this respect, is partially a code word for intertextual allusion and intradiscursive polemics. However, intertextuality is not unique to the trobar clus, for it also figures prominently in texts of the trobar leu, and the lyrical moments that follow the trobar.

For Roubaud, entrebescar embodies the poetic realization in the verse, rhyme, and melody of an aesthetic well developed in the trobar clus, an aesthetic that unites, through formal interweaving, latent aspects of the grand chant. Throughout his work, it becomes

---

les fixer" (*FI* 318). The hermetic difficulty of Marcabru's style clus relies on an allusive complexity that uses an appropriated popular speech to mount an attack on aristocratic powers in Occitania. Roubaud debunks the implication subtending this politically motivated poetics, namely that "la parole claire a toujours été aristocratique" (*FI* 317). Although he claims not to take a position in this debate ("Je ne prendrai pas parti dans cette discussion" [*FI* 317]), he is quick to recognize how easily popular language can be coopted to propagate dominant ideologies: "L'emploi du parler 'populaire' est une arme de clerc (Marcabru est pétri de Bible) qui tourne le langage cuit de manière tordue, imprécatoire, dissimulée et féroce, pour faire apparaître ce que l'amour a d'amoral et de décadent; il ne s'agit pas là d'une position révolutionnaire" (*FI* 318). Roubaud insists on the trobar's independence from religious ideologies, often remarking on certain poets' ironic stances toward the church; Marcabru's work does not conform to this model.

the basis for memory itself, it is "une esthétique de la *mémoire*" (*FI* 320). Raimbaut d'Orange, the founder of the trobar clus, approaches entrebescar as a means of thoughtfully constructing actively thinking texts:

> cars bruns e tenhz. motz entrebesc. pensiuz pensanz
> précieux sombres et teints   mots j'entrelace   pensif pensant
> (*FI* 320)

In this version of entrebescar the activity of "enlacing words to purify song" explicitly entails attention to verbal textures and rhythm. Dante discusses word texture in the grand chant in terms of sound, characterizing individual words as either *hirsute* (hard, grating to the ear) or *peigné* (elegant, pleasing melodies), and Roubaud weaves this qualitative framing into his own account. Textuality, in his analysis, also implies lexical frequency and discursive weight within the larger metatext of the trobar.

To describe the formal method of entrebescar as exemplified in the poetry of his favorite troubadours (Raimbaut d'Orange and Arnaut Daniel), Roubaud elaborates these textile metaphors, granting each word, rhyme or melody in a canso a unique color, or grain, which, through complex patterns of interweaving, becomes part of a much larger image or textual concept. Attempting a "chromatography" of the trobar, Roubaud explores a synesthesia of sound and color, combinations that lead to a mnemonic function important in the trobar, but also universal in poetry. In the following quotation, Roubaud compares the texture of the grand chant to medieval Irish tapestries: "On peut envisager l'image d'une forme dans un espace à plusieurs dimensions, disposée en lignes privilégiées, une sorte d'hyper-étoffe. Le mot, l'image proposée par le mot, font s'approcher un effet de l'étoffe, la tapisserie et aussi l'enluminure celte, les enchevêtrements peints du Livre de Kells, de l'art médiéval irlandais" (*FI* 320). In this comparison of textual and textile artistry, Roubaud identifies his preferred lineage of poems from the trobar clus, consisting of poems that interrogate, through negative representation, the "néant de l'amour." Unlike Marcabru's trobar clus, which complicates the grand chant by recasting popular speech in poetic discourse, the complex interweaving of Raimbaut's style relies instead on rhythmic references within the grand chant. As implied in both Raimbaut's verse and

Roubaud's comparison, lexical tone is a primary function of this rhythmical interreference. However, this is only one of many aspects considered in rhythmic echoes.

Also important in building poetic interreference is the use of meter, rhyme, and melody. By following the threads of increasingly complex forms of rhythmic constructions, Roubaud explains entrebescar as a method for embedding a directed memory of the tradition. Arnaut Daniel's sestina is essential in explaining how entrebescar functions as "une esthétique de la mémoire." Like Raimbaut d'Orange's "Ar resplan la flors enversa," Daniel's "Lo ferm voler q'el cor m'intra" is entirely composed of rimes estramps, so that each rhyme word is deferred until it is repeated in the next strophe. This delay poses difficulty to learning the song by heart, which effectively challenges its potential assimilation into the main current of an oral tradition. Moreover, the added difficulty of the permutational order of rhymes in this canso earns the sestina a unique status within the trobar.

There are several ways to describe the logic of differential reordering operative in "Lo ferm voler q'el cor m'intra." The simplest is to trace a spiral starting with the sixth rhyme word of a strophe back to the first in such a manner as to progressively repeat the middle rhyme words. If we represent six rhyme words by the numbers 1, 2, 3, 4, 5, 6, the movement of the permutation can be mapped thus (see figure 1):

FIGURE 1

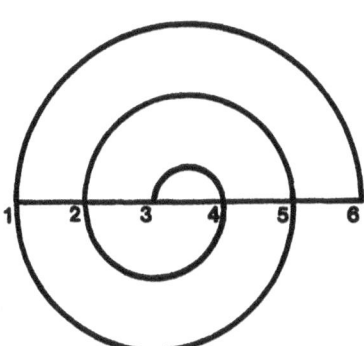

For Arnaut Daniel's sestina, the full permutational cycle of rhyme words, from the first to the last cobla, is as follows:

TABLE 1

I.	*intra. ongla. arma. verga. oncle. cambra.*
II.	*cambra. intra. oncle. ongla. verga. arma.*
III.	*arma. cambra. verga. intra. ongla. oncle.*
IV.	*oncle. arma. ongla. cambra. intra. verga*
V.	*verga. oncle. intra. arma. cambra. ongla*
VI.	*ongla. verga. cambra. oncle. arma. intra*

This combinatorial permutation is optimal because the number of elements and the number of permutations coincide; if a seventh strophe were to follow the sixth, the original order of the first would be reestablished. In a sense, that return to the initial order is implied by the form but not realized.

The rhythmical complexity of the sestina is exemplary of the trobar clus, for it requires, of poets and audiences alike, a sustained attention to the movement of the entire poem in order to reconstitute the complex textual image represented. Further developing his "chromatography" of the trobar, and illustrating the method of entrebescar, Roubaud invites readers to imagine the abstract design created through the logic of the sestina: "La sextine est essentielle à la compréhension de l'entrebescar. Donnons en effet à chaque mot-rime une couleur, plaçons chaque mot-rime sur un fil de cette couleur et la canso se trouvera entrelacée en lignes qui ne seront ni horizontales ni verticales, mais créerons le dessin abstrait des sons que seule la totalité de la canso déroulée à l'exécution permet de saisir, par la résolution cyclique, le retour à l'ordre initial étant laissé, et telle est l'essence de l'art clus, implicite, dans le prolongement virtuel de la voix, continuant à chanter intérieurement dans le silence qui suit la fin de la tornada" (*FI* 321). To visualize this "dessin abstrait" and to hear the "retour à l'ordre initial"—essentially a potential but absent loop in the form, a crucial figure in Roubaud's novel *La boucle*—requires a firm understanding of the form's function. Promulgated as a poet's poetry, the trobar clus of Raimbaut d'Orange and Arnaut Daniel demand a sophisticated approach to poetic composition. It presupposes knowledge not only of the thematic and lexical practices of the trobar, but also the ability to recognize the latent structures within a canso, as well as an ability to relate them between cansos–subtleties to which perhaps only poets themselves are attentive.

Because of its coblas estramps, "Lo ferm voler q'el cor m'intra" echoes and develops Raimbaut's "Ar resplan la flors enversa," with the difference of introducing the spiraling permutation. It is this type of linked formal embedding, present in all poetry, that Roubaud values in the craftsmanship of the trobar clus. Entrebescar represents an aesthetic of memory insofar as its complex interlacing and deferrals require a greater attention to order in the transmission, inscription, and reception of the song. Roubaud figures the constraints of this aesthetic according to the notion of a language game: "La méthode de l'entrebescar a ainsi deux conséquences, qu'on peut interpréter à partir de la notion de *jeu de langage* dans sa généralisation esthétique, le *jeu de la mémoire*, mais que je prends ici qu'en son acceptation courante: la première est l'inachèvement; la seconde, qui en un sens est la même, est la *non-répétition immediate*" (FI 321). If these two rules apply the trobar clus (and by extension, if they are axiomatic in tRoubaldian poetics) then their reception requires an active acknowledgment and a directed recollection of entrebescar techniques, one that increases distance between rhymes and organizes them according to increasingly subtle patterns.

ESTRIBOT

So far, my discussions of the sestina and the aesthetic of entrebescar have focused on purely structural concerns. I have tried to demonstrate that Roubaud values the incompletion and deferred rhyme of the trobar clus. However, the more enlarged sphere of this language game also includes intertextual references that recall thematic and rhetorical developments. Viewed as a countertext to the trobar leu, as its polar opposite on the axis of the trobar, this closed style proceeds by conflating distinctions and reversing fundamental principles of fin'amors.

In presenting the trobar clus in its relation to fin'amors, Roubaud links together a body of texts that explores, through contradiction and negative representation, the *néant* of poetry and love. His discussion pivots around problems of nothingness and absence, problems that cast love in an extreme mode of self-reflexive inquiry. The primary texts include Guillaume IX's "Faray un vers de dreit nien," Jaufre Rudel's "Lanquand li jorn son lonc en-mai" (the signature canso for *l'amor de lonh*); the "tenzos de non res" by Aimeric de Peghuilhan and Alberet de Sisteron; Raimbaut d'Orange's "Ar resplan la flors enversa"; and Daniel's "Lo ferm voler q'el cor m'intra." In each case, Roubaud identifies the poem within a critical poetic register: the enigma or the *devinhal*, whose functions include a critique of love. He calls these language games "je ne sais quoi" or estribot poems, texts that have the peculiar characteristic of praising an unknown thing or person. Voice in these poems resembles that of a *fada*, a hopeless and disoriented lover who is incapable of expressing anything but an unanswerable vow of love. However, these poems differ from those in which the poet is consumed by melancholia, for they are tempered by *mezura*, or poetic adroitness. And, unlike their counterparts in the style leu, their addressee, Amors, remains ultimately shrouded by the ineffable.

Citing Lynn Lawner's study, Roubaud links "Le vers de dreit nien," the earliest known *devinhal*, to strains of negative theology. In his analysis, the sequence of "je ne sais quoi" poems answers and develops Guillaume IX's ludic theological inquiry. Citing the philosophy of Cardinal Nicholas de Cusa (1400-1464) as an exemplary (and much later) negative theology, Roubaud indicates that estribot poems think about the persona of Amors through exclusion, contradiction, and the opposition of all things, according to a *via negativa*. "Dans son *De Pas-Autre* [*De Li non Aliud*], le Cusain approche l'idée de Dieu en montrant qu'il est plus que non non x pour tout x (x propriété quelconque) : non non x étant différent de x. Le Dieu du *De Li non Aliud* est un dieu intuitionniste" (FI 328). The transposition of negative theology onto the trobar may not be as simple as implied, for it entails a host of formal and ludic components. The fundamental move is to replace the name of God with the name of Amors, the persona served and defined in the elaboration of fin'amors. Roubaud's final remark on Nicolas de Cusa's work hints toward a conception of Amors that would necessarily maintain its expression as open-ended, as a potentiality, unachievable in the absolute. That conception proceeds through a process of double negation: "Telle est selon moi la stratégie du C(lus) : le non non A[mors]. L'amour existe non parce qu'il est ceci ou cela mais parce qu'il est plus que le contraire de ceci ou cela" (FI 329). In reading the privileged poems, Roubaud reiterates the surplus meaning produced beyond the contradiction of opposites. It is as if these nonsensical poems were simultaneously affirming and negating certain knowledge of amors through an elaborate style whose primary intention is to redefine the limits of language itself. Viewed as a language game, naming through double negatives simultaneously posits and questions the existence of love, and consequently the very existence of poetry itself.

Estribot poems are especially significant to the trobar clus, for they self-consciously test the limits of language and the meaning of fin'amors. In their radical questioning, they sharpen the trobar's relation to the possibility of nothingness, essentially reduced to the grand chant devoid of a dona, the trobar deprived of service. That is, by confronting amors with the possibility of absence, or loving in a void, estribot poems protect amors against the dilemma of an absent referent, while at the same time confronting that same possibility. In this sense, even if estribot poems integrate conventional elements of the canso, they often do so with the explicit effect of undermining conventional logic. And that form of destruction becomes a means of strengthening the discourse's tolerance to doubt and alterity. Regardless of the untenable oppositions they advance, enigma cansos remain raw affirmations of the possibility of poetry, of love, of their song. In other words, it is crucial to bear in mind that this extreme questioning takes place in verse, as part of the growth process of an art; the canso, the *sirventes*, the *tenson* provide a kind of shelter, or demarcated field where radical and ludic discursive inquiry may flourish, where the trobar clus and trobar leu may be hotly debated.

When Roubaud writes that "le trobar clus, lui-même, est un non re, un néant" (*FI* 325), he remotivates a poetic conception of language crystallized in Stéphane Mallarmé's "Crise de vers." In that essay, Mallarmé evokes a similar effect in poetic enunciations, whereby the idea of the named thing escapes linguistic nomination and continually renews a space for further poetic expression: "Le vers qui de plusieurs vocables refait un mot total, neuf, étranger à la langue et comme incantatoire, achève cet isolement de la parole : niant, d'un trait souverain, le hasard demeuré aux termes malgré l'artifice de leur retrempe alternée en le sens et la sonorité, et vous cause cette surprise de n'avoir ouï jamais tel fragment ordinaire d'élocution, en même temps que la réminiscence de l'objet nommé baigne dans une neuve atmosphère."[8] Although Roubaud argues that the trobar clus generally remotivates and renews the service to, and the expression of amors, he also shows that other key words of the trobar are refigured by the paradoxical contradictions of certain poems, for example all six rhyme words of Daniel's sestina, each of which is central to the style clus. This link to Mallarmé's poetic object is further implied by a brief comment Roubaud makes after citing Raimbaut d'Orange's "Ar resplan la flors enversa" as a quintessential example of the trobar clus. Mysteriously refraining from reading the namesake of his essay, Roubaud equates the surplus of the inverted style to a definition of love itself—"Pas-autre que fleur: Amors" (FI 331)—which echoes Mallarmé's famous description of an elusive flower: "Je dis : une fleur ! et, hors de l'oubli où ma voix relègue aucun contour, en tant que quelque chose d'autre que les calices sus, musicalement se lève, idée même et suave, l'absente de tous bouquets" (Œ, 279). Whereas Mallarmé's description applies to the idea named by a single word, rescued from the weight of its previous entrapments, Roubaud's description of the trobar clus and its method of entrebescar, applies to a progressive formal evolution within the trobar and its representation of amors. Nonetheless, the movement of both openings is similar. For Mallarmé the signifier is released from "le double état de la parole, brut ou immédiat ici, là essentiel" (Œ, 278), and for Roubaud the "forme formelle" of the trobar is enlarged through two opposing countertexts, the trobar leu and the trobar clus; in each case the poetic principle (l'idée, amors) is "purified" by a strategic manipulation (éloignement, entrebescar) within the formal presentation.

If I have drawn this comparison here between the critiques of these two poets, it is not to measure their respective views on innovation but rather to indicate that Roubaud's aesthetic of memory and his praise for difficult art of the trobar clus rehearse views advanced by other poets. I also want to suggest that what he most values in this experimentalist style is its opening as a poetic trajectory, one that engenders echoes in other poetic periods: "Ce qui compte pour l'interprétation d'ensemble du trobar n'est pas la polémique idéologique des débuts mais de l'appropriation par le trobar de l'essence formelle du clus pour la création d'une 'voie de poésie'

---

[8] Mallarmé, Oeuvres, 279; hereafter cited as Œ.

qui peut être retrouvée ailleurs, de manière assez universelle" (*FI* 319). If the trobar clus undertakes a poetic methodology that is figuratively contrary to the main current of the trobar, and if it deploys a formal method that resists easy memorization and assimilation into the oral discourse, precluding its contribution to the axiom of unisonority (pretz), it also posits an imperative of experimentation that both enriches and displaces the canon of the trobar. The style clus generates new avenues of creativity. Because this style takes the givens of its traditions, to turn them in on themselves, to multiply and interlace their formal properties, the trobar clus is both parodic and productive. Similar tendencies can also be traced in other poetic moments, especially those where specific formal concerns are broadly developed and robustly debated in the discourse.

Roubaud wants to trace the consequences of the trobar clus up to the contemporary poetic scene. Consequently, he pays close attention to how the sestina and the cobla, a fragment of the canso, pass through an Italian appropriation before becoming trigger forms in French poetry. In the next chapter, I shall discuss the atrophy of the trobar as form and comment on how its collapse resonates with the modern poetic conditions in France.

To consider the ratio of influence between tRoubaldian and Roubaldian poetics, in the second chapter I will continue to address Roubaud's reading of the trobar and address his ninetina "Tombeaux de Pétrarque." That poem confirms the unity of a poetic lineage that stretches from the Troubadours Raimbaut d'Orange and Arnaut Daniel, through Petrarch directly to Roubaud's mentor, the Oulipian Raymond Queneau. The sestina has undergone numerous resuscitations in the twentieth century, including many new uses that, through extension or perversion, either manage to crystallize or distort a memory of Arnaut Daniel's canso; my analysis of Roubaud's ninetina considers both the influence of these models and the manner in which Oulipian compositions reinforce and diversify form-embedded meaning.

Chapter Two

CRISTAL DU TROBAR: "TOMBEAUX DE PÉTRARQUE"

In Roubaud's view of literary history, the phenomenon of formal exhaustion is not steeped in the rhetoric of crisis, as it was at the turn of the twentieth century and thereafter. Rather, atrophy is a natural and positive development in the lives of forms. Exhaustion presents opportunities. It spurs research into new literary forms, some of them built from fragments of poetic history. The sonnet, for example, is one such remnant form–or, as Roubaud calls them, a *forme-mémoire*. Born of the canso's dissolution–essentially an isolated cobla–the sonnet transmits an intrinsic memory of the canso and the language of fin'amors. The sestina, by contrast, persists as a whole canso, as the culmination of the style clus. Underlining its singularity in the grand chant, Roubaud dubs Daniel's sestina the "cristal du trobar" for it condenses and encrypts an internal memory of a specific lineage of the trobar. And, once Petrarch adopts the form, essentially redefining it as distinct from the Italian *canzone*, he prolongs that lineage. For Roubaud, the sestina is "chargée de sens formel." Consequently, it becomes an illuminating link between the troubadours and French poetry.

Following the Albigensian Crusades, the French invasion, and the Inquisition of the thirteenth century, the trobar is silenced. "Il y a une diaspora des troubadours" (*FI* 335), leading them to Italy and Portugal, but the "gloire de la langue" in Occitania and in Provençal goes into decline, beginning a long period of subsistence: "C'est le moment du trobar comme survivance" (*FI* 336). Noting that "il est peu d'intérêt de parler de décadence'" (*FI* 335), Roubaud traces the rapid decline in fin'amors; they become indefensible or condemned in the works of thirteenth-century poets like Peire Cardenal, Guilhem de Montanhagol, and Guiraut Riquier. As the raison d'être of the trobar goes into decline so, too, does its poetic form. The canso decomposes as the social milieu that nourished it disappears, resulting in a starved and restrained poetic discourse. That era of subsistence–a lull in poetic production–is sustained by the exchange of shorter, impoverished poems. Relating his analysis of troubadour poetics to contemporary concerns, Roubaud compares this fragmentation to the birth of blank verse: "Un des traits, essentiel pour la suite, de cette décomposition de la forme est l'apparition chez les troubadours, dès la fin du 'moment,' de la *cobla isolée*. On n'a plus une canso, ou un sirventes mais une cobla seule, ou un échange de coblas. Un tel développement est comparable à l'apparition du vers libre par perte de rimes et de mesures imposées. La cobla isolée est une cobla qui ne rime plus avec d'autre dans une canso" (*FI* 340). In both cases, fragmentation produces new poetic forms that encrypt the traces of their destruction.[1] Here, the *cobla isolée*, this fragment of the canso, becomes an independent form and, by virtue of being crafted by Sicilian poets, eventually finds a renewed life as the sonnet (in its many shapes), thereby prolonging fin'amors. That is not to say that the sonnet is itself only a part of the canso, but rather that the canso is fragmentarily inscribed in the birth and elaboration of the sonnet.

Generalizing his hypothesis on the sonnet and its link to the trobar, Roubaud writes, "*Tous les sonnets sont des sonnets de Pétrarque et tous les sonnets de Pétrarque sont des mémoires de la canso*" (*FI* 344). Provocative in its simplicity, this axiom aligns all poetic history along a chain of memory linked by formal continuities and discontinuities. If "la présence et absence de la poésie des troubadours est une question qui dépasse la nostalgie" (*FI* 345), then the trobar's influence resides in the durability of its forms, and in a continuation of fin'amors, even if by a form external to the trobar. Carefully reminding us that "le spectre des troubadours hante la poésie" (*FI* 344), Roubaud juxtaposes the dissolution of their poetics and recent metrical crises in French poetry.

---

[1] This is Roubaud's thesis in *La vieillesse d'Alexandre*, where he shows that the vers libre is not liberated of its alexandrine antecedent but, rather, produced according to an aesthetic that unsuccessfully attempts to escape or subvert its influence. The memory image is therefore a negative imprint of the previously dominant form.

Never is the lesson of the trobar's decline more pertinent than when compared with the modernist disavowal of rhyme. Indeed, the rhetorical A-bomb that closes the trobar is emblematic of contemporary "endgame" poetics—as are other sites of disaster in Roubaud's work—and this helps explain why he closes *La fleur inverse* by reconnecting his arguments to the present context.

> Aujourd'hui, où la chute libératrice de la *rime* qui a fait la splendeur et le vertige du mouvement moderniste en poésie se trouve avoir précipité une crise qui n'est pas près de finir, les troubadours, poètes *mangés de rimes*, réapparaissent,
>
> au silence enroulé avec ironie.
>
> morceau de ligne du *Coup de dés* par quoi cet essai se retrouve à son début. (*FI* 346)

If the crisis facing modern poetry is fundamentally a question of survival, and if both the sonnet and the sestina evince the durability of the trobar, then the experience of the trobar may suggest new poetic solutions, or "voies poétiques," to contemporary poets. From Dada to Surrealism, from Denis Roche to Jean-Marie Gleize, avant-garde writers recursively adopt overtly hostile stances toward tradition as a means of vying for existence. In contrast, Roubaud's volitional archaism and his retracing of the sonnet and sestina as *formes mémoires* illustrate a more engaged approach to poetic history, one that seeks to imagine the European lyric as an interlinked matrix of influence, repetition, and innovation.

According to Roubaud the sestina transmits an "internal memory" of the canso; it constitutes a frayed but unbroken thread of poetic history: "La sextine est une forme mémoire de la canso: c'est une *mémoire interne*, car sa forme n'a d'environnement non abstrait compréhensible que dans le développement propre de la canso où elle est un aboutissement, un cristal de trobar. C'est pourquoi on peut, dans son histoire, suivre à la fois une fidélité exacerbée au champ lexical et conceptuel de l'amors, et une détérioration presque inévitable de la forme, les seules innovations (avant celle de Queneau qui lui donnera une définition abstraite susceptible de généralisation) étant des modifications qui montrent une incompréhension du 'pourquoi' de son mécanisme" (*FI* 343). The notion of an "internal memory" is both enticing and problematic. If all sestinas transmit memories of the trobar, is it solely by virtue of their form? And, if so, how is that memory distorted, deformed, or rehabilitated throughout the history of the sestina? Many sestinas, even the most influential ones, do not adopt this "fidélité exacerbée au champs lexical et conceptuel de l'amors."[2] So, what keeps the form from losing its connection to the trobar? And, to what degree does the notion of memory in Roubaud's model imply an understanding of the aesthetic of entrebescar? Or–turning these question toward Roubaud's work–is it by virtue of their formal interlacing that his compositions reconstruct memory?

When Roubaud directly relates difficulty and value, he is not simply defending his preference for difficult poems. He is also arguing that the difficulty of poetry is what assures its longevity. In *La fleur inverse* he stakes that argument on the difficult poems of the trobar, those consisting of stricter, more complex, and less common constraints. Although hard poems resist transparency and defy memorization, they also diversify and strengthen poetic discourse. Consequently, difficult poetic forms act as conduits for value. Mature fixed forms, like the sestina and sonnet, harbor in them the reshaping and renewal of tradition. By comparing the dissolution of the trobar to the ends of the dominant metrical form in France, and by locating the sestina as cristal du trobar, Roubaud retraces continuity and discontinuity in historical, form-invested poetry. Unapologetic, perhaps even playfully defiant about the resistance formalist poetry poses to assimilation, Roubaud prizes hard poems as treasure chests of memory, as key sites where language encodes consciousness rhythmically.

Since the sestina is the cristal du trobar and the trobar is his primary model, it follows that many of Roubaud's creative projects experiment with the logic of the sestina. The sestina, for example, is clearly inscribed into the structure of his *Hortense* novels. Though less directly, that form also subtends his *Projet* and the novel that recounts its destruction, *'le grand incendie de Londres'*. If Roubaud's sestinas rehearse an intentional memory of form, they also simultaneously articulate variations in its transmission and generalization, perhaps none more explicitly than "Tombeaux de

---

[2] Louis Zukofsky's sestina "Mantis," for example, recasts Daniel's form in an urban setting using rhyme words that do not recall theories of fin' amors (leaves/poor/it/you/lost/stone). Yet, "'Mantis,' an Interpretation," which illuminates the piece, refers to both Dante and the origin of the form. Zukofsky, *Complete Short Poetry*, 65-73.

Pétrarque." In this multi-layered poetic sepulcher, Roubaud reworks fragments of Petrarch's *Canzoniere* and, deploying Oulipian reasoning, recasts the sestina as a ninetina (a poem that is to the number nine what the sestina is to the number six). Here, as elsewhere, Roubaud aligns his work with elements of the trobar clus, and in doing so he signs his engagement with contemporary poetry as eminently tRoubaldian.

THE EXTREME CONTEMPORARY: *QUENINES* AND "TOMBEAUX DE PÉTRARQUE"

Throughout his work, Roubaud adopts numerous positions about poetry: what it is, where it is going, and how it relates to language and the world. Among these is his view that poetry is immanently contemporary, that "poetry is now" (*PM* 114). In discussing "Tombeaux de Pétrarque" and its inscription into the lineage of the trobar clus, I first consider the contemporaneity of language and describe how Roubaud situates poetry at the limits of language, or as the "extreme contemporary."

An essential question asked in and of poetry is how–or if–it relates to the presence of the material world. In "Poésie, contemporaine extrême" Roubaud recognizes that for some, "l'anachronisme de la poésie est radicale. Entre la poésie et l'univers, nulle contemporaneité, semble-t-il, ne subsiste."[3] Betraying his Wittgensteinian sympathies, Roubaud adopts an opposite point of view. He affirms that language writes the world and that the indispensable role of poetry is to write language into the world, and to write possible worlds in poetry. "La langue est le contemporain [. . .]: être dans le langage pour l'inscrire dans l'univers matériel. Tel est pour moi le contemporain dont l'extrême est la poésie. *Le langage est contemporain: la poésie est l'extrême contemporain*" (*EX* 182). To adopt the decision of "being *in* language" in an extreme manner, "comme archaïque, comme artisan, comme *joueur*," is to write one's contemporaneity, to radicalize poetry as an objective presence of language in the world. It is to write with the understanding that all poetry is the memory of a language, that all poetry is contemporaneous in a language, and that all poetry speaks in a continuous present.

---

[3] Roubaud (1988), *EX*.

In *Poésie, etcetera: ménage*, Roubaud couches these same attitudes in deceptively simple, almost satiric language. That "poetry is now" seems to have two consequences. First, it relates to how poetry speaks, or what it means. On this score Roubaud is categorical, claiming that poetry, as poetry, does not mean anything (*La poésie ne dit rien*" [PM 75]), or that "*La poésie dit ce qu'elle dit en le disant*" (PM 77). This does not preclude poetry from thinking, or from exploiting every possible means of meaning. Rather, it simply excludes poetry, as a discourse, from having to be sensical. In effect, what Roubaud proposes in *Poésie, etcetera: ménage* is a generalized version of what he said about estribot poems in *La fleur inverse*:

> Un poème qui dit de la pensée, dit aussi le contraire, de façon plus ou moins visible
> dit aussi autre chose, de façon plus ou moins visible; dit aussi la même pensée mais de manière redondante
> dit encore la meme pensée, mais par des moyens obliques, par des moyens formels. La seule exigence c'est que tout soit, poétiquement, *tenu*. (PM 94)

"Poetry is now" also describes the contemporaneity of language as a repository for memory. Once a poem enters language as memory, it remains potentially imminent, present to other poems in that language: "Ce que ça 'mean' c'est, en particulier, ceci: que l'*Odyssée*, La Chanson de la fleur inverse de Raimbaut d'Orange, la Divine Comédie, Le Vierge le vivace et le bel aujourd'hui, la Petite Cosmogonie Portative, Etat d'Anne-Marie Albiach sont 'maintenant,' des poèmes de maintenant; ceci pour chaque maintenant qui se présente" (PM 115 [sic]).

Four additional assertions accompany Roubaud's view of the contemporaneity of poetic language. First, poetry unavoidably requires doing violence to ordinary language. Second, there is no limit to linguistic extremity, just as there is no return. Third, innovation in language provides a perspective on the current state of language, providing a weathervane for its currency, its cultural force (this requirement simply guards against viewing contemporaneity as conditioned by impulse, or fashion). Fourth, empirically speaking, the only given is that there is contemporaneity in language; the question of accessing it in composition remains emblematic of problems associated with determining a center, or structure by which the field of poetry can be assessed (*EX* 183).

The extremity of Roubaud's stance is nearly always practical and concrete. By positing an objective or empirical approach to the evolution of forms through the statistical analysis of their concrete elements (ART), Roubaud defines the conditions of his own contemporaneity in language. In my view, it is according to that approach that one can best assess his work as innovative. For him, what is extreme in the making present of language is the ceaseless legitimation of poetry as a means of shaping the world, even when that reshaping includes contradiction, parology, and destruction: "La poésie comme contemporaine (et dans ce cas extrême-contemporaine) est une déclaration. [...] Déclaration d'amour et de droits, d'amour et détestation de la langue [...] et son extrémisme est de ne jamais céder sur cela" (*EX* 185). His formalist approach also helps reshape and revitalize what already silently inhabits the margins of poetic history and it illuminates the lineage he claims as his.

Granted that his manner of taking up residency in the contemporaneity of language deeply informs his research of, and investment in, literary forms (and vice versa), the extremity of Roubaud's stance within language may be best understood performatively, through his poetic compositions. If poetry is both the memory of and the extreme contemporary of language, how then do Roubaud's experiments with the sestina constitute innovations in his poetic heritage? What can they tell us about his approach to his poetic present? In "Tombeaux de Pétrarque" Roubaud optimizes the use of formal constraints as a means of building an effect of memory into his work. It is the self-reflexivity inscribed into Roubaud's formal practices, his form-motivated enactment of memory, which places his sestina compositions at the cutting edge of contemporary experimentation.

Commenting on recent sestina experiments, Roubaud notes that postmodern poetries often treat traditional forms derisively. Granted its illustrious history, from the Renaissance to the present, the sestina has been a kind test piece for poets.[4] The difficulty of the form incites contemporary experiments that both revere and revile its conventions.

> Une des caractéristiques du vingtième siècle (et du vingtième siècle récent) est l'apparition de nombreuses transformations des formes poétiques traditionnelles (il s'agit presque d'une explo-

---

[4] See Lartigue, *L'hélice d'écrire*.

sion); ces transformations sont à la fois des variations du modèle, des bouleversements (formes de décomposition parfois ironiques), des détournements, des pastiches, des inventions par analogie, des généralisations, des transpositions de langue à langue, d'auteur à auteur, de siècle à siècle. La *forme-sextine* n'a pas échappé à ce mouvement, parallèle au mouvement axiomatique en mathématiques, et parallèle aussi (mais allant à contre-courant) à celui qui vise à la destruction et à l'oubli de toutes formes sanctionnées par les traditions. On pourrait même dire qu'elle a été particulièrement touchée par ce phénomène. (*FI* 351)

Although, as I argue, each of these poetic transformations—variation, upheaval, diversion, pastiche, and invention—applies to "Tombeaux de Pétrarque," not all sestina experiments affect the memory in the same way. Indeed, if they lead to over-proliferation, or to the dissolution of the poem's formal properties, can experiments destroy or confound what's inscribed in a form?

Contemporaneity in language articulates tensions between convention and invention. The extremity of Roubaud's sestina experiments may be accounted for in the degree to which they recycle and renew the specific language of the form and in the degree to which they prolong, or repress, the discourse of fin'amors. "Tombeaux de Pétrarque" foregrounds a shifting memory of the sestina, both through the vocabulary of Petrarch's *Canzoniere* and through its use of *Quenines*.

QUENINES

As early as 1964, Raymond Queneau identifies the sestina as a "particularly potential" form (*BC* 329). Noting that the mechanics of its constraints are optimal, Queneau generalizes the form, first by identifying other numbers susceptible to the same permutation, and then by proposing a set of new poetic forms, known to Oulipians as *quenines*.[5] Quenines are poems that obey the same rules as Arnaut Daniel's sestina, but with a different quantity of rhyme words. The

---

[5] Not all numbers are susceptible to the quenine permutation; Queneau has located thirty-one among the first one hundred whole numbers (all of which are named in Oulipian theory, e.g. the *unine* or *monine*, the *bibine* or *didine*, etc.): 1 2 3 5 6 9 11 14 18 23 26 29 30 33 35 39 41 50 51 53 65 69 74 81 83 86 90 95 98 99.

ninetina, for example, isolates nine rhyme words (classically nouns) and reorders them according to the turning motion of the crystal du trobar. If each rhyme word were represented as a number, the permutations of the whole poem could be modeled in this way (see figure 2); each permutation completes the same spiraling motion as the sestina.

FIGURE 2

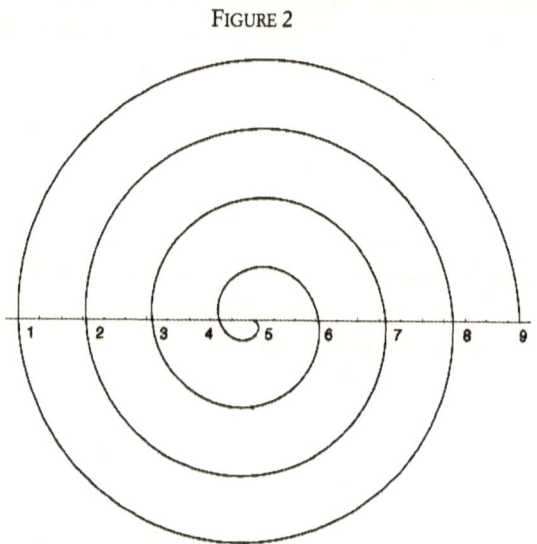

Here is the complete numerical model of the ninetina:

TABLE 2

123456789
918273645
594168327
752934816
671582493
369741258
835629174
487315962
246897531

Quenines require that the number of permutations and elements correspond; that is, in a ninetina, nine permutational steps are composed, followed by the envoi, or *tornada*. If a tenth stanza were written, the original order would be reestablished. The ninetina is of the ninth order, just as the sestina is of the sixth order.

The greater the length of quenines, the greater the difficulty. Consonant with Roubaud's preference of the style clus over the style leu, Oulipian theory supposes that difficult constraints produce meritorious texts.[6] But that difficulty also inflects on the relationship between poetry and memory. For example, because it introduces an optimal permutation in differentially distributing six rimes estramps over six stanzas, Arnaut Daniel's canso, "Lo ferm voler q'el cor m'intra," can be viewed as a refinement of Raimbaut d'Orange's "Ar resplan la flors enversa." Within the context of the grand chant, the additional constraint renders the memorization and performance of the song much more difficult. However, once that difficulty is mastered (inevitably through a comprehension of the form's logic), once its complexity is assimilated into tradition, difficulty hardens into durability, thereby improving a form's ability to transmit memory. Although the conditions for poetic transmission in the twentieth century do not rely as heavily on our abilit to memorize poems, I would suggest that, in writing a quenine loaded with words from Petrarch's *Canzoniere*, Roubaud resourcefully contributes to and extends the aesthetic of entrebescar inscribed in "Lo ferm voler q'el cor m'intra."

"TOMBEAUX DE PÉTRARQUE"

Originally published in 1975, "Tombeaux de Pétrarque" is now one of four "parties de poèmes" in *Dors* (1981), a book Roubaud calls "un programme de lecture" (*D* 33). In the text's user's manual, or *Indication*, Roubaud introduces as oral works the four poems of *Dors* ("Dors," "Tombeaux de Pétrarque," "Neuf éclats de l'âge des saints," and "La piste du vent"), as well as the essay that precedes them (*Dire la poésie*). They were all conceived "pour être transportés réellement par la voix."[7] Claiming that each text enjoys nearly autonomous modes of being, depending on whether it is read or heard, Roubaud instructs his reader to follow a peculiar sequence when reading the volume aloud: once one reaches the end of the fourth poem, "La piste du vent," the reading should contin-

---

[6] Motte, *Poetics of Experiment*, 19.
[7] Roubaud recorded a CD of the essay "Dire la poésie" and the poem "Tombeaux de Pétrarque," originally distributed in *Licorne 40* (1997).

ue in "Dors," but according to a specified sequence, "dans l'ordre inverse."[8] *Dors* is thus presented as a poem that experiments with serial combinations organized in a predetermined order. As such, it may be compared to minimalist compositions in music, for it includes similar effects of phrasal layering and strict restraint in the lexical field.

Like the final page of *La fleur inverse*, the end of this collection sends readers back to its beginning, implying a loop or a weave in the order of reading. In both cases Roubaud motivates a formally programmed re-reading. And, as noted, the figure of the loop is inscribed in the cyclical permutations of the quenines–"C'est là un des charmes de la sextine: la circularité potentielle mais non actuelle"; it is this potential circularity that leaves the audience of quenines almost hearing a return to the point of departure.[9] This trope of doubling back, or returning with a difference, recurs throughout Roubaud's works; it is, in a microscopic sense, the most basic element of rhyme as an act of memory; the expectation and recognition of a returning sound, determined in time by the rhythm of the piece. Serial compositions, both musical and poetic, present the same elements over and over again, but in a sequence of slightly differing order, thereby building, through minimal variation and multiple layering, a double effect of constancy and gradual change, or drift. In *Dors*, Roubaud attunes his readers to these sonorous effects and invites them to hear the coherence they provide to the collection as a whole.

"Je vais pleurant et désirant le jour" (*D* 37) is the phrase that most clearly establishes cohesion within *Dors*. It occurs in the poem "Dors" and, in a fragmented manner, in "Tombeaux" and the two other poems. Roubaud has multiple reasons for interweaving this verse throughout the context of his poem. To begin, it is an intentional echo

---

[8] Owing to separate intertexts, each poem of *Dors* proposes a different direction or branch of reading. "Dors" plays with a blank verse "dont l'inspiration est de William Carlos Williams, à travers Louis Zukofsky, mais s'éloignant à la fois de l'hasard spontané et du nombre" (*D* 34); "Neuf éclats de l'âge des saints" is a selection of translated Celtic fragments, most of which are said to have been found "en marges des livres sacrés" (*D* 37); in "La piste du vent," Roubaud offers versions of songs from four Native American languages: Pima, Winnebago, Navajo, and Zuni; "4 fois 4 poèmes empruntés à la poésie indienne terminent ce livre de poésie orale" (*D* 37). All citations from "Tombeaux" refer to the *Dors* edition and are followed by line numbers in the text. The entire poem is printed in the appendix.

[9] Roubaud (1992), "N-ines, autrement dit quenines," 7.

of Petrarch's *Canzoniere* ("vo lagrimando et disiando il giorno").[10] Not only does Roubaud indicate the specific textual locations of his citation, he takes advantage of the reference to cite Vasquin Philieul de Carpantras, a Grand Rhétoriqueur who was one of the first to translate Petrarch ("Vais larmoyant et desirant le jour" [D 35]) from whom he borrows the French translations. His quoting practices (or recitational practices) thus help motivate the "programme de lecture" of the text; they stage a history and incite a reconstruction of a textual trajectory passing through Petrarch's *Canzoniere*.

The organization and numerology of the *Canzoniere* have intrigued readers for centuries; Roubaud is no exception.[11] Given his attention to the sequentiality of reading in *Dors* (and his *Projet*), one may well ask what relationship there is between the mathematical organization of "Tombeaux de Pétrarque" and the *Rime sparse*. Roubaud indicates that the order of the poems of the *Canzoniere* exerts a direct influence on the form of "Tombeaux de Pétrarque." That order explicitly influences how he sets the lexical field of the *Rime sparse* into motion in his poem: "Chaque strophe-stèle est écrite en décasyllables à e muets libres (ils comptent ou ne comptent pas) et chaque décasyllabe enferme trois mots clés d'une des neuf sextines de Pétrarque (54 mots en tout en début, milieu et fin de vers), en respectant l'ordre de leur apparition dans le canzoniere et en construisant, par le mouvement de roue de ces mots une 'neuvine,' qui est au nombre neuf ce que la sextine est au six. La *neuvine* est une forme inventée par Raymond Queneau, dans laquelle tournent les sextines de Pétrarque, chacune résumée par ce qui en est le coeur, la liste ordonnée de ses six mots clés, dans l'ordre qui est celui de chaque dernière strophe" (D 34). In this description, Roubaud identifies enclosure and cyclical motion in each strophe-stèle (*stèle* refers to a monolithic stone monument bearing an inscription, a Greek or Egyptian gravestone). The compound expression *stanza-stela* aptly expresses the elaborate architectural construction characteristic of tombeaux, and it evokes if only by proximity the luminosity of a constellation, or an imaginary universe, a possible world where resonance between key words (*pierres vives*) is integral to the creative process. Like the sestina, Petrarch's words

---

[10] Petrarca, *Petrarch's Lyric Poems*, 57; hereafter all references and English translations are cited as *RS*.
[11] See Roubaud (1990), "La disposition numérologique," 215-40.

are "chargés de sens formel," and it is in their movement, in the way they relate to each other textually, that Roubaud inscribes his act of reading. Roubaud clearly distinguishes the stanza-stela and the words that inhabit them as discrete but strictly interrelated elements. "A mesure que le poème avance, de stèle en stèle, les mots clès de toutes les sextines se déplacent, dans l'ordre inverse de celui de Pétrarque, et mélangés, ou plutôt entrelacés, selon la neuvine. [...] On pourra observer que, de même que les 54 mots choisis par Pétrarque pour ses sextines sont des mots clés, non seulement des sextines mais de l'ensemble du *Canzoniere*, les mots clés choisis pour cet hommage gouvernent le sens et le déroulement de ses vers, constituant une interprétation, tout à fait personelle bien sûr, du 'chansonnier'" (*D* 36-37). To retrace how the context and connotation of each rhyme word influences meaning in the ninetina, one might attempt to account for their use throughout Petrarch's works. Such a study would inform a very close reading of the "Tombeaux," for it would make explicit the lyrical dye that colors each key word. Yet, it is not certain that such a microscopic reading would illuminate Roubaud's "entirely personal interpretation" of the *Canzoniere* or shed light on the way those words are used in the ninetina. However, considering the poem without taking into account their culminating role in the *Canzoniere* as sites of celebration and complaint would be to neglect an intended intertext.

RIME SPARSE

In *L'hélice d'écrire,* Pierre Lartigue notes that the fifty-four key words of "Tombeaux" transmit a specific poetic lineage, not merely because they play a unifying role in the *Canzoniere*, but also because they reflect the poetic attributes of the underlying model, the trobar:

> Le choix des mots refrains est intéressant. Les voici classés alphabétiquement:
> –*Alba, Alma, Anni, Aura*–*(Bosco, Boschi)*–*Chiome, Cielo, Corso*– *Fine, Fiori, Fiumi*–*Ghiaccio, Giorno*–*Lauro, Legno, Leito, Lume, Luna*–*Morte*–*Nebbia, Neve, Note, (Notte, Notti), Nove*–*Occhi, Onde*–*Parte, Piaggia, Pianto, Pioggia, Poggi, Porto, Porto, Pregio*– *Rami, Rime, Riva*–*Sciolta, Scogli, Selva, Sera, Sole, Stelle, Stile* –*Tempo, Terra*–*Valli, Vela, Venti, Versi, Vita.*

> Cinquante-quatre mots différents pour cinquante-quatre positions. Deux pluriels sont acceptés. On ne peut imaginer variété plus grande. Et les mots, d'autre part, sont les mots essentiels du chant courtois. (58)

If one of the strengths of the grand chant resides in the value it attributes to formal variety, then the sestina embodies that variety on a compact scale: end-rhymes enjoy optimal variance, both in terms of the distance between rhymes and of their timbres, for, classically, the six end-rhymes of one sestina do not rhyme. The variety Lartigue notes is also a diversity of sounds. Indeed, there are few strong rhymes in this list; it constitutes a quasi-vers estramp, a closed set, primed for permutation. These words are also already prime examples of motz clus, for the *Canzoniere* already contains and condenses the poetic history of the grand chant.[12]

In "Tombeaux," Roubaud's displacements begin with an Oulipian choice, one that he attributes to Queneau: "To approach language as if it could be mathematized." For Roubaud, all elements of language count and are to be counted. In order to mathematize language, one must first isolate its elements or atomize its parts, from the largest integers (e.g., books) to its smallest (e.g., letters). In "Littérature potentielle," Queneau shows how adding procedural constraints to such an approach can generate a wide variety of new poems. In one instance, he demonstrates that, with a smooth pass of the hand, a procedure called "haikuization" can effortlessly produce brand-new poems.

In this method of textual reproduction, one simply selects a poem, isolates the rhyme word(s) of every verse, and, leaving them in their original order, distills a new, shorter poem. Queneau takes Mallarmée's "Le vierge, le vivace, le bel aujourd'hui" as the parent poem, modifying its punctuation:

> Aujourd'hui
> Ivre,
> le givre
> Pas fui!

---

[12] Also see Roubaud (1996), "RVF 1-14." Here too Roubaud draws on the *Canzoniere* in composing a series of poems: "Des 14 premiers poèmes de *Rerum Vulgarum Fragmenta*, plus connus sous le nom de *Canzoniere*, ces poèmes ont été inspirés, à l'aide de prélèvements, ou quasi." Again, Roubaud's "prélèvements" in this series are motivated by rhythmic concerns accounting for the metrical, melodic, and lexical weight of select words.

> Lui
> se délivre...
> où vivre?
> L'Ennui...
>
> Agonie
> le nie,
> pris,
>
> assigne
> mépris,
> le Cygne. (*BC* 334)

    To isolate and recombine the rhyme words of a model poem, or a series of model poems, suggests derision and irreverence. The haikuizations Queneau exacts on Mallarmé's sonnets betray the playful spirit of Oulipian constraint. They are intended as amusement. Yet, through naïve demonstration, they also bring to light two byproducts: first, new poems that would otherwise remain dormant in classic works of literature; second, the recognition of the original poem's durability. In this case, the violence committed to the original texts may be viewed in a ludic light, for the swan appears not so taken, and happily reassigns contempt in response to this intoxicated procedure.

    While similar in spirit and practice, in "Tombeaux de Pétrarque," the haikuization is not the product of a simple, one-step procedure. It is considerably more complex in that each line integrates the rhyme words of Petrarch's sestinas. Consequently, the meaning and sonority of the text is condensed and compounded. Instead of isolating and presenting nine refrain words in their given order, as an independent poem, Roubaud assigns the fifty-four words of six separate rhyme series a spiraling permutation of their own, thereby winding six times as many rhyme words into his ninetina. In order to explain the constraints at work in "Tombeaux" it is useful to establish the order in which the rhyme words appear in Petrarch's nine sestinas.[13]

---

[13] Petrarch numbers his sestinas in order of appearance among the other 366 poems (sonnets, *canzoni*, madrigals) of the *Canzoniere*: 22, 30, 66, 80, 152, 214, 237, 239, and 332.

TABLE 3

i	1 terre	2 soleil	3 jour	4 étoiles	5 forêt	6 aube
ii	7 laurier	8 neige	9 années	10 cheveux	11 yeux	12 rive
iii	13 brume	14 vents	15 pluie	16 fleuves	17 vallées	18 glace
iv	19 vie	20 écueils	21 navires	22 but	23 port	24 voile
v	25 feuilles	26 lumière	27 ciel	28 collines	29 temps	30 branches
vi	31 lieu	32 neuf	33 prix	34 cours	35 légère	36 bois
vii	37 eaux	38 lune	39 nuit	40 bois	41 pente	42 soir
viii	43 air	44 fleurs	45 vers	46 âme	47 force	48 note
ix	49 joyeux	50 nuits	51 style	52 rimes	53 pleurs	54 mort

Before commenting on the combinatory Roubaud imposes on these six lists of rhyme words, it is worthy to note that in the French list there is a greater proximity of sounds–fleurs/pleurs; yeux/cheveux/joyeux–especially in cases where the plural and singular are included, as in bois, nuit(s). The effect is a loss of sonorous diversity. I return to the register of rhyme because by tracking both internal rhyme and interstrophic rhyme one can best map the constraints Roubaud adopts for his ninetina.

Normally, there are nine rhyme words in a ninetina, all of them appearing once per stanza, at the end of the line. In "Tombeaux" every line contains three rhyme words, one at the beginning, one in the middle, and one at the end. That is, in addition to loosely respecting a decasyllabic meter, each stanza contains $3 \times 9 = 27$ rhyme positions, and the whole poem (excluding the envoi) includes $27 \times 9 = 243$ rhyme positions. The combinatory selected by Roubaud organizes the key words into three separate sets, each of which obeys its own distinct mode of permutation: the distribution of sestina-lines follows the permutation of the regular ninetina; the internal or horizontal rhymes obey a permutation called the *sextine rétrograde*; and the columns of vertical rhymes create an effect of interlacing. The first two sets consist of the nine series (or lists) of rhyme words culled from the *Rime sparse*; I treat those sestina series first. The third set addresses rhyme from stanza to stanza; it consists of six series of nine words each.

In the first set, there are nine elements, the nine sestinas represented by the nine lists of rhyme words. Throughout the poem, Roubaud keeps these lists distinct and assigns the lines representing each sestina to a specific place in each stanza, according to the permutations of the quenine. That is, the first sestina (number 22 in the *Canzoniere*) appears as the first line in the first stanza, as the second in the second, as the fourth in the third, as the eight in the fourth, and so on, until it reaches the ninth line position in the ninth stanza.

But within each discrete series of rhyme words–set two–there is another permutation at work. Consider, for example, the last line of the first stanza: "Poisse la nuit comme rime   à la mort." A partial haikuization of Petrarch's last sestina, that line appears in the ninth line-position of the first stanza; it integrates three words from that poem–*nuit*, *rime*, and *mort*–but they are given in the same order as in the *Canzoniere*. Following the logic of a quenine, that same sestina is echoed in the first line of the second stanza, but this time by the three missing elements, *fleur*, *style*, *joyeux*: "Poisse des fleurs   ou dans le style joyeux." In this case, the word *poisse* makes the explicit link between the two coblas capcaudées; otherwise there is no overlap in the series. If, beginning with this series, we transcribe the appearance of these six words over the course of the poem we discover that although the stanzas respect the line distribution of the ninetina, the nine discrete series obey the permutation of the sextine rétrograde, a permutation that is an inversion of Daniel-Queneau.

Modeling the sextine rétrograde will facilitate an understanding of how it works in the entire poem. If we assign numbers to the lines just cited (*nuit* = 1, *rime* = 2, *mort* = 3, *fleur* = 4, *style* = 5, *joyeux* = 6), we can trace their reappearance over the course of the stanzas (I-IX); although the sextine rétrograde does not follow the spiraling motion of the classic sestina, moving from one line to the next involves rewriting every other element from left to right (2, 4, 6), and then writing what remains from right to left (5, 3, 1).

TABLE 4

I.	1 2 3	4 5 6	II.
III.	2 4 6	5 3 1	IV.
IV.	4 5 1	3 6 2	VI.
VII.	5 3 2	6 1 4	VIII.
IX.	3 6 4	1 2 5	
	6 1 5	2 4 3	

At each step, Roubaud includes only one half of the parent series. Consequently, the refrain lines remain partial and fragmentary. Also, as the roman numerals indicate, since there are nine coblas in

CRISTAL DU TROBAR: "TOMBEAUX DE PÉTRARQUE"

"Tombeaux," the implied structure remains unfinished; there are three triplets (in *italics*) that do not appear in the poem.

To picture how these constraints figure in the poem as a whole, I have tabulated the 243 rhyme positions, replacing the 54 rhyme words with the number that corresponds to their order of appearance in the *Canzoniere* (see table 5). That order is essential in understanding the implied meaning of the constraints in this poem, for it is both respected and inverted by the permutations.

TABLE 5

	A B C		E C A		E C B
I	*2 4 6* i	IV	39 42 **38**	VII	45 48 46
	8 10 12 ii		27 30 **26**		15 18 16
	14 16 18 iii		9 12 **8**		27 30 28
	20 22 24 iv		51 54 **50** ix		33 36 34
	26 28 30 v		15 18 **14**		9 12 10
	32 34 36 vi		21 24 **20**		<u>51 53 52</u> ix
	38 40 42 vii		45 48 **44**		*3 6 4* i
	44 ? 48 viii		*3 6 2* i		31 42 40
	<u>50 52 54</u> ix		33 36 **32**		21 24 22

	D E F		D E A		F A D
II	<u>44 51 49</u> ix	V	35 33 **32**	VIII	19 20 23
	5 3 1 i		41 39 **38**		43 44 47
	47 45 43		*5 3 2* i		37 38 41
	11 9 7		29 27 **26**		13 14 17
	41 39 37		47 45 **44**		*1 2 5* i
	17 15 13		11 9 **8**		25 26 29
	35 33 31		23 21 **20**		<u>49 50 44</u> ix
	23 21 19		<u>53 51 50</u> ix		31 32 35
	29 27 25		17 15 **14**		7 8 11

	B D F		C F B		C F D
III	28 29 25	VI	18 13 16	IX	12 7 11
	<u>52 53 49</u> ix		36 31 34		24 19 23
	22 23 19		<u>54 49 52</u> ix		36 31 35
	4 5 1 i		42 37 40		48 43 47
	34 35 31		24 19 22		<u>54 49 53</u> ix
	? 47 43		*6 1 4* i		42 37 41
	16 17 13		12 7 10		30 25 29
	10 11 7		30 25 28		18 13 17
	40 41 37		48 43 ?		*6 1 5* i

Although this figure does not take into account the many additional repetitions, rhymes, and echoes that are integral to the poem (e.g., the word *poisse* in lines 9 and 10), it details the exact placement of each rhyme word. For the moment, what most interests me in the ordering of the elements is how they relate to one another, and to their parent context, the *Rime sparse*. I will not address the exceptions to the rules, or clinamen, here.[14]

Each triplet represents one sestina taken in order of appearance in the *Rime sparse*, and the line permutation respects the form of the ninetina. In this sense, by the ordering of the individual lines, "Tombeaux" takes up and continues the sequence imposed by the *Canzoniere*. It applies the movement of the ninetina to the Petrarchan sestinas.

It may be argued that the relationship between the first and last stanzas, and between the first and last rhymes, is a privileged perspective in the composition of quenines, for in the steps that intercede, the rhyme words (in this case, rhyme lines) undergo a semiotic adventure, signifying slightly differently with every new return. Often, the meaning of the words motivates the first and last positions in a sestina. In Daniel's canso, for example, the first sestina, the first rhyme word is *intra* (enter), and the last is *cambra* (room); as the song progresses, *intra* works its way to the end of the series, and *cambra* enters the center of the final stanza. The nine-rhyme-series in Roubaud's ninetina entertains the same relationship. The elements of the first sestina (printed in italics and labeled i in table 5) progressively work their way around and through the other eight series and settle at the end of the ninth strophe. Similarly, the series defined by the ninth sestina (labeled ix and underlined in table 5) progressively works its way to the center of the final stèle. The nature of this intertwining holds true for each sestina series, as it does for each individual rhyme word in a simple quenine.

As already described, the structure of the sestina rétrograde determines the recombination of elements within the sestina series.

---

[14] There are three clinamen in the text. In the first, Roubaud interchanges the words *fleur* and *pleurs*. In the second, he writes *terre* where his constraints call for *soleil*. In the third, more complicated case, he replaces the word *âme* with the series *trame*, *flamme*, *rame* and (in the envoi) *arme*. These exceptions constitute versions of clinamen, or a formally programmed mistake. For a discussion of their significance in the poem, see Monika Elvira Laskowski-Caujolle and Jean-Jacques Poucel, "Descriptions de 'Tombeaux de Pétrarque.'"

One feature of that constraint is that it redistributes the rhyme-series over the space of two lines in succeeding stanzas, thereby extending the distance between the return of rhyme words. There is, in addition, a second formal effect that must be noted. Each rhyme-series appears in "Tombeaux" in the order of its final permutation in the *Canzoniere*. That is, the sestina-sequences established by the ninetina begin with the same disposition of elements found in each sixth stanza of the *Canzoniere*. For example, the ninth sestina series begins over the first two stanzas as I. (*nuits, rime, mort*) and II. (*fleur, style, joyeux*), which is the order of their final point of arrival in poem 332 of the *Rime sparse*, the double sestina "Mia beniga fortuna e'l viver lieto." By beginning with this last disposition of rhyme words, Roubaud could have completed the loop implied in each sestina series. Instead, the movement of the selected permutation reverses the order of rhyme in the parent context. By imposing an inversion in the constraint, he inscribes resistance to closure in the form itself. This contralinear movement of the sestina and the retrograde sestina may be easily understood by comparing the two numerical models:

TABLE 6

		Sestina	Retrograde Sestina
Cobla	I	1 2 3 4 5 6	2 4 6 5 3 1
	II	6 1 5 2 4 3	4 5 1 3 6 2
	III	3 6 4 1 2 5	5 3 2 6 1 4
	IV	5 3 2 6 1 4	3 6 4 1 2 5
	V	4 5 1 3 6 2	6 1 5 2 4 3
	VI	2 4 6 5 3 1	1 2 3 4 5 6

In a sense, the two structures are negative mirror images of each other, or palindromic opposites. The classic sestina begins where the retrograde ends, and vice versa; and they each retrace the same combinations in between.

Enclosing this backward movement within the rhyme lines (each of which independently follows the normal forward movement of the ninetina) strengthens the way the poem thematizes a resistance to, or reversal of, natural time (the coming of dawn, the passing of days), which, like the rhyme-lines, never ceases its forward march (I return to that aspect of the poem below). In addition, this formal backtracking of the permutations inscribed into these particular sestina series recalls Arnaut Daniel's famous signature:[15]

> *Ieu sui Arnautz quamas l'aura*
> *e chatz la lebre ab lo bou*
> *e nadi contra suberna.*
> Je suis Arnaut qui amasse le vent
> chasse le lièvre avec le bœuf
> et nage contre le courant. (*T* 236)

While the figure of "swimming against the current" might well refer to the trobar clus, and its tendency to resist the classifications of the trobar leu, in Roubaud's poem, there is an architectonic incorporation of going against the grain. Before explicitly linking this form-oriented revolt, or counter-current to the style and images of the poem, however, I wish to explore the third combinatorial set of the poem–arguably, the most important.

In most quenines, the phenomenon of rhyme (or key words) is organized vertically, from stanza to stanza. Until now, my description of the form has concentrated on the permutation of the nine appropriated sestina series. Since that combinatorial set redistributes elements within lines, we might refer to that form of internal line rhyme as horizontal; each half permutation of the retrograde sestina is written into a single verse, and the verses each hold within them the whirling rhymes of the *Rime sparse*. Since the phenomenon of rhyme is, strictly speaking, a question of time or distance–the return of the same at a later time–the horizontal-vertical metaphor describes only the appearance of the poem on the page. Nonetheless, evoking yet another interpretive metaphor, of text as textile, one can picture the first two sets of combinatorial permutations as belonging to the woof of "Tombeaux." In this model, each sestina

---

[15] The sonorous implication of this signature may be fundamental to Roubaud's personal interpretation of the *Rime sparse*, for it is where he hears a potential source for *Laura*: "'qu'amas l'aura' peut être interprété, par voisinage sonore, 'qui aime Laure' (Laura) et ce pourrait être cette proximité de sons qui a donné naissance par le jeu de l'imagination poétique, à la dame de Pétrarque ; car Pétrarque, qui emprunte à Daniel la forme de la sextine, qui la crée comme forme poétique autonome, lui donnant une place importante dans le *Canzoniere*, fait une allusion précise à cette canso dans sa sextine 'là ver l'aurora che sì dolce l'aura' où il se livre à cette identification de mots-sons" (*T* 236).

series represents a thread, with all nine threads being interwoven throughout the poem. In addition, each of these horizontal threads consists of six elements, smaller filaments colored by the sonority of each rhyme word; and these groups of filaments are wound around each other according to a logic that is precisely the inverse of the logic organizing the nine threads (or sestina series). In this sense, we can imagine the text as a tapestry, with threads that traverse back and forth as woof. To hold together, that same tapestry would necessarily have its warp, or horizontal threads. These constitute the third set of elements that Roubaud interlaces in "Tombeaux."

Each verse of "Tombeaux" includes three rhyme positions, one at the beginning, the middle, and the end of the line. Consequently, each stanza could entirely accommodate a three-way compound rhyme pattern. But, in mapping the rhyme schemes of the poem, one discovers *six* partial ninetina-series (labeled A, B, C, D, E, F in table 5). Characteristic of his tendency toward optimization and fragmentation, in a poem where phagocitation ("Ou le soleil mange les étoiles dans l'aube" [1]) accompanies maximal compacting ("Temps du ciel gavé de feuilles" [18]), Roubaud permutes twice as many elements as he allows for positions. The resulting sequence implies the alternating presence and absence of three rhyme strands, or the alternating dissimulation of three threads, hidden as strands of hair disappear and reappear in a braid.

By rhyme strand, I am referring to a sequence of words grouped vertically in each strophe. In the first strophe, for example, the A strand is *soleil, neige, vent, écueil, lumière, neuf, lune, fleur, nuit*, or written numerically (according to the *Canzoniere* list of table 2), 2, 8, 14, 20, 26, 32, 38, 44, 50. I have highlighted that strand throughout my diagram of the song to demonstrate that this series, like the other five, obeys the spiraling permutation of the quenine, even when it is not fully present in a strophe. That is, when is does reappear in stanzas IV, V, and VII, it does so as if it were the one and only strand of a normal quenine. If we examine the appearance of these six ninetina series, it is clear that the effect is very much that of weaving together, with the added characteristic of the *coblas capcaudées*. Like the rhyme words, each sequence appears either four or five times:

TABLE 7

I	A	B	C
II	D	E	F
III	B	D	F
IV	E	C	A
V	D	E	A
VI	C	F	B
VII	E	C	B
VIII	F	A	D
IX	C	F	D

In addition, this same sequence of strands, re-written as a series of six permutations, reveals a deeper ordering structure, the sextine rétrograde.

TABLE 8

A	B	C	D	E	F
B	D	F	E	C	A
D	E	A	C	F	B
E	C	B	F	A	D
C	F	D			

1	2	3	4	5	6
2	4	6	5	3	1
4	5	1	3	6	2
5	3	2	6	1	4
3	6	4	1	2	5
6	1	5	2	4	3

Once again, in the vertical rhyming structures, Roubaud manages to integrate the movement of the quenine, as well as the exact inverse of that movement; in that double movement, one observes a kind of grace.

The combinatorial constraints of "Tombeaux de Pétrarque" fragments and redistributes the series of rhymes of the *Rime sparse*; they divide and recombine each group of six refrain words and each group of nine rhyme words, so that they appear as multiple sets, ordered according to multiple permutations intersecting throughout the poem. The effect of the fragmented chains is the eschewal of full rhyme, of a regularly timed return of the same elements, or group of elements; three of the six constitutive parts are always absent, suspended in silence, until their return every other strophe, in different combinations. In short, to the ludic practice of Queneau's haikuization, and to the spiraling constraint of his preferred troubadour, Roubaud adds new elements of formal interweaving, or entrebescar.

What, one might ask, is the purpose, the effect, and the meaning of these complex and compound techniques of interlacing? How do they affect the rhythm of the poem? And how do they contribute to, or detract from, the production of meaning in the poem? Indeed, granted that the language of the poem is rather opaque, how can understanding the formal attributes of the text enrich the act of reading "Tombeaux" naïvely, as a poem?

In approaching these questions, one might consider the poetic function of a *tombeau*. In *Gradus*, Bernard Dupriez defines the genre as "recueil de vers et prose à la gloire du défunt," and in *A Dictionary of Literary Terms*, J. Cuddon defines an epitaph as "a kind of valediction which may be solemn, complimentary or even flippant."[16] "Tombeaux de Pétrarque" belongs to the class of elegy in which one poet honors and memorializes another in verse, as opposed to the more personal elegy for a loved one. In the first genre, the question of poetic influence is preeminent. In fact, especially since Baudelaire and Mallarmé, one of the aims of poets who laud and entomb precursors is winning their own renown, not solely through and against their distant masters but also among their poetic contemporaries. That is, like the modernist sestina form, the tombeau as genre has become a testing ground where what is carefully watched are the formal innovations in the architecture of the poem.[17] In reading the "Tombeaux" as elegy, there are two motifs: first, the intricate weaving of a resting place for the addressee, an attempt to enclose and protect the deceased; second, a revitalization of a precursor's works, staged through a reappropriation and a recontextualization of their poetic fragments.

The plural in the title implies multiplicity in the construction. It is safe to argue that the addressees of the poem are also implicitly plural. In many respects, "Tombeaux" responds to and echoes the pleas of pity replete in the *Canzoniere*. Consider, for example, this complaint taken from Petrarch's thirtieth poem, his second sestina:

---

[16] Dupriez, *Gradus*, 105; Cuddon, *Dictionary of Literary Terms*, 234.
[17] See Moncond'huy, "Tombeau poétique," 2-14.

> *sempre piangendo andrò per ogni riva,*
> *per far forse pietà venir ne gli occhi*
> *di tal che nascera à dopo mill'anni,*
> *se tanto viver po ben colto lauro.*
> always weeping I shall go along every shore,
> to make pity perhaps come to the eyes
> of someone who will be born a thousand years from now—
> if a well-tended laurel can live so long. (*RS* 33-36)

Written in 1974, exactly six hundred years after Petrarch's death (18 July 1374), "Tombeaux" almost directly responds to this lament. This carefully constructed re-citation of the grand chant through the *Canzoniere* sets up a complex game of echoing. That echo confirms a reception of the "well-tended laurel" and it ensures the longevity of its subjects paradoxically, by laying him (Petrarch)–or it (the *Canzoniere*), or her (Laura)–to rest: Brillons la vie … et … cumulons l'air et les fleurs … pour ces nuits de cent fleurs / ton rare lieu   rouvert neuf pour légère / t'entrer laurier frottée de neige sans yeux" (64-72). The "rare lieu   rouvert neuf" (opened in the line spacing) may refer to the *Canzoniere* as a textual space, and more precisely to the sestinas that Roubaud works into a self-reflexive constellation of words, forms, and style (indeed, playing on the sound, we might hear the line as "roue vers neuf," suggesting the transposition of the sestina as ninetina).

The question of the addressee, however, is not resolved by this textual link. If "Tombeaux" are panegyric homages to the author of *Rime sparse*, they are also, in Roubaud's words, an assassination: "L'éloge dissimule un assassinat" (*FI* 200). The overt borrowing of rhyme words is a kind of living ingestion, a *phagocitation*, on the part of both poets–Petrarch consuming and reciting the trobar, Roubaud reblending and reciting both Petrarch and the trobar–and the forms into which the ingested fragments are recast are, in a sense, doubly condensed.

In addition, because "l'éloge du mort ancien sert au silence sur le mort récent" (*FI* 200), a more personal homage might be at work in the construction of the "Tombeaux." It is of no small consequence that Roubaud writes to Petrarch in a form "invented" by his mentor, Raymond Queneau. In addition to crystallizing Petrarch's nine sestinas, this centenary ninetina surreptitiously serves as an occasion to obliquely pay homage to Queneau, who died just two years after the poem's composition.[18]

The plurality of the possible addressees is again figured in the body of the text. Judging from Roubaud's opening remarks, readers should look for two, if not more, sets of layering in reading "Tombeaux": "Les poèmes ont été conçus pour être dits, pour être transportés de la voix, et comme tels différent assez de leur disposition dans la page; les deux modes, ici, sont presque autonomes. Le poème dans le livre n'est pas une notation, une partition de la voix; les silences de la voix ne sont pas des traductions des blancs de la ligne; l'une et l'autre lecture construisent, imaginaire, un *double*, qui est cette poésie, absente de chaque poème, s'il est entendu ou lu, mais plutôt se situe derrière chacun, un peu   derrière chacun, à l'écart   oblique   et qui   derrière chacun   vous regarde" (*D* 33). Accordingly, neither the silent visual reading nor the recited aural reading leads directly to the object itself. Rather they both allude, separately, to the poem's absent double, "un *double* ... s'il est entendu ou lu, vous regarde." The actual poem is therefore a template for an imaginary poem that is the veritable object in question and that poem is granted agency in Roubaud's *indication*. In other words, a reading of the poem in the book, be it rhythmic or semantic, enables the perception of the poem outside the book, behind the written poem, and that *double*, as Roubaud puts it, is looking back at the reader from behind the present text.

As noted in Chapter 1, Mallarmé heavily influences this poetics of suggestion: "Une fleur! idée même et suave, absente de tous bouquets." Moreover, Raimbaut d'Orange's statement of method–"*cars bruns e tenhz. motz entrebesc. pensiuz pensanz*. Précieux sombres et teints mots j'entrelace pensifs pensant" (*FI* 320)–also informs the notion of a double that inhabits the concrete poem, actively thinking through its contrasts in texture. Even in the grammar of his introductory description, where he identifies two separate but interrelated reading operations ("l'une et l'autre"), he interlaces the main and relative clauses with a suspended hypothesis ("s'il est entendu ou

---

[18] Roubaud has composed another, more explicit quenine homage to Queneau in which he solves the combinative problem of the *octine*, a puzzle Queneau had imagined in *Bâtons, chiffres et lettres*, but for which he never actually found a solution. That poem is also fraught with mathematically motivated constraints. See Roubaud, "Novembre : 3-octine," in "N-ines," 13-14.

lu"), causing the effect of a bifurcating thought with one end: "Un *double* à l'écart qui vous regarde." Similar effects of suspense and multiple meanings animate the syntax of the poem.

Each strophe-stèle proposes a set of conditions applied to the descriptive state of the addressee(s). For example, the opening *cobla* of the ninetina proposes two possibilities: either a renewed life and the dawning of a new day or a frozen time, a shoring up and affixing of thread-like hair:

> Ou le soleil mange les étoiles dans l'aube
> ou dans la neige tes cheveux prendront rive
> comme les vents aux fleuves liés de glace
> si des écueils   but amer de ma voile
> une lumière   de collines   entre branches
> m'écarte neuf   j'aborde au cours d'un bois
> contre la lune   dans tes bois c'est le soir
> pas une fleur   que la trame   de ces notes
> poisse les nuits comme rimes   à la mort

The lack of punctuation, the numerous unmarked relative clauses, the insertion of blank space amid incomplete thoughts, and the abnormal word usage all contribute to linguistic opacity. The first three lines, for example, none of which contain blank spaces, read quite easily as a conditional either/or construction. The figurative meanings of the images here suggest the passage of time–and a resistance to its passing–marked by the disappearance of the stars due to the sun's dawning light. The absence of this cyclical renewal, it seems, would threaten the continued mutability of a chevelure-endowed addressee.[19]

The poem's next phrase poses more sustained difficulty. The first of six hypothetical constructions in the poem–and the first of nine "if" clauses–this sentence lacks grammatical order and may be construed as an estribot thought, a "je ne sais quoi" phrase whose

---

[19] In his "Vie brève de François Pétrarque," Roubaud briefly and comically glosses the young poet's vanity: "Pendant quelque temps Pétrarque et son jeune frère Gherardo vécurent en Avignon. Ils s'occupaient principalement de leurs vêtements et de leurs coiffures; inexperts dans le maniment des bigoudis ils marchaient nerveusement dans les rues, inquiets du mistral qui à tout instant menaçait de déranger l'ordre de leur chevelure. Leurs souliers étaient trop étroits. Ils étaient toujours habillés à la dernière mode" (Roubaud [1990], "La disposition numérologique," 218).

multiple meanings and fragments are scattered over three lines. If, as Roubaud states, an extreme poetic project entails doing violence to ordinary language, then these verses can be said to sabotage sentential linearity:

> si des écueils   but amer de ma voile
> une lumière   de collines   entre branches
> m'écarte neuf   j'aborde au cours d'un bois
> contre la lune   dans tes bois c'est le soir

After a little reconstruction, and some readerly violence, this section may be flattened out or paraphrased thus: "Si une lumière m'écarte des écueils, j'aborde…," positing the narrator's arrival in "un bois" that may or may not coincide with "tes bois." Even after having unwound this intricate word order, one finds additional semantic problems in this sentence. Does "une lumière" emanate from the woods? Or, considering the double meaning of *amer*, as both "bitter" and "seamark," does the light emanate from the sea? And, are the reefs a bitter end or a fateful desire?[20] Or, again, which combination takes precedence if the end result, "c'est le soir," is unchanged? Plus, given the lack of punctuation marks, where should the sentence come to an end? Here are four possible modes of punctuation demonstrating the parataxis of the second clause:

> Si une lumière m'écarte des écueils,
> –j'aborde.
> –j'aborde au cours d'un bois.
> –j'aborde au cour d'un bois, contre la lune.
> –j'aborde au cour d'un bois, contre la lune, dans tes bois.

A similar and reverse set of combinations exists for the next "complete" sentence–"c'est le soir." The possibilities for reading this po-

---

[20] It should be noted that Roubaud opts for the French word "but" over "fin" to replace Petrarch's "fine" (choosing "fin" would indeed have permitted the phrase "fin amer"–approaching fin'amors–instead of "but amer"). Does this choice indicate a goal-oriented composition, one whose closure is as necessary as it is ambiguous? Absolute closure, though concrete in terms of the poem or even in terms of the novels (see chapters 7 and 8), is viewed as impossible in the realm of signification, for this process depends on the poet-audience dialogue; plus, the polysemy already alluded to has the effect of resisting a final, singular meaning in the text.

em are thus very often plural, and frequently transgress boundaries between lines or between stanzas:

> ... que la trame   de ces notes
> poisse les nuits comme rimes   à la mort
>
> Poisse des fleurs...

These polysemic constructions lead to contradictory possible readings. How then are readers to make sense of this intentionally constructed language puzzle? Is this, one may ask, an idle exercise in combinatorial multiplicity, or is there some intrinsic value to this systematic suspension of defined sequentiality?

Without elaborating on the implicit value of play itself, I would like to elucidate how the polyvalent syntax and contradictory arguments of "Tombeaux" are directly inspired by the canso. In discussing the style clus of the "Vers de dreit nien" Roubaud comments that "l'efficacité de l'ironie de Guillaume IX tient à un caractère essentiel de la *forme canso*, caractère qui en fit un objet de scandale pour les érudits du second XIXe siècle, qui est de n'avoir aucun développement 'logique,' de juxtaposer des strophes dont l'enchaînement n'obéit à aucun principe de récit, à aucune argumentation motivée, où rien n'est préservé de la cohérence habituelle à la poésie depuis le XVIIe siècle" (*FI* 38). The "effet dévastateur" (*FI* 39) that Roubaud locates in the canso, and especially its manifestations as estribot, is also present in the "Tombeaux." The incoherence in the semantic development of "Tombeaux" is twofold. First, the order imposed on the list of words forces the poet to represent the same images (word-objects) under varying light, in a manner that is much more condensed than in regular quenines. Second, the sequence of conditional and imperative constructions, scattered as fragments (*Rime sparse*) within the poem, undermines any sense of logical or narrative linearity. In other words, though the fragments, verses and stanzas of "Tombeaux" follow one another on the page and in its recital, the images and ideas that inhabit them are not always linked according to a discernible logic. That is, unless–and this is what I am suggesting–the trobar clus and the aesthetic entrebescar are taken as convention.

Roubaud's version of the trobar clus endows the formal attributes of this writing style with a mnemonic charge, in part because its rhythmic constructions are more difficult to remember, and as such, they require that one possess a clear understanding of their structure in order to commit them to and recite them from memory. But Roubaud also praises the discursive value of formal continuities because they are the product of conversations between poets, between poetic works, and between poetic eras. Traditions are built on such conversations, in very much the same way that jazz musicians' riffing on the same tunes constitutes a body of standards. And their transmission into the continuous present of language constitutes a living form, a turning sphere of memory that supports and informs Roubaud's compositions. This aesthetic of entrebescar is especially subtle and challenging to read when the means of interweaving mixes citation and the technique of rimes estramps. The "ferm voler" of clus texts also sheds a darker light on the language of love, often turning axioms of love upside down.

In "Tombeaux," Roubaud rehearses and further complicates these stylistic qualities. As I have demonstrated, the aesthetic of entrebescar subtends the permutational structure of the verse order, the refrain fragments, and the braided rhyming chains. Those interweaving structures extend and vary the distance between individual rhymes without weakening the inter-stanza link of the cobla capcaudée. What's more, as I have just suggested, the aesthetic of entrelacement also permeates Roubaud's grammatical structures, and the development of the poem's argument, forcing readers to undo the knot of the polyvalent syntax. In order to emphasize how Roubaud incorporates the style clus, I shall briefly compare stylistic elements of "Tombeaux de Pétrarque" and Raimbaut d'Orange's "La fleur inverse."

Both poems flirt with notions of the impossible, each engaging in a calculated poetic game forged through a linguistic *jouissance*. I have already discussed some of the contradiction and undecidability found in the "Tombeaux." Consider now, as context to Roubaud's "style joyeux," Raimbaut's flower in verse:

> *Ar resplan la flors enversa . pels trencans rancx e pels tertres . cals flors neus gels e conglapis . que cots e destrenh e trenca . don vey morz quils critz brays siscles . en fuelhs en rams e en giscles . mas mi ten vert et jauzen joys . er quan vey secx los dolens croys.*

> Alors brille la fleur inverse   entre falaises tranchantes et collines
>   quelle fleur neige gel et glace   qui coupe et tourmente et
> tranche   dont meurent l'appels cris chants sifflets   en feuilles
> en rameaux en branches   mais me tient vert la joyeuse joie   et
> secs et douloureux les corbeaux. (*T* 144-45)

There is, to begin, a striking overlap in words common to both poems; an incomplete list of variants includes: *briller, fleur, inverse, tranche, collines, neige, glace, coupe, mourir, feuilles, branches, vert, joyeuse, siffle, rame*. That overlap echoes the richly sonorous landscape behind the *Canzoniere*. In addition, both poems invert or reverse a common notion that spring is the time of love. In effect they both directly argue that an inverted flower, or a hermetic poem "tient vert," that it preserves the purity of love, guards against the doubts of others, and proves the will of the poetic subject. That is, the inverted flower symbolizes the ability to resist destruction and the passage of time despite having blossomed early or outside the season of love. In this way, the longevity of song directly relates to forms of crystallization, and both poems motivate that symbolic field through images of snow, ice, and freezing. These images of crystallization or freezing recontextualize "Le vierge, le vivace, le bel aujourd'hui" (as well as its Quenellian haikuization) and bring into focus the volitional resistances at work in "Tombeaux." In the *tornada* of the "Tombeaux," as elsewhere throughout the poem, ice, rain, and snow help resist the disappearance of the addressee:

> Si la terre   bouclier d'étoiles de neige
> mange tes yeux   que la pluie que la glace
> arme ma vie   il y aura ce but
> épais joyeux   peut-être nuits tes rimes
> d'ici la mort.

Both poems therefore seek to preserve life with what most threatens it in the natural landscape of the trobar—ice, cold, snow, and sleet. The perspective of resistance is, however, changed in the context of these two poems. For Raimbaut, this inverted flower is an indissoluble symbol of love faced with the adversities of the "corbeaux," or *lausengiers* who speak against the poet's love and song: "La fleur inverse ... tient... secs et douloureux les corbeaux." In the context of the "Tombeaux," the poem resists the disappearance of an onlooker ("si la terre ... mange tes yeux"), and if that were to fail, ice and rain (or the writing of hard poems) would be recourse.

Raimbaut's formula–"jauzen joys"–alludes to amorous as well as poetic joys; that is, a *jouissance* associated with love play and textual play. Reiterating the reciprocity between the language of love and the love of language, Roubaud argues that in the grand chant playful word constructions –"joyous joy"–served to reinvest value in language. "L'invention de l'amour est sans doute, en grande partie, l'invention du *joi*. Ce pouvoir d'un mot, né dans le voisinage de la filiation phonétique de *joc*, le jeu, et de *gaudium*, entre l'oc et l'oïl, changeant, au-dessus de la fracture des langues, pour le français même, quelque temps au moins, jouissance en joie, a, pendant le siècle et demi du trobar, 'rémunéré le défaut des langues'" (*FI* 168). "Jauzen joys," cast in the context of the trobar clus, is not limited to the play of polysemy, melody and rhyme, but also expresses a *jouissance* associated with subverting the discourse's binary values. This healing and subversive play leaves Raimbaut "ferme enlaçé de joie" and impervious to his poetic opponents–or so he boasts:

> Quar enaissi m'o enversa . que bel plan mi semblon tertre . e tenc per flor lo conglapi . e-l cautz m'es vis que-l freit trenque. e-l tro mi son chant e siscle . e paro-m fulhat li giscle . aissi-m suy ferm lassatz en joy . que re non vey que-m sia croy
> Ainsi toutes choses j'inverse   belles plaines pour moi collines
>   et la fleur pour moi est glace   pour moi la chaleur le froid
> tranche   et le tonnerre chante et siffle   se couvrent de feuilles
> les branches   ainsi ferme enlaçé de joie   je ne vois plus rien
> des corbeaux (*T* 144-45).

These oppositions effectively play at questioning the conventional values inscribed into certain categories ("plaines/collines," "fleur/glace," "chaleur/froid," etc.), thereby subverting the clear (or leu) hierarchical order and valuing the quality of the song *as* song, as a testimony to a pure and ideal love. By the end of his canso, Raimbaut claims that love and joy have transcended the social order and overcome the naysayer, thereby uniting the distanced lovers: "*Doussa dona amors e joys. nos ajosten malgrat dels croys*" (*T* 144). But in the closing statement there is a return of the real which remasks the poet's jocularity behind the stark visage of the unlovable crow: "*Joglar gran ren ai menh de joy quar no-us veys e-n fas semblan croy*" (Joglar j'ai bien moins de joi sans vous voir mon visage est corbeau [*T* 144]). "Jauzen joys" in Raimbaut's canso therefore presents a textual play that short-circuits a reigning order of signification, even if only momentarily, for the purposes of an impossible love and *jouissance*.

In the "Tombeaux" Roubaud also presents a "ferm voler" and "jauzen joys" in the marriage of two opposites: "Le véritable antonyme de joi est *mort*" (*T* 172). "Tombeaux" presents an elegiac "style joyeux" whose central concern is to play on the inevitability of death as a closure. A technique in this style game is to alternate between an impossible resistance to and a fateful acceptance of mortality.

The theme of death is acutely approached in Petrarch's final, double sestina in the *Rime sparse*–"Mia benigna fortuna e'l viver lieto."[21] It is the only sestina to appear in the second part of the collection, composed after Laura's death and duly entitled "In morte di M. Laura." Formally speaking, the rhyme line culled from this ninth sestina occupies a privileged position in Roubaud's ninetina. Beginning as the last line of the first stanza, these six rhyme words ("nuit," "rime," "mort," "pleur," "style," "joyeux") are progressively displaced until they occupy the formal center of the last full stanza in "Tombeaux de Pétrarque"–unlike the sestina, each stanza of the ninetina provides a center position, the fifth line, which might be construed as a more concrete "cœur de la neuvine." While the fragments from the sixth sestina begin at the end of Petrarch's series, Roubaud recasts the rhyme words of this double sestina in such a manner that they wind their way to the center of his last stanza, culminating in "le coeur de la sextine" (*D* 34). Entombed in that final, center position, Roubaud repeats one of the rhyme words, thereby doubly marking the weight of that line: "d'être la mort   la mort au joyeux pleurs" (77).

It is ironic that the fragments of Petrarch's last sestina should wind their way to the "heart of hearts" in Roubaud's ninetina, for in this double sestina the Italian poet laments that owing to Laura's early death, his joyful, loving style has been transformed and that his now-worn, rude song is useless in recalling Laura to life. Already in Petrarch's poem there is an overtly ambiguous three-way relationship among the poet, his poems, and Death, whether it will be the death of an allegorical figure, the addressee, or the poet (di-

---

[21] The only earlier known "double sestina" was written by Dante and does not, strictly speaking, obey the rules of the sestina. See Lartigue, *L'hélice d'écrire*, 51-56.

rectly associated with the life and death of his verse). Petrarch's ninth sestina ends with the poet praying for death to put him to rest, and to free him from a pointless toil:

> *e'n aspro stile e'n angosciose rime*
> *prego che 'l pianto mio finisca Morte*
> and in harsh style and anguished rhymes
> I pray that my weeping may be ended by Death (75);

yet, this prayer may also be requesting the end of Death itself, stating more actively that writing puts an end to closure: "I pray that my weeping finish Death." In fact, though Petrarch bemoans the insufficiencies of poetry, and more precisely of rhyme, in overcoming death, the poem becomes a place for imagining the impossible.

Untenable oppositions, as I've pointed out, relate to stylistic strategies in Raimbaut's "Ar resplan la flors enversa." Similarly, paradox plays an important role in Roubaud's rewriting of elements of the *Canzoniere*. In both cases, textual jouissance resists the dominant signifying order, turning it upside down as a means of strengthening and diversifying the possible modes of being for poetic expression.

In "la flors enversa," Raimbaut inscribes his verses and love in an imaginary space exempt from worldly transformation, or interpretation by lesser singers:

> Qu'aillent mes vers qu'ainsi j'inverse
> que ne les tiennent bois ni collines
> là où nul ne ressent la glace
> où nul pouvoir du froid ne tranche
> mon chant ne veut pas de corbeaux (*T* 145).

For Roubaud, instead of being untenable, his verses present themselves as sonorous forms devoid of spirit ("Entends mes vers ils ont notes mais pas âme" [55]), and in their intention ("pour légère / t'entrer laurier" [72]) they espouse the qualities of what they tend to resist, death and darkness, figuring them as potentially recuperative symbols ("d'être la mort   la mort au joyeux pleurs" [77]). Although examples supporting this reading are immediately problematized by the overtly compact syntax, there are recurring moments where the poet's intention and method reveal themselves, as in the main clauses of the fourth cobla: "Découpe la nuit .../ ...si c'est ton style   mais de mort liées nuits / ...dépêtre tes vers" (43). This freeing of the addressee's verse ("ton rare lieu   rouvert neuf"

[71]), which is implicated in an economy of eating and reincorporating throughout the poem ("Ou le soleil mange tes yeux"; "Si la terre... / mange tes yeux" [1]), depends on the speaker's ability to hold back the passing of time or the dawning of light: "J'en fais mon style   mort à moitié de rimes / je happe jour   freine aube jusqu'en étoile" (61). In effect, where Petrarch laments darkness–"je vais pleurant et désirant le jour" (*D* 37)–Roubaud takes the inverse tack, crying of joy and wanting night.

Nuit, often attributed a negative value, takes on a positive connotation in "Tombeaux"; it becomes a leitmotif in Roubaud's work. Similarly, images of frost and ice, especially when associated with flowers–as they are in the opening sequence of *La boucle* (1993)–echo characteristics of the trobar clus, and its inversion of discursive principles. In effect, part of the richness of the fifty-four words Roubaud steals from Petrarch resides in their signaling the act of poetizing, both in their literal reference to the practice of song (*notes*, *rimes*, *style*, *vers*) and in their metaphoric reference to the products of writing (*fleur*, *laurier*, *feuilles*). If we extend this apodeictic function to the agrammaticality of the poetic figures, then we can say that the hypotactic link between resisting the dawning day in favor of freezing hair into ice-bound rivers symbolizes Roubaud's firm desire to both entomb as well as liberate the contexts of his addressees. That is, the crystallization of waters and the refraction of light through a diamondlike poetic form take on an emblematic metaliterary function in Roubaud's work. Like night and blackness, symbolic fields I address in reading *Quelque chose noir* in Chapter 6, crystallization participates in the purification of forms that are simultaneously under pressure and set into play.

From the "Tombeaux de Pétrarque" through *La fleur inverse*, two concomitant yet independent writing trajectories are present within tRoubaldian poetics. On the one hand, his expositions and compositions uncover, develop, and continue, in a critical and personal fashion, the stylistic trajectory of his chosen tradition, thereby inscribing a clear sense of historicity in his work. On the other, Roubaud approaches language and literature as if it were mathematizable; he methodically atomizes its parts and imposes constraint on the languages and its forms, thereby accentuating its artificial, arbitrary nature and heightening the reader's awareness of its potentiality.

Chapter Three

ϵ: SONNET OF SONNETS, AN OPEN SET

IN the tradition of the Western lyric, no single poetic form has exerted more influence than the sonnet. Written in virtually every European language, the sonnet has become the nervous system of the European lyrical tradition. And yet, because the sonnet has been shaped by so many intellectual and social movements from the late thirteenth century to the present, retaining both ideological and aesthetic traces of each period, some contemporary writers have renounced the sonnet and turned toward new, more experimental literary forms, poems whose potentials are not as proven or developed as the sonnet's. Members of the Oulipo have adopted a different stance with regard to the sonnet, sometimes demonstrating its inexhaustibility, sometimes pushing its productivity to new extremes.

Raymond Queneau's *Cent mille milliards de poèmes* (1961) is undoubtedly the seminal Oulipian sonnet experiment.[1] In this collection of ten sonnets, each line of each poem can replace the corresponding line in the other nine sonnets. The resulting interchangeability of lines, highlighted in the volume's presentation, produces a vertiginous number of potential poems–100,000,000,000,000, or 10^{14} (plus some)–enough to occupy multiple lifetimes of continuous reading, according to the calculations of François Le Lionnais.[2] In

---

[1] Queneau, *Cent mille milliards*.
[2] Each line of these ten poems is printed on an individual strip (*volet*) so that, keeping its strophic disposition, it can be read in combination with any disposition of lines from all ten poems. See Jouet, *Raymond Queneau*, for further possible combinations, including recombining hemistiches.

addition to creating more potential sonnets than all of the sonnets—or, for that matter, all the written material—that precede him historically, Queneau has also forcefully demonstrated a convincing point about fixed-form poetry: when all of the possible combinations of a fixed form seem exhausted, one need merely adopt additional constraints in order to renew both its productivity and its difficulty. Although simple, the constraint adopted in the composition of *Cent mille milliards de poèmes*—full metrical and semantic interchangeability between the lines of ten different sonnets—represents a lyrical project of unprecedented difficulty.

Although very different in terms of form, Queneau's *Cent mille milliards de poèmes* may be compared to Jacques Roubaud's first major book of poetry, his opening sonnet experiment, ϵ *(signe d'appartenance)*, of 1967. Both *Cent mille milliards de poèmes* and ϵ open with a short theoretical paratext, or "mode d'emploi," that explicitly draws attention to their Oulipian underpinnings. These "user's manuals" are integral to Oulipian texts and should be approached as theoretical statements for they explicitly attract the reader's critical attention and in turn occasion further theoretical reflection.[3] One function of these liminal texts is to establish the terms of the experiment performed in the text. Because of this status as literary laboratory, the Oulipian work transcends the distinction between literature and theory and presents poetry *as* poetics.

Also, both texts were originally published in distinguished collections at Gallimard, where Queneau was a renowned editor. In fact, as he recounts in *Poésie:* (2000), Roubaud first sent his manuscript to Queneau who, upon reading it and supporting its publication at Gallimard, invited him to join the Oulipo in 1966; Georges Perec quickly followed in 1967. That event was pivotal in Roubaud's development, not only because working with Queneau and Le Lionnais lent new perspective to his work, but also because he shared with Perec the excitement and disappointments of the Oulipo's first successes and crises. It was in that context that Roubaud continued to imagine the possibilities for his *Projet*, as well as the means to pursue its composition and presentation.

Experimentation underlies all Oulipian writing. By foregrounding the constraints adopted in composition, Oulipian texts stage a

---

[3] See Thomas, "README.DOC", 18-28, for a discussion of this aspect of ϵ.

contract with their readers; they set the terms of gaming. In this sense, the modes d'emploi propose a (set of) programmed reading(s) through which to test the actual experience of reading. Such experiments are cast in a collaborative spirit, for in decoding and evaluating them, readers are invited to imagine the conditions of their conception and to participate in the activity of making meaning. Whether this mode of active reading entails selecting preferred poems among the one hundred trillion possible in Queneau's text or negotiating the various reading trajectories indicated in Roubaud's ϵ, the pursuit of these Oulipian works incites readers to rethink the sonnet playfully, according to new perspectives.

In this chapter I study Roubaud's first sonnet cycle, ϵ *(signe d'appartenance)*, in its relation to the sonnet tradition and to discuss its importance in the poet's career. Perhaps even more central in Roubaud's poetics than the sestina, the sonnet form and sonnet tradition have animated the entirety of his career as a writer. Indeed, for more than forty years, he has been reading, copying, cataloguing and anthologizing sonnets.[4] These activities have influenced his writing, both in terms of his sonneteering and, necessarily, in his conception of the *Projet*. For this reason alone, it would be impossible to account for all that Roubaud has to say about the sonnet. Nonetheless, in many ways ϵ is emblematic of Roubaud's overall approach to traditional form.

In his first engagement with the sonnet form, Roubaud invites readers to question the field of the sonnet, claiming that "un sonnet appartient à l'espèce du sonnet" (*M9* 9). The silent, unpronounceable title ϵ–a mathematical symbol meaning "belonging to the set of"–opens his query on sonnets as a living form; the tenet of that approach itself predetermines that the investigation remains incomplete, ongoing. Working simultaneously to expand and debunk a centralized definition of the sonnet as a fixed form, Roubaud asserts that many poems entertain a familial relationship to the sonnet and that the sonnet form cannot be reduced to a closed set of rules.

---

[4] For his systematic analysis of Renaissance sonnets, see Roubaud (1990), "La forme du sonnet français," as well as the anthology, *Soleil du soleil* (1990). Other important Roubaldian sonnets are found in *Renga* (1971), *Les animaux de tout le monde* (1983), and *Les animaux de personne* (1991); Roubaud and Jouet (1993), "[∂]"; Roubaud (1999), *La forme d'une ville*; and Roubaud (2004), *Churchill 40*. For further sonnet works, please consult the full bibliography.

The composition of a sonnet requires satisfying a strict set of rules. Commonly, those rules are taken for granted. They include such categories as fourteen lines, quatrains of alternating rhymes, related tercets or a concluding couplet, traditional meter, and various indications about the way an argument, or subject, develops over the course of the poem. The precise nature in the sonnet makes the form neatly correspond to what Oulipians understand as a formal constraint. A fundamental precept in Oulipian theory has it that voluntary constraint is essential to the writer's vocation; it is productive and liberating because it is constricting. The transcultural, translinguistic and transhistorical proliferation of the sonnet illustrates this principle; the sonnet's constraints are in this sense generative, for they establish a set of obstacles that support the production of graceful poems. As a formal constraint, the sonnet establishes the mechanical workings of a "poetry machine" at which any author may try his or her hand. Such an approach is underscored by ϵ and may illuminate the collection as a sonnet of sonnets, as a united series of poems.

As I suggested in previous chapters, formal constraints can also transmit historically encoded memory, especially via historically important form. If the laws of sonnet form have become the vehicle of tradition, and if the modern sonnet bears the traces of its precursors, then Jacques Roubaud's sonnets are also a means of knowing, confronting, and continuing tradition. If approached with enough lucidity and speculation, a refiguring of such a dominant form may even affect how memory in language exerts force upon us. Indeed, to some extent, one senses that such high hopes animate the dream of the *Projet*. And, given the intensity with which Roubaud and his friends have continued his sonnet research, even after 1978 when he abandoned the *Projet*, it is clear that this form continues to be a privileged work site for both the Oulipo and Roubaud. In ϵ, however, Roubaud's adoption of the form is perhaps a bit less ambitious, though there too, it is already understood as a means of consciously reorganizing the anxiety of influence.

In an interview with Georges Perec that appeared shortly after the publication of ϵ, Roubaud describes his book as "un livre de sonnets," adding that "c'est aussi un livre sur le sonnet."[5] At his

---

[5] Roubaud and Perec, "Jacques Roubaud: sonnet," 6; hereafter cited as *S*.

point of departure, Roubaud situates the sonnet as not only "une grande forme," but also as *the* strategic form par excellence. Paradoxically, one of the characteristics that makes it so strategic is precisely its near interdiction among the young poets of Roubaud's generation. "Le choix du sonnet à la base s'explique par deux constatations élémentaires: d'une part il est à peu près admis qu'il est impossible aujourd'hui d'écrire un sonnet; d'autre part, le sonnet représente, dans la poésie à forme fixe (c'est-à-dire dans la poésie à contrainte, donc, pour moi, dans la poésie toute entière) l'expression la plus nette de la poésie occidentale. Interroger le sonnet c'était pour moi interroger une certaine possibilité de la poésie aujourd'hui, la recherche d'une voie nouvelle à partir d'une histoire, d'une tradition" (S 6). Interested in recounting "une histoire du sonnet" (S 6), ϵ does not simply rehearse the sonnet in its different historically attested forms but begins to imagine "toutes les formes possibles de sonnets" (S 7), introducing many that are entirely new. However, unlike the *Cent mille milliards de poèmes*, which consists almost entirely of classical sonnets, Roubaud's history eschews an orthodox form–"aucun de ces sonnets n'est canonique" (S 7)–and supplants it with deviant variations.[6] In short, ϵ presents a series of broadly varying texts that most readers would not immediately identify as sonnets. To the extent that they are sonnets, they might be best understood as marginal or non-sonnet sonnets, inventions that are inspired by, or borrowed from, the experiments of other sonneteers, composers, and writers of prose poetry.[7]

Perhaps it is because the fundamental constraints of a sonnet are so firmly rooted in poetic tradition that Roubaud so deeply questions them. Indeed, it should be noted that none of the poems in ϵ repeat the strophic pattern of traditional sonnets or of any other poem in the collection; each is unique in form. As a sonnet cycle, ϵ therefore bears little resemblance to its precursors and, in this respect, it is consistent with Roubaud's subsequent research on the

---

[6] Roubaud has pointed out that "la quasi-totalité sont des sonnets traditionnels (pas tous puisqu'en certains un même mot est utilisé deux fois à la rime) mais cela en fait quand même beaucoup" ([Roubaud] "La forme du sonnet français," 10).

[7] Roubaud names Charles Baudelaire, Ted Berrigan, Guido Cavalcanti, Blaise Cendrars, e. e. cummings, Alighieri Dante, Luis de Góngora, Giacomo da Lentino, Gerard Manley Hopkins, Rainer Maria Rilke, William Shakespeare, and Pierre Jean Jouve, whose French translations of Shakespeare serve as a model for Roubaud's prose sonnets.

sonnet: to propose sonnets that are as divergent as possible from the norm while remaining sonnets, and to conceptualize the form itself as abstract. To this end, Roubaud discards the notion that there is a fixed set of universal attributes to the sonnet. Rather, claiming that "la notion de sonnet unique est semblable à celle de la licorne" (*M9* 14), Roubaud imagines the sonnet form as a game in which the object is novelty, diversity, and singularity. It is in these terms that he stretches the boundaries of genre and tests just how far a form can be blurred before becoming unrecognizable in its traditional context: "Le sonnet est, par définition, une poésie à forme fixe, mais sa plasticité est telle que l'on peut étudier jusqu'à quel point on peut s'éloigner du sonnet tout en continuant à produire du sonnet, en d'autres termes, mesurer le degré d'intelligibilité de la forme sonnet" (*S* 6-7).

If Roubaud seeks to test the intelligibility of the sonnet, then his departures from the classical (or strict) sonnet must take place at every level (including the semantic, the metrical, the strophic, and the conceptual), while still including enough identifiable elements of the form. In one model, the singularity of the sonnet may be reduced to a dialectical argument: "Le premier quatrain pose, le second commente, le premier tercet nie, le second résoud" (*S* 7). In other models, the identity of the sonnet depends on subject matter, its presentation on the page, its tone, its relation to other sonnets. In contrast to these modes of conceiving coherence, the texts in ϵ come in varied tones, styles, shapes, and sizes, including "sonnets, sonnets courts, sonnets interrompus, sonnets en prose, sonnets courts en prose, citations, illustrations, grilles, blancs, noirs, poèmes, poèmes en prose" (ϵ 7). This collection therefore offers a series of poems whose multiple structures condition the play between a wide variety of sonnets and non-sonnets: "Les 'non-sonnets' désignent ce qu'un sonnet n'est pas" (*S* 7). Considered individually, the sonnets of ϵ are defined both in relation to an absent orthodox sonnet, and in relation to each other. "Ce sont," writes Roubaud on the opening page, "certains de ces rapports (ou absence de rapports) que nous proposons au lecteur" (ϵ 7). In order to enter this game of discernment, the work must first be approached as a whole, as a discrete set that includes texts belonging to the form called sonnet.

If Roubaud presents ϵ as an open set of hierarchically organized poems, as a predetermined sequence of poems, the open-endedness of the book questions the notion of a poetic collection. Explicitly pitting his book against a *recueil*, or loosely associated collection of poems, Roubaud tests the extent to which poems rely on each other for context and meaning. His self-conscious strategies situate ϵ in the tradition of sonnet cycles. Generally speaking, sonnet cycles are strictly organized by time, theme, or form, categories that present the work of poetry as a concentrated experience, re-collection, or ordering of songs; they are frequently associated with a period in the poet's life or conceived around a single personal or collective experience. In these cases, the notion of unity may be narrative in representing a life or the passing of season or an entire year. Or, in the tradition of the *Canzoniere*, it may also reflect the rules of composition present in its individual, constituent poems, as well as the precise order in which those poems are presented.[8]

In some respects the poetic book is again redefined, or rearticulated along a greater scale with the Mallarméan *Livre*. Even if it is ultimately elusive, that more inclusive model–an appropriate context to discussions of the *Projet*–boldly imagines potential coherence between literature, spirit, and the world. If it is productive to figure Roubaud's work as open and increasingly divergent, it is important to add a word of caution. Like Mallarmé, who obsessed over indeterminacy and chance in his refinement of poetry, Roubaud attempts to curb the influx of the haphazard into his work. "J'ai suggéré quatre modes de lectures possibles," says Roubaud, each of which dismisses aleatoric readings of the collection. In a sense, the work purports to impose its constraint upon the reader: "Disons que j'affirme ainsi mon hostilité au hasard" (*S* 7).

In principle, ϵ presents 361 texts bound together by a set of four crisscrossing structures. The mode d'emploi spells out the four strategies for reading these sets of sonnets. The first three reading programs invite us to imagine individual poems as elements in different series (or figures), and the fourth incites us to consider each text on its own, without bearing in mind its placement among the other matrices. Respectively, the first three reading strategies designate the poems as:

---

[8] Poetic precursors to ϵ may include Maurice Scève's *Délie*, Queneau's *Cent mille milliards de poèmes* or Petrarch's *Canzoniere*, though Roubaud does not situate them as such. In fact, he later commented on his limited knowledge of Petrarch during the period he was writing ϵ, "ce qui veut dire qu'en un sens je ne comprenais pas le sonnet" (Roubaud [1990], "La forme du sonnet français," 9).

1. the elements of diagrammed constellations of poems, metaphorical poems (schematically figured by the typographical arrangement of several titles) imagined in a spatial relation to each other;

2. the elements of an abstract poem, or series of poems composed of "paragraphs" based on a series of five mathematical symbols, either taken from symbolic set theory or invented for the occasion of this text; and

3. the elements used as game pieces in a specific match of the Japanese board game Go, typographically represented as black or white dots (stones) and associated with a numbered *go-ban* (diagrammed game) printed at the end of the text.

4. The fourth strategy, which I shall refer to as the discrete reading, occupies a muted place in the "mode d'emploi de ce livre." That sequence is structured by the reader who reads the poem in the order he or she sees fit.

As organizing structures, these linking programs locate each poem at a nodal point where separate readings intersect. They frame the volume as a network of composite poems whose wholes exceed the sum of their parts, for each sequence or group of poems constitutes an abstract or compound poems constructed of the same–but differently organized–elements. The mode d'emploi thus helps readers imagine every element, or every integer of the text, as simultaneously independent of, and integral to, multiple distinct and abstract structures. The poems, in other words, coexist in a plurality of discursive worlds: "Le seul moyen de rendre compte de [la] discrétion est de tracer dans le livre (précisément pour qu'il ne soit plus seulement un 'recueil') plusieurs chemins, d'établir une hiérarchie, une stratégie de la lecture telle que le sens, les résonances d'un poème isolé varient selon le mode de lecture adopté, telle qu'un groupe de poèmes constitue en soi un autre poème et que la relation vers/poème se retrouve dans une relation poèmes/livre, comme si le livre entier était un seul poème dont chaque vers serait un poème" (*S* 7). Placing his poems at the intersection of several different discursive worlds neatly characterizes Roubaud's conception of literature as a combinatorial mode of inquiry.

But what is the intended effect of these combinatory structures? First, the reading trajectories imply an architectural unity within the collection, a set of interlinked poems whose uniqueness is a condition of their predetermined sequence. Second, because it (potentially) participates in several overlapping reading chains, the tone of the isolated poem signifies in context, and this "resonance" changes according to the sequence in which it is read. Third, in describing ϵ as a "poem of poems," Roubaud reconfigures the relationships between the smaller elements of the book (verses/poems) and the larger forms that they construct (poem/book). Such displacements in the part-to-whole ratio may easily be extended to larger concepts (e.g., *Livre/Littérature*; poetry/language; language/consciousness). Extending the meaning of these relative relations, one might conceive of Roubaud's work as a demonstration of fractals, or Russian babushka dolls, where one structure fits snugly inside the next larger one along a trajectory of a two-way *mise en abyme*. This type of micro- to macro-text correlation is a recurrent trope in Roubaldian writing; it is implied in the crystallization of form and in the way poetry encodes or condenses a memory of language. In effect, one wonders if the conditions of imbrication Roubaud begins to explore in ϵ also inform the initial coherence of the *Projet*. In my view, ϵ provides the nascent experiment for the aesthetic of intersection and imbrication and, while determinations about the *Projet* are difficult to substantiate, this first sonnet cycle may hold clues about how the practice of that aesthetic takes shape in Roubaud's later works.

Regardless of how the mode d'emploi orients them, readers come to this collection of poems, or so-called sonnets, with many of the same questions: What are these poems about? Why are they so varied in style, length, form, and tone? To whom and why did Roubaud write them? What is the relationship of these poems to Roubaud's development as a writer? And what personal experiences do they address? Although each of these is an important and interesting question, until the publication of *Poésie:* (2000) the author's published notes provided incomplete answers. In fact, beyond glossing the textual strategies in ϵ and in *Mezura 9: Description du projet* (1979), Roubaud provided little illumination of the personal experiences behind this composition. On this score he kept silent. That silence partially motivated the unpronounceable title: ϵ.

A few years after the text's publication, Jacqueline Guéron wrote about the suicide of Jacques Roubaud's younger brother, Jean René Roubaud, in October 1961. Reframing that event as a central occasion for the book, her reading situates ϵ as a work of grieving, as well as a display of poetic bravura.⁹ In contrast, as late as 1979, Roubaud himself continued to speak about the book in purely formal terms–not as a work of therapy to deal with personal loss but as the product of a choice to write sonnets every day, a choice he made in 1962 as a consequence of having encountered a "vide absolu" in writing the "vers libre" (*M9* 5).

Given the importance Roubaud ascribes to poems that confront absolute nothingness, I would like to consider briefly the example of a poem of mourning set in vers libre. What interests me here is the relationship between verse form and the presentation of a "vide absolu," or how the experience of loss takes shape in one of the very first poems of ϵ, "je rêve":

> Je rêve que tu souris
> que je te parle à ma porte
> des livres que tu as lus
> du temps comme tu le sens
> c'est une nuit à Paris
> puis il pleut dans notre vin
> je rêve un jardin mouillé
> puis nous marchons dans la rue
> comme au retour de l'école
> au devant de notre chien
> adieu adieu l'âge des jeux
> l'âge de vents est fini
> et tout pouvait être mieux
> tout pouvait être différent
> je m'éveille dans les cris
> un fou avec dérision
> appelle Marie Marie
> et moi je suis dans ce noir
> et je sais que tu es mort
> et personne ne t'attend (ϵ 108-9)

Taken out of context this poem reads a little like a text from the Surrealist moment, for it includes elements commonly found in the golden age of French free verse: a conversationalist tone; a broad emotional register (from smiles to screams); the linking of discontinuous sequences (lack of punctuation); the description of a dream-

---

⁹ Guéron, "Lecture de Jacques Roubaud," 727-39.

scape; the depiction of madness; and anaphora in the final lines, which produces a culminating crescendo. The verse structure is variable (from six to eight syllables) and contains the basic characteristics of vers libre: it does not set a rhyming pattern, and each grammatical rhythmic unit is contained within the line itself. The poem as a whole is not intricately interwoven. Uncharacteristically confessional, this poem stands out in Roubaud's early verse. Like the other, less constructed poems of ϵ, it represents the experience of loss without providing, in itself, the kind of formal armature that supports most of Roubaud's other poems. The experience of vulnerability evinced in and as the poem might well have been a formative one for Roubaud, and it motivates his decision to set this poem into the various frames or the sequences of ϵ.

It was not until years later, in the context of '*le grand incendie de Londres*,' that Roubaud began to write more directly about how Jean René's death influenced his conception of ϵ and the *Projet*, the plans for which took shape at this time in Roubaud's life.[10] In my view, his silence strengthens the status of his work as living action. His insistent formalism and refusal to sentimentalize his experience as "grands élans du coeur," as Georges Perec puts it (*S* 6), characterizes Roubaud's discreet personality as well as his uncompromising will to shelter what is most private deep within his work. While unrewarding for readers who desire immediate transparency, Roubaud's formalism generously satisfies readers accustomed to more active modes of decoding.

First, Roubaud offers no simple or one-sided reduction of the text's significance. In a sense, the architectural framing of the poems serves as a mask, and readers are left to determine the reasons behind particular structures. The act of reading must confront the imposed constraints: one may read through them the way one looks

---

[10] In the context of grieving his second wife's early death, Roubaud intones the extent to which loss informs his personal voice. In the poem "Aphasie," in *Quelque chose noir*: "Devant ta mort je suis resté entièrement silencieux. / . . . / Je ne pouvais plus parler selon ma manière de dire qui est la poésie. / J'avais commencé à parler, en poésie, vingt-deux ans avant. / C'était après une autre mort. / Avant cette autre mort je ne savais comment dire. J'étais comme silencieux. Ainsi, pris entre deux 'bords' de mort" (*QN* 131-32). After this second profound mourning experience, Roubaud writes more freely about his brother, Jean René Roubaud, particularly in *La bibliothèque de Warburg* (2002), where he reproduces the letters his brother wrote before his suicide.

through a screen, one may focus a reading on the constraint as a screen, or, one may shuttle between these two approaches.

Second, if indeed it is a text of mourning, Roubaud's silence regarding this dimension participates in the poetics of multiplicity, incompletion, and interruption that permeates the collection's architecture. If he has proposed multiple strategies of holding these poems together, those strategies are only part of what informs each reading. Indeed, as soon as the sonnet is mentioned, the text takes on a potential light that requires little introduction. To some extent, the overtly constructed frameworks also deflect or challenge conventional modes of reading–reading for the confession being among them.

Third, to situate his poetic voice with regard to tradition while muting the import of personal experience restricts the reader to the literal space of the collection, with its various structuring games. This overtly self-conscious erasure signals the encoding of the deeply personal. It suggests that Roubaud uses formal constraints as a means of encrypting the personal.

Even when Roubaud does write about his decision to become a poet–"je m'étais voulu poète" (*M9* 6)–he nearly always casts his intentions as a consequence of his admiration of literary figures and (with reference to his study of mathematics) an oblique disengagement with the crisis of belatedness. Hardly ever does the young Roubaud directly link his poetic ambitions to a desire to translate his feelings about the world into words. This premeditated, idiosyncratic impersonality has led one critic to figure the poetic "je" of ϵ as double, incorporating both Roubaud's voice and that of literature itself.[11] That claim might be tempered by speaking only of the sonnet.

It is important to note the polemic effects of Roubaud's formalism, for the gaps created by this limited self-representation participate in the way ϵ and other Roubaldian works create meaning. On the one hand, Roubaud must be taken at his word–that ϵ is a book of sonnets, on the sonnet, written to the reader as an experiment in which the author explores his theoretical solutions to the poetic problems of his era (ϵ 7; *M9* 5-15). On the other hand, ϵ can be read as a personal book about a (poetic) death and rebirth, for, in

---

[11] Consenstein, "Rhythm of Irony," 9.

his translator's words, in these poems "we hear a very personal cry of loss at the death of a brother, and the troubled search of a poet coming to terms with the place of poetry in his own life."[12] The marked contrast between these two coexistent readings, what Perec calls the "comment" and the "pourquoi" of the book, establishes tensions that generate meaning.

To date, there have been three approaches to Roubaud's ϵ. Theoretical ones, like that adopted by Jean-Jacques Thomas, focus on the structural framework and constraints of the collection as a whole, analyzing its anti-aleatoric and programmatic functions. Others, exemplified by Peter Consenstein's "The Rhythm of Irony," offer a close reading of selected texts from the collection, mostly read without considering the intratextual dynamics of its hierarchical structure. In reading "Noyade" (ϵ 114), for example, Consenstein limits his analysis to the rhythmic role of the syllable "je," staging the appearance and disappearance of that syllable as a telling sign in the poet's use of form to cloak and reveal his personal experiences and emotive states. Third, other readings attempt to find meaning in the text through multiple strategies, retracing at once the abstract (dis)unity of the text, as well as the unstable character of greatly varied poetic voice. Each of these approaches negotiates the programmatic character of the text and its competition with the poems as statements of form, style, and voice. In this sense, readings of ϵ confront and bear the fruits of an Oulipian mixture of theory and praxis.

In her article "Lecture de Jacques Roubaud," Jacqueline Guéron stages a thematic reading of the whole text, a kind of story that she sees taking shape within the second structure, the paragraph-sonnets designated by mathematical symbols. That metaphoric journey begins with a "poetic suicide" and proceeds through three periods of poetic trial (substantiated by images of linguistic isolation and shipwreck, dialogues with other texts and poets [among them *Robinson Crusoe* and Franz Kafka's *Amerika*], and episodes of an autobiographical voyage to the United States) to culminate in a return to a literary project founded on the internal mirroring, the continuation, and the recapitulation of tradition. The five parts of her reading reflect the five paragraph-sonnets that Roubaud desig-

---

[12] Katheryn McDonald, trans., poems from ϵ by Jacques Roubaud, http://wings.buffalo.edu/epc/rift/rift04/roub0401.html, accessed on line May 1, 1995.

nates, but to make sense of the mathematical symbols structuring that five-part structure, Guéron frames her reading in an emblematic narrative. In this sense, she imposes additional hermeneutic strategies on the ones Roubaud proposes; or, alternately—and for my purposes the difference is not important—she teases that narrative out from the second reading program, though by recourse to reading strategies that precede the mode d'emploi.

Having outlined the hermeneutic difficulties of Roubaud's paratextual apparatus, I shall examine how the intersecting reading programs bear out consequences that are muted in the mode d'emploi. My discussion takes Roubaud's reading programs out of order: I first treat Go as an interpretive structure in the visual (1), sequential (3) and metaphoric (2) programs, and then briefly comment on the "paragraph-sonnets" (2).

The Japanese board game Go provides the template for two reading programs offered in the "mode d'emploi de ce livre." As part of the first reading strategy, it designates groups of poems as figures or abstract constellations defined by their spatial disposition. (Go is but one of several modes by which these spatial figures are designated.) Go also motivates the third principal reading program proposed by Roubaud. In that model, readers are invited to read poems in an order different from that in the text. That sequence is indicated by two textual particularities: each poem is accompanied by a Go number, printed above it; those numbers refer to a diagram representing a specific match, as well as a table of contents that lists the page number of each poem as a Go move. "Ce livre se compose, en principe, de 361 textes, qui sont les 180 pions blancs et les 181 pions noirs d'un jeu de go" (ϵ 7): the first indication given is that the poems of ϵ are, in theory, textual concretizations of the game's stones. In this respect, the poems are elements in a game metaphorically contained in the book and as the book and directly represented in the text, bearing a textual relation to the stones placed in a seemingly random previous match.

The analogies between book and game are vast. The basic functions of literature, as defined for centuries in the West, are to please and instruct. Similarly, board games serve the same double function; legend has it that Go was invented by the Chinese emperor Shun to enliven and amuse his son, Shokin. The design of both Go and poetry can be viewed as coded, specifically aimed at instruction and pleasure. To transpose the rules of Go into a book of sonnets is to construct a doubly encoded book.

Roubaud situates his idea for game-book with regard to an ever-present literary influence, Lewis Carroll. "J'ai emprunté à mon maître ... l'idée d'un livre-jeu, déroulement d'une partie d'un jeu" (*M9* 9). Roubaud emulates Carroll, but in a changed context: "J'ai fait de mes poèmes les pions d'une partie de Go, de même que Lewis Carroll a écrit *Derrière le miroir* comme une partie d'échecs" (*S* 7). Like chess, Go provides a subtext to both literary and philosophical investigations, most notably because of its combinative and agonistic sophistication, but also because of its traditional protocols (ranking system, game etiquette, courtly history). Although both games are mathematical in nature, Roubaud's choice of Go over chess is instrumental in revealing the conceptual strategies in ∈. There are salient differences between the two games. In chess, all the pieces are on the board when the match begins, and they are progressively removed during play. In Go, by contrast, the board begins blank and is progressively filled. Whereas each chess piece has its own movement and function, all Go stones serve one and the same function, to occupy space. To win at chess one must penetrate the opponent's defenses; to win at Go one must surround the opponent's defenses. In chess one wins by checkmate (by killing the king); in Go winning entails occupying the greater surface area on the board, or go-ban. Pursuing Warren Motte's observations about Go's writerly implications–that "quite often the game of Go itself serves as a pretext for other sorts of play"–I suggest that Roubaud's choice of Go over chess reflects metapoetic concerns.[13]

The rules of Go are few and simple, yet the complexity of play is exponential. Like writing itself, this complexity is recombinative. Here is a brief description of the game's four axioms: "First, two players (black and white) alternatively put their stones on any unoccupied intersection of the nineteen by nineteen line roster board. Any stone thus placed may not be moved except when it is captured. Second, if a stone or group of stones is completely surrounded by the enemy's stones, they are considered captured and are re-

---

[13] Motte, *Poetics of Experiment*, 58.

moved from the board. Third, each prisoner or territory captured counts as one point. Fourth, the situation called *ko*. If a configuration on a board is such that it would encourage the duplication of play the duplication is not allowed."[14] Since these rules apply to the third reading program, readers may wonder if or how they create meaning in the sequence of poems. And, granted that Go is given such a prominent role in the composition of the text, one might well take these rules as emblematic of Roubaud's general sonnet quest.

In my view, the way that this axis of inquiry plays out in ϵ is problematic. According to his own description, Roubaud envisions the transposition of Go rules and Go figures into writing as a metaphorical translation. Through a simple shift in frames of reference, each sonnet becomes a move in a game and playing a means of partaking. To draw the analogy as literally as possible, Roubaud claims that poems behave like the elements of Go play; he figures the blank page as an empty go-ban and the poems as the white and black stones: "Dans tout ce qui suit, on identifiera la représentation d'un texte sur une surface (papier) à la donnée traditionnelle d'un petit volume de nacre (pions blancs) ou de basalte (pions noirs)" (ϵ 7). Further developing this metaphor of the book as game board and the poems as play stones, Roubaud hierarchically organizes small groups of poems into configurations familiar to amateurs of Go.[15]

In these instances, his first and third reading programs coincide: the poetic figure, or diagram (principally a spatial element) takes as its surface the go-ban (a 19 × 19 grid) and the constellations of poems take on aspects of meaning from the figures in the game. To better explain, consider the example of the figure *ko* as it is presented in the text:

---

[14] Wimmer, "GO," 164-65.
[15] Although not all the presented groupings are common in Go games, their spacial disposition on the page symbolizes "une position possible des pions sur la table de jeu" (ϵ 8). For a detailed and humorous account of common strategy in Go, see Lusson, Perec, and Roubaud (1969), *Petit traité*; hereafter cited as *GO*.

FIGURE 3

2.2.4 Nuit devant la nuit

       KO
 Ko, qui signifie "éternité" ou "infini"
est, dans le jeu, une porte par où s'engoufreraient
tous les pions.

        •

      ménades

  •   o   •

 un hiver o glib le chien dit à guillaume

  o   o liebe. . .   o

 murailles. . .   fontaine
      o
      rêve   (ϵ 76)

Familiar to contemporary French readers, because it is the trademark symbol of books published by the P.O.L. publishing house, this configuration of dots (stones) is directly followed by the seven poems "corresponding" to the titles assigned to each position. Each poem therefore refers to its place in this schematic diagram of a common Go position (as well as to the other two sequences; this figure is 2.2.4 in the paragraph sequence).

 A basic understanding of the game's rules reveals that if "Nuit devant la nuit" were the actual position of stones in a game, the stone-poem "O glib o liebe. . ." could be captured by black, to which white could retort with a capture; subsequent moves would have to be played elsewhere before this one-for-one exchange could continue. In Go, this situation can lead to lengthy ko battles that demand simultaneous attention to different locations on the board. As such, this disposition of stones on the board could become a central focus, potentially exhausting all the stones.

 But how does this configuration of poems, this constellation of poem-stones, influence our reading of the poems? As in many of Roubaud's structured texts, the placement of the elements reveals their formal meaning. In the lexicon of Go, players speak of stable and unstable stones or groups of stones. A cursory reading of the poem "O glib o liebe..." demonstrates how this sonnet suits its unstable position in the ko configuration above (note the Go number that represents this poem's placement in yet another Go sequence, discussed below):

O glib o liebe...   O   [GO 69]

O glib o liebe source si tes eaux
seem song seem with their hundred folding herbs
sapides sous les jonquilles si neuves
où sifflent comme sifflent les roseaux

is it for me for us when lyin' above
you green on the marigold meadow
renversés sous les murmurant rideaux
de trembles gris nous jouons joute brève

or is it that from sauntering summer
in prairies drowned you hear the brooding birds
forever-owl or morrow nightingale

et débordant de mains fraîches tu pleures
qui crois versant douce tendresse neuve
apaiser le mal qu'ils portent au ciel (ϵ 79-80)

In this sonnet, the instability of the language resides in a no-man's-land of three languages. Its rhymes oscillate in imperfection (herbs/neuves, above/brève) or in isolation (morrow nightingale, summer, pleures). But it is difficult to determine the extent to which these instabilities are increased or engendered by the stone-poem's precarious placement in the ko configuration. In effect, its other attributes appear stable. The sonnet form is recognizable with the strophic divisions, the alternating rhyme, and the decasyllabic meter.

Yet, within this stable form, there is much movement. The ease with which the speaker passes from German to French to English to French implies games played by children learning languages. The poem speaks of childhood memories–make-believe jousting in fields–and the brooding sadness that such memories bring. It speaks of precious, fleeting moments, the kind that cannot be staged or revisited except in memory. Plus–another aspect that embodies instability–the poem stages the address implied by the birdsongs as a question ("seems song" "is it [sung] for me / us / you"? Or in "sauntering summer"?), thereby placing the memories and scenes in a precarious place. Further, that external influence of the Go configuration is alluded to in the poem. The "*forever*-owl," whose song participates in the questioning–indeed, we are not sure if it is his song, or that of the "morrow nightingale" that he (may) hear–may obliquely refer to the infinity of the ko position (forever asking "whoo"); and, in this way, the infinity in the ko figure might be aligned with the sky as: "une porte par où s'engoufreraient tous les *pleurs*."

This surface aspect of the constellation organization is also apparent in the sequence based on the Go game disputed by the two Japanese players, Masami Shinohara and Mitsou Takai. For this third reading strategy, readers are directed to follow the moves of an actual Go game, printed on a fold-out page in the appendix 4 of ϵ, and to consider the relationship between each stone and its corresponding poem within the sequence of the game (e.g., "[GO 69]," above).

Such a reading poses a variety of problems. In order for this sequence to sustain a secondary meaning directly related to what happened in that specific Go game, the reader would have to possess fluent command of Go strategy. Such subtleties are lost on the noninitiated. For these readers, the played stones and the printed poems bear a conceptual relationship only in that they share the same number, and they occupy a space on a reproduced record of the actual gaming surface. That is, although Roubaud alludes to a dialogue between the implied black and white players (ϵ 7), that dialogue is hardly identified by consistent stylistic differentiations in the poems or according to apostrophic address. Also, of the 157 moves represented from the actual game, only 84 of the corresponding poems bear the same color stone. There does not appear to be a systematic logic to this reversal of stone color, and the reader is left wondering what constraint determines the choice of white or black designation and how rigorously it was followed.[16] These

---

[16] A familiarity with Roubaud's writing will lead one to believe that there are hidden constraints at work here. Having taken into account Pierre Lusson and Jacques Roubaud's fundamental axiom regarding rhythm–"le rythme est la combinatoire séquentielle hiérarchisée du même et du différent" ("Le silence de la mathé-

contradictory representations frustrate a reading of the poems as a direct correlative to the game actually played. Indeed I wonder if the designation of a particular game of Go does not function, in a Perecquian spirit, as a bogus clue, or fausse piste.

Comparing a game of Go to a book of poetry represents a loose conceptual parallel. In effect, in the interview with Perec, Roubaud reveals that he imposed the Go sequence only after having completed one-third of the poems. He further discloses that in this sequence "l'ordre des pions est, en gros, identique à l'ordre de composition des poèmes" (*S* 7). Herein, I think, is revealed one of the parallels between the writing of the book and the "writing" of the game. That is, the only direct relationship between playing the stones and writing the poems is that they follow the same sequence: one poem = one move. In this sense, the Go sequence retraces what Roubaud has purposely erased elsewhere, the actual genesis of the text, which, if written every day, also serves as a record of the text's production.

In the *Petit traité invitant à la découverte de l'art subtil du go* (1969), Pierre Lusson, Georges Perec, and Jacques Roubaud celebrate the cultural wealth and strategic complexity of Go. Mockingly denouncing chess for its inability to yield a quantifiable victory, or for its lack of courtly tradition ("c'est pas un jeu qui rend poli" [*GO* 24]), they also liken the sequential play of Go to the act of writing itself. And what they admire in the Japanese tradition is the multivalence accorded to complex, or compound works. "Avec trente et une [syllabes] on fait, en cinq vers, un tanka; avec dix-sept un haïku de trois vers, et de quelques deux milles tankas, poèmes écrits par cents poètes, on construit, sur l'ordre de l'empereur, une anthologie qui est à la fois un animal fabuleux de papier, un puzzle impossible, un bouquet de dix mille fleurs, un jardin et une gigantesque partie de GO dont les poèmes, bons ou mauvais, anciens ou nouveaux... sont les pierres blanches et noires" (*GO* 15). According to Roubaud, these imperial anthologies provide a traditional

---

matique," 110)–I have mapped out the three separate but coexistent sequences of black and white stones in ∈ (the real game, the book game and the printed order of stones) in the hope of discovering some obvious interrelation. Although interesting, comparing these three rhythmic strands led to no precise conclusion. I have not analyzed them from a sophisticated mathematical perspective, a task for which I lack the relevant expertise.

model for the Go structures in ϵ, from which he has culled only the elementary constraints (*S* 7).[17] One of these justifies an aesthetic assumption about playing Go, that "l'enchevêtrement des pierres blanches et des pierres noires dessine des lignes, des réseaux, des zones agréables à regarder" (*GO* 41-42).

Another aspect aligning writing and Go involves the quasi-infinite possible combinations afforded by both activities. "Il n'existe qu'une seule activité à laquelle se puisse raisonnablement comparer le Go," write Lusson, Perec, and Roubaud, "on aura compris que c'est l'écriture" (*GO* 42). Offering a formidable number of possible combinations of play –"10^{750}, more than there are atoms in the universe"–, the game of Go opens, like writing itself, a "chemin infini" (*GO* 42), despite a limited number of elements (play-stones, moves; letters, ideas, forms).[18] Because play for the sake of play leads to no definitive ontological end and it is rooted in purposiveness without purpose, it harbors an intrinsic value, as does art in Kantian aesthetics. Roubaud accounts for this infinite possibility of play through a poetics based on multiple, intersecting organizing strategies, the diversity of poems, and an intentional strategy of incompletion.

Incompletion is most apparently emblazoned in the Go reading by the fact that the game textually transcribed in ϵ remains unfinished: only 157 of the 361 moves actually played appear. Claiming to avoid overdetermination in the composition, Roubaud figures this lacuna as a "voluntary imperfection" in the rendering of the game. Moreover, this self-imposed incompletion acts as reference to precursors whose poetics inhabit Roubaud's: "L'inachèvement est une face de l'imperfection volontaire. Elle prolonge, dans une direction un peu special, l'esthétique baudelairienne: erreurs, chevilles. Elles s'apparente aussi à celle de Zeami (no)" (*M9* 12).[19]

---

[17] Had this influence been more precise, one would seek to uncover a translation or cultural transcription of the linking techniques specific to Japanese court poetry and its imperial anthologies, the *Manyoshu* and *Shinkokinshu*. Before completing ϵ, Roubaud had become familiar with the constraints related to the composition of these anthologies and may have incorporated these concerns in his collection of "143 poems borrowed from Japanese," in *Mono no aware*. Also see Roubaud (1967), "Le *Manyoshu*," 3-24; Roubaud (1968), "Sur le *Shinkokinshu*," 73-106; Guéron, "Jacques Roubaud," 255-84.

[18] Wimmer, "GO," 164.

[19] Zeami is the fourteenth-century Japanese innovator of *no* theater. It is common for Roubaud, in the same instance, to mediate Western and Eastern poetic influences.

Similar types of imperfections can be found in the most faithful transcription of the model game: its numerical rendering (ϵ app. 4). For example, though their assigned locations bear a Go number and a textually present stone marker (•), the poems corresponding to the 79th and 156th moves of the game are omitted from the text (ϵ 102). And there are many printed poems that bear neither a stone marker nor a numbered position within the represented game (these, presumably, are excluded from the Go reading).

These imperfections and interruptions participate in the volume's overall intention, to engage the reader in a constantly shifting game whose end result must remain undecided. This perpetual tendency to look again from another direction, as if there were something more to be seen, to be said or felt, this constant search for what may yet make the speaker complete, is inscribed into the organizing principles of ϵ. That is, even when undertaken in good faith, the programmed reading trajectories cause consternation or frustration. An analysis of the book's second architectural structure, as a "sonnet of sonnets," will reinforce how Roubaud's voluntary imperfections help construct the signifying process of ϵ.

Working under the aegis of experiment, Roubaud advances the notion of the abstract sonnet. That is, he divides the sequence of his book into five "chapters," each of which is proposed as a "sonnet of sonnets" or a "paragraph-sonnet." These paragraph-sonnets are carefully numbered by poem, or sequence of poems, and these numbered sequences theoretically account for the composition of a (sequence of) sonnet(s). For example, "O glib, o liebe" appears in the sequence "Nuit devant la nuit," which is numbered 2.2.4, hence theoretically occupying the fourth position of the second segment of the second larger strophe. This organizing system, however, is neither simple nor complete, and the logic of the numerical sequences is anything but reassuring, especially to those not familiar with symbolic logic. Roubaud introduces this reading trajectory by stating that the sequences "s'insèrent dans un développement qu'explicite la table I de la page 155," but this appendix offers little explanation of the logic behind these numerical sequences; it merely provides a transcription of the numerical markers readers find as they read the collection from cover to cover.

Here, too, is an aesthetic of incompletion and imperfection, defining this set as open: "Les paragraphes doivent être considérés comme ouverts: certains textes ne sont pas donnés, certains le sont fragmentairement, tous pourront être ultérieurement modifiés, partiellement ou totalement" (ϵ 8). These openings contribute to intentional imperfections of the volume. In this numerical sequence, even blank spaces are numbered. Are these open spaces akin to the spaces between the strophes of traditional sonnets? Do they present a space for reflection and breath between the poems? Or, do they mark missing poems, poems that may be found later and inserted? Suggestive of poems to come, these spaces cast the economy of the text as a work in progress. Retaining such lacunae in the published version of ϵ also situates the reception of the text as necessarily incomplete.

Moreover, these voluntary imperfections create refractory effects retraceable in other Roubaldian publications. At the time of its publication, states Roubaud, not all of the texts had been written, "ne seront écrits" (S 7). He also states that there are several series of poems, published elsewhere, that, when located and graphed onto their marked places, may assume their potential roles in ϵ. For example, the series of poems "Prinsland" and "B. Y. Trois ou dix-neuf poèmes" or the poem "Sallèles" (S 7), all contribute, through an estranged relationship, to the complex architecture of ϵ.[20] Once again, like the missing classical sonnet, the blank spaces of ϵ refer to an absent form, or set of forms keeping in play a significant articulation between presence and absence, completion and incompletion. This interplay is echoed by the relationship between the overtly presented textual structures and the hermetical contents that they appear to cloak. Similar textual relationships take form between the places where Roubaud directly addresses his *Projet* (in M9 [1979] and *'le grand incendie de Londres'* [1989-]).

The title ϵ announces Roubaud's metaphoric use of symbols borrowed from set theory. Originally, Roubaud had selected the title *Eléments* but settled on the more theoretical symbol in order to underline the esoteric irony of his project. "Le titre finalement choisi manifeste l'ironie de la position lyrique assumée en chaque poème (elle est implicite *dans* toute l'histoire du sonnet) au moment même où elle s'exprime comme jeu d'une forme fixe, en principe impersonnelle, qui la nie. 'Bien que la raison soit commune, la masse des gens vit en ayant la pensée du coeur comme une chose particu-

---

[20] Roubaud (1967), "Prinsland," 28-37; Roubaud (1970), "B. Y.," 225-47.

lière' (Héraclite). Le signe d'appartenance, seul, imprononçable: qui? quoi? appartient à quoi?" (*M9* 12). Roubaud has therefore selected the title precisely because it is unpronounceable, a clever ruse for an object whose art is song–but also because the title effectively poses the questions that subtend each composition in the book, the "jeu d'une forme fixe" and its constitutive elements. Adopting a project of writing a "sonnet of sonnets" therefore has both its poetic and theoretical underpinnings, both of which relate to the author's ironic intentions.

"Le sonnet est comme le couteau de Lichtenberg," writes Roubaud; "changez la lame, c'est encore lui. Changez la manche, c'est toujours lui" (*M9* 8). It is this transformative capacity of the sonnet, of all fixed poetic forms, that funds Roubaud's research, for rather than narrowly defining its elements, he seeks to experience them broadly, modeling his work on the form's variability, not its norm. "S'il y a une théorie du sonnet, ses 'axiomes' semblent changer avec le temps; et les lieux" (*M9* 9); this first collection of sonnets boldly attempts to render an abstract model of this mutability, a model mediated by the axiomatic method of Bourbakian set theory.

This unconventional approach evokes the arbitrary character of the work. Roubaud's provocative figuration casts this second architectural organization as yet another game: "La méthode axiomatique transposée, le pseudo-bourbakisme appliqué à un objet aussi éloigné des mathématiques que le sonnet ont un caractère ludique évidente" (*M9* 9). Part of this ludic character lies in the theoretical (and questionable) assertion that mathematics (or artificial languages) can effectively provide the template for literary innovations whose import recapitulates, alters, or advances traditional notions of literature and form. To be sure, mathematics and mathematical thinking are key organizing elements in Roubaud's work, but the extent to which the implications of set theory are translatable to formal literary concerns is also questioned by the poet who advances his own title as a puzzle, or extended analogy: "Par extension, symbole de l'appartenance du monde de 'l'être au monde'" (ϵ 11).

In addition to confronting the loss of his brother in 1966, while he was writing ϵ Roubaud was also completing his doctoral thesis in mathematics, *Morphismes rationnels et algébriques dans les types d'A-algèbres discrètes à une dimension* (1967). An expertise in mathematics is required to fully understand this work, not to mention to relate it to Roubaud's literary projects–an expertise that I lack. Still, the introductory remarks to Roubaud's dissertation reveal that in his academic pursuits he contemplated questions similar to those pondered in his poetic undertaking: "L'objet du présent travail est la définition et l'étude de certaines familles de morphismes, que nous appelons 'morphismes rationnels et algébriques' d'une catégorie. Il s'agit de généraliser la notion de série formelle définie par un système d'équations linéaires à une classe de structures algébriques assez vaste et d'y étendre, à l'aide d'hypothèses convenables, certains calculs et résultats du cas 'modèle'." If one were to replace the word *morphisme* here with *sonnets*, these sentences would provide an accurate general description of Roubaud's appeal to mathematical symbolism in ϵ.

In writing and researching simultaneously the formal languages of set theory, linguistics, and the sonnet, Roubaud orients the direction of his subsequent writing projects, each of which proposes a unique blend of mathematics and literature. "1967 marque donc pour moi un double aboutissement: une thèse unissant catégories et langues formels. La réflexion sur les problèmes formels de la poésie, d'une part, sur la mathématique des constructions syntaxiques m'a ainsi conduit à un rapprochement, encore partiel [1979], des deux activités, en apparence absolument antithétiques; c'est à la consolidation de cette "chaîne de proximités" que je m'emploie, dès ce moment" (*M9* 22). Roubaud thus relegates the mathematical theory behind this volume's title to a secondary, exploratory level; it nonetheless remains an important structuring tool, even if, like the structure of Go, its effect on the coherence of the book is primarily superficial.

The idea of making poetic language signify through the rules of a game is akin to making poetry signify through a formal language, like symbolic logic. What, we may ask, are Roubaud's intentions in cross-pollinating two types of discourse? Is he invested in producing a third, hybrid discourse? Or, is he attempting to measure the parallels and incommensurability of natural, literary, and formal languages? Or, in a more Oulipian spirit, do these intersecting discourses provide new generative models by which poetic forms are to be reinvented and enacted?

Roubaud downplays the extent to which the formal languages of set theory or Go actually shape the meaning of the poems in ϵ. Like the visual constellations, the sonnet-paragraphs and the Go sequences provide context; they may be reduced to "la discipline métaphorique d'un geste et d'une organisation de surface" (*M9* 12). The procured effect is a purely conceptual relation between the poems: "La contrainte fut alors, pour un sonnet, de *s'accorder* avec d'autres selon ce mode de 'convenance,' concorde ou discorde assez inhabituelle entre les poèmes" (*M9* 10). But even that conceptual order must be read metaphorically. In effect, in "Description du *Projet*" Roubaud explains that set theory and Go influenced his early thinking about literature and that "les nécessités de *dire*, en sonnets de telles figures (par exemple, celle du 'ko,' métaphoriquement l'éternité) commencèrent à orienter mon travail" (*M9* 10). That is, the syntax of formal languages takes on metaphoric meanings in Roubaud's writing. Consequently, in some cases their logic becomes axiomatic. The ko rule in Go, for example, states that if a configuration on a board is such that it would encourage the duplication of play, immediate duplication is not allowed. A similar precept animates Oulipian inquiry: the notion of unicity. Oulipians believe that once invented and realized, it is senseless to repeat any given constraint, or combination of constraints. That is, the Oulipo favors the elaboration of diverse forms, not the proliferation of fixed forms.

Roubaud's use of formal language and generative grammar implies research of what the evolutionary biologist Conrad Waddington has termed an epigenetic landscape. This model attempts to imagine all the possible genetic transformations of a given organism or form, in this case the sonnet as pure form. In offering an analysis of actually attested sonnets, Roubaud provides an abstract environment in which the various possible but not actual developments of the sonnet may be imagined, thereby diversifying our understanding of the sonnet tradition and its remarkable mutability. Pursuing the limits of distortion of the form Roubaud proposes deformations of the sonnet, linking together a great variety of deviant forms buttressed by their structured context. The prose sonnet, for example, is "an aberrant form." Yet, when it is linked in a chain of sonnets whose interconnection makes a larger conceptual or abstract sonnet, the contextualization reinforces the form's plausibility.

The final trajectory offered in ϵ is a reading of each text individually: "On peut enfin, sans tenir compte de ce qui précède, se contenter de lire ou d'observer isolément chaque texte" (ϵ 9). This fourth reading trajectory is relatively muted in the "user's manual," as if it were offered as an afterthought. But how does it interact with the first three? Does reading of a single poem from this collection "sans tenir compte de ce qui précède" contradict and refuse other programs? And can any sonnet reading entirely ignore its context–"une histoire du sonnet"? The very notion of writing a sonnet necessarily entails knowing what a sonnet is. To "pay no heed to what has preceded," a textbook avant-garde maneuver, is therefore to willfully forget the constraints that have influenced and formed the literary framework. Oulipian writing, most notably Roubaud's, reminds us that willed repression is neither possible, nor finally interesting in that the force of the new relies on the momentum of the old. In a microcosmic way, Roubaud's fourth reading technique, the discrete reading, condenses the relationship of the new poem to tradition by offsetting the single poem from the other sequences of the collection.

Given the variety of its organizing structures, ϵ has not one center but, rather, multiple, interrelated centers. The play between the individual elements of the text and its conception as a whole, or as multiple wholes, initiates conditions of play between the exact and the general, between the linguistically precise and vague, between presence and absence, between totality (*le tout*) and nothingness, notions that are important in modern poetics generally, and in Roubaud's *Projet* more specifically.

If Roubaud's first collection of poems attempts to recapitulate "une histoire du sonnet," this ambitious abstraction also provides the structural architecture for a playful and enigmatic tension between the concrete and the abstract, the minute and the gigantesque, the personal and the universal. The poems that are absent or not finished, the sets of sonnets that are left open, the quasi-infinite potential combinations in Go and in writing itself, all refer to the incompletion of a personal life reflected in the open "symbole d'appartenance au monde de 'l'être au monde'" (ϵ 110). In the literary work, as in life itself, closure is inevitable, and the structural forms used in ϵ both echo and contradict that end.

CHAPTER FOUR

CONSTRAINT AND READING IN *TRENTE ET UN AU CUBE*

THE idea of a synthetic book is given new dimension in Jacques Roubaud's third poetic work, *Trente et un au cube* (1973), where he presents an overt conception of poetry as volume, as a measured space. Partially inspired by the Japanese tanka, Roubaud's poetic "cube" foregrounds how formal constraints engender textual meaning. Exploring alternative modes of poetic production, this work also illustrates Roubaud's blending of European and Japanese literary aesthetics.

Trente et un au cube is composed of thirty-one poems of thirty-one lines of thirty-one syllables. The simplest thing one could say in describing that book is that *Trente et un au cube* is about reading *Trente et un au cube*. Reading the work as a poetic treatise on the art of poetry is fundamental to understanding how Roubaud turns literary self-referentiality into a study of poetic rhythm and memory.

In *Description du projet* (1979), Roubaud lays bare some of the goals motivating his research and creative activities. Among them, Roubaud espouses the following idea from the English writer John Thomson: "*Whatever else I may be talking about, I am talking also about language itself*" (M9 23). For Roubaud, it is not precise enough to claim, along with Roland Barthes, that "la littérature parle d'elle-même." Wishing to prove the thesis that "*la poésie est mémoire de la langue,*" Roubaud prefers to stress the dialogic relationship between literature and its languages: "*La littérature parle du langage*" (M9 23). For him, the operative aspect of transformations in language may be isolated in rhythm, and this partially explains why Roubaud revises contemporaneous views of literary self-referentiality. Roubaud's interest in language focuses on its status as monument, as vehicle of memory. He seeks to renew the monumental language of poetry and therefore interrogates "l'objet des langues comme source de mémoire" (M9 24).

The title, *Trente et un au cube*, is calculated. It declares, in an unconventional manner, what the poem contains; it advertises the poem's status as a measured quantity, as a volume: theoretically, 31 cubic syllables, or 29,791 metrical positions. The title thus opens a book whose principal referent is form as contents. The specular relationship between the poem's form and its name has led Peter Consenstein to describe the book as "an immediately transparent object" whose straightforward self-referentiality alludes to an aesthetic of "hyper-reality."[1] This first impression points to the possibility of associating Roubaud's intentionally directed aesthetic with other, very different modes of self-referentiality. This type of association may occur at the outset, for Oulipian and specifically Roubaldian methodologies *do* engage a self-referential aesthetic based on the arbitrary nature of signs. As I hope to make clear, however, Roubaud's attention to constraint as rhythm does not align his experiments with the proliferation of aleatoric meaning or with an abolition of "History." On the contrary, his intentional mathematization of the arbitrary, literally spelled out in *Trente et un au cube*, demonstrates the extent to which motivated self-referentiality can articulate a controlled memory and displacement of literary convention. In short, the title names, describes, and advertises the work as an experiment under the constraints of a fixed quantity, drawing attention to the actual *counting* behind its composition.

To situate the importance of counting in each poem, the author devotes an entire page to that poem's number, printing the numeral at the center of an otherwise blank page. To draw further attention to the value of numbers and the process of counting, Roubaud begins the first poem by making explicit who is counting, what they are counting, and for whom counting counts: "JE DÉTIENS MILLION de / syllabes comptées pour toi" (1.1).[2] The first words of this poem

---

[1] Consenstein, "Rhythm and Meaning," 261; hereafter cited as *PC*.
[2] For the sake of concision I refer to quotations by locating first the poem number and then the line number, separated by a period. The single backslash (/) indicates an internal line break between fragments. Double backslashes indicate a break between lines and triple backslashes a break between strophes. For example, "dans le blanc, / tu n'étais plus qu'un point de /// brûlure" (25.17-18). When skipping between fragments, often necessary in reconstructing syntactical continuity, I mark the skip with an ellipsis: e.g., "faut-il / que . . . tu saches mes raisons?" (1.16, 17). When referring to quotations found between the poems, I provide the page num-

foreground the enumeration of syllables, both those presented and those withheld ("JE DÉTIENS"). Metrical counting is thus explicitly put into relief against what the poem is about: "JE DÉTIENS MILLION de / syllabes comptées pour toi / /// *disposées pour la contemplation par l'esprit / de la parole pour soi / au dessus delà le sens*" (1.1, 10). Counting, in short, is the name of the game in this first poem.

If the relationship among poet, poem, and reader is predicated on concise counting, then semantic meaning, by contrast, is represented as a secondary concern. Words in this context are presented for contemplative value, as distinct from referential meaning: "*disposées pour la contemplation par l'esprit / de la parole pour soi / au dessus delà le sens.*" To claim, however, that the poem does away with a concern for reference, that its author and reader count words solely for numerical value, for their "mise en durée" (1.6), is to overlook the semiotics of meter. The question of meaning here is intricately interwoven in the poem's metrical pattern and consequently engenders the determinative question negotiated by the highly constructed positions–"je" / "tu"–of the text. Simplified, this question amounts to nothing more than a game of authorial hide-and-seek: "faut-il // que tu saches mes raisons?" (1.16, 17). In other words, I would argue that Roubaud's aesthetic of contemplative form ("*la parole pour soi*") only *seems* indifferent to content. It is in the play of interstices in the text, in the gaps created by its formal constraints, that the poet inscribes meaning in the poem.

The vanguard of the arbitrary sign, integral to postmodern aesthetics, is articulated in *Trente et un au cube* through a bold transfiguration of the Japanese tanka: "La référence numérique à 31 vise, d'une part, la tradition japonaise" (*M9* 45). The tanka is a thirty-one syllable poem. In Chinese and Japanese, poetry explicitly overlaps with visual arts; consequently tanka explicitly integrate elements of drawing. When transposed into Western languages, the tanka most frequently consists of five lines that do not rhyme. They follow a rhythmic pattern of pure syllabic meter: the first line consists of five syllables, the second of seven, the third of five, and the fourth and fifth of seven (5 7 5 7 7). Loosely speaking, five lines respecting this syllabic distribution can be said to resemble the Japanese tanka, at least in appearance.

---

ber following the abbreviation *31*: e.g., "*even now the stress and buoyancy and abundance of the water is before my eyes*" (31 16).

Trente et un au cube imitates this poetic structure, except that Roubaud generalizes the form, giving it other dimensions. Instead of writing a short poem of thirty-one syllables, Roubaud factors the tanka's minimal metrical constraints into a much longer compound poem that is divided into thirty-one shorter poems. Each of these poems is then divided into five stanza groupings, of 5 7 5 7 7 lines, respectively; each stanza is marked by a blank line. And each line is divided into five segments of pure syllabic groupings, also based on the tanka's 5 7 5 7 7 syllabic distribution; in this case, each medial caesura is textually marked by blank spaces. Having thus "cubed" the numerical structure of the tanka, Roubaud composes a new form of three-dimensional text, a tanka of tanka.

What relation does this verse form have to the French poetic tradition? And how might Roubaud's adoption of the form pose interesting questions about French prosody? The tanka, unlike its shortened relative the haiku, has been imitated relatively little in Western literature. Because of his tendency to engage with "les grandes formes," Roubaud's choice may not seem obvious, especially since the tanka is exterior to his own canon. In terms of Japanese poetic forms, however, the tanka is arguably the most revered, for it predates the haiku or renga and plays an essential role in the imperial anthologies, monuments in Japanese literary culture. What's more, because French and Japanese are unaccentuated languages, based on pure syllabic prosody, theoretically speaking their verse structures are intercommunicable. For these reasons, in an Oulipian perspective, the tanka offers a particularly potential form.

Speaking of his interests in Japanese verse forms, Roubaud suggests that through a departure from the norms of French prosody he can most effectively come to know and change them: "C'est en examinant les conditions du choix de la forme dans une tradition étrangère, celles de la multiplication des essais et les modifications apportées au modèle emprunté qu'on peut, je crois, saisir le mieux ce qu'est une forme poétique" (*M9* 14). What is operative in Roubaud's adoption of foreign forms is the poetic license he appropriates in adjusting their constraints to suit his experimental ends. He writes tanka in French in order better to perceive and instill contrast into French prosodic constraints. In this respect, the tanka found in *Trente et un au cube* are not, in a strict sense, representative of traditional tanka; rather, they are a motivated echo of the borrowed form, a compound appropriation and approximation of Japanese tanka.

If Roubaud's interest in medieval Provençal poetry is foundational to his work, his study of Japanese form is no less rigorous. In the articles "Le 'Manyoshu' et la première poésie lyrique japonaise" (1967), and "Sur le Shinkokinshu, huitième anthologie japonaise" (1968), Roubaud writes a brief history and formal analysis of the art of the tanka. And, his anthologized "translations"–*Mono no aware: Le sentiment des choses (cent quarante-trois poèmes empruntés au japonais)* (1970)–illustrate how that poetics embodies an intrinsic harmony between the human spirit and poetic forms.[3] In each of these works Roubaud addresses specific formal aspects of Japanese poetics and experiments, at times working from the original language (with the assistance of an expert in the field), at times working from–even reproducing–contemporary English language translations and studies. Hence, although *Trente et un au cube* renders a transformed version of the tanka, Roubaud's knowledge of the traditional form is not insignificant.

But how does the Japanese model influence Roubaud's transposition of the tanka into French? And, more generally, how do foreign constraints enrich Roubaud's poetic engagement with poetry as a memory of language? If writing under constraint forces language to construct the world in different ways, then to import constraints from afar is a strategic means of renewal and hybridization. In effect, the search for change is central to Roubaud's adaptation of the tanka, and his maximizing use of the form constructs a new type of rhythm in *Trente et un au cube*.

Rhythm is often described as a natural condition in any language. In *An Introduction to Japanese Court Poetry*, Earl Miner investigates the organic nature of rhythm, comparing French and Japanese poetic meter, but finds the notion of origin elusive. "It is clear that each prosodic system is natural to its language, but it is very unclear why. The Japanese definition of syllabic line length into alternating fives and sevens seems very natural once it grows out of the formlessness of primitive song. But the cause of what seems natural is obscure, like the reason for the alexandrine in French" (21). The notion that a metrical constraint is natural to a given language, that it reflects the native rhythm of that language, raises more questions than it answers. The idea of an innate rhythm is all the more suspect when associated with national character and identities. Rhythm

---

[3] See Guéron, "Analyse d'un discourse," 255-84.

and meter, like signification, are historical constructs; they impart meaning according to an implicit tension between individual creativity and the historical forces of convention.

The 5 7 5 7 7 syllabic distribution in Japanese meter, like the twelve-position alexandrine in French, is the result of complex, historically grounded developments in literary convention. Classical Japanese poetry, in contrast to its Provençal counterpart, gained eminence in medieval imperial courts. The cultural elite codified its aesthetic in order to teach codes of amorous behavior. It enjoyed the privilege of imperial protection and it thrived under the purview of power. While these histories are too vast to address here, I will suggest that Japanese tanka attracts Roubaud precisely because, like the trobar, its central concern is love, and it was generated under nearly ideal, agonistic discursive conditions. Plus, like the idealized invention of poetic love in Provençal, Japanese court poetry has enjoyed thirteen centuries of uninterrupted reign in the Japanese language.

Taken as a *forme-mémoire*, the privileged form of the Japanese lyric could potentially transmit centuries of poetic know-how. In addition, the parallels between its historical formation and those of European court poetry point to a shared experience of constraint, social structure, and a poetics of desire. With these possibilities in mind, then, a reading of *Trente et un au cube* must probe the effect of a tanka of tanka, of a form that maximizes the metrical matrix and formal underpinnings of that memorial form. To what extent does reformulating and translating the tanka's basic constraints reflect the art of tanka? And what takes its place in Roubaud's versions of tanka poetics?

According to Miner, in early Japanese court poetry there is a marked tension between the expression of profound and sincere sentiment and the artifice used for such expression. The two terms used to distinguish the poles in this tension are *kotoba* (words) and *kokoro* (heart). Because courtly poetic discourse had become strictly codified in form and occasion, belated poets sought to renovate the old models, or old occasions, with new feeling, without losing their grounding in traditional contexts. Innovation in early Japanese court poetry therefore became a matter of "old words, new heart" (Miner 35). In Western poetic discourse, the tension between traditional form and novel expression is articulated analogously, and Roubaud's adoption of the Japanese model is not without reference to these familiar problems. In fact, his exploration of the Japanese medieval lyric decontextualizes tensions between fixed forms of occasion (*kotoba*) and new modes of lyrical expression (*kokoro*). His integration of Japanese poetics animates the shifting relationship between conventional artifice, new formalisms, and a poetics of pathos, or pure emotion.

The hybridization of traditions in *Trente et un au cube* stages questions regarding context and continuity. Some of Roubaud's readers are quick to point out the inherent difficulties. For example, in "La poésie et ses techniques," Alain Bosquet reviews Roubaud's "innovation obscurantiste" skeptically, claiming that, faced with the book's difficult formalism, the reader is deprived of a lyrical context within which to read the poem: "Le lecteur n'est pas prévenu: qu'il se méfie donc ou, au contraire, qu'il fasse l'inutile effort d'essayer plusieurs clefs mentales face à combien de serrures invisibles?"[4] For Bosquet, the text's *Verfremdungseffekt* is repellent. While demonstrating what Roubaud calls "la surdité bien connue de son auteur" (*M9* 46), Bosquet's remark does indicate the extent to which an appreciation of poetry relies on context.

Lyrical context, in both Japanese and Western tradition, relies on two forms of reference: the phenomenal (the poem's reference to human experience of the world, most often mediated by some form of mimetic representation) and the intertextual (the relationship between the poem, its technical art, and other poems, situating the work in a literary lineage). In the Japanese tradition, short poetry is classically situational. That is, the tanka, like the haiku, seeks to condense an integral experience into few words.[5] In early tanka

---

[4] Bosquet, "La poésie," 100-104.
[5] For the sake of illustration, I include a traditional tanka as it is presented in *Mono no aware*, including the title and roman print transcription of Roubaud's French translation:

> *ama gumo ni*
>   *chikaku hikari te*
>   *naru kami no*
> *mireba kashikoshi*
>   *mineba kanashi mo*
>
>   une femme
>   comme le dieu du tonnerre
>   illuminant près
> des nuages du ciel
>   quand je te vois j'ai peur
>   quand je ne te vois pas j'ai mal   (*MW* 71)

the poetic occasion is inspired by a variety of court-related situations, more commonly romance than war. Although tanka and haiku typically represent human experience in a lyrical mode (a world highly ordered by courtly life), as poetic subjects became increasingly codified and formalized, the poems' mimetic pretext gave way to modes of reflection on the art of representation. Miner points out that the feelings represented in the mature tanka have remained an intricate part of the poetic context, though their reality had become conventionally formulaic: "The belief that there must be some real situation behind the composition of a poem is a very enduring attitude, even while the thirst for actuality is often satisfied by what is transparently fictional" (Miner 27).

In *Trente et un au cube* Roubaud echoes and parodies this situational context, offering in each of his thirty-one poems a meditation on a particular scene. In some of these poems, Roubaud imitates conventional topoi of the Japanese tanka, notably in his descriptions of vegetation and landscapes, such as in the poems "LA MENTHE POUSSAIT," "RÉCIT DU SUREAUX," and "OR DANS CE JARDIN" (6, 7, 8). In these pages, Roubaud's subject matter may be read as pretext to a contemplative reflection on the poem itself. For example, the eighth poem conflates the literal and literary garden: "OR DANS CE JARDIN / les flammes courtoisement / les averses brandies par d'excellents archers / les fleurs dans ce jardin les // fruits s'agençaient ou / se combinaient / en jeux variables dans ce / jardin couvert de / figures" (8. 1-3). Roubaud's poetic moments are, then, like many of the Japanese tanka, almost purely situational and intended to facilitate a description, representation, or enactment of an "état de vision" (16. 11). Each of these "states of seeing," a figure emblazoned into the process of reading itself, communicates the effects of a concrete experience that often simultaneously shares mundane and esoteric points of reference.

Other Japanese conceits in *Trente et un au cube* may be noted in its construction of time and its incorporation of formal linking techniques similar to those found in the imperial anthologies, as exemplified in the *Manyoshu* and the *Shinkokinshu*.[6] An important and

---

[6] There are twenty-one other Japanese imperial anthologies, but I limit my reference to these two, for they are the only ones on which Roubaud has published critical analyses.

interesting aspect of these anthologies is the manner in which they interlink a vast number of poems into an integral chain of poems, which in turn becomes a complex, multidimensional poem. The anthologizing of Japanese tanka is linked to its problematization of content and form, or subject and context, for, in Earl Miner's words, "a court poem is five lines in search of a context" (Miner 28). These monumental anthologies offer a context in which tanka by many poets of different generations can be read as a single strand, or tightly constructed sequence. They condense and recount the terms of poetic taste; they provide a record of changes across poetic eras.

Short poems are thus compiled in a "temporal progression [that] was natural to the love poems, which were arranged in the pattern of a courtly love affair" (Miner 28). These love affairs frequently follow the seasonal rhythms of a calendar year. Roubaud's thirty-first poem, "UNE ANNÉE FINIT," seems to echo this organizational principle. Furthermore, by repeating the theme and question established in the first poem, this final poem marks the potential circularity of the collection:

> mais di- // ras-tu où est la / réponse je ne vois ici que des miettes / pour te suivre à travers le / cri des nuits mais diras-tu // je ne vois pas la / moindre lueur démontrable / cela est vrai ma / réponse n'est qu'une fuite / je détiens millions de syl- // labes placées pour / toi qui dorment ou me répandent je puise selon mes lignes des chaînes plausibles sous mes contraintes // pourtant j'ai répondu la réponse est là prise / dans le mouvement / d'ensemble: désordre clair / derrière la voix battante (31. 27-31)

The return, in this final sequence, to the question posed in the first poem ("faut-il que tu saches mes raisons?"), along with the repetition of the opening theme ("JE DÉTIENS MILLIONS de / syllabes comptées pour toi"), draws attention to the poem's progression through time, reiterating, like the numbers that locate each poem, the volume's sequentiality and circularity.

Temporal progression in Japanese imperial anthologies soon gave way to complications. "The basic temporal progressions were in time augmented by spatial progressions, and later by techniques of association that integrated poems into a whole even when progression was infeasible" (Miner 29). In other words, in composing the imperial anthologies. Japanese poets and scholars used more abstract, sometimes intentionally non-linear linking techniques to establish a collection's continuity. These highly formalized modes of interlinking poems are of particular interest to Roubaud, first because of their novelty in modern analyses of Japanese poetics: "The detailed principles of integration through association and progression have been rediscovered only in recent years, in what must be considered one of the major literary discoveries of our generation" (Miner 30). Roubaud's translations of Japanese poems and his introduction to their poetic principles–work that is strongly influenced by Miner and other English-language research–help disseminate some historical context to Francophone audiences. Second, for Roubaud, the linking techniques found in the Japanese imperial anthologies provide a new formal syntax that can be generalized and applied to literary compositions. It is very much along these lines that we might best approach *Trente et un au cube*, and what it might contribute to Roubaud's *Projet*.[7]

In his article on the *Shinkokinshu*, Roubaud discusses a variety of linking techniques and analyzes their development. He explains the practice of linking by "categories of phenomenon" in successive poems (*shinku*); the use of a pivot-word whose double meaning is engendered by different parsings (*kake kotoba*); the use of "pillow-words" (*makura kotoba*) which are five-syllable modifiers echoing older poems; and the repetition of related words in associated contexts (*engo*). Roubaud's interest in these linking techniques traces two phenomena: the collective authorship of a national monument based on "reminiscent associations," and the progressive fragmentation and recombination of short poetic forms, from the tanka to the haiku and renga.

To pursue Japanese influences in *Trente et un au cube*, one might retrace how these linking techniques are connected to the distant Oriental context. In such a study, Roubaud's poem would be considered as a Japanese work, shuttling between languages, presumably

---

[7] It is relevant to note that Roubaud locates another such formal syntax of memory in the "arborescent" prose of the Arthurian romances, which are interconnected through shared episodes and tangential interference. These abstract structures of memory become explicit figures of constraint in Roubaud's late prose works, *'le grand incendie de Londres'* (1989), *La boucle* (1995), *Mathématique:* (1997), *Poésie:* (2000), and *La bibliothèque de Warburg* (2002). In this sense, the aesthetic of entrebescar is enriched by at least two intertexts: the Japanese imperial anthology, and the memory prose of Arthurian romance.

by way of translation (as I have tried to do in retracing the Provençal style clus via Petrarch). But *Trente et un au cube* poses questions about convention and technique that are intricately linked to the processes of translation and reading. Is it possible, for example, to translate a poetic aesthetic from an entirely different culture and language without seriously deforming and reducing it? Can one inscribe the memory of one language into another? Can such a memory be transmitted via a foreign form? Is not a "romanicized" version of Japanese poetic techniques (including the notions of kotoba and kokoro) already partially determined by the poetic conventions of the Western language in question? From a strategic point of view, by conflating two very different poetic traditions, Roubaud displaces the norms of one context with the techniques of the other. And deciding what belongs to which tradition may become tricky.

Peter Consenstein has initiated a study of the Asian influences in *Trente et un au cube*, focusing particularly on the linking techniques known as *engo*, or word repetition, in differing contexts (PC 275-77). In that discussion, Consenstein renders explicit the repetition of final words or phrases of one poem at the beginning of the following poem. I have already cited an example of this type of repetition in pointing to the potential circularity inscribed between the last and first poem (in the phrase "je détiens millions de syllabes"). But how does one specify the origin of this technique as principally Japanese? Indeed, a similar linking technique is already integral to the tradition of the canso (in the cobla capcaudée), and other similar ones preexist elsewhere in the French poetic landscape. Those resemblances make it difficult to distinguish native linking techniques from their Japanese versions.

Consider, for example, the use of *makura kotoba*, or pillow words. Because analogous techniques exist in the Western tradition—for example, the refrain in the ballad, or an often cited alexandrine, or a cliché image—and because each language constructs its own memory through poetry, it would be difficult to establish the Asian purity of linking techniques. In effect, makura kotoba also resembles intertextual techniques that already permeate the condition of poetic memory in French. Certainly, there are technical differences in Japanese and French linking techniques, and those distinctions may clarify and enrich the use of key phrases in building a memory of tradition. But likening Roubaud's use of fragment repetition to the use of makura kotoba in Japanese imperial anthologies may be stretching matters. In the imperial anthologies a team of poets and scholars stitches together the works of numerous authors from various centuries. In Roubaud's case, although he may be generously citing from a diversity of sources in *Trente et un au cube*, or may be developing from poem to poem an effect of internal citation, and repetition, there is little sense in which his work can transmit a direct memory of Japanese poetics; few of his French readers would in fact possess access to that memory. Equating Roubaud's technique with engo or makura kotoba therefore deforms the original use and context of the terms; and yet, alternatively, their comparison may sharpen our understanding of association in literary memory.

Similar conflations enrich a classification of Roubaud's own linking techniques. For example, the thirtieth poem, "JE T'ENFERMERAI," presents a singular example of an internal linking technique. Each successive line in this poem refers to the situation represented in each successive poem in the collection, thereby serving the double function of recapitulating each poem and of providing a delineated table of contents. In that poem, the first line refers to the content and movement of the first poem, the second line to the second poem, and so on, until the last line foresees closure in the last poem. If the thirtieth poem functions as a linking technique inspired by Japanese poetics, it would be difficult for a French reader to identify that motif as such. The critic, in choosing the appropriate descriptive term, is constrained by the text's novelty and self-conscious heterogeneity; in cross-pollinating these two literary traditions, the poet cunningly questions a possible convergence in the monumentality of both.

Roubaud catalogues another element of this heterogeneity on the last page of *Trente et un au cube*. Here, the author explicitly acknowledges the sources of his intertextual influences, most of which are not directly associated with the Japanese tradition. The names of these fifty-nine individuals–poets, mathematicians, philosophers, and composers, given without explanation–appear as in the credits of a film, "dans l'ordre de leur *première* intervention" (131), implying that these citations are plural, interspersed, and cumulative. Such incursions are marked in several ways: first, in direct quotations from the artist (either italicized in the poem or inscribed as incipit on one of the inter-pages separating the poems, often in the original language accompanied by a French translation); second, in a direct mention of the interlocutor's name; and third, perhaps less evidently, in veiled imitations of their technical art crafted into the poem itself. Or, as is commonly the case, in a combination of all three.[8]

Delineated in groupings that imitate the collection's 5 7 5 7 7 rule, this list of contributors further complicates the memorial context of *Trente et un au cube*. In its form, the text invites readers to consider the influence of a Japanese poetics in Roubaud's choice of the tanka and to confront these erudite concerns with commentary

---

[8] In the twelfth poem, VIENT LE REPOS TOUT, we observe how these intertextual, interdisciplinary influences are incorporated into the text. Nicolas Bourbaki is given as inspiration for this particular poem. The very structure of the poem establishes an underlying, repetitive structure, like the series in a numerical set. Translated into verbal syntax, this series is repeated six times, each time marking a great or slight difference that foregrounds the underlying concerns of caesurae and syllable count. A comparison of the first and twenty-seventh line of this poem illustrates how the slight variations focus the reader's attention on the combinative sequence in play in the composition:

> VIENT LE REPOS TOUT / dans la nuit vacille tout / se charge de lignes / les formes matérielles comme / l'idée de noir chaque courbe (12. 1) vient le repos tout / dans la nuit hésite tout / se lie de silence / les herbes compliqués comme / la pluie de noir chaque pierre (12. 27)

The syntactic parallelism, intact in all six repetitions, demonstrates the recurrence of a linguistic structure independent of, but transformed by, the metrical count imposed on the line. In these two lines, the syntactical structure and the metrical structure coincide, but there is a displacement of certain words. This substitution, present in each step of the six permutations, imposes a variation independent of and complemented by the strict metrical parsing (the number of syllables in these six sequences varies between 128 and 204). Here are the first thirty-two syllables of the second permutation; notice how the shifting in metrical position forces a shift in the imposition of the caesura, hence a variety in the length of the syntactical segments:

> vient le repos tout dans la / nuit s'effrite tout / se charge de signe les pentes immobiles comme // l'issue de noir chaque / forme (12. 6-7)

In the first two examples, 31 syllables construct the parallel tankas; in the third example, owing to the metrical variance (7 + 5 + 14 // + 5 +1), 32 syllables are counted (four silent [e]s in the third segment). These changes repeatedly foreground the rhythmic structures operative in the poem's production and reception. These changes also illustrate the distinction between what is referred to as meter (the line and segment length; the syllable positions), structured prose, oral language, and, as an element of each of these, rhythm, which all work together in revealing the formal underpinnings of the composition. Of particular interest in this poem is how this Bourbakian series systematically displaces the notion of unity and wholeness conjured by the repeated dissolution of the "tout."

from an additional set of voices. That is, as poetic form and literary moment, each poem speaks of itself in plural and often different or contradictory terms. Noting these challenges, Consenstein also remarks that "Roubaud never explores one question at a time, he prefers to juxtapose different yet similar phenomena" (PC 297). This multidimensionality, conceived progressively in the development of Roubaud's works, synthesizes differing signifying contexts. As a result it is tempting but misleading to privilege an account of one strategic intention over the others; for example, the combinative art of Japanese linking techniques over the combinative art of the Troubadour canso, both of which remain important concerns in Roubaud's shifting conception of the *Projet*.

Consequently, it *is* appropriate to apply the notions of Japanese linking techniques to a reading of *Trente et un au cube*. These techniques are integral to a close reading of the poem as a whole and relevant to the cumulative manner in which Roubaud constructs multidimensional constraints in other compositions. Nonetheless, it is important to recognize the shift that these principles undergo when rendered in French, as opposed to Japanese. In short, given the explicit influence of other literary voices, *Trente et un au cube*'s heterogeneity presents a peculiar polyvalence that eludes conventionally structured readings. In order further to demonstrate the wealth of perspectives offered in this volume, I shall continue to interrogate its metrical meaning from a mathematical point of view.

Beyond providing the measure of an explicit symmetry, the cubed root (31^3) reflects the numerical play subtending the conception of the collection. For a mathematician, the tanka appeals because it consists of prime numbers; thirty-one, and each of the segment divisions (5 7 5 7 7). As a self-proclaimed fanatic of numbers, or "métromane," Roubaud elaborates a numerical metaphysics associated with certain numbers and certain series of numbers. In some cases his pet numbers play an important role in traditional poetic forms. In this case, however, the mathematical beauty of the text is supported with the use of prime numbers, which François Le Lionnais characterized as "anges rebelles."[9] Roubaud explains:

---

[9] In "Raymond Queneau et l'amalgame des mathématiques et de la littérature," Le Lionnais discusses Raymond Queneau's fascination with arithmetic curiosities and reveals how this interest, as much theoretical as idiosyncratic, subtends many of

"Le choix du nombre, 31, implique également une 'métaphysique' arithmétique du nombre premier, puisque 31 est premier de nombre et sa 'décomposition' à la japonaise en fait la somme d'un nombre premier de nombres premiers" (*M9* 45). In this respect, Roubaud conceives of the segments, lines and groupings of his poem as prime, and therefore unique. Although he often attributes added significance to the numbers chosen in his compositions, he limits this significance to their functions as whole numbers or to the role each number plays in a poetic tradition. In this sense, Roubaud grants numbers no "magical powers" other than those associated with arithmetic or their recollection of poetic forms. In his works, numbers determine the text's structural matrix, they contribute to its formal meaning, and they relay connection between the history of mathematics and poetry; but there is only strained proof that they constitute a coherent, underground metaphysics.

The best discussion of the mathematical matrix in *Trente et un au cube* is Jean-Jacques Thomas's "Chances Aren't: Roubaud's Numerical Poe-tricks."[10] Thomas approaches Roubaud's text from the perspective of generative grammar. In that theory, two pairs of concepts have operative value. The first pair opposes *competence* (the formalized and finite set of the transformational rules of grammar as accepted by an ideal speaker-hearer) to *performance* (the actual application of these rules). The second pair opposes the *deep structure* (an artificial base of the sentence to which no transformation has been applied) to the *surface structure* (the actual occurrence of an uttered sentence, including its transformation). Deemphasizing the use of the tanka, Thomas concentrates on how the number 31 provides an "abstract theoretical principle of the text as a whole" (184).

Queneau's works. Roubaud shares and develops Queneau's fascination with numbers, and *Trente et un au cube* presents a simple example of how Queneau's hyperprime numbers have been worked into a poetic composition. Le Lionnais explains this class of whole numbers in the following manner: "Un dégustateur de nombres entiers ne peut pas ne pas ambitionner d'affronter les affres et les délices de ces anges rebelles que sont les nombres premiers. Raymond en avait imaginé une catégorie qu'il avait baptisée les *nombres hyperpremiers*. Un nombre hyperpremier à droite (resp. à gauche) est un nombre premier écrit en numération décimale (mais on voit rapidement que touts les chiffres pairs sont exclus) et tel que si on retranche un ou plusieurs chiffres consécutifs en partant de la droite (resp. de la gauche), la partie restée intacte est toujours un nombre premier" (*ALP* 37).

[10] Thomas, "Chances Aren't," 177-91.

According to Thomas, this *"numerical principle* does not work solely at a superficial (*macroquantic*) level, but is embedded deeper in the abstract transformational process which intervenes between the primary and the secondary system." In other words, the pure mathematical organization of each line and poem, as well as of the entire text, has a generative property: it is the rule that "manifests the conversion from a numerical order to an alphabetical one, the passage from one symbolic to another without any waste" (185). Asserting that "in *Trente et un au cube*, the number 31 plays the role of competence," Thomas characterizes "the systematization built around 31 [as] a main part of the literality of this text," for "it not only formalizes the external structure but at the same time generates it, assuring the wholeness of the text as an autonomous and integrated system" (186-87).

Thomas emphasizes that "these are not 'let's pretend' rules," that poetry is "no longer in the external form," and that Roubaud's new poetic *écriture* "is entrenched in principles" (189, 190). This analysis underscores the role numerical constraints play in determining textual interpretation. On the one hand, the numerical principle draws attention to the procedure of composition that the poet adopts, thereby foregrounding the technical craftsmanship of writing. On the other hand, both Thomas and Consenstein remark that the number 31 and combinations of its subsets (notably segments of 5 and 7, which allude to the alexandrine) determine how the surface structure of the text signifies with respect to the French poetic context. Both critics recount how the poet's use of the mute *e* prompts readings that rely on conventional metrical strategies in French. A simple example discussed by Thomas appears in the very first segment of the first line. This segment—"JE DÉTIENS MILLION DE"—exceeds the five metrical positions allotted. Thomas strategically reads the first "je" of the poem in an *uncounted*, or *empty*, metrical position (188), a reading that enables him to argue that the recurrence of very similar sequences in the thirty-first poem—"je détiens million" and "je détiens million de syl" (31. 18, 29)—performs the "re-establishment of *je*" in the text. In an argument that further relies on conventional notions of syllabic stress in French verse, Thomas identifies what he calls a "thematic isotopy" played out in the metrical relationships of the "je" and "tu" in the text.

Approaching this problem with the perspective that "one cannot be sure of the absolute method of counting the 'mute *e*' in this work," Consenstein questions the stability of Thomas's argument (*PC* 295). He claims that Thomas "seems to have overlooked" Roubaud's description of how the lines are to be counted: "Chaque voyelle non élidée est 1, chaque e muet (élidé ou non) est 1 ou 0 (au choix)" (*M9* 45). Because Roubaud lets his readers decide how to count the mute *e*, a measure of undecidability remains. Consenstein takes issue with Thomas for overlooking Roubaud's instructions and for having failed to "take responsibility for his own choices" in counting (*PC* 297 n27). He claims that Thomas's argument for a disappearing, and reappearing "je" is arbitrary, and that it should be recognized as such. Moot as this point may seem, Consenstein's argument maintains multiple ways of counting metrical positions, allowing the discovery of experimental combinations to the discretion of individual readers.

Consenstein's critique is, however, not detrimental to Thomas's analysis of *Trente et un au cube*. It merely establishes that the generative system underlying the text is not entirely "autonomous and closed," as Thomas asserts, but rather an intentionally open, dynamic system conditioned by modalities of variation, or clinamen.[11] Moreover, in studying the "juxtaposition of the 'je' and the 'tu' in the text, Consenstein goes to some length to demonstrate that these two pronouns "rhythmically counterbalance each other," an argument which further supports Thomas's view of "thematic isotopy" (298-303).

---

[11] Ibid., 190. In his analysis of *Trente et un au cube*, Consenstein has considered the role of the clinamen in the places where the 5-7-5-7-7 syllable distribution is violated. This study begins to uncover the manner in which the combination of a 5-7 segment echoes and refers to the alexandrine, an engagement that is complicated by pivotal uses of the counted and uncounted "mute *e*" (∂). For the Oulipo, use of the clinamen, a conscious swerve incorporated into the rendering of one or several poetic constraints, imparts strategic intentions. In Roubaud's case these are most frequently associated with formal problems rooted in tradition. The exceptional combinations of 5-7 segments therefore have two functions. On one hand they function extratextually, raising questions about the continued sway of the alexandrine in contemporary French poetics. On the other, they function intratextually, flagging specific sites where the form has been violated for intentional purposes (sometimes related to the expression of other competing constraints, sometimes supporting the expression of a semantic point). For an analysis of clinamen in *Trente et un au cube*, see *PC* 303-9.

The discrepancies between these two readings are of minor importance, for underlying both lines of argument is the notion that the text has been determined according to the principle of numerical constraint, which the poet either follows or subverts. More important here is the degree to which these critics must rely on formalized and traditional notions of scansion when faced with such metrical novelty. Although *Trente et un au cube* makes explicit reference to its mathematical matrices, it provides no static model against which to measure its realization. Preemptively foreseeing the critical gestures of metricians, Roubaud's volume figures new forms of rhythmic measure. Thomas and Consenstein have both responded by demonstrating the extent to which systematized, conventional scansion facilitates readings of *Trente et un au cube* that count.

Not all readings are as responsive. In "La poésie et ses techniques," Alain Bosquet characterizes the poems' numerical constraints as evidence of the author's "manque de confiance."[12] Grumbling about having to unfold the page of each poem to read its contents (a concrete particularity that would intrigue most readers of poetry), he asks: "La page imprimée sert-elle à rêver ou à camoufler des verités d'ordre exclusivement scientifique?" (100). In order to reveal the pure poetic merit of Jacques Roubaud's style, Bosquet asserts that "the text of the most uncontestable poet of this generation" must be "reglued, reconstituted, resutured, in order to apprehend its full ardor" (101-2). As a solution to the problem, he reprints a selection of the nineteenth poem, omitting the segment and line breaks, as if Roubaud's book were composed of unmetered prose.

To discount the numerical matrices underlying this text is to denature an important aspect of its poetic presentation. In a canny response to Bosquet's articles, Roubaud composes a supplementary

---

[12] "La poésie et ses techniques," 100-04. In this article Bosquet praises Roubaud's innovations but tempers his approval by stating that "le malheur est que, pour le lecteur de bonne volonté moyenne, Jacques Roubaud se barricade dans ses livres et en interdit l'accès." He complains that this volume lacks a "mode d'emploi" and questions why it was not printed on larger paper to facilitate "une lecture normale." He concludes in asserting that Roubaud is "un poète à recopier avec des moyens techniques très pauvres, très essentiels," an imperative he immediately fulfills by reprinting and repunctuating the first stanza of the volume's fourth poem, "LA BOUCHE EST DOUBLE et." See also Bosquet, "Jacques Roubaud," 16.

text entitled "Poème de présentation composé pour une lecture de *Trente et un au cube* à Shakespeare et C." [13] Reclaiming the spacing in his poems, Roubaud emphasizes the metrical segments by printing the poem in separate columns of 5 7 5 7 7 syllables each, the long lines appearing this time on facing pages. As the first line of this mocking "mode d'emploi" suggests, meaning in the poem largely depends on a willingness to listen and to understand, both of which are underlined in the French verb *entendre*: "cela signifiait / ce que chacun voulait vous / l'entendre et moi / l'entendre aussi mais parmi / vous c'est cela voyez vous" (168-69). Yet listening for meaning poses problems here, for if one were to hear this line without having read it, it might be difficult to decide on the conjugation of *vouloir*, as it sounds like *vous* could also be its subject (*voulez-vous l'entendre*). Might it be Bosquet's unwillingness to listen to these line breaks that prompts Roubaud's charge of "la surdité bien connue de son auteur" (*M9* 46)? Or is Roubaud punning here on the stuttering, almost sobbing rhythm that his metrical scansion imposes?

Deaf to this rhythm game, Bosquet complains that Roubaud's spacing techniques force pauses and ruptures that are uncustomary in French poetry. These ruptures are especially clear where Roubaud divides a word to respect the syllabic constraint. Since the poetic line in French is traditionally defined by its respect for syntactic and metrical unity, it comes as no surprise that Bosquet should advise readers to overlook the distraction of the segment breaks, for he hopes to refamiliarize a text whose beauty is compromised, in his opinion, by its experimental entrapments. As each poem in the volume attests, however, and as the supplemental poem repeats, Roubaud writes these five caesurae into an extraordinarily long line precisely to encourage a displaced reading experience; it is that new rhythm that becomes the vehicle for pure emotion.

In the supplemental poem, beginning "cela signifiait," Roubaud explains that these syllabic constraints open new possibilities for him as writer, and for the "tu" in the poem (a personal pronoun that refers to both the poet's beloved and to his reader). Throughout these poems, "je," or the speaking subject, toys with disentangling the reader, the textual "vous," from the beloved addressee, "elle," both of whom are conflated in the second person apostro-

---

[13] Roubaud, "Poème de présentation," 167-71.

phe, "toi." Even in this riddle poem, Roubaud affirms that his experiment was undertaken in a spirit of love songs, to speak of his loved one in order better to hear her: "la marche ancienne / de celui qui parle / de qui l'occupe pour l'entendre." He challenges his reader to do the same.

> Moi j'avais pris sur / ce chemin indispensable / en l'absence du machin communicatoire / dans la transparence // duquel chacun as / pire la marche ancienne / de celui qui parle / dans le bruit qui l'entoure de / de qui l'occupe pour l'entendre // vous pouviez ouvrir / les oreilles suivre du / doigt ce que cela / disait de toi l'entendre ou / le réfléchir mais toi? // et c'était tout ce / la que c'était toi partout / ici toi le tout / de toi et c'était cela / que cela signifiait. (28-31, 170-71)

In this poem's closing lines, Roubaud again solicits his reader's collaboration in creating meaning by virtue of rhythm, in the way the line wends around pauses, leaving openings where what is not said might be heard. And that collaboration is predicated on respecting and listening to the spaces that separate the counted segments of the lines, the blanks that punctuate the rhythm of each poem. Here again, the very condition of "toi" in the text is ordained by its bordering on a typeset blankness: "toi partout / ici toi le tout / de toi." This insistence on the role of the blank between "je" and "tu" is repeated throughout *Trente et un au cube*, and therefore bears closer analysis.

OÙ VIVIONS NOUS?

As stated, counting is a continuous concern in *Trente et un au cube*. Like reading itself, the conditions for counting in this text are marked by undecidable spaces, by open and blank spaces separating the segments, the lines, the strophes, and the poems themselves. In fact, the volume's overall organization is based on space occupancy, on the numbered spacing of sound and silence. The identity of each poem is therefore decided by its place among the other thirty poems, and that identity depends on its distinctness from the surrounding poems, a distinction facilitated by the whiteness between poems. From the beginning the reader is positioned according to the familiar second-person pronoun "tu," and the dialogue between the "je" and "tu" in the text frames the intrigue of the entire volume as a Roubaud textual game of authorial hide-and-seek. This dialogue, like the numerical disposition of 5 7 5 7 7, can be heard or understood only through an attention to its silences, the blank spaces that structure it.

In discussing the role of the blank space in *Trente et un au cube*, one is first faced with a choice of poems. Each poem makes at least one explicit reference to the blank space that separates individual line segments, and the following poems explicitly address the role of the line break in their titles: J'ARRANGE LE BLANC (11), DANS UNE PAUSE ABSTRAITE (15), QUE VOIR? L'IMMOBILE (24), AUJOURD'HUI EST BLANC (25). I have chosen to take a closer look at OU VIVIONS NOUS? (18) because it has not, to my knowledge, received particular critical attention, and because it aptly represents the amorous dialogue that runs as a constant theme through the collection.

By way of introduction to OU VIVIONS NOUS? I suggest that blank space in a poetic text is structured space. The significance of empty space in a poem relates to the tone, content, and rhythm of the printed space that surrounds or interrupts the blankness of the page. If the poetic line depends on spacing for metrical purposes, these openings in syntagma must be considered prosodic: line cutting (*la coupure*) is a technique of verse. Space, moreover, contributes to how the text counts time, for it establishes a period of waiting, a suspended breath in the continuity of the poem, an interruption to both the syntactic and rhythmic flow.

Many recent poets have developed techniques around the concrete functions of blank space, silence, and images of whiteness. Studies of spacing in modern poets have also led to a broader understanding of the overlap between visual art and language art. Whiteness and its counterpart blackness have often been read metaphorically as a means of representing, within a historical perspective, the boundaries around what has been written (signified through representation) and what has not or cannot be written, respectively. If one were to approach Roubaud's *Trente et un au cube* from this perspective, it might be suggested that the use of the tanka and quotations from the chosen intertext historically marks the forms and methods Roubaud adopts in the printed word. As this is a text dominated by blank space (more than half of the book consists of almost entirely blank pages), it might also be suggested that Roubaud actively writes white space against print as a means of testing boundaries. It is in the movement between these contrasting spaces that Roubaud invites his reader into a subtle, playful dialogue.

According to Maurice Blanchot in *L'entretien infini*, dialogue, like all forms of intelligible discourse, is conditioned by interruption: "L'interruption est nécessaire à toute suite de paroles; l'intermittence rend possible le devenir; la discontinuité assure la continuité de l'entente."[14] Interruption in the flow of words is what both separates and unites distinct syntagma, both as white spaces between printed words and as pauses between spoken words. Blanchot suggests a typology of the functions of these interruptions, distinguishing the manner in which these silent pauses establish relationships between the interlocutors in a literary discourse.

For Blanchot, interruption is, in one respect, tangible, reducible to the typographic or phonic pauses that define the position of each speaking subject: "l'arrêt-intervalle est comparable à la pause ordinaire qui permet le 'tour à tour' d'un entretien. Elle est la respiration du discours" (*EI* 107-8). In *Trente et un au cube*, this first type of interruption is, in part, punctuated by syllabic groupings, whose ungrammatical sequences establish a rhythm of fits and starts. These pauses are unconventional, in that they ignore concerns of syntactical unity; they are more or less regular in occurence, and thus establish a specific rhythm of respiration: "désordre sûr, véridique / à travers la voix battante" (1.31).

However, in a literary discourse, there is yet another Roubaud interruption, one conditioned by the material and physical distance that separates author and reader, a silence whose beginning is marked by writing, and whose end may be marked by a reception or reading of that writing. "Mais," continues Blanchot, "il y a une autre sorte d'interruption, plus énigmatique et plus grave. Elle introduit l'attente qui mesure la distance entre deux interlocuteurs, non pas la distance réductible, mais l'irréductible" (*EI* 108). This second kind of spacing, irreducible to the ordinary pause between speakers, or between syllabic groups, describes the layers of lyrical apostrophe inscribed in *Trente et un au cube*. Blanchot has postulated the following typology of its functions:

---

[14] Maurice Blanchot, *L'entretien infini*, 107; hereafter cited as *EI*.

> Dans l'espace interrelationnel, je puis chercher à communiquer avec quelqu'un de quatre manières : une première fois, en le considérant comme une possibilité objective du monde et selon les façons de l'objectivité; une seconde fois, en le regardant comme un autre moi, fort différent peut-être, mais dont la différence passe par une identité première, celle de deux êtres ayant l'égal pouvoir de parler en première personne; une troisième fois, non plus dans une relation médiate de connaissance impersonnelle ou de compréhension personnelle, mais dans une tentative de relation immédiate, le même et l'autre prétendant se perdre l'un dans l'autre ou se rapprocher l'un de l'autre selon la proximité du tutoiement qui oublie ou efface la distance. Reste une autre modalité (sans mode). Cette fois, il ne s'agit plus d'une recherche unificatrice. Je ne veux plus reconnaître en l'autre celui ou cela qu'une mesure encore commune, l'appartenance à un espace commun, tient dans un rapport de continuité ou d'unité avec moi. Maintenant, ce qui est en jeu, c'est l'étrangeté entre nous, et non pas seulement cette part obscure qui échappe à notre mutuelle connaissance et n'est rein de plus que l'obscurité de la position dans le moi–la singularité du moi singulier–, étrangeté qui est encore très relative (un moi est toujours proche d'un moi, même dans la différence, la compétition, le désir et le besoin). (*EI* 108-9)

Blanchot's typology of interruption schematically proposes the dialogic relationship between author and reader. The function of interruption, as it is defined here, enriches Roubaud's methodical questioning of poetic writing, for in the potential subject-positions proposed, the question of alterity becomes essential to the question of the book itself, and more specifically the question of the book as voluminous space.

In *Trente et un au cube*, the lyrical dialogue between the speaker and the addressee can be viewed in light of this fourth type of interruption, as a desire-laden space fashioned to accommodate the becoming of an "obscure" relationship between self-consciousness and the consciousness of the other: "Altérité qui se tient sous la nomination du neutre" (*EI* 109). The interruptions in the lines of each poem, syntactical interruption, morphological interruptions, rhythmic interruptions, impose an arbitrary pause, a marked emptiness around which the counting in the poem, the accounting for between the speaking "je" and the listening "tu," reach not only for each other, but also for the otherness in themselves through the silence and space opened and maintained in the dialogue. And that dialogue of doubles is again supported, or echoed, in the textual dialogue between the poems and the inscriptions that interrupt the blank inter-pages.

What, one may ask, is the content of the relationship between the author and reader of this text? Roubaud colors the textual game of hide-and-seek, predicated on counting, with a variety of intertextual influences, and adopts versatile postures in his address to the reader, "tu." There are two interrelated threads common to all the poems. First, the author/reader relationship lends erotic content to the collection; both positions are constructed around mutual desire and around the stammerings, the stutterings that struggle to pronounce the parts and whole of that desire. Second, as this amorous dialogue is limited to text, all the poems contain explicit metaliterary games; and those games align the acts of reading and writing with the acts of flirting, lovemaking, crying, wanting and wanting to be wanted. Fittingly, the playscape of the dialogue is also structured hierarchically, with the authorial voice playing hard to get, or keeping a tight rein on the rules of play. For example, in avoiding a direct answer to the principal question ("what are my reasons for writing these poems?") the speaking voice coyly reminds us that it is the author who fashions the reader's role in the collection: "vois mes sifflets de silice / mon matériel mes jeux d'orgues // cela qui pénètre / décisivement en toi / cela te façonne" (1.22-23).

But Roubaud's reference to how the text mediates a complicit author-reader relationship is often much subtler, revealing his sensitivity for crafting intimate poems. As an example of how this interspace is conditioned by mystery and erotic desire, consider "OU VIVIONS NOUS?" (reprinted here with original spacing):

OU VIVIONS NOUS? dans   une ville funèbre et   dans cette ville au   bout des heures nous dormions   dans un lit grand tous les deux
ensemble souvent   dans le tien derrière des   lames métalliques   (orientables vers le haut   ou vers le bas par des cor-
dons blancs) d'un gris pâle   quelquefois dans le mien sous   des volets de bois   à deux battants quelquefois   encore seuls (nuits de la
trame contre les   nuits du dessin) nous dormions   dans cette funèbre ville des heures durables   au bout de la chasse diurne
mais avant de dormir toujours entre tes draps   les miens je te touchais je te touchais des doigts   des jambes de la bouche et

de paroles à   ton oreille contre ta   joue en te touchant   en même temps de mes mains   nue et chaude entre les draps
par la parole ou   les mains l'enchevêtrement   des corps défaisait   obliterait la funèbre   mécanique diurne la
sourde usure des   choses en vacarme la   perte de substance   dans le travail les rencontres   distraites les soliloques
inversement on   se touchait aussi quand les   jours revenaient quand   les pigeons s'enroulaient dans   leurs périodes désolées
les jours de bleu ou   de pluie très proche par les   chuintements des lames   parallèles ou la loi   des ombres le jour venant
on se touchaint toujours de jambes de doigts de paroles le sommeil   enveloppé ainsi préservé d'un couloir de jeux
notre sommeil ainsi rendu sourd de la cire   vivante de la   nudité et des paroles   cachées comme galaxies

sous une poussière   sidérale or nous vivions dans cette ville   glaciale et pour dormir les   soirs je descendais du nord
vers toi vers ton lit   grand où t'étendre nue où   te toucher des doigts   des genoux du front de la   bouche par un continent
de rues gelées ou   chaudes sur le bruit des rues   je disposais l'invisibilité de ta voix   voix ligne de protection
dans ta voix tangible   je marchais divisant un   territoire clos   ta voix contre feu brousaille   m'accompagnait de bout en
bout filtrant le noir   les bruits épais et semblables   ta voix profondément me séparait en elle   mon chemin se finissait

quand nous dormions un   peu de lumière traversait les volets ou   les lames jointes par ricochets de photons sur la
surface lisse et diffusion dans les poussières   lumière faible et   variable (un mouvement   dans d'autres chambres cour ou
minuterie d'escalier) dans cette lumière   je m'éveillais lourd   de ta chaleur un silence   à bourdonnement de bois
un silence d'arbre   m'engourdissait immobile   et toi dalle tiède   pomme de flamme ménine   toi saveur de soie cédrat
dormante semblait   n'être plus là je croyais   des temps revenus   d'ailleurs d'un fond très obscur   où des   feuilles tombaient
sur moi dans le noir   un vieux temps manipulé   selon des circuits   incomprehensibles dans   la machine du sommeil
ensuite la nuit   reprenait son ordre tu   bougeais toute tiède   de nouveau la lumière apparaissait avec ses bruits

quelquefois seul   dans l'obscurité continue   agitée de points   lumineux imperceptibles   dans la noirceur désolée
attendant le jour   des dénombrements à   des échafaudages   de futures en îles dans   l'obscurité froide seul
je faisais récit   de notre vie entre ces   murs réunissant   jours ou nuits pour une durée autre (traverses d'encre
où l'oeil s'accélère   dans une course de forêt) : où vivions nous?   dans cette ville funèbre   et dans cette ville la
nuit tu te tournais   pour me toucher dans le noir   de tes seins de tes   cuisses de la bouche tu   te tournais et m'embrassais
et me touchais chaude   sous le peu de lumière entraînée jusque sur   nous à travers lames ou   volets fermés perméables
tu te tournais vers   moi endormie la lumière   soulevaient les lames   insignifiante traversait   dans la ville faible

The question of place being central, the poem itself may be said to mimic its setting. That is, the "ville funèbre" and the dimly lit rooms that the poet describes can be read as images that describe the space of the poem itself. This parallel is suggested in the images of the window shades and shutter slats that metaphorically represent the long, thin lines, or wider, dense stanzas printed across the opened double page, which suggests an opened window. Furthermore, the mechanicity of these images articulates how a division between the outside and inside, between day and night, between public and private space, is modulated by "des cor- / dons blancs" (18.2-3) that adjust the aperture of shades or shutters permitting the passage of light.

An attention to the mechanicity of these window shades is echoed and reinforced by the poet's almost scientific observation of the physical properties of light: "un / peu de lumière traversait les volets ou / les lames jointes par ricochets de photons sur la // surface lisse" (18.18-19). The effect of the "lumière faible et / variable" (18.19) described in the poem becomes metaliterary in that the description is also reflected in the play of light on the page itself. The parallels between the play of light in the room and on the page become explicit near the poem's end–"je faisais récit / de notre vie pour une durée autre (traverse d'encre // où l'oeil s'accélère / dans une course" (18.27-28)–but they are suggested throughout. For example, "je descendais du nord // vers toi vers ton lit" (18.13-14) implies a downward movement repeated in the manner the eye descends the page while reading.

A striking parallel is also established in the relationship between sound and the mechanisms regulating light: shades and shutters in the room, and metrical constraint in the poem itself. In the representation of the speaker's memory, the act of touching is triggered by light and sound as mediated by these filters: "les jours de bleu ou / de pluie très proche par les / chuintements des lames / parallèles ou la loi des ombres le jour venant // on se touchait" (18.10-11). The whispering of the parallel shades provides an objective echo of the amorous "paroles" exchanged between the lovers; it is the noise and light draw them from their solitary sleep toward "l'enchevêtrement / des corps" (18.7), and in their touching their sleep is preserved, "préservé d'un couloir de jeux" (18.11). It seems that these whispering shades, like the poet's assembling of sounds themselves, are pitted against the deafening sounds of the city and its "funèbre / mécanique" (18.7), as if the poem's embedded rhythm were capable of undoing "la / sourde usure des / choses en vacarme la / perte de substance" (18.7-8).

The narrator presents this struggle against the "nuits de la // trame" (18.3-4), against "les rencontres / distraites les soliloques" (18.8), as an attempt to recall the presence of an erotic touch in a continuous past. Echoing the whispers of the shades at dawn, or the "silence / à bourdonnement de bois" (18.20) in the dead of night, he recounts not only the rhythm of these days and nights marked by lovemaking, but also how in their midst he formulated what would become their song, thereby providing a record of how that love and its memory would be preserved: "sur le bruit des rues / je disposais l'invisibilité de ta / voix ligne de protection // dans ta voix tangible / je marchais divisant un / territoire clos / ta voix profondément me séparait en elle" (18.15-17). This recalled disposition of an "invisible voice" *over* the street noises, "filtrant le noir"–the blackness of night *and* of the print on the page–like the formulation of this couple's story ("je faisais récit"; 18.29), points to the "dénombrements" and "échafaudages" that structure the questioning of the poetic space of "OU VIVIONS NOUS?" That is, in this recollection of where "we" were living, it is as if the poet has inscribed the rhythm of the poem that here attests to a remembrance of those rooms, as well as the lovemaking that took place there.

Furthermore, the objective description of the light shades and the metrical constraint also point to how touching, sexual and textual, is mediated by body parts and words. This double entendre between the textual and sexual touch is put into relief most in the opening, or gap, between the first and second line groupings. This textual effect charges the waiting period between the lines represented by the blank or light-interrupting night: "mais avant de dormir toujours entre tes draps / les miens je te touchais des doigts / des jambes de la bouche et /// de paroles à / ton oreille contre ta / joue en te touchant / en même temps des mains / nue et chaude entre les draps" (18.5-6). Playing on the tactile in text and sex, Roubaud culminates the erotic play in the poetic word (*parole*) snugly tucked between the folded sheets of paper, and all its other points of contact–mouth, eye, ear, counting fingers– reiterate the reciprocal relationship between Roubaud's love (of) poetry.

This reciprocal game illustrates Jean-Jacques Thomas's "thematic isotopy." It might be observed that in this poem there is a movement in agency from "je te touchais" (18.5) to "inversement on / se touchait" (18.9, 11), ending in a longer sequence of "tu te tournais / pour me toucher dans le noir" (18.29-31). I would like to suggest that even though Roubaud enthusiastically objectifies his addressee as if ruminating through personal, bittersweet memories ("toi dalle tiède / pomme de flamme ménine / toi saveur de soie de cédrat" [18.21]), this progression of agency in the poem is part of the game he plays with his constructed reader, constantly shifting the perspective of control "selon des circuits / incompréhensibles" (18.23).

Reflexivity in this text therefore continuously engages a desire-motivated dialogue between author and reader that provides the collection with a common theme. Presented in the form of a puzzle, in which readers are entreated to decipher what are at times very difficult syntactical constructions, this dialogue often puns on the oral or written medium of the game. To give an example of this wordplay, I turn to the first stanza of "LA BOUCHE EST DOUBLE" (4), a poem that recalls the idea of an ideal love song, a song that imitates the intermingling of kissing tongues by paraphrasing the closing passage of Bernart Marti's canso "Bel m'es lai latz la fontana": *"ainsi je vais enlaçant / les mots et affinant la mélodie / comme la langue est enlacée / à la langue dans le baiser"* (T 107):

> LA BOUCHE EST DOUBLE et / la langue est double dans la / bouche et dans la double / bouche naît l'unique langue / langue des baiser et du // chant. la langue du / chant dans la bouche est double et / dans la bouche la / langue s'enlace à la langue / double langue d'une, // un instant, unique; / bouche qui n'est rien sans autre / bouche; langue qui / langue vraiment que double / à la naissance du chant. // que le chant condense / révèle resserre porte / fixe par mimique / par choix de mélodie coupes / dans la forêt de ses sons. // que le chant traverse / décide illimine lance / change par violence / par douce persuasion / répétitive, fusion. (4.1-5)

Here again, perhaps more directly than in "OU VIVIONS NOUS?," Roubaud offers his readers an active role in the game of poetry. The very act of poeticizing is equated with kissing, as well as a metaphoric intertwining of voices; poetry is proposed as a feast of song and touch. Nonetheless, these games, we are reminded, are strictly determined for both reader and writer, for they are compositions "qui vont leur chemin dans l'ordre / de mes contraintes" (1.30).

The "duplicity" of the mouth, the word, the poem, the page, and the book, as they are presented here, is recursively performed in reading *Trente et un au cube*. This performative element emphasizes the importance of reciprocity for the life of poetry and that of its amateurs: "bouche qui n'est rien sans autre / bouche" (4.3). Creators of an active, living form of poetry, structured by both arcane principles and foreign constraints, Roubaud and his collaborative reader share in exploring a synthesis of diverse poetic concerns. Although the game of reading often focuses on the composition and comprehension of the poems themselves, both "OU VIVIONS NOUS?" and "LA BOUCHE EST DOUBLE" demonstrate that, as primary content, the poems depict various moments in an elaborate textual love affair.

The combination of tanka in a self-reflexive, ludic text colored by a wealth of interwoven poetic styles substantiates Roubaud's search for a maximal or synthetic form. *Trente et un au cube* offers the first collection in which constraint is cast in a continuously reflexive mode, turned in on itself, and grafted to multiple rhythmic and thematic contexts. Offering an intentionally motivated literary game, the most ambitious goal of Roubaud's second major experimental work might be to displace existing poetic conditions, whereas its most consistent method is to amuse and seduce while fastidiously fulfilling the commitment of its formal constraint, all the while forging a new stammering rhythm suited for maneuvering an amorous textual dialogue.

For Roubaud, the synthetic book is engendered through formal constraints, and those constraints become substantive in the process of meaning. In *Trente et un au cube* the prime number 31, and its threefold application to poems, lines and syllables, asserts the work's singularity. But the constraints also provide generous hospitality to other codes, including Japanese linking techniques and a host of interrupting cited voices. The play of meaning in *Trente et un au cube* is largely determined by this synthesis of constraints; the result is as much a tanka of tanka as it is a singularly sustained contemporary canso. Because Roubaud culls fragmented citations, poetic principles, and textual motivators from diverse moments of literary history, he enriches the already hybrid character of this cube and recasts its components into a crystallized form, thereby renewing both the contemporary context and access to the source material. Given the volitional quality of Roubaud's writing, it is perhaps not enough to underline how *Trente et un au cube* commands the authority of the traditions that it leans on; one must also emphasize that the games undertaken in the writing and reading of this work are largely motivated by the author's insistent questioning of, and his indefatigable incursions into, poetic history.

CHAPTER FIVE

THE WRITING OF LIFESTYLE: *AUTOBIOGRAPHIE, CHAPITRE DIX*

IN *Autobiographie, chapitre dix* (1977), Jacques Roubaud constructs an ironic narrative of his "real life" as a poet. His purported aim in this book is to recite, condense, and overcome tendencies dominant in the verse of Surrealism and Dada. Embracing the principle that "*la vie est unique,* mais les paroles d'avant la mémoire font ce qu'on en dit" (*A* jacket notes), Roubaud confines the material of his first published autobiography to 317 fragments more or less copied directly from 84 books of poetry published by 35 poets in the 18 years preceding his birth, 1914-32. Subtitled *poèmes avec des moments de repos en prose*, this cento probes conventional notions of the novel, the lyric, and autobiography while repairing what Roubaud calls a catastrophe in the history of French verse.

As the title indicates, *Autobiographie* is a difficult book to classify. Conceived as the third of six *romans formels*, this collection recounts an episode in an autobiographical story that is encoded in the text's form.[1] The idea of a novel in poetry begs a consideration of genre. Classically, the epic or long narrative poem is said to be the precursor to both the novel and the short lyric. One difference between lyrical and narrative modes of expression is summed up in the presumption that the novel as a genre is freer, or unfettered by the types of convention inherent in the lyric and long narrative poems. More recently, though, regenerative developments in novelistic discourse have been viewed as a consequence of the form's self-dis-

---

[1] Roubaud's first two *romans formels* are *Etoffe* (1975) and *Mezura* (1975). To my knowledge, Roubaud does not identify any of his later compositions as the fourth, fifth, or sixth volume in this cycle.

covery through modes of dialogue.² Maintaining that similar conditions for innovation inhabit both the novel and the lyric, Roubaud and other Oulipians approach both forms of writing as coextensive. In many ways, this understanding is based on Raymond Queneau's theory of the novel.

In "Technique du roman," Queneau laments that "le roman, depuis qu'il existe, a échappé à toute loi," adding that "pour ma part, je ne saurais m'incliner devant un pareil laisser faire" (*BC* 27-28). Instead, he makes the art of the novel a continuation of poetic art by introducing entirely arbitrary numerical structures into his novels. For example, in *Le chiendent* there are 91 sections (7 × 13 = 91), for reasons that are entirely motivated by Queneau's fondness of numbers and the personal meanings they foster for him.³ This emphasis on bringing formal constraints into the composition of novels characterizes Queneau's reaction to a literary catastrophe of his time, the general disuse of fixed forms: "Si la ballade et le rondeau sont péris, il me paraît qu'en opposition à ce désastre une rigueur accrue doit se manifester dans l'exercice de la prose" (*BC* 28). Though he does not directly make the connection here, the 'disaster' Queneau describes implies the falsely liberating tendencies of automatic writing techniques in vogue during the heyday of Surrealism. It is along this trajectory of reaction that Queneau eventually claims that all literature should be volitional in nature, in no way ruled by chance.

For his part, Jacques Roubaud also challenges distinctions of genre by constantly shifting perspectives in the types of constraint he applies to each work. In this case, instead of bringing poetic forms into the novel, he imposes some strategies of prose onto poetic technique. This inversion of his mentor's call for constraint in the novel is neatly summed up in a problematic definition of poetry cited in *Autobiographie*: "La poésie est la continuation de la prose

---

² See Bakhtin, "Epic and the Novel," in *Dialogic Imagination*.
³ In addition to being a triangular number in Pythagorean mathematics, Queneau ascribes the following modalities of meaning to this choice: "91 étant la somme des treize premiers nombres et sa somme étant 1, c'est donc à la fois le nombre de la mort des êtres et celui de leur retour à l'existence.... je voyais dans le 13 un nombre bénéfique parce qu'il niait le bonheur; quant à 7, je le prenais, et puis le prends encore, comme image numérique de moi-même, puisque mon nom et mes deux prénoms se composent chacun de sept lettres et que je suis né un 21 (3 × 7)" (*BC* 29).

par d'autres moyens" (*A* 157). Originally borrowed from Carl von Clausewitz, who famously summed up the relationship between *diplomacy* and *war* in this fashion, this quasi-maxim, transformed through recombinatory, suggests that prose and poetry are practically interchangeable, at least in terms of technique.

Early in his career as a writer, Roubaud wrote several sustained experiments that define and explore modalities of constraint for prose *in* poetry, as opposed to the more familiar category of prose poetry. These *romans formels* seek to realize specific aspects of the *Projet*; because they illustrate Roubaud's drive to explore all possible combinations of genres, they should be thought of as distinct, both in terms of their individual strategies and with regard to the novels and the prose writings that occupy Roubaud later.[4] In the opening pages of *Mezura*, the first of these *romans formels*, Roubaud explains how numbers help him rethink constraints for prose in poetry: "Si le *poème en prose* peut emprunter des brides et des cadences à la métrique qui le baigne, la *prose en poésie* en revanche, dont on offre dans ce qui suit un exemple, se doit de répudier toute scansion régulière; ce qui ne peut guère être atteint que par la soumission à une contrainte du type de celle qui joue ici" (*Mezura* 3). Not surprisingly, the constraint Roubaud adopts in that work ensures that the text's appearance of being verse will be overthrown by its utter lack of rhythm. The constraint is simple: in *Mezura*, Roubaud sets the syllabic line length of the entire text to the first one thousand numbers of π, thereby doing away with recursivity altogether. To apply this constraint to the composition of prose in poetry pushes irregular meter onto new ground, and demonstrates how irregular verse can be exactly controlled by strict and clearly determined measures.

In *Autobiographie, chapitre dix*, Roubaud further complicates questions of form by actively shuttling among the properties of prose, regulated verse, and free verse, adding to the mix problems of narrative, fact, and fiction. If the subtitle announces the work's hybridity, it also draws puzzling distinctions: *poèmes avec des moments de repos en prose*. First, in this chapter of Roubaud's autobi-

---

[4] The Hortense novel cycle and *'le grand incendie de Londres'* novel cycle explore this question by integrating poetic constraints into prose in an explicitly Quenellian fashion. See also Chaillou, Deguy, Delay, Michel, Roche, and Roubaud, *L'hexaméron*.

ography—normally a sort of story, fictional or not—there is something called poetry. Then, there is something else, something extra presented alongside, in prose: moments of rest. The prose/poetry distinction is classical, formal, and perhaps too simple for Roubaud's purposes. But the temporal term complicates matters, as if it were drawing distinctions in how we experience what is written in poetry and what is written in prose. In addition, the moments in prose are moments of *rest* (*repos*), presumably different from what's found in the poems where greater activity is associated with *work* or *play*.

The anagram *repos/prose* flags Roubaud's use of combinatory in his compositional techniques and triggers the polysemy of both terms. Taken from the Latin verb *repausare* (to replace or pause again), the French noun *repos* means both the act of resting and the time elapsed during rest. It also denotes a state of (mental) inactivity; a state of peace or tranquility; and, in music or poetry, a rhythmic or syntactic pause in the melodic phrase. Each of these meanings has resonance in *Autobiographie*, yet this last sense of repos, as a caesura in the poetic line, is particularly pertinent, for it inscribes prose in an incursive relationship to poetry. In addition, when associated with the transitive verb *reposer* (to place or pose again), repos also names the act of recopying the words of others. If prose connotes an easier mode of reading and writing, the *moments de repos en prose* also suggest moments of copying or plagiarism.

Whether performed entirely unconsciously or approached with the self-reflexivity of an exacting art form, the process of literary citation consists of recontextualizing the *déjà dit*, perhaps even to shed light on the way precursors influence literary (re)creation. For Roubaud, remotivating the words of other poets becomes a means of exploring literary potential through form itself. In each of his works, he aims to engender specific citational economies that encode formal meanings, for the process of (re)citation is also that of remembrance, and to copy is, in some sense, a means of erasure and destruction.

Within the French poetic tradition, the prose/poetry distinction recalls the formal experiments of early modernist prose poems like Charles Baudelaire's *Spleen de Paris* (1857), Lautréamont's *Chants de Maldoror* (1868), Arthur Rimbaud's *Une saison en enfer* (1873) and *Les Illuminations* (1886), and Stéphane Mallarmé's *Divagations* (1897). These compositions, whose nomination as poetry in the form of prose (*poèmes en prose*) announces their fallen and hybrid status, are particularly important developments in tradition, in part because of their timing. They mark a shift away from the monumental verse forms embodied in the purportedly exhausted alexandrine, toward a new period of experimentation that runs through Dada and Surrealism to the present. This era of modernist experiment in poetic composition continues to characterize contemporary French poetry, for the monumentality of the traditional verse forms has not entirely weakened in the French poetic consciousness. Or, to put it differently, granted that the force of traditional rhythmic patterns proper to the French language persists in the French memory of rhythm, or in the deep structure of that poetic language–even if some see it as being stuck in a stagnant state of repos–many of the formal experiments undertaken since the death of Victor Hugo can still be understood in terms of a need to escape or diversify the dominant rhythm.[5] A comparative reading of Baudelaire's prose and verse, as well as a close reading of Mallarmé's reflections on rhythm, demonstrates that late Romantic and early Symbolist *poèmes en prose* were not so much proof of a search for new subjects as they were evidence of a search for different rhythmic structures, or new forms.

The first uses of vers libre in French might be viewed as a kind of compromise between the use of prose and the use of verse. It seems, at first, to distinguish itself from both forms of writing. Unlike traditional verse, the vers libre refuses regular scansion, inciting Mallarmé to call it "polymorphe."[6] Unlike the prose poem, however, the vers libre retains key elements of verse, and thus overtly proposes a search for new rhythmic structures, but against trajectory already determined by the conventions of lineation, syllabic count, and (lack of) rhyme. Claiming a priori its difference from the prose poem, the vers libre therefore presents itself as both the continuation and the refusal of traditional verse. This double status may explain why it is so well suited to early twentieth-century avant-garde movements.

Yet, from its inception onward, the purported freedom of the vers libre was under scrutiny. Even though Mallarmé heralds the novelty of this verse form–"Toute la nouveauté s'installe, relative-

---

[5] For an analysis of why Victor Hugo persists as a key figure of traditional verse, or the "père-vers," see Johnson, *Défigurations*.

[6] Mallarmé, "Crise de vers," Œ, 272.

ment au vers libre" (Œ 272)–his praise of poets like Moréas, Khan, Verhaeren, and Dujardin is eclipsed by his distrust of a liberated, unconstrained verse: "Selon moi jaillit tard une condition vraie ou la possibilité, de s'exprimer non seulement, mais de se moduler, à son gré" (Œ 273). And, for his part, Mallarmé does not compose what we now understand as vers libre, but continues to write increasingly hermetic versions of traditional verse, or an altogether innovative kind of verse in *Un coup de dès*, where space and not syllables become the rhythmic standard and where the structure is rigorously organized around thinking about the poetic book.

Eighty years later, in *La vieillesse d'Alexandre* (1978), an essay written at the same time as *Autobiographie, chapitre dix*, Roubaud plots the life of the French vers libre form and, in doing so, confirms Mallarmé's distrust of newfound freedom.[7] According to Roubaud, early vers libre poems in France produce a kind of negative model of the alexandrine, a shadow verse form whose only rule is actively avoiding the characteristics of classical verse forms. Roubaud demonstrates that it is this massive repression or forced forgetting of traditional meters that paradoxically ensures their survival and return.

Originally heralded as avant-garde, as a revolt against the orthodox monument that it refuses to imitate–rhyme and twelve-position lines are virtually forbidden to classical vers libristes–vers libre offers a relatively poor rhythmic field and therefore limits the poet's freedom of formal expression. That is, the dependent identity of the form, its negative mode of existence, limits its flexibility as a formal code. Stating the central argument of his thesis, Roubaud explains the irony of this paradox: "Le paradoxe du vers libre: à savoir qu'il ne l'est pas et que, loin de réussir à délivrer la poésie française des contraintes qui historiquement pèsent sur elle, son adoption a réussi en définitive à leur assurer un sursis en les maintenant sous une forme dissimulée; il se révèle être un instrument privilégié de la survie de l'ancien. Cet échec du vers libre éclate inséparablement de son triomphe" (*VA* 15). In short, the ultimate

---

[7] The vers libre referred to in *La vieillesse d'Alexandre* differs, both historically and formally, from what Roubaud calls *le vers libre international,* which is a more modern poetic form of "free circulation" that draws on a multilingual and multicultural heritage and does not bear the imprint of specific moves away from traditional models (*VA* 204-5).

failure of the vers libre is a consequence of its triumphant success; in purely poetic terms, the proliferation of vers libre encourages a facile and negative poetic template that facilitates the return of the ghosts repressed in tradition and conventional verse form. In reading the story of the vers libre in this way, Roubaud restates a central tenet of Oulipian polemics: authors consciously writing under constraint are freer than authors who are unaware of the subliminal constraints at work in their writing. The implication is that early practitioners of French free verse unwittingly ensure the continued dominance of the alexandrine.

This adds a layer of irony to the Oulipo's imitation and mockery of Surrealist and Dada manifestoes. Although he parodies the exigencies of the avant-garde, with its unchecked fervor for self-reinvention, his imitation, appropriation, and arrangement of their work cunningly reenacts and recuperates their innovative gesture. Instead of disavowing the past, like a disinherited Romantic poet, Roubaud claims that there is no real originality, that we are all products of our past, that all attempts at self-representation are futile, adding that an "honest" autobiography should not seek to be creative or inventive but should consist entirely of re-citations of the past or "re-prise" from the matter that has made one a poet (*M9* 49). Turning his eye and ear inward, toward the recent poems he learned as a student, Roubaud simply steals the work of his immediate poetic precursors, committing an act of blatant plagiarism.

This disavowal of originality, feigned or sincere, must also be read as an ironic and polemical stance with regard to his chosen source texts, most of which are associated with the rise of Surrealism. Warren Motte has convincingly argued that the two *bêtes noires* of the Oulipo are the notions of inspiration and chance as valid compositional principles. Both are foundational to Surrealists. Asserting that Queneau's formal aesthetic is "diametrically opposed" to Surrealist aesthetics, Motte sees Oulipian theory as a symmetrical inversion of Surrealist principles. Succinctly put, "the Surrealist insistence on inspiration becomes in Quenellian poetics a valorization of practice; the idea of genius gives way to an advocacy of craftsmanship; chance is transmogrified into determination."[8]

---

[8] Motte, "Raymond Queneau," 196.

If Oulipian aesthetics reflect an inversion or mirror image of Surrealist practices, and if Surrealist metrics reflect a negative model for traditional verse form, two questions must be asked of Roubaud's recycled vers libre. First, does revising select vers libre in a new form reveal, condense, and correct that period's triumphant failure (as discussed in *La vieillesse d'Alexandre*)? And, second, does *Autobiographie* illustrate the foundational tenets of an Oulipian work; does the book force readers to take cognizance of constraint in the experiment while simultaneously tapping into new potentials for the source material and the experimental form? Both questions address issues of poetic influence. On the one hand, like all poets, Roubaud confronts the influence of tradition from a belated position. And, like all poets of his generation, his view of tradition is marked not only by successive avant-gardes, but comes at a period in time when many contemporary thinkers and writers are theorizing the end of poetry, or, in Denis Roche's case, its inadmissibility. On the other hand, Roubaud also negotiates a separate source of influence that is more relevant, if as contemporary: the theoretical and methodological influence of the Oulipo of which he is, by 1977, an important proponent. Since these two sources of influence are intertwined in his work, one must approach them simultaneously, beginning again with Queneau.

Queneau's break with Surrealism, first documented in *Un cadavre* (1930), a surprisingly virulent attack on André Breton, initiates his historical exploration of radical formalists. That research agenda eventually leads him to develop the deeply ludic and structured aesthetic of his early novels, and later, following François Le Lionnais's initiative, the Oulipo. Rejecting the Surrealist program was critical for Queneau, as it was for Michel Leiris and others, because it confirmed important differences in his artistic practice. In addition, Queneau's relation to Breton was affected by the break, and what would follow would necessarily differ in nature from the Surrealist experience.

For Roubaud the Surrealist period belongs to the most recent past, but it is a past in which he did not directly participate, for it took place before his coming of age. For him, this classic era of the vers libre still remains a keystone moment in his apprenticeship as a poet, in part because he knows the poetry of that era well and perhaps in part because his adolescent poetry was written in the Surrealist mold.

The relationship between Queneau and Roubaud, by contrast, is one of direct influence and collaboration. Largely responsible for the publication of Roubaud's first major work, ϵ (*signe d'appartenance*) (1967), Queneau was instrumental in initiating Roubaud into the Ouvroir de Littérature Potentielle and later encouraged his literary and mathematical investigations (*M9* 12). Granted the generous dynamics of this student/mentor relationship, one might argue that Queneau remains Roubaud's strongest poetic precursor, in a Bloomian sense.[9] And yet, precisely because Oulipian method encrypts poetic consciousness in formal codes, discerning ratios of influence in Oulipian writing necessarily becomes a more complex issue.

As I mentioned in previous chapters, Roubaud identifies a wide variety of poetic models, the most important of which–the troubadours–are neither contemporary, nor strictly of the French language. He calls the first model his voluntary archaism and, like his engagement with foreign forms, it is the model's distance from the contemporary scene that best figures Roubaud's strategies of incursion into the present. If choosing ancient and foreign models is an attempt to skirt contemporary influences in French poetics, if that strategy is a means of infusing the present with inspiration from elsewhere, Roubaud's rewriting of poems written on the eve of his birth represents a return to what is bred in the bone. That is, the decision to revisit the poems composed during and just after WW I adds contemporary dimensions to his collection of models. Yet, like his other chosen models, this period is characterized by a kind of poetic explosion, a prolific discovery of new modes of writing poetry, with the exception that this explosion was, in Roubaud's view, detrimental to poetry's vocation as the memory of a language.

Broadly speaking, poetry from Guillaume Apollinaire to Blaise Cendrars to André Breton is thematically marked by a rapidly changing modern world, new media, new adventures, and the horrific violence of war. Poetic form integrates these dramatic changes

---

[9] Bloom, *Anxiety of Influence*. Although Bloom's theory of influence is foundational, one may consider that the dynamics of writing under constraint makes authors more conscious of influence. Along these lines, it is pertinent to remark that the "famille quenouillarde"–as Jouet has called it–has toyed openly with Queneau's figure as an Oulipapa, most prominently perhaps in the following theorem proposed by Jacques Roubaud: "L'oulipo est *un roman non écrit* de Queneau" "L'auteur oulipien" (in Contat, *L'auteur et le manuscrit*, 83).

through the use of countless new techniques. While unquestionably impressive in scope and variety, those new techniques tend to erase appreciation for what precedes them; or so Roubaud would imply in this poem that foretells of forgetting the trials of loss in war while longing for songs in peace:

              IMMORTELLE MALADIE

       les poissons de ta chaleur s'en
       voleront en fraction infinitésimales

       la respiration mourra de sa
       belle mort et nous
       qui avons grandi dans le bruit des
       coups de pioche (*A* 132)

But even when he is addressing the atrocities of war, the senselessness of life, or the suicide of poets, Roubaud always keeps a firm eye on the present or insists on looking toward the future, thereby reviving and changing the texts he cites. Here, for example, the closing sequence–"et nous / qui avons grandi dans le bruit des / coups de pioche"–might recontextualize war time death for a WW II audience, or, for that matter, any wartime childhood.

Although the Holocaust is not often *directly* addressed in this work, Roubaud's trademark image of catastrophe, the Great Fire of London of 1666, first mentioned in *Autobiographie*, serves as an emblem of his impulse to write, just as they had for Pierre Reverdy: "Les entreprises humaines ne sont que des sottises; mais que penser des hommes qui s'obstinent à construire leur demeure au sein de capitales exposées à tant de dangers? / je me suis retiré à la campagne" (*A* 142).[10] The sociohistorical developments of the eighteen years prior to Roubaud's birth remain background concerns in *Autobiographie*; they help figure, if distantly, the historical importance of this period in the poet's literary apprenticeship.

Far more apparent in the construction of *Autobiographie* is the appropriation of particular words, phrases, and verses selected from

---

[10] In this passage, Roubaud also appears to be translating the work of twelfth-century Japanese hermit Kamo no Chomei, *Ten Foot Square Hut and Tales of the Heike*.

the source texts. The presentation of quotations, all lacking explicit textual reference and rarely enclosed in quotation marks, represents the principal work completed in this collection. Because this presentation is informed by the research undertaken in *La vieillesse d'Alexandre*, it may be argued that the formal aspects of the texts considered are more intentionally brought to light than their thematic ones, and it is from this perspective that I approach *Autobiographie*.

The art of citation takes on a particular character in Oulipian practice. Having adopted as one of their foundational precepts the research and elaboration of already extant forms (*anoulipisme*), Oulipians call prior compositions of their appropriated forms incidents of "plagiarism by anticipation" (*LP* 23). The irony of this playful nomination is doubled when Roubaud describes *Autobiographie* as an extended cento, for the strategy specific to this type of composition is the art of plagiarism itself.

In an interview that appeared shortly after the publication of *Autobiographie*, Roubaud states that all writing is always already a repetition and suggests that his choice of source texts sets boundaries in this particular site of plagiarism. "Tout ce que l'on dit dans un poème a déjà été dit des millions de fois, du moins dans son matériau, la langue. Je pense qu'un poème dit d'autant mieux ce qu'il dit que si ce qu'il dit a été beaucoup dit. Ce qui change d'un poète à l'autre, d'un poème à l'autre, c'est essentiellement la façon de mettre ensemble ces briques qui sont le bien commun. Mon intervention à moi n'est que l'agencement de ces paroles qui ont appartenu à d'autres et que j'essaye de faire miennes, au moins pour le temps de cette poésie."[11] Accepting his linguistically belated position, Roubaud claims that the poem most effectively communicates its object through the recognition of its own inevitable plagiarism. That is, by being conscious that what is being said in the poem has already been said countless times, the poet appropriates a heightened sense of freedom, for he need not account for all the previous formulations of a thought or expect to invent an entirely new poetic image, but can content himself in recontextualizing chosen moments of *déjà dit*. So runs his argument in *Autobiographie*, where he combines this consciousness of the past with an ironic regard for

---

[11] Roubaud (1997), interview with Pierre Lartigue, "Mandarin au cube," 160.

his precursors: "Combien singulière est notre situation, à nous autres mortels. chacun de nous est sur la terre pour une courte visite. sa vie extérieure et intérieure dépend du travail de ses contemporains, au sens philosophique du terme. / Avoir conscience de cela contribue à adoucir d'une manière bienfaisante le sentiment de responsabilité qui laisse place à l'humour" (*A* 112). There is not, in Roubaud's conception of poetic influence, a sense in which the poet must entirely reinvent his language or his art in order to establish his voice as an artist. On the contrary, to recognize that creative existence depends on conditions of dialogue with one's contemporaries is to emphasize a viable (and playful) work ethic.

What does Roubaud mean by "contemporains au sens philosophique du terme"? His conception of contemporaneity differs from what is generally understood by this term. In "Poésie, contemporaine extrême," Roubaud considers possible directions in current French poetics, defining the contemporary not as the work of living artists but as the state of language itself: "*le langage est contemporain.*"[12] By this he means that the contemporary does not limit itself to a place in time but depends, rather, upon the concrete extant uses of language, which includes all uses of the past in a broader sense.

In *Autobiographie*, the contemporary is limited to a choice of source texts. Describing this choice as an itinerary of readings, Roubaud posits his existence as poet as an appropriation and transformation of poetic language prior to his birth. "Les mots des poètes sont les matériaux de la biographie d'un poète; ce sont les mots de sa langue et les mots de sa vie, mais les uns et les autres se réfractent à travers la poésie qui l'a précédée, celle qu'il a lue, aimée ou détestée. Ainsi les poèmes qui m'ont *servi* pour *Autobiographie, chapitre dix* font parti de mon existence en tant que poète" (*M9* 49). Two salient positions are adopted in this description of the work. First, a poet's words may be equated with his life. This conception of existence limits the writer's life to a verbal field: a poet's words become his worlds, the concrete manifestations of his life; they constitute his being. Such a stark conception of the biography does not originate with Roubaud, for it is also formulated by Louis Zukofsky,

---

[12] Roubaud (1988), *EX*, 181.

one of Roubaud's favorite American poets, who said of his long poem *"A"*: "The words of this book are my life."[13] And, more recently, a similar thought has been reiterated in Lyn Hejinian's poetic autobiography, a work in progress entitled *My Life*.[14] In equating their work with an autobiographical mode of writing, these poets share a deliberately formal approach to language, for the experience of language, more than any other, provides a tangible and real condition for being.

Second, this conception of biography asserts that the development of writers is predicated not only on what has preceded them but, more precisely, on what they have (or have not) read. Reduced to its *degré zéro*, this precept states not only that you are what you write, but that you can write only what you have read, for it is from this experience of language that the words of your life and (life) work are drawn. For Roubaud, the experience of living in language, or of reading his precursors, is characterized as refractive, suggesting an oblique dispersal in his manner of reading: "Les mots de sa langue et les mots de sa vie se réfractent à travers la poésie qui l'a précédée, celle qu'il a lue, aimée ou détéstée" (*M9* 49). But his reading and rewriting of "la période la plus créatrice du vers libre" does not seek to further disperse the poetic techniques of the era. Instead, Roubaud reorganizes them in a decidedly measured form.

An awareness of strategic remotivation is apparent throughout *Autobiographie*; it begins, for example, in the very first collage, where the poet addresses the conditions of engaging with a poetic horizon:

> il faudrait savoir
> se rouler
> sur cet horizon
>
> comme sur le sable pourquoi
> manteau vert? (*A* 8)

Set in a deserted landscape, a train station in New Mexico, this particular moment, inspired by "une mélancolie inexprimable" (*A* 8),

---

[13] Zukofsky, *"A" 1-12*; quoted by Roubaud (*M9* 49).
[14] Hejinian, *My Life*.

begins the tale of the narrator's search for poems, or the tale of his putting existing poems into an altered form (here a poem of twenty-four positions divided in the following sequence: 5 3 5 8 3). Typically fragmentary and opaque, this first collage orients the reader in questioning the ensuing engagement with the poetic horizon.

Though Roubaud maintains a kind of love-hate relationship with the poems of his youth, he manages to adopt a productive, if ironic, regard for them. His take on the recent past is idiosyncratically objectivist in that he takes his antecedents' writings as building blocks in his own literary project, and then refashions them to build his own fable. It is not surprising, moreover, that we find analogous modes of unabashed borrowing and self-fashioning in many of Roubaud's models, most pertinently in the work of Louis Zukofsky. By anchoring the source of his method in the work of others, Roubaud overtly understates his powers of invention; he modestly characterizes his literary identity as a consequence of reading, transcribing, and arranging.

In fact, pushing this objective view of literary influence to an extreme, in his conception of an autobiographical work he emphasizes that in order to provide a faithful representation of one's life, all invention should be avoided: "Le plus souvent, en écrivant des poèmes, le poète affabule sur la relation de la poésie antérieure dont il se construit lui-même. Mais si le 'pacte autobiographique' est une affirmation de vérité (même impossible), une autobiographie poétique doit éviter toute invention. Je n'ai pas inventé les poèmes d'*Autobiographie*. Je les ai pris dans ma mémoire de poésie, dans les livres que j'ai choisis pour en parler" (*M9* 49). On the grounds of using only the real elements given to him in his readings, Roubaud claims to avoid making his story up, thereby eschewing fable altogether. His autobiography therefore remains true and fulfills as closely as possible the "impossible" autobiographical pact. Polemical as this stance may be, in the composition of *Autobiographie* there is substantial evidence that this ethic of non-invention is not entirely upheld. A study of Roubaud's deviations reveals, I think, traces of his intentional poetic misprision.

First, as Roubaud himself states, in his choice of poets, books, and years of publication the author has already limited the vocabulary with which he recounts his life story. The exigencies of making the collage impose subjective choices that necessarily constitute a reasoned intervention. But as Roubaud's description of the text makes clear, the reasoning behind that intervention remains encoded within the 317 moments that the *Autobiographie* recounts: "Les textes de ma relation appartiennent à la période la plus 'créatrice' du vers libre. En les racontant comme ma vie, j'ai réfléchi et tenu compte de ce qu'était le vers libre pour moi et j'en ai fait une *critique*, en modifiant, dans mes poèmes non inventés, le rapport du vers aux mots, aux phrases qui le composent. Là, et bien sûr dans le choix des moments restitués (comme dans toute autobiographie) comme dans la progression de la présentation, est mon intervention propre, en ce livre" (*M9* 49). Here again, Roubaud presents the program of reading as a dialogic game wherein the goal is to uncover ratios of difference between the original poem and its restored form. The first step in that game is the recovery of the source poems, followed by a study of sequencing in the 317 moments that constitute *Autobiographie*.[15] A further step in that game is decoding how the collage itself critiques and restores the *vers libre*.

Thankfully, any attempt to pursue these invitations immediately reveals the author's disingenuousness, for *Autobiographie* does not entirely fulfill the conditions set forth in the paratextual remarks. There are, for example, quotations in the book taken from texts published both prior to and after the said eighteen years (1914-32), notably phrases from Plato (*A* 161), from Aristotle (*A* 166), from Marcabru's *Vita breve* (*A* 184), from an anonymous tenth-century Irish hermit, and from Raymond Queneau's 1975 *Morale élémentaire* (*A* 7). Also, there are many incidents in the text where the narrator directly addresses the reader in a metanarrative mode, as if to justify what has occurred in the work or else to mystify where the composition is leading, much like the direct address of a narrator in a novel.

For example, very early in the collection the narrator states: "Je vous ai longuement entretenu de ma famille et je n'y reviendrai plus" (*A* 19). This statement is not strictly true, for in the preceding pages the narration consists of very fragmentary moments of a life (in which there are only brief references to a grandfather [*A* 8] and descriptions of what may be construed as a childhood home [*A*

---

[15] A complete source study of *Autobiographie* has been undertaken. See Baudart, "La poésie."

15])). However, if the text consists entirely of poetic antecedents, then, in a fabulistic manner, all of its citations originate in the protagonist's family. Hence, this pledge to no longer speak of his family is immediately violated in the very next sentences: "Ma cousine traversait les rues avec un bourbaki sous le bras. 'l'algèbre, nous expliquait-elle, pénètre par osmose.' Nous passâmes notre baccalauréat avec zéro dans toutes les matières, par le simple jeu des coefficients" (*A* 19).

Further on in the narration, which is disjointed because of its disparate sequences of poetry followed by prose followed by poetry, the narrator turns directly to his readers and, in a tone reminiscent of *Tristram Shandy*, *Jacques le fataliste* and Blaise Cendrars's trans-Siberian compagnon, he feigns to share in their probable sense of disorientation. "Si tu ne m'as pas, cher lecteur, abandonné depuis longtemps en route, peut-être te demandes-tu où nous en sommes? question légitime. Moi aussi je me le demande. Autant qu'il m'en souvienne, je t'ai parlé de ma famille, de la guerre, de mes amours. tu m'as accompagné dans mes voyages. tu as partagé avec moi le vin de la joie, le pain de l'absence (et vice versa), le sel de la douleur; tu en as été ému, peut-être. Mais, enfin tout cela c'est du passé. la vie continue. Que va-t-il arriver MAINTENANT?" (*A* 82). In adopting this air of improvisation–"moi aussi je me le demande" and "que va-t-il arriver MAINTENANT?"–Roubaud simulates the "unconstrained" works that he is citing, aligning them with the unpredictable in real life: "la vie continue." This affected tone of improvisation helps contribute to the myth of an "honest" autobiography, for it suggests that the cited texts follow an aleatoric progression in the development of the book. It is *as if* they unfold haphazardly, in the way that Surrealist automatic writing supposedly presents an unfiltered account of subconscious linguistic machinations. This imitation is put into greater relief once the source texts are considered, for many are themselves riddled with questions of identity, interrogating in their own right forms of self-representation.

Further developing an objectivist practice of the autobiography, some moments of the collection clearly parody what Roubaud calls "tous les automates 'flip-flop' de l'avant garde" (*M9* 7). For example, proposing his own borrowed version of a Dada manifesto, Roubaud distills the following account of a self-absorbed vanguard poet:

MANIFESTE DAGDA

[1]   pour lancer un manifeste il faut vouloir
[2]   j'écris un manifeste et je ne veux rien
[3]   je parle toujours de moi puisque je veux convaincre; j'ai le droit d'entraîner d'autres dans mon fleuve
[4]   je me trouve très sympathique.
[5]   je glisse entre la mort et les phosphates indécis
[6]   regardez-moi bien! : je suis idiot! je suis vous (*A* 162)

In cutting these phrases out of the Dada manifesto, Roubaud mockingly alters their meaning, emphasizing a portrait of the artist as an empty vessel, whose source of inspiration presents itself in conceited, solipsistic self-parody.

Continuing this self-parody, the narrator emblazons the artist's complete lack of originality as an implicit condition for manufacturing the text. Such examples appear in the introduction to Roubaud's sampling from Tristan Tzara's *L'homme approximatif*.[16] The text is introduced with the following prose remarks, intended to conjure the impression of improvisation: "ce que je dis a l'air en désordre mais ne l'est pas. je dis les choses tout en ordre comme elles sont arrivées. les choses arrivent et passent; et quand elles sont passées, on les raconte. la vie. bien sûr, on a parfois du mal a se reconnaître: / *moi approximatif*" (*A* 100). Here again the text claims its quotient of verisimilitude by equating progression with the course of events in real life, "la vie." But in this case the poet adds a narrative twist, pointing to the fact that the story itself depends on memory and that occasionally problems of self-recognition occur. To illustrate the distortion of remembrance and forgetting, in quoting the first text from Tzara's work, Roubaud omits most of the parent text and condenses one hundred lines in the following three:

I   les cloches sonnent sans raison et moi
        aussi. mousses coussins clairs des eaux
            [assises dans le soleil
        je me vide devant vous poche (*A* 100)

Such bouts of forgetfulness and identity loss–"perdu à l'intérieur de moi / même. là ou personne ne s'aventure sauf l' / oubli" (*A* 105)–

---

[16] Tzara, *L'homme approximatif*.

corrupt the promise of an honest autobiography, or do they? In effect, the central pledge in this passage–characteristic of other autobiographical statements found, for example, in *'le grand incendie de Londres'*–is not to recount what happened, but rather to recount a remembrance of what happened. It is the distortions of memory, controlled as they may be in Roubaud's co-opting, that illustrate the living memory of poet, and the impertinence of linearity.

In one respect this depiction of the foggy-headed writer echoes the narrator of Georges Perec's *W ou le souvenir d'enfance*, whose story, or search for an autobiography, begins with the motif of amnesia: "Je n'ai pas de souvenir d'enfance. Cette absence d'histoire m'a longtemps rassuré: sa sécheresse objective, son évidence apparente, son innocence, me protégeait 'je n'ai pas de souvenir d'enfance': je posais cette affirmation avec assurance, avec presque une sorte de défi."[17] In complement to Perec, whose writings erect an edifice of constantly shifting, unverifiable memories, Roubaud's *Autobiographie* is entirely drawn from real memories, both textual and formative. But in Roubaud's case, all recollection of those memories changes them, puts them into movement, and thereby characterizes the autobiographical mode of writing as a controlled stream-of-consciousness narration in which the truth value is located in the *telling* and not in the *story* itself. As in Perec's *W*, the narrator's apparently objective take on history structures both the narration and the ways it deforms the past.

The penchant for witty alterations, reminiscent of the Oulipian translation technique known as "S + 7," is first and perhaps immediately evident in the freehand transformation and reduction of chosen titles.[18] In addition to examples already cited, Tristan Tzara's *De nos oiseaux* becomes DE MES OISEAUX; Paul Eluard's *Les nécessités de la vie et les conséquences des rêves* is abbreviated as NECESSITE ET CONSEQUENCES; *L'allure poétique* is recast as

---

[17] Perec, *W*, 13.
[18] Occasionally confused with Surrealist procedures of writing, the Oulipo invented S + 7 as a kind of antidote to *automatisme* and chance operation. The technique is entirely arbitrary: take any text, isolate the substantives (s) and then rewrite the text, replacing all nouns with the seventh noun to follow in a dictionary of choice. Clearly, freedom intervenes in the choice of text and dictionary, but once those elements are decided the technique is mechanically–but not automatically–executed.

> L'A
> L
> LIVRE POETIQUE;

André Breton's *Revolver aux cheveux blancs* is rewritten as LE BROWNING AUX TRESSES NOIRES. These slight alterations play on obvious acts of imitation and destruction. Similar forms of homage and parody are apparent in the recollected texts.

Consider, for example, the manner in which Roubaud transforms Robert Desnos's famous poem "Rrose Sélavy."[19] In *Autobiographie*, Roubaud anagrammatically rewrites the title of this polysemic work as "AVENTURE DE LASER VIROSE, OU L'ART SORT; VISEZ-LE (EXTRAIT)." Roubaud's travesty of Desnos's poem also presents a brief advertisement—"*l'auteur ne pourrait, sans les obfusquer, nommer les biographes de Laser Virose. Les esprits curieux pourront les décoder au numéro 13*" (*A* 169)–echoing the manner Desnos identifies of Marcel Duchamp who adopted the name "Rrose Sélavy" for his alter-ego. In this fashion, the imitating text collaborates with its source text and continues Desnos's self-conscious burlesque.

In citing selected lines from the original poem, Roubaud deviates from their meaning. These heteroparodies consist largely of repeating the same verse, maintaining the syntactical structure but making alterations that poke fun at the original text.[20] This particular poem lends itself particularly well to such wordplay because it is already rife with spoonerisms, idiomatic tics, and derided clichés. Here are three examples: in Desnos's text we read

> 8. Au pays de Rrose Sélavy on aime les fous et les loups sans foi ni loi, (*CB* 34)

whereas Roubaud's version reads

> 8 au pays de laser virose on aime les foins et les lions sans feu ni lieu. (*A* 169)

---

[19] Desnos, *Corps et bien*, 31-46; hereafter cited as *CB*.

[20] Describing parody as an essential form of potentiality in literary creation, Jacques Bens distinguished between two forms: *heteroparody*, where one imitates the works of another author, and *homoparody*, where an author makes reference to his own works. See Bens, "Queneau oulipien" (*ALP* 30).

In the revised utopia of the artisanal Oulipian, madmen and wolves are edited out and replaced with "foins" and "lions." Similarly, Roubaud replaces "foi" and "loi" with "feu" and "lieu," extending the text's recombinative wordplay. While the ethics of the land may have shifted, the translation extends the original text's phonetic symmetry. A contiguous verse in Desnos's text reads

> 24. Croyez-vous que Rrose Sélavy connaisse ces jeux de fous qui mettent le feu aux joues? (*CB* 34)

which Roubaud renders as

> 24. Laser Virose joue des doigts pour faire la joie des douces (A 170)

In Roubaud's *re-prise* the sound [wa], omitted from the instance cited above (number 8), returns in the form of a spoonerism. This shift in the wordplay engenders an altered meaning in the remembrance of Desnos's poem.

Note that Desnos's aphorism already incorporates a reference to the Surrealist icon of *l'amour fou* as well as a veiled reference to Louis Aragon's *Feu de joie* (1920). Both versions, therefore, thematically address love games, but Roubaud's revision deviates the immoderation of *l'amour fou* ("jeux de fous") toward a game of measure and counting ("Laser Virose joue des doigts"), which also leads to seductive pleasure ("le feu aux joues," "la joie des douces"–*le jeu de douze*). With this subtle reworking, Roubaud turns his reading of Desnos's construction away from a mad, lawless love toward more measured language gaming.

The art of quoting also demonstrates Roubaud's concern with making his text fit into his own story, toward which he is of course equally ironic. Making reference to both Aragon and Alexandre Dumas, Desnos cites the acts of reading and collecting in "Rrose Sélavy":

> 16. Aragon recueille *in extremis* l'âme d'Aramis sur un lit d'estragon (*CB* 34)

to which Roubaud responds by updating authors, switching the adventure novel's character, and matching two unlikely bedfellows:

> 16 Sollers recueille in extenso les aveux de Porthos dans le lit de Barthes (*A* 170)[21]

Here again, in replacing the names in the original verse Roubaud draws from both its structure and its meaning to engender, in his version, a new slant, whose tendency toward punning imitates the source referencing and wordplay found in the original. In addition, the characters chosen are not surprising targets for Roubaud: both are prominent members of the *Tel Quel* group, and both openly declared their dislike of poetry.[22]

As a final example of this process of distortion, consider Roubaud's version of Blaise Cendrars's *Dix-neuf poèmes élastiques*.[23] From this series of nineteen poems, Roubaud borrows and cuts out particular words and phrases. Unlike the cut-up techniques used by William Burroughs or John Cage, in which chance plays a prominent role, Roubaud's cutouts are entirely volitional.[24] In selecting words and phrases from the parent text, Roubaud respects their order of appearance, teasing out of the original a poem that echoes the first in a distorted form. The resulting poem is then both a stolen poem and a preservation of the earlier poem, a new text that recalls yet betrays the original.

From a formal point of view, it is important to note that the basic idea of elasticity in line length is preserved in the shortened versions. Here is the culminating poem in Cendrars's collection, a poem approaching the portrait as a dynamic form of construction. I have italicized the verses that Roubaud cuts out.

---

[21] See Barthes, *Sollers*.

[22] The antagonism suggested in this passage could reflect an episode of recent history in which the collective *Change* (cofounded by Roubaud and Jean-Pierre Faye), a diverse group of intellectuals, set out to redefine interdisciplinary thought at the same time as, and in competition with, members the journal *Tel Quel*. See Forest, *Histoire de Tel Quel*, 342-56.

[23] Cendrars, *Monde entier* (1947, 1967); hereafter references to the 1967 edition are cited as *ME*.

[24] See Perloff, *Radical Artifice*, 150-61; Motte, "Burroughs," 203-23. Perloff argues that Cage's borrowings are intentional, aligning them with Oulipian procedures. Unlike Roubaud's, Cage's work relies heavily on chance operations. Adding his own slant to randomly selected phrases, Cage claims to say what he intends: "In the nature of the use of chance operations is the belief that all answers answer all questions. The nonhomogeneity that characterizes the source material of these lectures suggests that anything says what you have to say, that meaning is in the breath, that without thinking we can tell what is being said without understanding it" (Cage, *I-IV,* 6).

19. *Construction*
De la couleur, de la couleur et des couleurs...
Voici Léger qui grandi comme *le soleil de l'époque
  tertiaire*
Et qui durcit
Et qui fixe
La nature morte
La *croûte terrestre*
Le liquide
Le *brumeux*
Tout ce qui se térnit
La *géométrie* nuageuse
Le *fil à plomb* qui se résorbe
Ossification.
Locomotion.
Tout grouille
L'esprit s'anime soudain et *s'habille à son tour* comme
  les animaux et les plantes
Prodigieusement
Et voici
La peinture devient cette chose énorme qui bouge
La roue
La vie
La machine
L'âme humaine
Une culasse de 75
Mon portrait (ME 104-5)

For the most part, the lines of this poem obey what Roubaud identifies as the four negative rules of the *vers libre standard*: they are mostly single poetic segments (they do not contain caesura), and they are unpunctuated, unmetered and unrhymed (VA 121-32). Plus, composed of various line lengths, from two to twenty syllables–avoiding twelve, of course–Cendrars's poem performs the elasticity denoted in the title. Similarly, reflecting the asymmetrical dynamism apparent in the poem's form, the self-portrait is construed as a contradictory and vague construction: "Cette chose énorme qui bouge."

Although he radically alters the original, Roubaud echoes the basic poetic structure of the composition. He adds a break in the sequence of lines to divide the poem into two stanzas of asymmetrical lines:

CONSTRUCTION

Soleil d'époque tertiaire
croûte terrestre
brumeuse

géométrie du fil à plomb
l'esprit s'habille à son tour:
mon portrait

(ELASTIC-POEMS, 19) (*A* 94)

Recondensing the parent poem, Roubaud's "Construction" repeats the variance in line length (7/5/2//8/7/3) and reiterates the transitory status of the "brumeuse" self-portrait. By and large, Roubaud's collages imitate the vers libre standard of this period, in that there is an unspoken and conscious avoidance of traditional metrics, or even of lines consisting of systematically divided metrical positions.

Thus, in *Autobiographie* the work of rewriting is specifically directed by the source texts: Roubaud's engagement with the vers libre establishes his point of departure from his recent poetic past and demonstrates how he reads particular poets from this moment in French poetic history. Roubaud's récit formel does not propose a virulent attack on Surrealism, or even an end to the vers libre that it recites, condenses, and deforms. On the contrary, Roubaud's incursion into that particular poetic moment measures the degree to which his own writing draws on, and differs from, the Surrealists and Dadaists. What could be more derisive of the classic age of free verse than to confine its liberated vanguardism to a calculated form?

It is within the sequence of poems themselves that Roubaud organizes an underlying numerical structure. Among the formal observations presented in *La vieillesse d'Alexandre*, Roubaud remarks that the vers libre standard differs from traditional verse in its *unicity*, in its ability to stand alone, unanswered on the page: "Chaque vers dans le mètre libre est un tout, un signe poétique plein" (*VA* 122). *Autobiographie* respects this unicity by separating each heading, poem, or prose piece in the book into 317 clearly delineated, numbered, and isolated moments. But, according to Roubaud, the vers libre knows no architecturally constructed books: "Aucun poète classique du vers libre, aucun livre, aucun poème même n'impose un vers divisé en deux ou plusieurs morceaux par un procédé quelconque" (*VA* 123). Structuring a sense of difference, Roubaud presents his citations in a series of moments (317 is a prime number) divided into six notebooks, each of which contains an architecturally significant number. In the first notebook, there are 44 moments; in the second through fifth notebooks there are 41 moments; and in the sixth there are half as many as in the first five put together, or 104 moments.

In the forty-fourth moment of prose we find a "note from the editor," which novelistically reveals a link between the book's numerical structure and the author's autobiographical project:

> PROSE QUARANTE-QUATRIEME
>
> *Note de l'éditeur : cette prose manque dans le manuscrit.* Algernon D. Clifford *et* Octave de Cayley, *dans leur livre récent sur "l'autobiographie"* (L. N. I. T. Press, 1976), *indiquent que le titre de cette prose devait être: prose du calendrier. Ils ajoutent : "nous ignorons pourquoi cette prose n'a pas été écrite; peut-être parce que toute autobiographie, par définition, ne peut être qu'inachevée"* (sic). (A 120)

The given clue, that the forty-fourth moment should have been entitled "calendar prose," confirms the matrix according to which the book is organized. Composed in 1976, *Autobiographie, chapitre dix* marks Roubaud's forty-fourth year, the exact quantity of moments numbered in the first notebook. Thus, in the sequence of "moments," each of which consists of an act of quotation, we find inscribed references to the author's age, as well as a reiteration of incompletion as an a priori condition to the autobiography.

Other references to dates and calendar units structure particular poems, or sequences of poems. "LES MOIS: UN POÈME DE DOUZE VERS" (*A* 121), for example, simultaneously refers to the twelve months of the year and to the series of self-portraits–"les moi(s)"– presented in the work. Or the series of poems parenthetically entitled "ROME HEBDOS" (*A* 85-87, 115-16) emblazons the conceit of journal writing, adapted from texts by Cendrars, as part of the autobiographical project. But the most salient reference to the calendar year situates the time period over which *Autobiographie* was composed, and sets the temporal itinerary for Roubaud's appropriations. Among the later prose moments of the collection we read the following calendar clue: "*Moi, Jacques Roubaud, j'ai écrit ces pensées dans ma retraite, entre le sixième jour du dernier mois de l'année ... et le cinquième du même mois de l'année suivante / pensez à moi / avec indulgence*" (*A* 150). Significant as the second moment in the book where Roubaud inscribes his own name, this signature alludes to the poet's date of birth (December 5, 1932) as well as to the period over which the book was composed.

This period of composition is telling in that 1976, like the poet's year of birth, is a leap year. There are therefore 366 days during which Roubaud composed this series of poems. This is precisely the same number of poems, and poetic moments, found in one of Roubaud's key pretexts, Petrarch's *Rime sparse*, whose numerological disposition is the object of one of Roubaud's studies.[25] Although Roubaud's composition does not also contain 366 moments, this calendrical reference aligns his composition with this distant model; there are 317 sonnets in Petrarch's book of poems. The fact that there are 317 moments in *Autobiographie* may simply help contribute to the notion that all autobiographies are inevitably incomplete, as are the poets' deviations from precursory moments in literary heritage, but it also poses questions about the 49 missing poems.

In short, Roubaud insistently cloaks the liberated form in a counted, measured, and divided book, thereby violating Surrealist and Dada precepts. He playfully resists the parent moment in a fashion that illustrates how the autobiography tracks his own volitional self-(re)creation. To tell the story of one's life is to recreate that life under the conditions of the narration itself, conditions which are never quite total or all-inclusive. Roubaud's parody of the autobiographical mode of narration emphasizes that all representation is fundamentally limited by the constraint of choices, conscious or unconscious. His rewriting of memory firmly denies a confessional or personal mode, opting rather for form-motivated engagements with the precursory poetic moment. By restructuring his memory of the vers libre in *Autobiographie*, Roubaud situates writing under constraint in an oblique relation to poetic liberation; he brings to light that the act of self-(re)creation through poetic narration, an automatism of the avant-garde, is an infinitely recursive act.

---

[25] Roubaud, "La disposition numérologique," 215-40.

Autobiographie, chapitre dix confirms Roubaud's ironic regard for early twentieth-century French poetry; his indefatigable self-figurations culminate in complex reformulations of the final directions in his entire life's work, which culminates and dissipates in the *Projet*. In each of his works, in their self-conscious quest of more elaborate forms, Roubaud constantly reformulates the potential for a literary life, opting to seek new modes of recombination, new techniques of composition. In his formal essays, he seeks the same kind of potentials in reading past poetic moments, canonical or not. And finally, in his expository essay *Description du projet* (1979), as in his most recent novel cycle, '*le grand incendie de Londres*,' Roubaud tirelessly lays bare and reappraises the impossibility of completing his literary autobiography. This impossibility may in part result from the infinity of the ambitious and hypothetical work he conceived of as a young man, but it is also intricately interwoven with the flipside of literary heritage, that one's works do not end with death; "complete" or not, Roubaud's writings will become part of the heritage he adopts and adapts, the poems he remembers and recovers. These latter self-formulations differ from *Autobiographie* in that their irony is not specifically aimed at one period of poetic composition, but rather cast as a meditation on and memory of the developments that contribute to the succession of literary life.

CHAPTER SIX

DEATH, MOURNING, ELEGY: *QUELQUE CHOSE NOIR*

WHEN *Quelque chose noir* was published, in 1986, critics praised the work's readability.[1] Noting Jacques Roubaud's consistent formalist stance, reviewers lauded the personal quality of the poems and their direct address of the experience of loss.[2] One reader even claimed that Roubaud was cured of his "fallacieuses avant-gardes" and that he was now capable of composing poems unfettered by extraneous formal or mathematical concerns.[3] If one does find a shift in language, verse form, and frame of reference in *Quelque chose noir*, the change does not indicate a loosening in the poet's compositional rigor. On the contrary, the spare language of *Quelque chose noir* presents a work of grieving that resolutely resists conventional elegiac rhetoric and casts memorialization in a minimized and exacting poetic discourse.

Jacques Roubaud's second wife, Alix Cléo Roubaud (née Blanchette), died January 28, 1983, of a pulmonary embolism. Since childhood she had been afflicted with asthma. An active photogra-

---

[1] Roubaud (1986), *Quelque chose noir;* translated as *Some Thing Black.*
[2] See Bosquet, "Jacques Roubaud," 85-86; Edwards, "After a Death," 1050; Rosello, "Jacques Roubaud," 914-15; Savigneau, "*Quelque chose noir,*" 11.
[3] Alain Bosquet's review of *Quelque chose noir* offers an apology for Roubaud's formalism: "Les premiers recueils de Jacques Roubaud montraient un souci d'enveloppe originale, soit scientifique, soit structuraliste. Le poème était peut-être offert au lecteur: il lui était en même temps soustrait." Bosquet presents *Quelque chose noir* as a departure from this aesthetic: "*Quelque chose noir* abandonne radicalement cette attitude hautaine, pour exprimer un drame vécu, dont il n'a plus l'inutile pudeur de se cacher. De la douleur exemplaire, Jacques Roubaud, enfin débarrassé des fallacieuses avant-gardes, a franchi toutes les étapes" (Bosquet, "Jacques Roubaud," 85-86).

pher and student of philosophy, Alix Cléo lived thirty-one years. During the two and a half years following her death, Jacques Roubaud fell into silence; he retreated from the world, spoke little, if at all, and did not write any poetry. In 1984, he edited and published the last four years of his late wife's diaries.[4]

In this work of mourning–where "work" is both the process and product of grieving–Roubaud establishes an important relationship between death, writing, and language.[5] Already in ϵ, Roubaud actively integrated the process of mourning his brother's death with the process of inventing himself as a writer. Similarly, in *Quelque chose noir*, Roubaud evokes the relationship between death, writing and mourning, noting that his license to speak as poet is framed by two personal losses: "Avant cette autre mort je ne savais comment dire. j'étais comme silencieux. Ainsi, pris entre deux 'bords' de mort" (*QN* 132). While his work is often concerned with remembrance, memorials, and remotivating a certain poetic ethos, it is these two "borders" of death, by virtue of their intimacy, that crucially contain the relationship between experience, memory, and representation in Roubaud's poetry.

The title–some thing black–distinctly names what is to be found in the book, even if this object is purposefully indefinite. Black, the quality that colors the theme of the collection, may denote the ink of the printed page, though it may also connote the mood of mourning. The named object, however, the black thing itself, remains obscure, suggesting slippage between the literary work and the work of grieving. Moreover, the undetermined quantity of the black thing contributes to the sense of uncertainty in the title. This level of indeterminacy in the title immediately draws attention to instability of linguistic meaning.

Borrowed from Alix Cléo's photographic series entitled "Si quelque chose noir" (1980), Roubaud's title confirms the actual occurrence of something black, presumably Alix Cléo's death. It might consequently be read as a statement of fact, as the reiterative confirmation of what is conditional in "Si quelque chose noir": the eventual possibility of an indeterminate event. In this respect *Quelque chose noir* is written in direct response not only to Alix

---

[4] Alix Cléo Roubaud, *Journal*; hereafter cited as *Journal*.
[5] I am borrowing this formulation of the elegy from Peter Sacks's study of the genre, *The English Elegy*, to which I am indebted.

Cléo's photography and writing, but also in response to the specificity of her dying, to her having meditated, accepted, and succumbed to her own death. As such, in an aesthetic realm, the whole collection continues their amorous dialogue, including their reflections on its possible end.

Conscious of her imminent death, Alix Cléo's photographs and diaries represent her own meditations on death, often in a mode that addresses Jacques, her intimate reader, directly. The compulsion to represent and rehearse her own death confirms Alix Cléo's certain awareness of its imminence–and implies that she must have been in extraordinary pain, an element that is muted in both her and his writings. Although her writings are largely addressed to her husband in the second person, it is unclear if he read them prior to her death. As illustrated in this journal entry from August of 1980 (twenty-eight months before she died), her sense of her impending death deepens the couple's dialogue, perhaps coloring it with an added sense of urgency:

je vais mourir.

Tu vas me perdre mon amour.

Je n'ai jamais aimé que toi.

Je mérite la mort.
Je mérite la mort,stupide,inutile amoureuse.

Tu me verras morte Jacques Roubaud.On viendra te chercher.Tu identifieras mon cadavre.

Tu ne sais rien de Dieu.

prépare-toi à ma mort.

tu m'aimes pour les raisons de la vie–sottement tu oublies les raisons de la mort. (*Journal* 53-54)

Almost as if it had been planned, years after these lines were written, in *Quelque chose noir*, Roubaud writes on the difference between the sight of a death and memorializing the deceased. The modalities of that writing are marked by Alix Cléo's journalistic writing, by her meditations on "la mince pélicule mentale de ta mort, de ma mort" (*Journal* 9).

It is as if Roubaud draws his modality of work directly from the objects left behind after death. Some examples are striking in their correspondence. Describing the terms under which she keeps her journal, Alix Cléo discovers an absolute correspondence between loving and speaking that love: "Curieuse adéquation, pour une fois adéquation exacte de l'amour même,l'amour rêvé,l'amour vécu, l'amour même même.Identique à lui-même même" (*Journal* 14). In working through his loss, Roubaud refashions this statement, citing it as recognition of another absolute: "Pour une fois adéquation de la mort même à la mort rêvée, la mort vécue, la mort même même. identique à elle même même" (*QN* 15).[6]

In addition to writing her journal, Alix Cléo had also been confronting and imagining her death through her preferred medium, photography. The series of photographs "Si quelque chose noir" explores visual representation of her passage through life toward death. Absent from most of this series, Roubaud is pictured in the last of these photographs. In that black and white photograph, both lovers are captured lying in a stone-floored room with a single window, in the last light of the day. Both figures are naked, and he is pictured as a resting bed for Alix Cléo's body, as if his living form were a sepulcher or a tomb for his wife's being.

Given the age difference between Jacques and Alix Cléo, one might think that the question of mortality would be posed in terms of his death. But in Alix Cléo's writings, worries regarding death are almost always related to her own, not to her husband's. Still, in her diary, she writes of having given Roubaud a photographic image of his own death: "Evidemment, ce n'était pas un cadeau ordinaire celui de te livrer,à deux heures du dimanche après-midi,l'image de ta mort" (*Journal* 13). This reversal is interesting because it underlines the extent to which the poet's creative survival is challenged by his loss. Indeed, nothing reminds us of our own mortality more powerfully than the loss of a loved one. While she repeatedly con-

---

[6] Benoît Conort locates the origin of these puzzling lines in Ludwig Wittgenstein's discussion of tautology: "Nous nous trouvons là au coeur de certaines propositions du *Tractatus logico-philosophicus* à propos de la tautologie, spécialement qui énonce que lorsque 'la proposition est vraie pour la totalité des possibilités de vérité des propositions élémentaires les conditions de vérité sont tautologiques.' Et, de même, si la proposition montre ce qu'elle dit, 'la tautologie résulte de toutes les propositions: elle ne dit rien.' La tautologie a pour effet (et pour but) de dire l'impossibilité de la représentation. Elle ne rend possible que l'image de l'image, une représentation seconde, 'la tombe de la photographie prélevée de la tombe'" (*QN* 46). See Conort, "Tramer le deuil," 56.

fronted her own mortality, and while she represented herself in these postures of meditation, Alix Cléo forces Roubaud to think through her death and what it means to him: "tu m'aimes pour les raisons de la vie–sottement tu oublies les raisons de la mort" (*Journal* 54). Consequently, in *Quelque chose noir*, as in the first volume of *'le grand incendie de Londres,'* Roubaud begins an extended meditation on her writings and photographs, on the manner in which she had arranged their life together. While meditating in turn on these gifts of death, Roubaud appropriates and slightly alters phrases from Alix Cléo's diaries–"Évidemment ce n'était pas un cadeau ordinaire. celui de me livrer, à cinq heures du matin, un vendredi, l'image de ta mort" (*QN* 16)–rendering explicit the dialogue between the two.

While Alix Cléo's photographs are partially reproduced in the English translation of the text, those images are entirely omitted from the Gallimard edition. In a sense, that absence concretizes the experience of loss by divorcing the text from its occasion. This gesture participates in a poetics of absence and restraint found elsewhere in the poems. The missing images signify more by their absence and contribute to an austerity that tests the value of words against the process of grieving. That is, loss is concretely built into the absence of the central referent and its effects are heightened through a scarcity of poetic images and declarations of emotion. In Roubaud's mourning process, grief finds a clear expression in a kind of sober, propositional language that simultaneously observes, analyzes, and performs the poet's continued love.

Within the tradition of Western poetry, *elegy* has two distinct meanings. Technically it refers to a specific verse form, the elegiac distich, as well as a poetic lament written on the occasion of a loss, conventionally the death of an exemplary person, often a leader, friend, or loved one. The function of elegy has traditionally been to lament and praise the deceased and to console the survivors, and unlike the tombeau poétique it often addresses more intimate interpersonal relations. *Quelque chose noir* presents a reduced version of elegy, for it resists the conventional rhetoric of lament, praise, and memorialization. I do not mean that *Quelque chose noir* presents an anti-elegy or a lament cast in an ironic tone, but rather that in this composition Roubaud makes use of elegiac rhetoric in a selective and restrained fashion. This reduction prompts particular stylistic choices whose rigor structures the minimalist art of the entire collection.

Usually, personal elegies are relatively short poems; *Quelque chose noir* is rather long. The collection consists of nine sections containing nine poems of nine lines.[7] These eighty-one poems are followed by an envoi entitled "Rien," dated two years prior to the other poems (1983). Although length is by no means a definitive consideration, it is important to note that this composition is closer in length to Rilke's *Duino Elegien* than to Milton's *Lycidas*. Given this length and the dates of composition, Roubaud's poem is no funerary eulogy, but belongs, rather, to the class of meditational or epideictic elegies.

The modern elegy is informed by the pastoral elegy. Like most contemporary elegies, *Quelque chose noir* undercuts that classical genre's conventions. Roubaud's poem is set in a modern, urban context, not a pastoral one. There are no marked emotional outbursts and no processions of mourners. Nor are there appeals to myths, gods, or transcendental metamorphoses or resurrections. Instead, Roubaud's lament is solitary, stoic, and atheistic. He forgoes the forced pomp and noise of celebratory elegies to mourn in a quieter, more delicate poetic space:

> Je reviendrais, de quelques pas en arrière, je serais
> > dans un espace
> > différent, en un sens précaire. (*QN* 30)

Still, *Quelque chose noir* does rehearse the basic movement of the elegy. Echoing Dante's descent in the *Inferno*, Roubaud retraces a descent into memories–"On y descend par une spirale, une damnation. / Toutes stations que maintenant je descends en enfer, par le souvenir" (*QN* 82, 83)–followed, in the envoi, by a regard, if not an ascent, toward the heavens: "Ce morceau de ciel / désormais / t'est dévolu" (*QN* 147). This final movement toward consolation remains incomplete, however, for it is mediated by a cautious and self-conscious use of language. The concerns structuring this constraint are complex. In one sense, Roubaud is reluctant to surrender his memories to language; in addition, he must do so to survive

---

[7] For an analysis of numerical constraint in *Quelque chose noir* see Conort, "Le chiffre de la mort," 195-213.

the loss symbolically and emerge from his silence. Behind the self-consciousness of the work, one may identify its strongest link to the elegiac tradition, namely its distrust and interrogation of poetic figuration.

The collection opens with a poem entitled "Méditation du 12/5/85," presumably written over two years after Alix Cléo's death. This poem presents two juxtaposed scenes: the end of the poet's two-year silence and an image of the initial scene of death, which marks the beginning of that silence. These lines also introduce the story of the poems that follow. In them Roubaud refuses the elegy's principal aim, consolation.

> Je me trouvai devant ce silence   inarticulé   un peu comme le bois   certains   en de semblables moments   ont pensé   déchiffrer l'esprit dans quelque rémanence   cela fut pour eux une consolation   ou du redoublement de l'horreur   pas moi.
>
> Il y avait du sang lourd sous ta peau   dans ta main   tombé au bout des doigts   je ne le voyais pas humain. (*QN* 11)

Rejecting consolation, the poem returns to the initial image of death. The image of the hand, no longer human because inanimate, suggests the poet's first gaze on the deceased, or the reader's first glimpse of something black: "Du sang s'était alourdi au bout des doigts. comme un fond de guinness dans un verre" (*QN* 13). The infinite recurrence of this and other macabre images prompts the process of writing:

> Cette image se présente pour la millième fois   à neuf   avec la même violence   elle ne peut pas ne pas se répéter indéfiniment   ces tirages photographiques internes   je n'ai pas le choix maintenant. (*QN* 11)

The repetition of this disturbing image of death–always as if it new, and always at the site of the number nine–intact more than two years after the event, incites Roubaud's account of grief. By its sheer tenacity and repetition, indeed by its insistent novelty ("cette image se présente pour la millième fois   à neuf"), this *souvenir* leads the poet to break his silence ("je n'ai pas le choix   maintenant") in order to separate horror from living memories.

Roubaud's account of his memories is strikingly self-conscious and analytical. As lament, it imparts an understated emotional range. It is as if the poetic "I" of these poems is silenced by the loss; as if nothing in life matters to him any longer–"Rien ne m'influence dans la noirceur." Consequently, his elegy avoids all exaggerated rhetoric. The delicate issues of blame, regret, and resurrection are each addressed in turn, but in an understated, minimal discourse. The scarcity of extreme feelings is echoed in the rarity of transformational metaphors and figurative metamorphoses so common to the elegiac lyric. Indeed, when Roubaud does describe Alix Cléo or the works she has left behind, he employs the simplest, most direct, literal language. From the very beginning, this aesthetic of restraint is rendered explicit and intentional: "Je ne m'exerce à aucune comparaison   je n'avance aucune hypothèse" (*QN* 11).

Despite the painful recurrence of images recalling loss, Roubaud openly resists any symbolic figuration intended to replace Alix Cléo. Such an explicit refusal underscores the functions and limits of language in addressing loss. Adopting resistance as a theme in the poems, Roubaud foregrounds *what* the poems represent and *how* they make use of words. This interrogation of language, depicted *in* and *as* the composition, provides an experimental context in which Roubaud explores new modes of literary grieving.

In practice, Roubaud records his grief through a ritual of daily meditative writing, or diary entries. The poems often present the quotidian details of the mourner setting about the work of grieving. That daily practice becomes an allegory of the literary techniques deployed in the poems themselves. Typically, the day begins early: "Quand je me réveille il fait noir: toujours." (*QN* 33); "Dès que je me lève (quatre heure et demie, cinq heures), je prends mon bol sur la table de la cuisine. Je l'ai posé là la veille, pour minimiser le bruit de mes déplacements" (*QN* 27). The minimal movements calculated here are not practiced out of respect for the sleeping ("Être silencieux n'a plus la moindre importance" (*QN* 27). Rather, the ritual is maintained in a refusal to accept the death of habit, as if the ritual were sustaining a possible reality: "Je continue à le faire, jour après jour, moins par habitude, que par refus de la mort d'une habitude" (*QN* 27). The precarious, minimal movement is further echoed by the lacklustre, lukewarm, generic-brand instant coffee: "Je remplis mon bol au robinet d'eau chaude de l'évier / Le liquide est un peu amer, un peu carmélisé, pas agréable" (*QN*

27). Roubaud's insistence on the mediocrity of his name-brand coffee mix (Zama) reiterates the extent to which the poems draw from, and remain anchored, in a banal quotidian experience. [8]

The passages in which Roubaud describes the mundane in his daily life are particularly significant in their wealth of black images, for these images lend atmosphere and tone to the work of mourning. As, for example, in this description of his morning coffee: "À la surface du liquide, des archipels de poudre brune deviennent des îles noires bordées d'une boue crémeuse qui sombre lentement, horribles"; "Je l'avale et je reste un moment immobile à regarder, au fond du bol, la tache noire d'un reste de poudre mal dissoute" (*QN* 28). These small, evocative images of blackness recur, in varying form, throughout *Quelque chose noir*, each time suggesting and obscuring something extra but absent.

Tracing the passage of time, these daily meditations on the experience of mourning also challenge the role of language in the work of grieving. Roubaud begins interrogation by isolating and thinking about certain statements. In the "Méditation du 21/7/85," for example, he sets propositions apart in quotation marks in order to measure their value:

> On ne peut pas me dire: "sa mort est à la fois l'instant qui précède et celui qui succède à ton regard. tu ne le verras jamais."
>
> On ne peut pas me dire: "il faut le taire." (*QN* 22)

The quotes put the value of these thoughts under scrutiny. This metalinguistic approach to poetic statement casts the elegy as a self-referential language game, measuring the value of elocution in the work of mourning. Similar deictic gestures occur without explicit quotation marks, as, for example, in the last lines of the first poem of the collection:

> On ne peut pas me dire   parle et attend une seule chose de la parole   elle ne sera pas pensée. (*QN* 12)

---

[8] The presentation of the everyday becomes privileged material in the minimalist aesthetic of American painters and sculptors and, more recently, in the writings of authors in the U.S., France, and elsewhere. See Motte, *Small Worlds: Minimalism in Contemporary French Literature*.

What the poems say, what thoughts they make available, is an essential concern for the mourning subject. Consequently, the reduction in language presented in *Quelque chose noir* underlines the extent to which the poems fail to represent the development of thoughts or memories and succeed more in presenting their end:

> Voilà le bout   le bout où il n'y a aucune vérité   qu'une palme de feuilles en espace   avec ses encombrements. (*QN* 12)

Perhaps more than presenting poems about the lost loved one, then, *Quelque chose noir* explores a specific resistance to the traditional excesses of elegiac figuration. Nonetheless, because of its reduced structure, the poem imposes a formal closure that represents the lamented death. This closure being necessary, the poems seek less to represent the finality of Alix Cléo Roubaud's life than to present the poet's labor in searching for a language of survival and a language of mourning. By "survival" I simply mean successfully overcoming, through poetic creation, the silence that follows death.

Roubaud's silence is alluded to throughout *Quelque chose noir*. It is measured in segments of time (as in the title "1983: janvier. 1985: juin" [*QN* 33], and the line "Je n'ai pas pu parler pendant presque trente mois" [*QN* 131]), or in recurrent moments ("Dans les centaines de matins noirs je me suis réfugié" [*QN* 33]). It is figured by the ineffectiveness of words ("En moi regnait la désolation. comme conversant à voix basse. / Mais les paroles n'avaient pas la force de franchir" [*QN* 18]), and associated with an inability to read or write poetry ("Le registre rythmique de la parole me fait horreur. / Je ne parviens pas à ouvrir un seul livre contenant de la poésie" [*QN* 33]; "Impossible d'écrire, marié(e) à une morte" [*QN* 63]). Silence is further figured in a pronounced use of open spacing. There is a surplus of white space, or blankness, separating the individual lines of each poem, as well as the individual segments within each line. The sparse use of figurative language, along with the *espacement* of the poems, lends force to the depiction of silence, intermittently broken by the imprint of writing. One might say that the world of this immovable "I" is marked by a self-prescribed silence and by an absence recalled in images and memories inspired by death: "Je suis habitant de la mort idiote" (*QN* 35); that his *raison d'être* as well as his *raison d'écrire* is to speak the death that he inhabits: "Mais ta mort en moi progresse   lente   incompréhensiblement" (*QN* 136). Tracing the slow progress of death through the language of these poems is the object of my study.

The gap between the actual loss and symbolic figuration is a problematic element of the elegy. In *The English Elegy*, Peter Sacks claims that "[o]ne of the least well observed elements of the genre is this enforced accommodation between the mourning self on the one hand and the very words of grief and fictions of consolation on the other" (*EE* 2). Sacks's point is that the effectiveness of rhetorical figurations and memorializations conventional to the elegiac tradition is often left unquestioned in the poem itself, for this type of immortalization through poetry is supported by convention. For his part, Roubaud sensitizes readers to the limits of his language ("le langage n'a pas de pouvoir" [*QN* 67]), resolutely denying that representation affords resurrection: ("Je ne t'ai pas sauvée de la nuit difficile" [*QN* 20]). In this denial, and in the lyrical choices that accompany it, Roubaud self-consciously questions how poetry can bear witness to his wife's living traces. The search leads Roubaud to pursue a highly restrained strategy of writing whose goal is to create precise and indeterminate poetic statements that inscribe his memories without finalizing their absent referent.

The collection unfolds in a commemorative, at times erotic landscape whose warmth is direct and declarative–"Son jean, ses seins, ses chaussettes, ses fesses, ses baskets / Ceci est une aventure sentimentale." But in this "Portrait en méditation, III," for example, in which generic descriptions of Alix Cléo evoke her "absence intermittente," the poem's object proves elusive. That is, the possible manifestation of her living memory–"si toutefois elle criait / une douleur mentale traversant Paris désert (août)"–is only admitted as "Inaudible" (*QN* 69).

Roubaud's interrogation of symbolic figuration is rooted in a refusal of comparisons common in panegyric rhetoric: "Je ne m'exerce à aucun souvenir. je ne m'autorise aucune évocation" (*QN* 21). These refusals resolutely avoid inscribing discernible images of Alix Cléo. In this context, visual images impart a redundant quality. Metaphors, similes, and metonymies are avoided as viable modes of lament, for, like the photographs left behind by Alix Cléo, they repeat the closure that coincides with her death. These modes of representation are themselves repetitions of death. They reiterate "La mort même même. identique à elle même même" (*QN* 16). In

"L'histoire n'a pas de souvenirs" Roubaud explains how emblems of Alix Cléo are stale hindrances to his mourning process:

> Chaque image de toi–je parle de celles qui sont dans mes mains, devant mes yeux, sur le papier–chaque image touche la trace d'une reconnaissance, l'illumine,
>
> Mais elle est pourtant révolue, elles sont révolues, chacune et toutes, ne constituent en leurs configurations aucune vie, aucun sens, aucune leçon, aucun but.
>
> Ta voix se déplaçant en bruissant dans le magnétophone, j'entends les efforts de ton souffle, dans la nuit, devant le magnétophone à ton lit.
>
> Je l'entends après des centaines de nuits inchangée et pourtant il n'y a rien en elle du présent, rien que la magie mécanique ait pu, par la mimésis en limailles, translater d'aucun moments, pleins, séparés, difficiles de souffle, révolus, pour être là en ton nom, comme un recours.
>
> Et c'est pourquoi peut-être, tu es en elles, vue, et voix, le plus irrémédiablement, morte.
>
> Et c'est pourquoi aussi la vie qui te reste, s'il te reste, est imprimée en moi, suaire, entremêlée en moi, refusant de se défaire. (*QN* 112-13)

Belonging to historical moments unraveled in the past, the photographs, the voice recordings, and other objects that Alix Cléo invested with meaning are now only reminders of her death. For Roubaud the "magie mécanique" of the artifact, including the poetic image, fails to evoke the presence of the deceased and serves only to illuminate and, at length, degrade the memories reproduced.

It is as if the entire personal world of the poet is iterating closure. From the arrangement of objects in their apartment to the sights, sounds and experiences they shared together, the world itself speaks this end. Initially, Roubaud seems to have wanted to avoid the finality of these images: "Je voulais détourner son regard à jamais. je voulais être seul au monde à ne pas avoir vu du tout l'image de ta mort" (*QN* 15). Over time, however, confronting these images of closure becomes possible and even necessary to the creation of a poetic representation that bears witness to Roubaud's living memories.

To express these memories, Roubaud must first overcome the limits presented by the inherited images: "Je peux réellement affronter ton image, ta 'semblance,' comme on disait autrefois. difficilement, mais je le peux." (*QN* 34) It is only through the process of accepting the irremediable coincidence of the actual death and the remnant images of Alix Cléo that Roubaud is able to formulate a lyrical mode of writing that disassociates his memories from the image of death. In order to do so, however, Roubaud does not explore the universe of closure; he writes that "La proposition 'tu es morte,' elle, n'a besoin d'aucun univers de discours," for this reiteration of her certain death also affords no meaning or direction in his effort to emerge from numbness and silence: "Elle ne restitue aucun sens" (*QN* 129). That is, without dwelling on closure, he attempts to create and maintain as potential a poetic space inhabited by the other, nonrepresentational traces still alive within him: "Les autres traces, venues d'autres sens, ne sont qu'en moi. Quand je trébuche dessus, j'étouffe" (*QN* 34). The challenge of writing mourning lies in inventing a style that somehow presents and preserves memories. The urgency of this invention is a question of symbolic survival, associated here with the difficulty of breathing–"j'étouffe"–suffered by the asthmatic Alix Cléo.

Roubaud consequently resists a fundamental property of language: to represent, define, and deform its object. In writing the remnant traces that subsist within him, he avoids naming or describing them directly. Inversely, he refuses to condemn them to silence. In the last few verses of "L'histoire n'a pas de souvenirs" Roubaud depicts these supplementary traces as having an agency of their own, as if their preservation and utility to mourning were predicated on remaining unwritten, "refusant de se défaire."

> Et c'est pourquoi aussi la vie qui te reste, s'il te reste, est imprimée en moi, suaire, entremêlée en moi, refusant de se défaire.
>
> Et de céder comme ta chair à la complaisante décomposition non imaginable, et de s'immobiliser comme l'image et la parole dans les parenthèses documentaires. Cette vie qui est cela:
>
> Ton odeur, ton goût, le toucher de toi. (*QN* 113)

These traces, other than sight and sound, are only broadly designated (*odeur, goût, toucher*), classified generally so as to avoid the closure and decay of specific renderings. There are two stylistic elements at work here that recur elsewhere in *Quelque chose noir*, both of which point to the conditional conjunction (*Si*) omitted from Alix Cléo's title. First, the conditional clause "s'il te reste" qualifies the possibility of continued life. Second, the run-on sentence ("la vie est imprimée en moi refusant de se défaire de céder de s'immobiliser") suspends and multiplies its subject by means of interrupted syntax. The effect produced by these constructions is to render "la vie qui te reste" conditional, plural, and indeterminate, located only in negative terms, as what refuses to reveal itself.

How can Roubaud propose a new life for Alix Cléo? How could he fashion a poem or space that would memorialize without finalizing? How, in short, can he describe his memories without defining them, without altering them through representation? In keeping with his commitment to self-conscious and volitional literature, Roubaud formulates their potential answers through a poetics of constraint that establishes, for him, the functions of a new elegy. To this end, he mutes the traditional rhetoric of the elegy and tests the utility of propositional speech in the form of a language game. He creates "Une sorte de logique pour laquelle tu aurais construit un sens   moi une syntaxe, un modèle, des calculs" (*QN* 49). Presented as a strategy of intentional writing, the poems often read as prolegomena for the discursive techniques they develop.

Consider, for example, this exposition of "Le ton," where Roubaud points to the gap between the need for and the value of words in grieving death. Indeed, Roubaud breaks a silence of mourning, but in the precarious space of his poems the utility of each syllable is carefully measured:

> *Le ton*
>
> Il est convenu que la tonalité sera sinistre
>
> Ou bien il sera, directement, question d'autre chose
>
> Dans le registre lyrique, élégiaque, l'horreur culminera métriquement (mort métrique). ou bien par la disjonction et la suspension
>
> Du moins si on écoute jusque-là, ou lit
>
> Il est convenable de s'en tenir aux genres attendus: évocation, imprécation, futur antérieur : rituels.

> Il y a ainsi des engendrements de sentiments disponibles dont je ne sais pas me servir
>
> Je suis devant les mots avec mécontentement
>
> Très longtemps je n'ai même pas pu m'en approcher
>
> Maintenant, je les entends et je les crache. (*QN* 126)

In this poem, appearing near the end of the collection, the poet continues to explain his poem in a future mode, how it will present itself: "la tonalité sera sinistre," "le registre, lyrique, élégiaque"; what it will be about: "il sera, directement, question d'autre chose"; and what effect is intended in eschewing a regular verse form: "mort métrique." Accompanying his dissatisfaction with words, one notes an apparent indifference toward conventional modes of expression ("Il est convenu que..." and "Il est convenable que...") as well as a need to rid himself of the words that come to him: "je les entends et je les crache." Ritual conformity to expected genres is adopted in the tone of the poem, acknowledging their "engendrements de sentiments disponibles" but respecting their techniques in an involuted and strategically constricted manner: "Voilà le bout   le bout où il n'y a aucune vérité   qu'une palme de feuilles en espace   avec ses   encombrements" (*QN* 12).

Comparison is largely refused in the poems, with slight exception. In "Méditation de l'indistinction, de l'hérésie," Roubaud spells out the proposed discursive constraints to be respected in his account of grief:

> Il y a trois suppositions. la première, ce n'est pas trop d'y mettre un ordre, c'est qu'*il n'y a plus*. je ne la nommerai pas.
>
> Une deuxième supposition, c'est que *rien ne saurait se dire*.
>
> Une autre supposition enfin, c'est que *rien désormais ne lui ressemble*. cette supposition destitute tout ce qui fait lien. (*QN* 75)

From these three givens, Roubaud deduces the linguistic constraints of *Quelque chose noir*: "de ces suppositions se déduisent des propositions comme une chaîne" (*QN* 75). In the first supposition–"*il n'y a plus*"–there is no grammatical object. What is missing is replaced by a refusal to name Alix Cléo: "je ne la nommerai pas." This omission underlines the principal discursive strategies: to avoid reiterating death and to create a possible world in which a potential life for Alix Cléo can be meditated and expanded.[9]

The second supposition, "*rien ne saurait se dire*," reflects Roubaud's interest in the ineffable. More than other artistic mediums, language must signify something, even if it represents its referents indirectly. Representing nothingness linguistically is therefore difficult, for it addresses an epistemological problem. Although nothingness may exist–and mourning in love may indeed be a phenomenological experience that contextualizes nothingness–its expression in the matter of language, because rendered complete in that medium, remains unpresentable. This second supposition takes on several meanings. Roubaud may be saying that after his loss nothing is worthy of speech, that there is nothing worth saying. Or–and I think this is the more operative meaning for the collection–Roubaud invests his poetic discourse in the notion that, while nothingness is real, it is strictly unknowable, undefinable, and consequently not able to be represented. In short, "nothingness" (like its inverse, "totality") names an absolute and particularly *potential* notion, a kind of infinite imaginary space into which symbolic creation makes egress only by way of suggestion.

The third supposition locates Roubaud's most cogently formulated statement of consolation: "*rien désormais ne lui ressemble.*" Nothingness, in this context, takes on the positive quality of potential because of its indeterminacy. Accordingly, direct forms of comparison are avoided, confining description of Alix Cléo to appositions that amount to "nothing." For Roubaud, nothing in this world measures or resembles Alix Cléo: "on conclura qu'il n'y a que du dissemblable et de là, qu'il n'y a aucun rapport, qu'aucun rapport n'est définissable" (*QN* 75). Roubaud is willing to inscribe the memory of Alix Cléo only in what is indistinct, dissimilar to everything, stateless (*QN* 87), and identical only to itself (*QN* 77). Obeying this particular semantic constraint enables Roubaud to inscribe the essence of his memories in a set of poetic propositions that designates without defining.

---

[9] David Lewis's work on possible worlds is a clear influence in *Quelque chose noir*, as well as in Roubaud's subsequent collection, *La pluralité des mondes de Lewis* (1987-1990). See also David Lewis, *On the Plurality of Worlds*.

The final words of *Quelque chose noir*, for example, illustrate how this proposition is realized in Roubaud's elegy. Dated two years prior to the other poems, the *envoi* describes a pause before the sun sets over a "patch of sky" dedicated to Alix Cléo ("ce morceau de ciel / désormais / t'est dévolu" [*QN* 147]). In this pause, Roubaud inscribes a release of absence that likens Alix Cléo's eyes to nothingness: "le soleil, là / hésite / // avant que la terre / émette // tant d'absence / que tes yeux / s'approchent // de rien" (*QN* 147-48). Reminiscent of Shakespeare's mistress whose eyes are nothing like the sun, Roubaud's mistress's eyes are like nothing at all. From this description, and others like it, one learns more about the poet's gaze, more about his mode of perceiving memory, than about the woman praised. His resolution to consign memory to indistinction, irresemblance, and infinitude presents the work of mourning as an experiment in representing nothingness: "Ta mort m'a été montrée. Voici: rien   et son envers: rien" (*QN* 66). The poetic force of this experiment targets the indirect production of a "nothing," of an indeterminate potential for life: "Tout se suspend au point où surgit un dissemblable. et de là quelque chose, mais quelque chose noir" (*QN* 76). Representing this point at which everything is eclipsed, "le point familier du doute de tout" (*QN* 20), therefore becomes Roubaud's main aesthetic goal. In this performative moment, Roubaud offers the trace of an extant nothingness–"Quelque chose noir qui se referme. et se boucle. une déposition pure, inaccomplie" (*QN* 76)–as testimony to mourning: "Gouffre pur de l'amour" (*QN* 15).

These indeterminate evocations do not, however, amount to a set of elaborate mannerisms evoking an ideal Alix Cléo in an infinitely signifying verbal game. "Il pourrait me venir à l'esprit de te comparer à un corps noir," postulates Roubaud, considering a comparison of (the memory of) his lost love to the trace of language: "Je pourrais mais je ne m'y résigne pas" (*QN* 85). Instead, Roubaud invests meaning in her nonbeing, her negative being, her singular nothingness: "Je m'acharne à inscrire *rien-toi* avec exactitude, ce bipôle impossible, à parcourir autour, de ceci, ces phrases de neuf que je nomme poèmes" (*QN* 85). Again, this nothingness is drawn from the powerful experience of her absence, an absence that Roubaud construes as a form of being: "ton existence était si forte. elle était devenue une forme d'être" (*QN* 18). Rendering this inscription of nothingness as specific as possible structures the constraint of this elegy: "Rien ne m'influence dans la noirceur" (*QN* 11).

The key textual technique in this evocation is the use of apostrophe as a propositional form of modal logic. Direct second-person address is the privileged form of enunciation in *Quelque chose noir*: Roubaud apostrophizes Alix Cléo in lieu of directly describing and praising her. Apostrophe alone unites and possibly preserves the divergent and decaying sense of Alix Cléo and the dialogue they share: "Je vais me détourner [de l'image de ta mort] et inscrire les mots de l'adresse   les mots de l'adresse qui sont l'unique manière de constituer   encore une identité qui soit tienne sans cloisons" (*QN* 61). Her proper names, Alix Cléo, as well as the familiar second person pronouns *tu* and *toi* might be said to conjure an absolute and pure notion of the addressee while simultaneously pointing to her absence.

There is something indestructible, incorruptible about the proper noun. In mourning, Roubaud repeats his young wife's name to himself: "Je dis toujours ton nom   ton nom en moi   comme si tu étais" (*QN* 136). Because it directly invokes its addressee, apostrophe performs (the possibility of) the presence of one addressee. In this simple and direct address, Roubaud is present to Alix Cléo without bringing her into relation in the world. In naming her, in saying her name, he affirms her being beyond the decay of analogy: "En te nommant je voudrais te donner une stabilité hors de toute atteinte" (*QN* 87). The name's immutability becomes a performative function of apostrophe: "Ton nom est trace irréductible. Il n'y a pas de négation possible de ton nom. Te nommer c'est faire briller la presence d'un être antérieur à la disparition" (*QN* 88, 87). But apostrophe does not afford a continuous presence, for the economy of perfomance demands that "presence" occur in a locus of absence: "tu y apparais à l'endroit où seule tu es absente" (*QN* 84).

This mode of nomination differs from the visual traces of Alix Cléo in that each iteration provides a possible world for its addressee, if only in a linguistic realm. The last four lines of "Je vais me détourner" suggest how iteration itself lends life to her one indestructible trace–her name:

> Incapable je suis désormais de ralentir   autrement qu'en le prononçant les dérives divergentes des syllabes de ton nom qui
>
> Quand il n'était pas pour moi cette désignation rigide   se répétait dans un monde possible   par la seule vertu d'une
>
> Parole   autour d'un corps vivant
>
> Alix Cleo Roubaud. (*QN* 62)

For Roubaud, to hold back or slow down the "dérives divergentes" of her name is to create a kind of consolation; it is to think and propose a discursive world in which Alix Cléo may live.

In several poems, Roubaud plays with the pronunciation of his wife's name. Emphasizing the orality of apostrophe, Roubaud's phonic play explicitly triggers memories associated with erotic pleasure–"Ces souvenirs sont les plus sombres de tous" (*QN* 116). In "Pexa et hirsuta," for example, Roubaud draws an analogy between Alix Cléo's physical and verbal nudity. In this analogy he locates an enunciatory pleasure animated by Dante's opposition of smooth (*peignées*) and harsh (*hirsutes*) syllables:

> Hirsute la fragmentation de tes prénoms,
>
> Je les disais toujours ensemble, l'un heurtant l'autre: Alix Cleo.
>
> Où le signe voyelle manquant était celui de : 'nue.' (*QN* 61)

Here, he uses her name without the accent. The "nudity" of the name helps figure the pure transparency and luminosity of the *nom propre* in *Quelque chose noir*.[10] And the collision of the two harsh consonants [k], balanced by the liquid consonants [l], provides a figure of Roubaud's desire, a figure cast as a phonic performance and a visual grapheme.

> Ce qu'il y avait d'hirsute dans ta nudité n'était pas ta chevelure basse très noire autour de l'humide où la langue passait en t'écoulant
>
> Pas ta nudité mais ton nom. Au milieu de jouir de toi le dire. (*QN* 64)

Each time he refers to her name, he describes the drama of repeating the sounds to himself in a possible world. Yet, in the poems themselves, there is more *description* of the status given the name than occasions where the name is actually written or pronounced.

In these descriptions, Roubaud asserts that with each enunciation the name breathes another life, thereby repeating the event of

---

[10] That the French word *propre* also means "clean" lends ironic effect to the privileged status of the *nom propre* in *Quelque chose noir*, for in his use of the name Roubaud researches a pure possible life for Alix Cléo, who had depicted life as impure: "'Sale vie, sale vie mélangée à la mort'" (*QN* 80).

absence: "Il y a ton nom. je peux le dire. je peux rayer la biffure qui le bare, en lettres, pesantes du lieu / et tu y apparais à l'endroit où seule tu es absente" (*QN* 84). The name thus becomes a means to speak a unique absence without altering the meanings of Alix Cléo, without comparisons. It becomes the vehicle of a nonlife or *via negativa*. As such, the name must remain free of comparison; it must remain, in a sense, pure: "Ton nom ne se supprime pas (mais il restera sans description, qui viendrait briser cette solidité pour en faire un énoncé maléable, moins exigeant, veule, dérisoire, et pour tout dire, faux)" (*QN* 88). This demand for rigor with the use of the proper name may explain why it appears only twice in the entire collection.

Also, as with the pronunciation of the proper name, there is a game set up in the potential life of nomination. Here I am referring to the title of the last four poems in the collection, "Nonvie, I-IV," where the sound of nonlife (a negative attribution of existence) coincides with the sound of noun- or name-life (*nom-vie*); like this final series, "Alix Cléo" is composed of four syllables or parts.

A more common form of apostrophe in *Quelque chose noir* is the use of the second-person subject pronoun, *tu*. Here, too, we trace a poetics based on sonorous play, often in muted tones:

> "Vous" était notre mode d'adresse. l'avait été.
> Morte je ne pouvais plus dire que: "tu." (*QN* 18)

The choice of pronoun reiterates singularity (as opposed to *vous*, which suggests both formality and plurality). In this singularity one might read an emblem of Roubaud's world, of our world, whose very existence is contingent on its unicity. For Roubaud the unicity of his world is confirmed in the singularity of one death: "Tu disais : 'le singulier est idiot'" (*QN* 79); "je suis habitant de la mort idiote" (*QN* 35). And, inversely, the possibility of thinking abstract lives for Alix Cléo is contingent upon a precise expression of her (unique) absence: "tu y apparais à l'endroit où seule tu es absente" (*QN* 84). In other words, Roubaud's apostrophe specifically constructs the discursive conditions of possible worlds for one being: "Alix Cléo." But the singularity of the world where he writes and repeats her name is confirmed by the certainty of her death. In this world her possible existence is silenced.

Being a homophone with the past participle of the verb *taire* (to silence), *tu* pronounces (names) the silence created by the eschewed modes of representation. That is, presented in a metapoetic context (where the status of each enunciation is calculated, measured for its utility in furthering a continued consciousness of the deceased), apostrophe takes the place of other modes of speaking that are quieted.

Furthermore, the stress pronoun *toi* also bears weight. Like the proper noun and the second-person subject pronoun, *toi* functions as a graphic image of Alix Cléo, reiterating the appearance of her absence. Its phonic environment recalls the "golfe de toits" that Roubaud describes in meditating on her last photographs: "ce que l'on voit, là, dans le golfe de toits ce qu'on voit / est, précisément, ce qui maintenant manque / Toi" (*QN* 91-92). The image of the "golfe de toits" functions as a *mise-en-abyme* of Alix Cléo, a rhyme of the "toi" [*twa*] in which her non-existence is repeatedly invoked. It is almost as if this image becomes emblematic of Alix Cléo's tomb: "Dans les villes, on ne sait pas qu'il y a un toit. / Une tombe, il faut se forcer pour aller voir" (*QN* 135).

Toi is also associated with the number three (*trois*) which, being a factor of nine, subtends the collection's organization. In *Quelque chose noir*, important things come in threes. First, the givens behind the constraints adopted: "Il y a trois suppositions": "*il n'y a plus*," "*rien ne saurait se dire*," "*rien désormais ne lui est semblable*" (*QN* 75). Second, the presentation of mourning is divided into three steps: "imitations sous les trois modalités / Perceptions délibérations décisions" (*QN* 95). Third, for Roubaud, there are three forms of images that reiterate Alix Cléo's death: her creations (photography and writings), her dead body, and their apartment, marked by its "agencement d'objets   le tien" (*QN* 61). Each of these are united in the apostrophic *toi*: "Ce sont   trois fois toi   trois des irréductiblement séparés   déplacés de toi perdu en une diaspora qu'unit seule ce pronom :   toi" (*QN* 61). Although impersonal, the subject and stress pronouns are used more readily than the proper name in Roubaud's apostrophe.

Apostrophe is the central poetic practice of *Quelque chose noir*, for, through invoking Alix Cléo, Roubaud also solicits the reader's participation as audience to his virtual dialogue. The conditions of this dialogue most succinctly reflect the conditions of consolation afforded by possible worlds: "Un poème se place toujours dans les conditions d'un dialogue virtuel" (*QN* 124). All poems, like the concept of possible worlds, propose an hypothesis: "L'hypothèse d'une rencontre   l'hypothèse d'une réponse de quelqu'un" (*QN* 124). The hypothesis of possible worlds proposes an infinite number of other worlds whose existence, like our own, is contingent upon being logically consistent. Although a hypothetical dialogue and the hypothesis of an infinity of possible worlds greatly differ, Roubaud's poems provide an example of how the latter philosophical proposition may help figure and enrich poetic discourse.

For Roubaud, the consideration of multiple worlds where Alix Cléo might live takes the form of a poem; in the poem, in the life of the poem itself, he qualifies these possible worlds.

> Un poème se place toujours dans les conditions d'un dialogue virtuel
>
> Même dans la page: la réponse supposée par la ligne, les déplacements, les formats
>
> Quelque chose va sortir   du silence, de la ponctuation, du blanc   remonter jusqu'à moi
>
> Quelqu'un de vivant, de nommé: un poème d'amour (*QN* 124)

The possibility of a reply, of a resurgent "Quelque chose" or "Quelqu'un" is factored into the concrete presentation of words on the page (*ligne, ponctuation, blanc*). The disposition of language is structured around the possibility of giving voice (life) to an absent and impossible being or thing "Dans l'espace minime" (*QN* 36): "Quelque chose noir se referme. et se boucle. une déposition pure, inaccomplie" (*QN* 76). The reader witnesses and participates in the presentation of this purely speculative hypothesis. But the reader's reception does not provide consolation; rather, our recognition of the impossibility of the addressee's reception, and perhaps our cooperation in doubting that impossibility, is what opens our imagination of (im)possible worlds. That this poem is intended as a dead letter becomes one of its most explicit and potential conditions:

> Même quand l'omission, l'indirection, l'adresse pronominale rendent possible cette translation: qu'un lecteur soit devant la page, devant la voix du poème comme au moment de sa naissance
>
> Ou de sa réception: lecteur lecteur   ou   lecteur auteur
>
> Ce poème t'est adressé et ne rencontrera rien. (*QN* 124)

In missing the poem's addressee, the possible worlds it suggests are kept open. And each reading bears witness to the hypothesis of this continued dialogue.

In imagining possible worlds where Alix Cléo is alive, however, Roubaud does not stray from his mourning apostrophe. Instead, he describes novel(s) in which recounting an adventure coincides with the unfolding or occurrence of that adventure. Respecting this constraint aligns the reality in which the story is read with the reality of the fictive story; that is, the constraint conceptualizes the notion of parallel universes whose reality might be thought of as interchangeable. Here is how the idea of these novels is presented:

> Il y a quelqu'un, un homme. Il n'est pas nommé. Il y a sa jeune femme, qui est morte.
>
> Le roman se passe dans plusieurs mondes possibles. Dans certains, la jeune femme n'est pas morte.
>
> Le temps est le présent. le temps de chaque monde possible est le présent. (QN 51)

The novel therefore takes place (*se passe*) in several possible worlds. Among these are the one where it is written and read, our world, the only one that is certain.

What would happen if the two were to communicate, if the apostrophe were to be heard? Roubaud considers the question, revealing the consequences it would have for his text:

> Un homme abandonné, à cause d'une mort, reçoit un coup de téléphone. Ce coup de téléphone est un appel de la femme aimée, et morte. [...]
>
> Mais que dira-t-il? que s'est-il passé dans ce monde là en trente mois? que lui dira-t-elle? comment entrerait-il dans ce monde où l'horreur n'a pas eu lieu, ce monde à la mort abolie, où la lutte continue contre la mort, où ils s'obstinent à ce combat qui ici, dans le monde où il est encore au moment où il décroche l'appareil, a été perdu? (QN 53)

This hypothesis presents an aporia, a contradiction in the consistency of this or the other possible world, rendering one of them impossible: "Ce monde n'aura pas été." It is therefore necessary, for the work of mourning, that the poem propose an open-ended hypothesis: "Le téléphone ne sonne pas. Tant qu'il ne sonne pas le nouveau monde, le monde possible est encore possible" (*QN* 54). Similarly the work of grieving itself depends on the possibility of other worlds: "Quand il n'y a plus qu'un seul monde, où elle est morte, le roman est fini" (*QN* 52). Consigning his work thus to a "Gouffre pur de l'amour" (*QN* 15), Roubaud pledges to continue his calculated expression of faith until his own end: "Quand ta mort sera finie. je serai mort" (*QN* 67).

Among the traditional elements of the elegy not included in *Quelque chose noir*, I have noted Roubaud's refusal of consolation through metaphoric language or an appeal to transcendence. Conventionally, the narrative movement of the elegy traces a descent into grief followed by an ascent into some kind of consolation, often concluded by some form of immortalizing resurrection, a constellation. In *Quelque chose noir*, there is little movement away from the image of death. There is no resurrection, no symbol other than the proper noun (Alix Cléo) to replace the lost loved one. *Quelque chose noir* presents the process of grieving, stripped bare of all certainty in symbolic reification. It presents a process that is perpetually incomplete, for the surviving subject does not transfer emotional attachment from the deceased loved one to another object or person. On the contrary, through the refusal of symbolic and visual images, absence is given new form. And, re-enacting that absence through apostrophe becomes a means of writing survival for the poet and his loved one.

Instead of impoverishing Roubaud's poetic account of grief, the austere language in *Quelque chose noir* enriches the discursive world where possible lives for Alix Cléo are proposed. The parsimony of Roubaud's language paradoxically broadens the referent's signifying horizon. By espousing this restrained poetic discourse sustained as an "espace minime," Roubaud intones that less is more. Lessening in Roubaud's poems is concretized in the rejection of the consolation provided by metaphor and metonymy; it is realized in the modal affirmation of the nonexistence and irresemblance of the poem's unique referent; and its perpetuation is confined to the performative act of apostrophe, reiterated in each new reading. All these discursive reductions inscribe a potential mode of *becoming* for Alix Cléo.

The lyrical value of these verbal constraints is supported by the return of rhythmic compositions in the poem's later movements. In the poem "Dans cet arbre" one observes the continued absence of representational complication, as well as a return of rhythm into the apostrophic discourse:

> Descends et dors   dans cet arbre, dans cet arbre.
>
> Repousse la terre   dans cet arbre, dans cet arbre.
>
> Écope la terre   dans cet arbre, dans cet arbre.
>
> Désinvente le noir   dans cet arbre, dans cet arbre.
>
> Reconstruis des jambes   dans cet arbre, dans cet arbre.
>
> Décline les poussières   dans cet arbre, dans cet arbre.
>
> Coupe la lumière   dans cet arbre, dans cet arbre.
>
> Emplis les orbites   dans cet arbre, dans cet arbre.
>
> Écris, écris toi vivante   dans cet arbre. (*QN* 139)

What is striking about this poem, along with others grouped in the last set of nine, is how clearly it expresses the evolution of Roubaud's mourning process. Recovering from the horror inspired by the rhythmic register of speech (*QN* 33), the poetic "I" of *Quelque chose noir* invents and puts into practice a form of writing animated by the same loss that instigates the work's conception. This self-referential (metapoetic) trope is a common topos to the elegiac tradition, and it characterizes a recurrent feature of Jacques Roubaud's literary innovations.

In *Quelque chose noir*, Roubaud adopts the elegy's fundamental condition, the absence of a loved one, as the work's generating principle. Beyond providing an exquisitely modern and philosophical work of grieving, *Quelque chose noir* draws attention to how linguistic constructs limit or expand our experience of literary representations.

Chapter Seven

METAFICTIONAL PLAY IN *LA BELLE HORTENSE*

La belle Hortense, L'enlèvement d'Hortense, and *L'exil d'Hortense* are the first three installments of a six-volume novel project. The first of two structurally integrated prose cyles, the Hortense novels recount the adventures of a beautiful heroine, Hortense, and her progressively complicated involvement with the royal family of Poldevia, a fictional Balkan state.[1] An enchanting trilogy on love, crime, and urban living, the *Hortense* series reflects Roubaud's continued interest in, and mastery of, metaliterary techniques, though in this case they are practiced within the popular genre of the detective novel.

In previous chapters on Roubaud's poetry, I have discussed how his engagement with poetic genres, especially fixed forms, pursues a critical recollection of select literary lineages. How does the influence of tradition differ in the case of the novel?

In "Technique du roman" (1937), Raymond Queneau addresses this question in a fashion that opens a new playing field for Oulipian novelists like Italo Calvino, Jacques Jouet, Harry Mathews, Georges Perec, and Jacques Roubaud. Claiming that "le roman, depuis qu'il existe, a échappé à toute loi" (*BC* 27), Queneau explains that he imposes rigorous constraints in three of his early novels, *Le chiendent* (1933), *Gueule de Pierre* (1934) and *Les derniers jours* (1936). A self-proclaimed metromaniac, Queneau conceives of constraint as necessarily mathematical. Confessing that "il m'a été insupportable de laisser au hasard le soin de fixer le nombre des

---

[1] The second synthetic prose work alluded to here is entitled *'le grand incendie de Londres'* and is discussed in chapter 8.

chapitres de ces romans" (*BC* 29), he reveals the entirely idiosyncratic reasoning behind his novels' numerical ordering (each number chosen reflects the author's personal, autobiographical whimsy). His argument is that the novel's continued relevance, like poetry's, relies on the practice of intentional and conscious techniques: "Si la ballade et le rondeau sont péris, il me paraît qu'en opposition à ce désastre une rigueur accrue doit se manifester dans l'exercice de la prose" (*BC* 28).

Queneau's call for rigor in the formal composition of novels is directly answered by members of the Oulipo and indirectly by practitioners of the *nouveau roman*. Subsequent experiments in the novel are not limited to mathematical constraints, and each realizes a novel-form generated from a set of predetermined, often arbitrary rules that encrypt the author's aesthetic idiosyncrasies. These rules can be very simple or very complex and often articulate meaning on several levels. Georges Perec's *La disparition* provides the quintessential example of the extraordinarily simple yet extremely difficult constraint. A lipogram in *e*–that is, a text written without the letter *e* (the most common letter in the French language)–this three-hundred-page mystery about the disappearance of Anton Voyl hinges on the disappearance of the letter *e*; each time one of the characters realizes the link between the missing character and the missing letter they, too, are eliminated. Perec's use of the lipogram eloquently unites form and content by staging the disappearance(s) both in the story and in the telling of the story. In this respect, *La disparition* exemplifies the essentially metaliterary character of writing under constraint, an axiom dubbed the Roubaud principle: "Un texte écrit suivant une contrainte parle de cette contrainte" (*AL* 90).

To write novels under constraint can be approached as a means of mixing novel and poetry. Queneau's imperative–"une rigueur accrue doit se manifester dans l'exercice de la prose"–is aimed at resuscitating already mature literary forms. Formal experimentation attempts to revive and renew a literature whose practiced forms are used up or worn out. The question of the novel's vitality is repeatedly posed in Western literature and, in a contemporary setting, it continually refigures the recursive debate between modernists and classicists. Taking Roubaud's *La belle Hortense* as example, I explore the ludic character and critical contemporaneity of Oulipian metafiction and examine how Roubaud's novel both confirms and questions innovations in novelistic discourse.

In the prefatory remarks to *Essais critiques*, Roland Barthes evokes the fundamental challenge of innovative literature.[2] Recognizing the combinatorial nature of narrative art, Barthes claims that literature is composed of very few basic emotional states, infinitely recombined with varying subtlety: "L'affectivité qui est au fond de toute littérature ne comporte qu'un nombre dérisoirement réduit de fonctions: *Je désire, je souffre, je m'indigne, je conteste, j'aime, je veux être aimé, j'ai peur de mourir*, c'est avec cela qu'il faut faire une littérature infinie" (*ES* 14). Barthes's observations repeat the tautology that everything worth saying has always already been said millions of times. This infinite repetition invokes the fatigue of language and literature; there is, in one sense, no point to repeating the same old tired stories century after century. Yet Barthes's investment in style, in the infinite mutability of a lover's discourse and the rhetorician's art, valorizes the perpetual renewal of the creative process, be it the writer's labor or the reader's collaboration. That is, according to Barthes, the challenge of innovation is to overcome conventional ways of telling and reading stories, to overcome the "déjà dit": "On entend souvent dire que l'art a pour charge d'*exprimer l'inexprimable*: c'est le contraire qu'il faut dire (sans nulle intention de paradoxe): toute la tâche de l'art est d'*inexprimer l'exprimable*, d'enlever à la langue du monde, qui est la pauvre et puissante langue des passions, une parole *autre*, une parole *exacte*" (*ES* 15). This view of innovation as a struggle against received forms of articulation broadly resumes actual developments in twentieth-century novelistic writing.

With the end of literature and the beginning of writing (*écriture*), contemporary French writers have sought to undermine totality in the literary work, the preeminence of the author's voice, and, contiguously, the mediating role of the literary critic. The "death of the author," as Barthes formulates it, traces technical developments in literary style, such that the author's subjectivity is displaced and replaced by the active and liberated reader.[3] Stéphane Mallarmé's "disparition élocutoire du poète," as well as his call to "céder l'initiative aux mots," are among the earliest and most influential depictions of these modernist styles. James Joyce's *Ulysses* and *Finnegans*

---

[2] Barthes, *Essais critiques*; hereafter cited as *ES*.
[3] Barthes, "The Death of the Author," in *Image-Music-Text*, 142-48.

Wake are often cited as seminal examples of the impersonal art form of this century, for their use of varied narrative and metaliterary techniques exemplify techniques of the modern novel. His use of stream-of-consciousness narration, in particular, is representative of a narrative style in which authorial voice is disguised, replaced by other elements of the narrative itself. But to what degree do these stylistic refinements represent fundamental changes in our understanding of the novel?

According to Queneau, the essential elements of the novel have not changed greatly since the form's inception in the classical period: "[The *Iliad* and the *Odyssey*] have one thing in common: one finds in them nearly all the techniques of the novel. It doesn't seem to me that anyone has discovered much that's new since."[4] Couched more in praise of Homer than as denigration of the modern novel, Queneau's remark questions what developments have kept the novel vital. Ian Watt suggests that the novel's birth and maturation, like much of the criticism that has accompanied it, centers around realism.[5] But the degree to which the novel produces a realist account of the world or history is often challenged in questioning crises, in instances of what Lucien Dällenbach has termed "Le récit spéculaire," where narration mirrors or doubles the conditions of its own exegesis. These self-conscious moments blur the distinction between representations of reality and fiction in the novel. Like the French alexandrine verse form, the novel has matured (especially during the eighteenth and nineteenth centuries) through self-conscious exploration of its production process.

Felt to be simultaneously destructive and regenerative by some writers, this maturation leads to a kind of literary endgame. Seeking to restore the novel's former vitality or to transform the form altogether, novelists have explored narrative self-reflexivity to make it new again. As the drive for innovation has incited a radicalization of novelistic experiments, many, like John Barth, have praised the literature of exhaustion.[6] The experiments of Queneau and Roubaud, I think, are grounded in such a conscious attempt to push the boundaries of narrative self-reflexivity in the novel.

---

[4] Queneau, "Interviews with Georges Charbonnier," 22.
[5] Watt, *Rise of the Novel*.
[6] See Barth, "Literature of Exhaustion," 162.

In *Narcissistic Narrative*, Linda Hutcheon has suggested that metafictional narratives prolong the question of the novel.[7] Elaborating an allegorical reading of Ovid's myth of Narcissus in which she identifies the novel form with the self-absorbed Narcissus, Hutcheon argues that the character's metamorphosis (the form's transformational self-reflexivity) guarantees an important rebirth. In her reading, "Ovid and the niads and dryads who lament Narcissus' change are seen ironically as representative of those critics who lament the death of the novel–refusing to accept that the form of the novel might just have changed" (*NN* 8). These (poorly identified) "Ovidian critics" resist the passing of the realist novel, arguing that "like Narcissus, the novel began to lose those attractive features–of action, of personality–which had made it so beloved to become absorbed in a deeper self-reflective state which–and herein lay the fear–threatened to deny the novel's existence as a realistic narrative of something outside itself" (*NN* 13). Hutcheon responds to this rhetoric of crisis in the novel by noting that "Narcissus lives on–in *two* forms, one (his own) in the underworld, and one (as a flower) that, while different in form, does bear his name" (*NN* 8).

This continued life is condensed in what Hutcheon terms the "metafictional paradox," the coexistence of the novel as it *was*, and as it *is* now practiced: "More and more the reader is made aware of the fact that the existence of verbal and structural materials conditions the formation of images, that the human imagination is exercised in working with these materials–perhaps still at the service of some human meaning and value outside themselves" (*NN* 14). This different perspective on language, and the construction of reality–a critical focus of Michel Foucault's study of representation and power in discourse–becomes integral to the art of metanarrative writing.

According to Queneau, the novel's metafictional impulse has permeated the form since its inception.[8] Moreover, Mikhail Bakhtin's seminal essays on dialogism in novelistic discourse have demonstrated how, throughout its history, the novel has relied on parody as a means of development and innovation.[9] Accordingly, metafictional practices in the novel are not unique to the modern period. Bakhtin, Barth, Barthes, Hutcheon, Queneau and other writers

---

[7] Hutcheon, *Narcissistic Narrative*; hereafter cited as *NN*.
[8] Queneau, "Interviews with Georges Charbonnier," 23.
[9] Bakhtin, *Dialogic Imagination*.

agree that Miguel de Cervantes' *Don Quixote*, Laurence Sterne's *Tristram Shandy*, and Denis Diderot's *Jacques le fataliste* are pivotal texts for the modern novel, for each of these texts *overtly* thematizes the conditions of production and reception proper to narration; that is, they stage the hermeneutic activity of novelistic discourse at the center of the work's plot. These novels also share an additional stylistic element that is further elaborated by Oulipian novelistic writing and has come to be associated with the literature of exhaustion: they thematize narrative in an ironic mode.

Philosophically associated with post-Hegelian nihilism, metaliterary irony has become a privileged mode of interrogating the teleological dialectics of the literary work, especially with regard to authorial subjectivity and novelistic articulations of the real and imaginary. Evoking a long tradition of comic metanarrative novels, Oulipian fiction playfully evaluates the relationship between the real and fictional worlds of novelistic writing. In addition to questioning the discursive status of literary actants (writer, editor, reader, and critic), Oulipian fiction also interrogates the relation between the novel and other literary genres, often introducing formal techniques of poetry in the novel. Roubaud's particular brand of metafiction also parodies contemporary literary theory of the novel, thereby mocking the supposed authority of the critical discourse over the literary one. Adopting metaliterary irony as a mode of narration in *La belle Hortense* allows Roubaud to consolidate and further elaborate the self-consciousness of novelistic discourse, while simultaneously expanding that field of metafictional inquiry.

Self-conscious narrative is the most prominent feature of Roubaud's Hortense novels, where no aspect of the novelistic tradition escapes parody. The diversity and breadth of this parody serves two complementary functions: first, to elucidate, enumerate, and condense conventional novelistic techniques; second, to elicit laughter. Alluding to Roubaud's use of pastiche, burlesque, and travesty, Susan Ireland, who has written eloquently on the Hortense novels, maintains that "his novels 'exorcise' the past by providing a comic version of the 'serious' canon."[10] It is, I think, by making fun of the novelistic canon that Roubaud most convincingly consolidates the form and assures its continued vitality.

---

[10] Susan Ireland, "Jacques Roubaud," 181. See also Ireland, "The Comic World of Jacques Roubaud," 22-31.

Illustrating the idea that "one only writes by continuing other writings" throughout *La belle Hortense*, Roubaud uses varied intertextual references, the diversity of which confirms his approach to the novel as an eclectic genre.[11] These references, ranging from popular television to complex mathematics, from ancient and modern philosophy to classical music, help frame the novel's characters and the contemporary setting of the story.[12] Their variety, it seems, is justified by the "Author's" self-imposed didactic role, a role he assumes overtly, as if to indicate why he is doing what he is doing while he is doing it: "Un des rôles du romancier, depuis que le roman existe, n'est-il pas d'augmenter le niveau de culture générale des lecteurs?" (*BH* 111).

Within this variety, no genre figures as prominently in *La belle Hortense* as the novel itself. And intertextuality in the work begins with Raymond Queneau's *Pierrot mon ami* (see *BH* 94, 110, 124 for direct references to that novel). In the epilogue of this 1943 novel, the hero, Pierrot, reflects on the type of novel that his story could have produced. It is from this passage that Roubaud draws the inspiration for his Hortense novels: "Il voyait le roman que cela aurait pu faire, un roman policier avec un crime, un coupable et un détective" (*Pierrot* 210-11). Though not a linear continuation of Pierrot's story, Roubaud's novels borrow parts of Queneau's setting to create the potential novel hidden within the parent text. At the end of *Pierrot mon ami*, the protagonist is left to tend to a chapel built in honor of a Poldevian prince who died near the "Uni-Park." In Roubaud's novel, oil has been struck under "la place Quenelieff," enriching the Poldevian nobility who live in a distant, imaginary kingdom structured by a confluence of canonical texts. Succession to the Poldevian throne, disputed by six nearly identical princes, becomes a central motif in this novel cycle. Although few of Que-

---

[11] Roubaud (1985), "What Have They Done to Us?," 20.
[12] Here is a list of artists and thinkers whose names appear in *La belle Hortense* (in order of appearance): Emile Zola (10), Nicolas de Cusa (12), Louis Marchand (39), Jehan Alain (40), Abbé Migne (41, 250), J. S. Bach (42), Arnaut Daniel (45), Plato and Schopenhauer (80), Freud (80), Spinoza (82), Alexandre Dumas (85), Raymond Queneau (95, 124, 144), Max Planck (97), Louis Veuillot (100), Epictète (100), Jane Austen (111, 209), St. Colombe (113), Desargue and Pappus (116), Pierre Getzler (119), Guyomard (119), Alfred Hitchcock (123), Gongora (140), Crébillon fils (143), Victor Hugo and Joseph Conrad (172), Frank Harris (174), Krafft-Ebing and Havelock Ellis (174), Humphrey Bogart, James Cagney, and Edward G. Robinson (180), Perry Mason (180), Sextus Empiricus (182).

neau's main characters reappear in Roubaud's novels, the Poldevian chapel and the princes associated with it, become primary thematic and formal elements in the Hortense novels.

Presented as both a love story and a detective novel, *La belle Hortense* recounts the adventures of a beautiful young philosophy student living in a pseudo-Parisian setting where a succession of enigmatic crimes, "La Terreur des Quincailliers," is puzzling an illustrious, if quirky, detective, "l'inspecteur Blognard," and his Pyrrhonic sidekick, Arapède.[13] The crimes are generative, for in them are emblazoned the geometry, mathematics, and humor that subtend the novel's composition.

The first thing one notices about these crimes is that they are not staples of detective fiction. On 35 occasions, someone has broken into different neighborhood hardware stores in the middle of the night. Each time the thief has attached 53 cooking pots to the ceiling in such a fashion that after departing unnoticed with the loot –miniature statuettes of the Poldevian Venus–all the pots simultaneously fall to the ground, creating a terrible racket that announces yet another theft.[14]

The farcical nature of this crime, accentuated by the mock sobriety of the detective's investigation, flags Roubaud's parodic intention: to exaggerate the irrelevance of the crime and to underscore metaliterary play in the game of detection. That is, the absurdity of the crimes confirms Roubaud's burlesque approach to detective fiction. And yet, despite this parody, he eschews the highbrow "who cares whodunit" stance, preferring instead to depict the narrative techniques of the *roman policier* as form motivated.[15] The hardboiled pattern inscribed in the crimes elucidates the formal grace of Roubaud's narrative art. Through its specific details, this series of crimes reveals the constraints subtending the Hortense novels, and these constraints become layered codes in the game of detection.

---

[13] The neighborhood after which Roubaud models this setting is the Marais in Paris, the fourth arrondissement, where Jacques and Alix Cléo Roubaud lived together. For a study of Parisian place names, see Delignon, "Jeux de pistes dans *La Belle Hortense*," 59-63.

[14] In addition to being a *nombre de Queneau* and playing an important role in Georges Perec's unfinished novel *"53 jours,"* the number fifty-three bears an added significance for *La belle Hortense*: Jacques Roubaud was fifty-three years old when he composed this novel.

[15] See Wilson, "Who Cares Who Killed Roger Ackroyd?," 35-40.

Like all novels of detection, *La belle Hortense* is presented in the form of a puzzle. In the hermeneutics of detection, the characters and readers are invited both to solve the mystery and to reflect upon literary sleuthing. The novel's "Narrator" rehearses the clues left by the mysterious criminal. Monsieur Mornacier–an anagram of "romancier"–is a journalist who earns a participatory role in Blognard's investigation by revealing to the detectives, and the readers, the key to the pattern of crimes. Hoping to acquire an inside view of the controversial investigation, a position he plans to exploit to write novels based on the famous inspector's successes, Mornacier reformulates the following deductions about the Terreur des Quincailliers:[16]

> En disposant, au moyen de petits drapeaux, les 34 quincailleries frappées sur le plan de la Ville, je vis de manière aveuglante que le criminel avait décrit un parcours en spirale; cette spirale était très nette et chaque fois, il avait choisi la quincaillerie la plus proche du tracé de la spirale; plus précisément encore, il se dirigeait, à rebours, vers le centre de la spirale. Mais j'avais trouvé autre chose (de plus important encore à mes yeux): en comptant, sur les photos des boutiques sinistres, les casseroles qui étaient tombées à terre, et en tenant compte de quelques variations dues à la qualité des clichés et aux bonds imprévisibles de quelques casseroles hors du champ de vision de l'appareil dans un cas, je découvris que leur nombre était très vraisemblablement toujours le même, et *que ce nombre était 53*; ce qui voulait dire que les parcours en spirale du criminel le conduisait au 53 de la rue des Citoyens, dans la maison même que j'habitais! (*BH* 54-56)

The revelation that the crimes trace a spiral in the city becomes pivotal for solving the mystery. The spiral is a favorite motif of Roubaud's, for it is the figure implied in his preferred fixed form, the sestina. In this canso form, six rhyme words reappear according to a strict combinatorial permutation that is most easily retraced by drawing a spiral through their changing order. This poetic form enacts six permutational movements in the shape of a spiral (starting with the last integer, followed by the first one of that series and me-

---

[16] The criminal and literary evidence is reviewed remarkably frequently in *La belle Hortense*: thrice by the "Author," once by the "Narrator," and continually by the inspector.

thodically working its way toward the center) in such a fashion that a sixth permutation would reestablish the original order of the elements (see Chapter 1).

The logic of the sestina, emblazoned into each Hortense novel, provides a poetic, numeric, and comic substructure to the narration. Poetic, because adapting fixed forms to prose theoretically inscribes rhyme and rhythm in the narration. Numeric, because the key numbers of the sestina generate certain occurrences in the novel (primarily integers divisible by six, especially 36 and 366–though exceptions are frequent, and telling, in *La belle Hortense*). And comic, because the movement, permutations, origins, and logic of the sestina incite numerous self-reflexive jokes spun into the narration.

In this world of ridiculous crime and parodic crime-stoppers, the generative poetic form becomes an instrument of ratiocination. It is the sestina-spiral in *La belle Hortense* that leads Mornacier to the site of the final crime. And, in *L'enlèvement d'Hortense*, the form's permutations help Blognard identify the villainous usurper of the Poldevian throne–the prince in question appears once too frequently, out of the predetermined order (*EH* 279). Although the form is relatively subterranean at first, as the trilogy progresses its presence becomes increasingly overt and parodic, occasioning a torrent of puns. In this context, the slightest comment returns our attention to the spiraling sestina, as in Blognard's anticipatory "Ça prend tournure, ça prend tournure" (*BH* 160).

Not surprisingly, the succession to the Poldevian throne is itself subject to the spiraling permutation of the sestina. That is, the sons of six different Poldevian families share the kingship according to the rule established in the thirteenth century by Arnaut Danieldzoï. In this manner, the throne changes family every generation, and every sixth generation the same family regains the throne (*BH* 44-6). The sestina thus becomes a parodic figure for authoritative order within the narrative form. The spiral shape is also repeated as a means of telling the otherwise identical princes apart. Each prince, the "Author" explains, bears a birthmark on their left buttock in the shape of a snail, the spiral shape of which explains its status as the sacred animal of Poldevia.

METAFICTIONAL PLAY IN *LA BELLE HORTENSE* 209

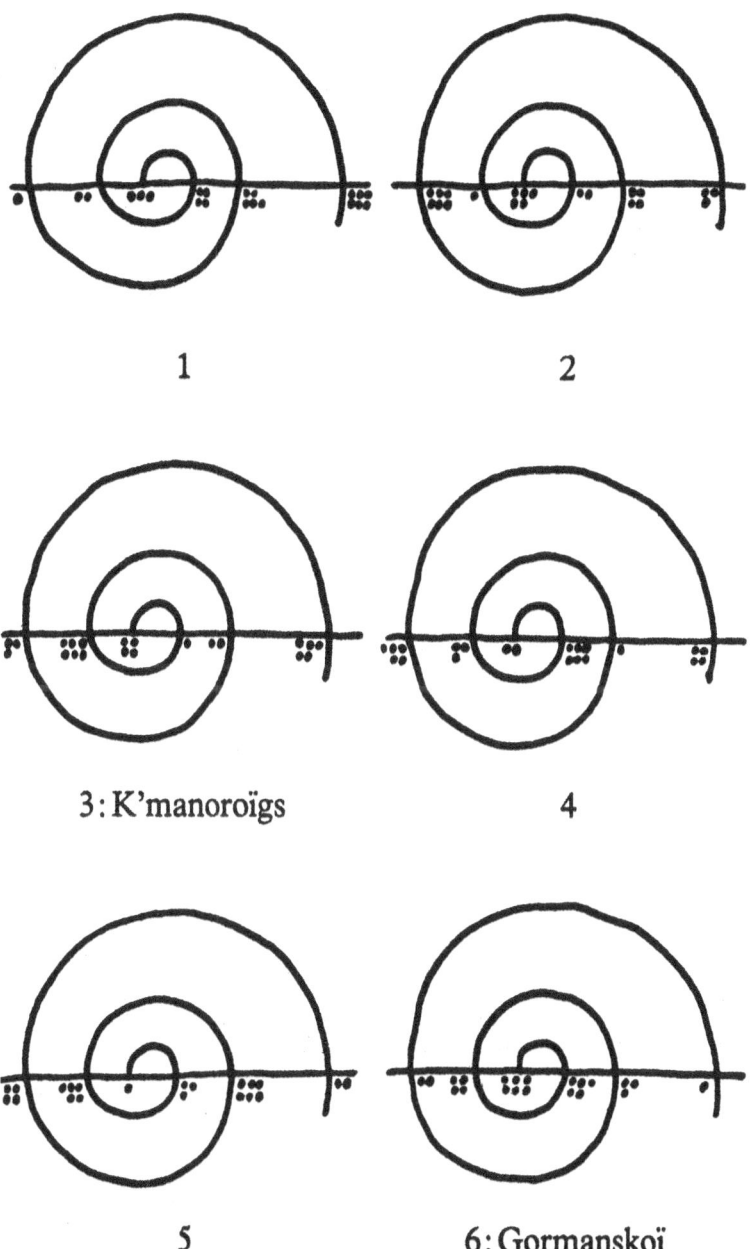

1

2

3: K'manoroïgs

4

5

6: Gormanskoï

These birthmarks differ only in the distribution of dots within the escargot, which are the only visible means of distinguishing the princes. This complication occasions several funny scenes in which Hortense, who, after falling in love with one of the otherwise nearly indistinguishable princes, must tell them apart without viewing their behinds.

Roubaud's generative use of the sestina recalls the form's creator ("le plus extraordinaire limier du siècle" [*BH* 62]) and illustrates Queneau's vision of imposing rigorous formal constraint on the novel. As in his poetry, where intertextual reference establishes links to tradition, Roubaud pays homage to his novelistic precursors while twisting the novel form into a sestina. The intentional visibility of the constraint contributes to the inventiveness of the Hortense novels. Queneau and Perec had already worked on conflating poetic constraint in the novel, Perec explicitly adapting the quenine, as in *La vie mode d'emploi*.[17] The movement of the sestina has figured in other narrative moments, as, for example, in the spiral descent into Dante's *Inferno*. Plus, the generative role of the sestina remains so consistent and overt throughout the Hortense novels that it functions as an ever-present leitmotiv. Such explicit allusions to the sestina occur in music, geometrical shapes, recipes, mathematical permutations, sequences of events and character appearances in the novels. The reappearance of the novel's generative form manifests a new *mise en abyme* of the narrative and authorial rules.

Not all of the sestina's applications are made explicit, however, and herein lies the subtlety of this constraint-generated novel. On the one hand, the *idea* of the constraint is advertised, but, on the other, the *way* it is implemented in creating the novel is hidden. In *La belle Hortense* in particular, it is difficult to identify the particular elements Roubaud has inserted as "rhyme words," first because these elements are very different in nature, and second because the numerical ordering of *La belle Hortense* poses more questions than it answers.

Returning to Queneau, we observe that the particular novelistic elements chosen to create order and rhythm can greatly vary in type: "Je me suis fixé des règles aussi strictes que celles du sonnet. Les personnages n'apparaissent pas et ne disparaissent pas au hasard,

---

[17] See Perec, "Quatre figures," 50-53; Perec, *Cahiers des charges de la vie*; and Roubaud (1995), "Hypothèses génétiques," 9-23.

de même les lieux, les différentes modes d'expression. On peut faire rimer des situations ou des personnages comme on fait rimer des mots, on peut même se contenter d'alliteration" (*BC* 42). The quantifiable elements of the novel vary in Queneau's description, ranging from character to setting to rhetorical style. As in poetry, where rhyme and rhythm are determined according to repetition and meter, the intentional arrangement of tangible narrative techniques lends additional structure to the novel. But because narrative rhyme and rhythm are less codified than the prosodic, the repetitions might be more difficult to identify. Moreover, as is illustrated in Perec's *La vie mode d'emploi*, there can be a very large number of isolated elements worked into each sequence of any given novel, each obeying its own permutational ordering. In a series as long as the Hortense novels, or Roubaud's more recent *'le grand incendie de Londres,'* identifying each of these integers proves indeed difficult, and yet their movement, explicitly spelled out in the form, provides a narrative substructure that brings to the novelistic discourse mnemonic techniques normally reserved for poetry.

In addition, the precise structure of the sestina is not strictly followed. Instead of presenting six parts of six chapters each (a form respected in the two subsequent novels), *La belle Hortense* presents four sections of seven chapters, each demarcated by a kind of intermission in the narration (which Roubaud calls the "entre-deux-chapitres"). This incongruence between the evoked form and the presented form alludes to a derivative quenine used in the novel's production, and indicates a purposeful open-endedness in the form.[18] Once Roubaud has established a certain pattern of combination he systematically distorts that pattern, often relying on programmed structures to affect that distortion. The process of firming up the unity of his novelistic universe is thus complicated and deferred, for just when it looks like the structures will take hold and complete their determined path, Roubaud shifts gears, adds additional constraints, and changes the underlying conditions of the detection game.

---

[18] The number seven is a numerical self-portrait of Raymond Queneau because both his names have seven letters (*BC* 29). For an analysis of *La belle Hortense* read as a quenine based on the number seven, see Catherine Rannoux, "*La belle Hortense* de J. Roubaud," 65-75. See also Roubaud (1992), "N-nines, autrement dit quenines"; (1993), "N-nines, autrement dit quenines (encore)."

Similar variations may be found in previous Oulipian works. In *Les derniers jours*, for example, Queneau excludes eleven chapters in order to create a syncopated rhythm in his novel (*BC* 33). That is, after having imagined a complete and symmetrical novel form, Queneau subtracts some of its elements so as to create imbalances and aporia in the structure. In *La belle Hortense* the incoherence between the named and presented form is echoed in the plot's imperfect denouement; at the "end" of the novel, Inspector Blognard wrongly arrests the eminent professor Philibert Orwells, leaving the mystery suspended, falsely solved. This mistake is echoed in the numerical structuring of the novel's chapters. If indeed this novel is based on the number seven and if it obeys the permutations of the sestina, the novel comes to a premature end, having performed only 4/7 of the required permutations. In this respect, the self-reflexive constraint reveals its own disguise, for its early end bears consequences in the unfolding of the plot.[19]

Not all of the metafictional play in *La belle Hortense* corresponds to the novel's generative form. Much of the metafictional commentary here benefits from the genre's dialogic discourse, particularly exploiting the textual roles of the "Author," "Narrator" and implied "Reader." Toying with the acclaimed notion that the author is dead, Roubaud animates his narration by drawing explicit attention to the manipulation of each formally constructed subject position. Comically pitting each narrative voice against the others, he lays bare the narrative devices used or eschewed in his novel and engages his audience in a masterful review of novelistic encoding. But what gives Roubaud's prose its distinctive ease is the levity with which he parodies narrative art, making of its critique an interactive game.

Although witty and at times cunning, Roubaud's approach to metaliterary commentary is rarely condescending. From beginning to end, the text rehearses its formal properties in a generous and playful tone. For example, one of the first characters to be introduced is the owner of the neighborhood grocery, Eusèbe. His ap-

---

[19] Even a cursory reading of the novel reveals this cyclical ending, for the novel's closing lines repeat the first meeting between Hortense and her lover, except that in this meeting the woman is named Carole, and the bus where another Poldevian prince approaches her is moving on an axis perpendicular to the one where Hortense mets her prince. In this passage, Roubaud suggests simultaneous, perpendicular possible worlds instead of parallel novelistic universes.

pearance occasions the narrative's first of many digressions, the parenthetical introduction of the storytellers: "Nous profiterons de ce court répit pour faire le portrait d'Eusèbe (par *nous*, je veux dire le ou plutôt les narrateurs de cette histoire, puisque toute l'histoire suppose non pas un, mais une foule de narrateurs implicites ou explicites)" (*BH* 8). This host of narrators corresponds, naturally, to the equally well-defined narratee, the story's *vous*: "(par *vous*, nous désignons, bien entendu et pour toute la suite du roman, *le* Lecteur –dont le portrait générique ou robot, orne le bureau du directeur commercial de notre maison d'édition–, et nous le vouvoyons par respect)" (*BH* 12). The dialogic contract, implicit in the act of reading, lays the groundwork for numerous distinctions playfully established in the narrative. First and foremost, the writer insists on respecting narrative polyphony: "Moi, Jacques Roubaud, je ne suis ici que celui qui tient la plume, en l'occurence un feutre noir 'Pilot Razor Point' à pointe fine et c'est pourquoi je dis *nous*, ce qui est un pluriel de modestie. Il y a dans ce roman, par ailleurs, autant vous le révéler tout de suite, un Narrateur qui est un personnage de l'histoire. Il apparaîtra dès le deuxième chapitre, et il dira *je*, comme les narrateurs le font généralement dans les romans. Mais je vous invite à ne pas le confondre avec moi, qui suis l'Auteur" (*BH* 8). The status of the different voices is rendered more precise throughout the novel's development. Although here distinguished from the narrator, on other occasions the "Author" appears as both part of and external to the plot. For example, in rebuffing a smart aleck who once wrote that "on ne peut pas se mettre à la fenêtre pour se regarder passer dans la rue," the "Auteur" proceeds to explain how in this novel it is indeed possible: "Mais attention, il y a 'moi' et 'moi.' Appelons, si vous le voulez bien, moi$_1$ celui (moi) qui est dans le *Gudule-Bar*. Moi$_1$ regarde et raconte ce qui se passe. Moi$_2$ est toujours moi, l'Auteur, mais un moi entrant directement dans le récit, un moi de chair et d'os autant que d'oeil et de pensée" (*EH* 45-46). Part of the game initiated here entails juggling who is and who is not a direct actant in the principal story line.

Parodying Rimbaud and Baudelaire, Roubaud problematizes the question by implicating the reader: "Si 'je' est un Autre, n'est-il pas Pas-Autre que toi, Lecteur, mon semblable, mon frère" (*EH* 12). Here, too, Roubaud creates a duplicitous role for the implied reader, inviting him or her to come to terms with their own textual subjectivity: "En ce qui vous concerne, c'est encore plus compliqué, et je vous laisse vous dépatouiller des implications topologiques et existentielles de votre situation" (*EH* 46). In *L'enlèvement d'Hortense*, the reader also becomes actant in the plot; so much so that he or she is added to the pool of suspects. Feigning to swear off writing the type of detective novel in which the reader is the criminal (*EH* 151), the "Author" proceeds to blame the reader for having left a garden gate unlatched, an oversight that leads to the tragic murder of Balbustre, a cherished dog.

The atmosphere of this metanarrative play remains frivolous and unpredictable throughout the Hortense novels. Roubaud cultivates the appearance of having created an astute implied reader who questions the detective's rationale, only to dismiss his or her queries as poorly thought out and irrelevant (*BH* 234-35). Creating the semblance of a liberated and proactive reader implicitly mocks poststructuralist theories that tout the death of the author as a prerequisite to the freedom of the reader. Self-consciously toying with Barthes's notion, Roubaud's narrative insists on the writer's authority over his implied reader. But this insistence is ironically cast, always alluding to the authorial voice as pure construct: "Je le sais parce que c'est moi l'Auteur et que je sais tout, et vous le savez parce que je vous le dis" (*EH* 73). Roubaud's construction of the author and implied reader sets up a quasi-agonistic dynamic in which the reader is depicted as constantly trying to catch up with the novelist's reasoning or to find some way of debunking his mistakes (*BH* 234-35). The novel cycle leaves off with the writer affirming his authority over both the text and the (implied) reader: "Le lecteur n'aura pas encore rejoint l'Auteur, vlan!" (*XH* 259).

Such antagonistic posturing also characterizes the textual interactions between the "Author," "Narrator," "Editor," and "Reader."[20] Animating the implicit textual choices of the narration, Roubaud establishes an openly competitive relationship between Mornacier and the implied author. This competition naturally revolves around each character's ability as a writer. For example, after having produced a

---

[20] I shall not comment on the dialogue between the constructed author and his market-savvy publisher. But it is pertinent to note that their satirical exchanges serve to comically thematize the work's publication, promotion, and legal authenticity. In that vein, one must also remark that the Hortense novels changed publishing houses, from Ramsay to Seghers, and that Paul Fournel, another member of Oulipo, may have been instrumental in the series' acceptance by both houses.

stylistically flat metaphor describing his emotive reactions to another character's shopping habits, Mornacier interjects that "dans mon métier, il faut savoir placer de belles phrases, c'est pas l'Auteur qui l'aurait trouvée, celle-là" (*BH* 21). But the Narrator is repeatedly put in his place as the author's instrument, both by the "Author" (*BH* 28, 65-66) and his reluctant "Reader" (*BH* 60). And, in the narration, he comes to recognize his subservience to the omniscient author: "Comme je sens que vous êtes vous-même dans un état de grande impatience, que vous brûlez de connaître le sens de mes paroles sibyllines (et comme d'ailleurs l'Auteur ne me laissera pas vous faire attendre plus longtemps) je ne vais pas vous faire attendre plus longtemps; je vais vous dire ce que j'avais découvert" (*BH* 53).

In addition to this ludic antagonism, Roubaud's author amuses his audience by denigrating the narrator, belittling the limits of his literary ideas. Mornacier's project–to become involved with the investigation for the self-aggrandizing purpose of writing a bestseller based on Blognard–is identified by the author as pure plagiarism, stolen from another detective novel. This lack of originality earns the following mock indignation: "Par dessus le marché, copier toute la scène dans un autre roman! Si c'est ça que le Narrateur imagine être la tâche du romancier, ça promet pour la littérature française! Nous reprenons donc, mais c'est maintenant, comme il se doit, le Narrateur qui parle et dit ce qu'il doit dire, en son propre nom" (*BH* 60). The irony of this remark is that Roubaud insistently justifies authority in the narration by copying the construction of forms and comparing his work to received novelistic masterpieces; he therefore mocks his own practices in these remarks. In short, this feigned indignation levels the precise criticism (praise) against M. Mornacier that one could level against Roubaud ("ça promet pour la littérature"), making this metacommentary doubly ironic.

Roubaud also frequently refers to tradition negatively, by eschewing potential narrative techniques. For example, when the heroine drops in on her philosophy professor to ask for an extension on her thesis, her gaze occasions the following reflections: "Hortense en profita pour examiner attentivement la pièce (ce qui aurait pu être pour nous l'occasion d'une description perspicace et panoramique, mettant en évidence les traits essentiels du caractère des deux personnages, le regardant et le regardé, par le truchement d'un choix d'objet judicieux, mais nous nous refuserons cette facilité, dont nos prédécesseurs du XIXe siècle ont usé et abusé, transformant les apparences bourgeoises en autant de 'paysages moralisés')" (*BH* 165). Eschewed in the actual narrative, the "paysages moralisés" allude nonetheless to Roubaud's reliance on conventional novelistic encoding. A similar such allusion to nineteenth-century novels occurs when a dinner scene is portrayed as an avoidance of what it would have been if written by Zola (*BH* 106).

On other occasions, readers are invited to rethink the difficulties of establishing a coherent sense of time in the narration (*BH* 112): "Nous aurions beaucoup aimé pouvoir poser quelques questions à nos collègues à ce sujet; particulièrement à Alexandre Dumas; sauter d'un seul coup *vingt ans après*, quel tour de force!" (*BH* 85). Or we are simply referred to other novels for more details about particular events, like the effects of the storm that occurs before the denouement: "Toutes les fenêtres mal fermées claquèrent, les dégâts commencèrent sérieusement (*cf.* Victor Hugo et Conrad pour plus de détails)" (*BH* 172).

Throughout the story, novelistic convention plays so strong a role that the author shamefacedly admits to not knowing what is referred to in some of the conceits he employs: "Nous ignorons ce qu'est le rotin mais il y a toujours une chaise en rotin dans de telles circonstances romanesques" (*BH* 117). It is with irony that Roubaud imposes these novelistic codes on his "Auteur, Jacques Roubaud." Be they worn from overuse, discarded because outdated, or advertised as unavoidable or newfangled, narrative techniques are rendered explicit at every turn.

In one of the finest moments of the novel, Roubaud's author offers an apology for having put his inevitably gendered reader in the morally questionable position of the voyeur. Once the Poldevian prince has managed to seduce Hortense, she lies naked on her bed waiting for their love to be consummated (eloquently condensed in the phrase "et le chapitre s'acheva" [*BH* 141]). This occasion is seized to paint a portrait of the beautiful heroine: "Nous nous excusons du fait que ce portrait n'est pas présenté dans les conditions idéales, où le lecteur serait seul avec Hortense, et pourrait la contempler à loisir. Nous nous excusons, d'autre part, de mettre le lecteur dans une situation de voyeur, il n'y a rien à faire et de toute façon, si ce n'était pas le jeune homme en question, ce serait sans doute un autre, peut-être même pas jeune du tout, ce serait l'Auteur seul peut-être, et de toute façon nous serions en train de regarder ensemble cette belle jeune femme étendue, nue, sur son lit" (*BH* 138). As with many of the other metanarrative comments, the fictive author draws attention to his own limitations as a writer, emphasizing the degree to which the novelistic discourse itself exerts force on the shape and perspective of the story. In this case, Roubaud mockingly presents the construction of voyeurism–along with its gendering–as unavoidably constrained. The construction of sexual desire in *La belle Hortense* might therefore also be viewed as a reflection and recapitulation of conventional literary conceits. Moreover, Roubaud's construction of literary desire, both in terms of the relationship between reader and text and the narrative tensions that unfold between Hortense and her host of princes, reiterates Roubaud's reading of *fin' amors*.

In this respect, Roubaud's author persona effectively illustrates the constraints that Michel Foucault identifies as implicit in our cultural construction of the author: "The author does not precede the works; he is a certain functional principle by which one limits, excludes and chooses; in short, by which one impedes the free composition, decomposition, and recomposition of fiction."[21] He embodies, in *La belle Hortense*, as does each of the other narrative voices, the manner in which narration is driven by a compliance with, or a disregard for, the expectations of narrativity. Roubaud's "Auteur's" travesty of these narrative codes, his ludicrous insistence on his story's originality and his recursive recital of the predetermined authorial function, serve to mock the demystification of the text's formal constructs. That is, by postulating an authorial voice that both slyly and self-righteously recapitulates a culturally constructed "author," Roubaud employs metanarrative strategies to preempt the critic.

In short, a metadiscourse provides effective tools for narrativity to reflect on the similarities and differences in representations of reality and fiction. Roubaud's *La belle Hortense* deploys metanarrative games to further the novel's formal elaboration. The embedded constraint of the sestina plays the central role in this formal elaboration. Roubaud's parodic tone and continual reference to novelistic conventions plays with metanarrative conventions themselves, demonstrating the extent to which their interrogation of culturally con-

---

[21] Michel Foucault, "What Is an Author?," in *The Foucault Reader*, 118-19.

structed discursive actants, such as the "Author," "Narrator" and "Reader," is also subject to its own codification through tradition. Further developing a specifically Oulipian branch of metafiction, Roubaud's experiments with narrative prose enrich the novel tradition with formal and thematic concerns taken from other literary contexts, thereby expanding the field of metaliterary inquiry. His experiments with the novel, like much of his work on poetic traditions, prolong the question of the form's vitality, all the while providing new structures that accommodate a lively and enchanting sense of irony.

CHAPTER EIGHT

MEMORY, DESTRUCTION, AND PRESENCE:
RE-CREATION IN *LE GRAND INCENDIE DE LONDRES*

PERCIVAL Bartlebooth, the hero of Georges Perec's *La vie mode d'emploi* (1978), leads an exemplary life. Independently wealthy, he decides to spend ten years learning to paint, twenty years sailing the world painting five hundred watercolors, and twenty years assembling another five hundred jigsaw puzzles made from his paintings. Once reassembled, the watercolors are reconstituted, extracted from the puzzles, sent back to where they were painted, and destroyed in their waters of origin. In theory, Bartlebooth's lifework, and the industry of his helpers, will have left no trace. Each image will have been twice composed, and twice decomposed; yet, once completed, no evidence of the project will remain.

Bartlebooth's project is a radical one, painstaking in its demand for detail and quality, beautiful in its ultimate purposelessness, and extreme in its self-destruction. In effect, this hero's project may well be read as a work of art in itself, as a long performance piece: it is unerringly faithful to the principles of art for art's sake; it illustrates the rigors of creation under constraint; and it valorizes the *process* over the *product* of creation. In short, Bartlebooth's lifestyle and lifework, the centerpiece of Perec's novel, provide a compelling model of ascetic aestheticism.

At the end of Perec's novel, Bartlebooth's project ends in failure. After nearly twenty years of assembling the puzzles that Gaspard Winckler has prepared for him, the now blind Bartlebooth dies holding the last piece to his 439th puzzle: it bears the shape of a W, but the remaining blank calls for the shape of an X. Even as the epilogue traces the diaspora of the novel's other characters, the enigma of this final scene is left suspended, inspiring perhaps allegorical readings of the novel. This incompletion may also be read as exemplary, for Bartlebooth's demise forces us to reflect upon the relationship between the puzzle, the puzzle maker, and the puzzle solver, calling further into question the intentions of his and Perec's enterprise.

Twenty years after the publication of *La vie mode d'emploi*, Jacques Roubaud began publishing a novel cycle that recounts the ambition of another hero who has also embarked on a long aesthetic project. Like Perec's hero, Roubaud's main character fails to complete the project he had formulated in his youth. Unlike Perec's novel, however, Roubaud's novel *begins* with the declaration of failure, which becomes the occasion and condition for the novel *'le grand incendie de Londres'* (1989): "En traçant aujourd'hui sur le papier la première de ces lignes de prose (je les imagine nombreuses), je suis parfaitement conscient du fait que je porte un coup mortel, définitif, à ce qui, conçu au début de ma trentième année comme alternative à la disparition volontaire, a été pendant plus de vingt ans le projet de mon existence" (*GI* 7). Narrated in the first person, this pseudo-autobiographical novel recounts Jacques Roubaud's failure to complete his own self-imposed *Projet*, a project that is both deeply personal and profoundly engaged with the remembrance and innovation of literary traditions. As in *La vie mode d'emploi*, the rhetoric of failure here invites us to reread, analyze, and reconstruct the methods, means, and intentions of the original project. Roubaud's novel project is also peculiar in that in retelling the story of his lifelong *Projet*, he does not seek to recuperate what has failed, nor to complete what has been left undone. Rather he explicitly intends to destroy his *Projet*. This reflection on failure is therefore not so much an abandonment of the project, or a justification for its failure as it is an intentional ruining of the work. As I argue in this chapter, however, this initial rhetoric of failure quickly lays the groundwork for a dynamic economy of metafictional narration whose formal vitality serves to prolong, in an altered form, the poet's lifework.

The comparison between Jacques Roubaud's and Percival Bartlebooth's projects underlines the relationship between *'le grand incendie de Londres'* and Roubaud's original *Projet*. The most apparent difference between the two projects is that Bartlebooth's is purely confined to the world of fiction, whereas, in principle, Roubaud's project is real, at least in part, incorporating many of his publications since 1967. But this distinction becomes problematic when Roubaud describes the role *Le Grand Incendie de Londres* was supposed to play in the completed *Projet*. According to his original plan, the novel *Le Grand Incendie de Londres* (capitalized) was to become the crowning jewel of the project, a kind of autobiographical story of the form itself, "racontant le *Projet*, réel, comme s'il était fictif, donnant enfin à l'edifice du *Projet* un toit qui lui aurait assuré l'ombre nécessaire à sa protection esthétique" (*GI* 7). That is, in its first conceptual form, the novel would have fictionalized and safely circumscribed the otherwise disparate elements of Roubaud's literary research, borrowings, compositions, and inventions. And yet, his *'le grand incendie de Londres,'* spelled more modestly with lowercase letters and set within single quotation marks, is presented as a replacement for what *Le Grand Incendie de Londres* would have been.[1] That is, this novel is not openly presented as a stand-in for the first, but rather as a "récit de mémoire" that attempts to describe, explain, and distort what the original novel would and could have been. It is through the written exercise of remembrance and description, through a "mise en destruction" (*GI* 411) of the *Projet* and *Le Grand Incendie de Londres*, that Roubaud establishes the terms of *'le grand incendie de Londres.'*

Before looking more closely at the novels that have appeared in the cycle, I shall briefly reconsider the *Projet* and the role imagined for *Le Grand Incendie de Londres* therein. *Le Projet*, as Roubaud defines it, has developed around a central thesis–"*La poésie est mémoire de la langue*" (*M9* 23)–that he supports through a wide variety of literary activities. Although distinct in their approach, each activity contributes a discrete formal meaning to Roubaud's *Projet*. Work on this project, in other words, always concerns memory, literature, and their relationship to form. Each extant work in Roubaud's *Projet* demonstrates the central thesis from a different perspective.

The foreword to *'le grand incendie de Londres'* states that the original novel "aurait eu une place singulière dans la construction d'ensemble, distinct du *Projet* donnant enfin à l'édifice du *Projet* un toit" (*GI* 7). This structural metaphor places the idealized novel in a capital position, as a protective covering over all the other ele-

---

[1] In this chapter, the two novels–the actual publication (*'le grand incendie de Londres'*) and the novel it replaces (*Le Grand Incendie de Londres*)–are distinguished according to those spellings.

ments included in the *Projet*. Conceived as a "*biographie du projet*" (*M9* 79), the novel was intended to trace the life of the project, but *as if* it never existed, *as if* the *Projet* were in fact fictional. Fiction, in Roubaud's plan, is therefore viewed as more impervious to aesthetic decay than other forms of writing.

The idea and umbrella title of the novel may then have served Roubaud as a safety mechanism. No matter what was to come of the *Projet*, its internal contradictions and disparate parts would be resolved or hermeneutically contained in the potential novel called *Le Grand Incendie de Londres*. The project would, in any case, amount to a kind of accomplishment in that novel. From its inception, however, the success of the *Projet* was always questionable. As early as 1979 Roubaud admitted that his *Projet* "est à bien des égards utopiques" (*M9* 3), which implies that *completion* was already considered dubious, if not altogether undesirable. In short, the *Projet* and *Le Grand Incendie de Londres*, the two absent and abstract pretexts to the actual '*le grand incendie de Londres*,' were, from their inception, slated to fail. And this failure would be double: "*Le Grand Incendie de Londres* n'a pas été écrit parce que le *Projet* a échoué, parce qu'il ne pouvait qu'échouer" (*GI* 8).

Given the programmed incompletion of the *Projet*, the rhetoric of failure with which Roubaud opens '*le grand incendie de Londres*' must be read carefully. The gesture of destroying the project and planned novel–"je porte un coup mortel [au] projet de mon existence" (*GI* 7)–in order to write about what it could have been might effectively be a way of recasting the virtual novel and the *Projet* in a real world of fiction. In this model, there would be two books, read simultaneously: the virtual *Le Grand Incendie de Londres*, read through its replacement, its counterfeit shadow-version: '*le grand incendie de Londres*.' The formal construction of the novel, as I will demonstrate, supports and encourages this reading strategy. The actual novel is organized in such a fashion that the abolished novel ends where the concrete one begins, and the concrete one ends where the abolished one begins.

A primary narrative condition for this implied duplicity–constructed like a palindrome–is that one novel is created *at the same time* that the other one is destroyed.[2] To maintain the formal imma-

---

[2] A palindrome is "a written locution that reads the same backward or forward" (Motte, *Oulipo*, 200). The notion of the palindrome reappears in different

nence of *'le grand incendie de Londres'* Roubaud composes his novel under a set of disclosed constraints (there are hidden constraints as well). The declared constraints set the genesis of the novel in what might be best understood as an absolute present where the temporality of writing and reading directly coincide. Linearity is articulated through the concatenation of "moments de prose," each composed under three conditions: a) that they not follow a preestablished narrative plan; b) that they recount what they recount truthfully; and c) that they not undergo revision or rewriting. In these moments of prose, Roubaud openly reflects on the conditions of both his failed and his current writing projects, thereby casting his narrative in a subgenre of metafiction.

A self-begetting novel takes as its central plot line its own genesis as novel.[3] In some cases that process takes on a decidedly mysterious character. Roubaud emphasizes this aspect of his narration by repeatedly suggesting that his is a *roman à thèse* (GI 178), only then to draw a blank over what that thesis would be: "*'le grand incendie de Londres'* sera .. .." (GI 29). This blank is presented as a necessary narrative condition in the novel (GI 183), for it opens and continually re-poses the question of the novel's form and, by extension, its formal meaning. Once Roubaud completes and publishes the six projected volumes of *'le grand incendie de Londres,'* the fundamental question that will have to have been addressed is to what

---

forms. There are moments when the narrator discusses the structure of the palindrome (GI 169-71) and moments where an experience is described as palindromic, as in this return leg of a bus trip: "Je relis le même paysage qu'à l'aller, palindromiquement" (GI 243). The palindrome also appears in the numerical structure of the text. One example of palindromic numbers is prominent in the date April 21, 1983. That date marks the 1,178th day since Alix Cléo's death, a number of particular importance since Roubaud and Alix had known each other exactly 1,178 days (GI 365-66). Finally, the palindrome is emblazoned in the presentation of the work's foundational "assertions" in the chapter "Rêve, décision, 'Projet.'" In that chapter, the ninety-nine "assertions" (theoretical principles intended to apply to Le Grand Incendie de Londres) are presented twice, first in their reverse order (from 99 to 1), separated by ample commentary, and then in their sequential order (from 1 to 99 [the 31st assertion is missing]). The palindrome serves as metaphor for the activity of recollecting in reverse, beginning with the most recent event and going backward from there. Moreover, the palindrome also describes how the descriptive, analytical, real novel (*'le grand incendie de Londres'*) retraces events and activities of its virtual, fictional counterpart (Le Grand Incendie de Londres)–this distinction becomes massively salient in the text's tendencies toward digression and bifurcation.

[3] The term "self-begetting novel" was coined by Stephen G. Kellman in *The Self-Begetting Novel*. De Ferrari makes excellent use of this figure in her reading of *'le grand incendie de Londres.'*

degree the actual novel effectively replaces (or provides for) what Roubaud hoped it would have been; or, to what degree it accounts for the *Projet*'s ruin.[4] The modulation in temporality, from the past conditional to the future anterior, made in moments of the absolute present, articulates both the process of the hero's sentimental education in the novel and the condition of the novel's genesis.

Like the Hortense novels, *'le grand incendie de Londres'* was conceived as a six-volume prose cycle. To date, Roubaud has published five installments of *'le grand incendie de Londres'*: *Destruction* (1989), *La boucle* (1993) *Mathématique: (récit)* (1997), *Poésie: (récit)* (2000), and *La bibliothèque de Warburg (version mixte)* (2002).[5] The entire prose work also bears a descriptive subtitle: *Récit, avec incises et bifurcations*. Accordingly, each volume is divided into three main parts. In principle, the first is a series of chapters–six in the first two volumes, four in the third, fourteen in the fourth, seven in the fifth–composed of a determined number of short narrated fragments.[6] Next, there are numbered series of *incises* or short digressions directly related to something said in one of the numbered prose moments; these are brief explications grafted to the main story, supplements that complement but do not return to the principal

---

[4] Although this question subtends the entirety of Roubaud's novel, its outcome, along with the hidden constraints of the novel, may not fully come to light until the entire six novels are published. And even then, its illumination, like Perec's novel, may pose other enigmas. My chapter *begins* uncovering some of the reading strategies inscribed in the first volumes of novel cycle. Important changes in form, style, and tone mark a strong evolution in the means of production used in the five first volumes. I do not attempt to exhaustively discuss those changes here. Instead, I discuss the novel's early construction, how it predicates its own (future) genesis, and how it illustrates aspects of Roubaud's evolving poetics.

[5] The first volume bears the title of the entire prose cycle as well as the subtitle, *Destruction*. For the sake of clarity, I refer to the first volume as *GI*. The other volumes are abbreviated in my text as *B*, *M:*, *P:*, and *BW*, respectively.

[6] The foreshortened volume four indicates a continued poetics of incompletion in Roubaud's project. And yet, as this parenthetical remark indicates, changes in the work's structure are not always intentional: "(Ajouté en 1995: Je signalerai enfin que, pour des raisons indépendantes de ma volonté un blocage insurmontable de plus d'une année, le présent volume ne représente que la première partie de cette troisième branche)" (*M:* 42). In addition, in branches four and five, *M:* and *BW*, Roubaud has initiated other changes in the format and regiment of writing, some of which have been forced upon Roubaud out of editorial concerns. These changes point to a poetics of distortion, a means of representing the irreversible drift in his memory-scape, as well as a more simple phenomenon: as the artist and his world evolve, so do his works, and their means of production; one goal of *'le grand incendie de Londres'* is to provide a record of those changes.

narrative.[7] Last, there are additional series of numbered narrative fragments called *bifurcations*. These provide alternative narrative trajectories that deviate significantly from the direction of the central narrative. Unlike the incises, the bifurcations elucidate and alter events or narrative conditions established in the chapters. In this respect, they can double back on what has already been written with a transformative effect (B 509-10), exposing what has already been written in a new light. In addition to these incisions and bifurcations, this prose includes an abundance of reflexive parenthetical remarks, often justifying narrative choices.

These various forms of narrative interruptions and digressions –fundamental conditions of every volume or branch of this extended prose work–are consequences of the first disclosed constraints: to write an account of the failed project without following a predetermined structure–"je me refuse la distance protectrice d'une construction réfléchie" (*GI* 30)–and without editing the text once it has been written. These initial constraints reflect Roubaud's commitment to avoiding the traps that had foiled his previous attempts in writing *Le Grand Incendie de Londres*. They are designed, in other words, to encourage a continuous production of the text. Roubaud states that continuous production serves as a therapeutic means of writing through a double anxiety: the anxiety over not being able to advance in his novel project and, in the early stages, the personal anguish related to his wife's early death. Writing alone assuages Roubaud's disquietude: "Et j'écris seulement pour poursuivre, pour échapper à l'angoisse qui m'attend dès que je m'interromps, dès que je suspends leur progression incertaine et maladroite, pour que ce recommencement, après tant d'inquiétude et de paralysie, ne soit pas à son tour un simple faux départ de l'entreprise de prose à laquelle je m'efforce, vainement, depuis tant d'années" (*GI* 13). The textual insertions provide a means of negotiating the demands of continuous production; they reflect the necessity of writing through the anguish of loss and unfulfilled potential.

Committed to not reworking the narrative as he writes it, Roubaud opts to add changes and digressions in subsequent moments of prose. This decision is made clear in the narration, and it

---

[7] In Roubaud's words, "Les 'incises' sont des insertions locales qui se terminent en impasse (on ne va pas plus loin)." Roubaud (1995), "Nécessité et condition," in *Littérature et informatique*, 293-300; hereafter cited as *LI*.

contributes to the variety of metaliterary commentary generating the work: "En avançant dans la prose je rencontre, presque à chaque pas, l'impossibilité de la maintenir sur une ligne unique, de la diriger dans un seul sens. A tout moment j'éprouve, comme quand on raconte, en vrai, pour quelqu'un, et d'autant plus si on raconte (comme c'est le cas ici) à quelqu'un d'éloigné, que beaucoup de noms ou de circonstances risquent de surprendre (et il est nécessaire alors de les rapprocher de lui par une explication, sous peine de n'être pas compris), j'ai besoin, donc, d'expliquer, de m'arrêter pour accrocher, au fil ténu de la narration, la lampe d'un éclaircissement indispensable" (*GI* 33). At first, the insertions serve to reveal the choices normally concealed in constructing a story "en vrai": "je n'ai pas voulu dissimuler qu'il y a eu choix" (*GI* 36). This choice privileges the process of the novel's production over its completion as aesthetic object.

As the body of the work develops, however, the insertions begin to play an important role in accomplishing the destructive goals of the first volume. Roubaud adopts Alix Cléo's axiom "*raconter un projet l'annule*" (*GI* 32) as a means of exposing, describing, and dissolving his memories. The insertions thus explore and exhaust every possible narrative divergence that presents itself to the writer/narrator: "J'ai décidé que toutes ces branches, routes, rivières, sentiers d'os, nervures du récit, je les parcourrais, mais à mon pas de prose narrative accompagnant le marcheur" (*GI* 35). In his exhaustive enterprise, Roubaud attempts to describe each aspect of the *Projet* objectively, truthfully, and by touching upon them he claims to nullify them. Echoing Mallarmé's remarks on the ends of versification, one might even say that through description "il a touché au Projet."

Imitating Chrétien de Troyes's *Lancelot en prose,* Roubaud classifies his prose work as an "arborescent prose," a term employed by other members of the Oulipo.[8] The term designates a narrative form that includes digressive and combinatoric divergences in the normally rectilinear progression of narration. In '*le grand incendie de Londres,*' Roubaud evokes a visual image to represent the "arborescent form" of his novel. He imagines that each branch of '*le*

---

[8] See Le Lionnais, "Une nouvelle policière en arbre"; Raymond Queneau, "Un conte à votre façon"; Paul Fournel and J.-P. Enard, "L'arbre à théâtre" (*LP* 272-80).

grand incendie de Londres' could be manually copied onto a very large piece of paper, each in a single black line (in which the chapter segments would be separated by a visible blank). Each corresponding insertion would then be written in a different color, such that it branched off from its segment of origin. The resulting image would be one large treelike structure with six primary "branches," representing each of the intended volumes of *Le Grand Incendie de Londres*; and from each of those primary branches would extend smaller branches, sometimes digressive, sometimes crossing again the main narrative.[9] In this system of writing, the reader is free to choose a preferred reading trajectory–"j'imagine un lecteur devant ce 'grand incendie de Londres' mural. Je le vois choisir un itinéraire de lecture, s'approcher" (*GI* 40)–and even encouraged, the first time around, to omit the insertions (*B* 253).

Roubaud first begins using arborescent sequences in *Graal théâtre* (1977) and *Graal fiction* (1978), directly linking his versions of memory prose to Arthurian romances.[10] These medieval tales are key pretexts, for, in Roubaud's reading, they constitute a literary moment whose cultural, historic, and stylistic unity complement the coherence of the trobar, but in a prose form (*FI* 63). For Roubaud, a literary tradition's durability relies on the indissociable interweaving of texts, an *entrelacement*, which in turn provides a vital field of memory. The use of insertions in *'le grand incendie de Londres'* imitates the intertextuality that Roubaud values in both the troubadour tradition and medieval Arthurian romances, but crafted with Oulipian constraints: "Le roman aurait donc été comme un croisement de *Lancelot en prose* (le modèle médiéval d'une prose de l'entrelacement) et de roman oulipien" (*GI* 202). That is, the system of insertions grafted to Roubaud's main story establishes a matrix of short texts that constitute elements of the same body of literature. The temporality of this prose is modeled after the intertextuality of Arthurian romances and its troubadour equivalent: "La prose de la mémoire, cette 'sparterie' (comme l'a écrit autrefois Ferdinand Lot dans son *Etude sur le 'Lancelot en prose'*) tiendrait chacun de ses fils coprésents d'une manière absolue" (*GI* 222). The internal weaving of the novel is therefore intended to produce a "prose de la mé-

---

[9] A depiction of the arborescent structure of *La boucle* can be viewed in Consenstein, "Memory and Oulipian Constraint," 19.

[10] Roubaud and Delay (1977), *Graal théâtre*; Roubaud (1978), *Graal fiction*.

moire," a prose in which diegetic time is split three ways among an absolute present tense of the description, a past perfect tense of the described, and a future anterior tense of the work under construction or *le livre à venir*. To better understand these temporalities and how they affect textual memory in *'le grand incendie de Londres,'* a more detailed account of the descriptive modality in the moments of prose is necessary.

Each moment of prose in *'le grand incendie de Londres'* is numbered, purportedly in its order of composition. As such, they present a journalistic log of the work's genesis. Roubaud qualifies the practice of separating and numbering each narrative fragment of the book as "des procédés tout à fait ordinaires de fragmentation d'un texte," adding that "il n'y a rien à en dire de particulier" (*GI* 280). This last remark may appear disingenuous, for this numerical sequence provides the most linear sense of the work's progression, and it is through the numbered paragraphs that readers most easily orient a reading of the insertions. Moreover, since some numbers are loaded with meaning in Roubaud's poetic practices, they also exert an influence on what is said in their corresponding numbered fragment–not to mention the fact that in the later branches of this prose Roubaud assiduously accounts for the number of lines in each moment of prose, and its subsequent subdivisions (see *BW*). However, the accumulative progression practiced in the first volumes relates solely to the concatenation of isolated fragments and not necessarily to a linear progression in narrative time. In fact, throughout the composition of *'le grand incendie de Londres,'* each descriptive moment is set in the present tense of its own composition, thereby simultaneously providing a record of its writing and, in an anterior mode, a record of what is recollected through the description. As a first requirement, then, the moments of prose are intended to provide a record of the experience of recollecting and writing down the memory of *Le Grand Incendie de Londres*, the absent but still potential story of the *Projet* that could have been. In short, Roubaud records his process of recollection: "Je voudrais, en somme, conserver quasi immuables les conditions d'une expérience le plus possible quotidienne de prose; que le lieu en soit presque invariable, le temps fixe; que les signes que j'écris, et qui s'ajoutent, se poussent l'un l'autre dans mon cahier, s'arrêtent sur cette image de quasi-permanence, soient comme tracés en elle, enfermés entres ses bords. Et j'essaierai de le faire apparaître, chemin faisant, par la description" (*GI* 14-15). The moments of prose are therefore intended to describe and affix the time and place of their composition, drawing the reader into the writer's "chambre (*stanza*) verbale" (*GI* 44).

Roubaud underlines the metanarrative status of description by focusing on the daily, concrete experience of writing. These include descriptions of the place of writing (his apartments), as well as the mode of inscription. Initially written by hand, using pens of four different colors, Roubaud then composes the work on a Macintosh computer, which provides for complications in the typographic presentation of the storytelling (*B, M:, P:, BW*).[11]

The temporality of these moments is therefore highly constructed: "Chaque *moment de prose* est aussi 'moment' en cela; il a l'immobilité concentrée et 'oisive' (comme dit Wittgenstein) d'une *piction* (ce mot-valise, fait de l'anglais 'picture' et de 'fiction,' s'oppose à *image*). Il ne bouge pas" (*GI* 281). This immobility, however, relates only to the placement of the fragments, for the events that they describe often take place much earlier or later along the continuum of chronological time, not unlike the effect of rhyme words or familiar rhythms in poetry. This highly structured and exquisitely dynamic temporality, quite different from that of a classical serial novel, challenges conventional modes of storytelling. Instead of building on what has already been said, this narrative pursues its yarn by constantly starting afresh. In fact, in the first three branches of the novel, key moments of prose explicitly restate their status as a new departure (*recommencements*) in the process of recollection.

These continual beginnings reflect the state of immanence characteristic of the self-begetting novel, for its textual terms are created and recreated in every new moment of prose. To the extent that each moment is a short text unto itself a *petit récit* or a kind of lyrical reminiscence about the failed project, the text imi-

---

[11] Those modes of production change again in the fourth and fifth branches. Beginning with *Poésie:* through *La bibliothèque de Warburg*, during the process of composition, Roubaud counts each print line in every moment, making explicit a numbering process that may also inhabit the first volumes. In the recent versions (*BW*), currently published in altered and fragmented forms, the presentation includes five colors and five levels of indentation that structure digression in a fashion that is unaccounted for in the first three branches. These changes in presentation help distort and transform (access to) the field of memory written into *'le grand incendie de Londres.'* Moreover, as Roubaud's early handwritten manuscripts indicate, the system of colors and indentation may have already been present in the earliest stages of composition.

tates a poetic collection in which readers may find a new beginning with each new poem. "Ces bonds continuels dans mon livre que représen-tent virtuellement les *bifurcations*, les *incises*, toutes les espèces du genre *insertion*, sont l'équivalent d'un des privilèges absolus de la lecture: pouvoir en ouvrant un livre, être aussitôt n'importe où (privilège qui, dans la pratique, est surtout utilisé par le lecteur de poésie, beaucoup moins par le lecteur de romans)" (*GI* 48). A coherence in the experience of writing and reading might be seen as separate from narrative linearity. Formal unity here also becomes a function of tone and style, both of which vary from moment to moment, the way tone and style vary in synthetic poetry anthologies or architectural sonnet cycles.[12] Instead of progressing in a single line from beginning to end, the narrative process of *'le grand incendie de Londres'* functions more like *un recueil*, in which self-reflexive meditation is captured in isolated moments of prose. Yet, as the conditions of the novel's composition change with each new fragment (and the conditions of each new branch), reading for plot forces one to retrace the experience of writing at the same rate and in the same order of composition. Consequently, as they are thematized in the work, writing and reading are organized according to a constant present tense of description: "Et j'essaierai de le faire apparaître, chemin faisant, par la description" (*GI* 14-15). Roubaud calls this present tense of writing and reading a reflection of the "real time" of his narrative. "Le temps de la narration, dans cette branche première, est *vrai*. Je vous présente, et vous lisez (selon votre propre présent), en ce moment même des pages qui sont disposées exactement selon la succession des instants de leur écriture, et j'y raconte aussi comment je raconte ce que vous lisez" (*GI* 49). The real time of the text therefore coincides with moments of being where Roubaud describes both the failed *Projet* and how he undertakes its narration.

---

[12] *Le Grand Incendie de Londres* was to include a fixed set of poetic styles. Roubaud invents these ten styles by borrowing and adapting poetic terms from Kamo no Chomei, a thirteenth-century Japanese poet (see *GI* 216-19). Further research into these stylistic configurations may provide evidence of a weave, or internal rhythmic architecture, based on the recurrence of these styles. But determining how to mark such idiosyncratic styles poses formidable challenges, for elements of literary style are far more subjective than, for example, the more objectively isolated syntagmata of language.

An example from the first branch will help illustrate how this mode of temporality is constructed. Chapter five, "Rêve, décision, 'Projet'," states that the initial idea for the *Projet* and *Le Grand Incendie de Londres* came to Roubaud in a dream in 1961; he reproduces written accounts of the dream, all the while describing the transformative effect that the inscription of the dream had on both the memory of the dream and the experience of remembering the dream: "En posant le rêve, je le fais s'évanouir, comme tout rêve: mais d'un évanouissement particulier, puisque le rêve est déjà évanoui, comme tout rêve, et depuis longtemps (dix-neuf ans). Ce qui s'évanouit maintenant (je parle du "maintenant" qu'est la disposition du rêve sur le papier) n'est pas le rêve, mais son souvenir. Car le souvenir, lui aussi, une fois posé, s'évanouit. Il s'évanouit, sans doute, parce que souvenir du rêve. Mais il s'évanouit aussi parce que, je le crois, tout souvenir raconté ou écrit s'évanouit. Il ne peut plus demeurer que le souvenir de sa déposition, de sa trace devenue noire" (*GI* 154). Written in the present tense, this description addresses what "le *texte* du rêve" (*GI* 150) does, rather than what it says. Symbolism in the dream is categorically downplayed. Instead it is the dream's formal inaccessibility, and the effect of its destruction once written, that engenders further commentary. Moreover, the fragment relates the dream's inscription as if it were part of the same moment of prose, as if it were written simultaneously: "En posant le rêve je parle du 'maintenant' qu'est la disposition du rêve sur le papier." However, the "text of the dream" first appears in the previous moment of prose (written three days earlier) and was originally written in 1980. Yet, Roubaud's intention is that every moment of prose in his novel share the same absolute present, a present tense contained within the confines of his book, a present tense dedicated to the description, elucidation, and destruction of memory.

Modeled after his readings of Arthurian romances and the trobar, Roubaud interlaces the varying moments of his text. The moment of composition becomes enmeshed with the moment remembered, which, in turn, is said to determine what the work will become in a future moment (alluding in part to the work's reception, but also, in the interim, to the mutation of the work's formal rules from volume to volume). The three temporalities are intended to remain distinct in their interlacing. The project is attenuated through description in the past perfect tense. Writing and reading moments in *'le grand incendie de Londres'* take place in a textual present tense. The completion of the work, what it will have become once it is finished, is postponed through a future anterior tense, a projection formulated in the repeated programmatic phrase "*'le grand incendie de Londres'* est .. .." Like the intertwined narratives found in *Lancelot en prose*, the fragments of *'le grand incendie de Londres'* are cast as a "prose de la mémoire" in which each narrative moment is made accessible in an absolute present of writing each recollection.

This absolute present is problematic in that changes take place in the course of the text's composition. That is, along the way, Roubaud decides to alter the conditions of composition, thereby marking various temporal stages in the text's genesis. For example, in *La boucle* he adopts new kinds of insertions (*les entre-deux-branches*) and in *Poésie:* the number of chapters, and each of their elements, is assiduously measured–frequently pointing to the numerical structures of the sonnet and Roubaud's initial engagement with that form. Other similar changes take place through the practice of inscribing memories. In many of the remembered scenes, for instance Roubaud uncovers embedded memories that are made accessible through the exercise of writing. That is to say, each present moment of composition also becomes a moment of potential revelation. *La boucle* is particularly rich with layers of intentional remembering. In that branch, Roubaud revisits key childhood memories that he figures as *images-mémoires*–like the opening image of a frosty windowpane, reminiscent of crystals–as well as old photographs (which he terms *pictions* because of their ability to engender memories).[13]

These "memory-images" often undermine or over-elaborate preestablished sequences in the narration, frequently contradicting chronology. The image of the frosty windowpane, for example, is strongly associated with Raimbaut d'Orange's poem "La fleur in-

---

[13] Roubaud makes explicit that even though these memory images appear after his description of the *Projet* in the text's first branch, they are intended as anterior to the récit. It is the translation in their status, from "souvenir" to "mémoire," that is depicted as simultaneous to other moments in *'le grand incendie de Londres'*: "Je maintiendrai ceci seulement: toutes les images constitutives de cette branche, des **images-souvenirs** devenant des **images-mémoire** du fait même de leur insertion dans la continuité constructive de la narration, sont situées dans un passé antérieur au triple constitué du *rêve*, de la *décision* et du **Projet** qui est au centre de la première branche" (*B* 509).

verse" and the sestina as "crystal du trobar," thereby effecting resonances throughout Roubaud's work and the *Projet*. These resonances rhetorically preclude a narrative or temporal sequence other than the mobile present of each moment of prose. They elaborate a system of echoes that is simultaneous in 'le grand incendie de Londres' and, by extension, in Roubaud's oeuvre as a whole. The resulting slippage between the present moments of prose reflects a key goal of Roubaud's narrative: to depict the temporal displacement of the central narrative voice to thereby cast self-portraiture as unavoidably ephemeral. Roubaud explains by stating that he wants to play temporal contradictions against his narrator's voice. "La coexistence de présents aussi incompatibles que péremptoires (tout présent, je l'ai dit, est péremptoire, c'est sa jeunesse) dans 'le grand incendie de Londres' achevé sera (serait), je crois, une différence réelle (sans valeur particulière mais réelle) avec les principales variétés de romans réellement existants, et donnera sans doute naissance à quelques paradoxes narratifs que je voudrais apprendre à faire jouer, contre la monotonie inévitable de ma voix" (*GI* 48). By playing the present of one moment against the present of another moment, Roubaud's text "devrait avoir des effets sur la mémoire du lecteur," effects that would mirror the manner in which the inscription of memories affects the *Projet:* the "destruction" of what *Le Grand Incendie de Londres* would have been.

The narrative paradoxes in the novel's fragments are not explicitly aimed at frustrating the novel's reception: "Le jeu ne devrait pas, dans ces conditions, être générateur de contradictions senties comme embarrassantes" (*GI* 49). On the contrary, Roubaud presents them in such a fashion that tracing the dissolution of memories thematically organizes the concatenation of the individual prose moments. That is, the narrative conditions that thematize remembrance and the attenuation of the *Projet* are openly presented as a textual game inseparable from the novel's form: "Ce ne sont, en définitive, que des conditions personnelles de fonctionnement dans un *jeu de langage*, auquel vous êtes convivé, et qui dépendent en grande partie des circonstances même de la mise en route du récit" (*GI* 49). One wonders, however, if Roubaud foresees the progressively shifting interrelation between the moments as stable upon the completion the work, or–and this is far more likely given the shifting conditions of production–if the memory-effect on the author will be something closer to a progressive distortion, a blurring of distinctions, and, if his readers will experience an inverse effect, that of a deeper clarity and perception of to how all the pieces of the *Projet* hold together.

Early readings of '*le grand incendie de Londres*' respond directly to this thematizing of memory and destruction in Roubaud's prose moments. Guillermina De Ferrari, for example, observes that "the constant deconstruction of the *roman de mémoire* by the self-begetting novel can be read as the principal constraint in '*le grand incendie de Londres*'" (262). While, in my view, De Ferrari eloquently and judiciously retraces Roubaud's strategies in '*le grand incendie de Londres*,' her use of the term constraint does not strictly correspond to the Oulipian notion.[14] Rather, in '*le grand incendie de Londres*' there are sets of constraints that, when textually realized, engender the de(con)struction of both the novel and the memories it recounts; the self-de(con)struction of the novel is not, strictly speaking, a form of constraint; it is an effect engendered through Roubaud's use of constraint.

Other readings have also focused on the effects of Roubaud's formal memory.[15] Elizabeth Cardonne-Arlyck has responded to his *jeu de langage*, remarking that "[l]a mémoire devient dans le récit où elle se fixe le double d'elle-même, son propre reflet, la marque de son annulation" (93). Cardonne-Arlyck argues that the mirroring effect established in shuttling between moments of prose, between what the work could have been and what the work will have become, remains an operative modality of reading '*le grand incendie de Londres*.' Through its object (*Projet*) and its self-reflexive mode of composition, the *roman de mémoire* simultaneously destroys and constructs an absent but immanently potential literary work. The dissolution of memories, in other terms, leaves a ruin of the *Projet*,

---

[14] To draw a distinction between the text's conscious and unconscious levels, De Ferrari cites two forms of constraints: those that are revealed and those that are hidden in the text's composition. If Roubaud dissimulates the use of certain constraints in his novel, his choice to do so is explicit and volitional, especially in the fifth branch. In this sense, the concealed constraints do not belong to an unconscious layering of the text for Roubaud. To the contrary, their practice and the silence that surrounds them is entirely volitional, as is the practice of setting in false constraints and the misleading appearances of constraints. Here too Roubaud is further elaborating the boundaries of Oulipian clinamen. See Motte, "Raymond Queneau," 193-209.

[15] Cardonne-Arlyck, "Poésie, forme de vie," 89-101; Barberger, "*La boucle*," 91-100; Samoyault, "Autobiographie," 101-14.

a written trace from which the project's history may be inferred, if not eventually recuperated. Each memory's destruction provides a testament of *Le Grand Incendie de Londres*, bearing witness to a life practice that Roubaud calls *une forme de vie*. It is in the degree to which *'le grand incendie de Londres'* represents the *Projet* as a form of life that Roubaud succeeds in contextualizing the shifting vitality of his memory.

In choosing to classify his work as *récit*, Roubaud challenges the normative genres to which his work belongs: "J'essaye, on le voit, de maintenir à mon livre ce que j'imagine être une certaine originalité, au moins classificatoire" (*B* 285). In addition to labeling his writing a "prose de la mémoire" or "un traité de la mémoire à l'imitation d'un roman" (*GI* 100), Roubaud makes clear what is *not* intended: "Il ne s'agit pas, à l'évidence, d'un roman, ni d'un conte, ni d'un essai" (*B* 285), adding elsewhere that "la situation différentielle" implicit in writing the text precludes its being "poésie" (*GI* 309). However, the one literary genre that most closely resembles *'le grand incendie de Londres'* remains the autobiography, and Roubaud reluctantly recognizes this possible classification: "Ecarter l'hypothèse d'une aspiration par le genre de l'autobiographie semble plus difficile" (*B* 285). Not surprisingly, most studies of the novel have reflected on this approximation: "In Roubaud's novel, the borderline between fiction and reality is blurred to the point where the possibility to consider it an autobiographical novel cannot be discarded."[16]

Perhaps best characterized as a programmatic self-portraiture, all the narrative material in *'le grand incendie de Londres'* is of an autobiographical nature. In the chapter "Portrait de l'artiste absent," we learn a series of facts about the narrator: his self-consciousness about being tall (*GI* 122), his shaving habits (*GI* 129), his love of swimming (*GI* 135) and counting (*GI* 138), and his ludic self-identification as "*Homo lisens* (si j'ose ce barbarisme franco-latin)," a man defined by his reading activities (*GI* 141). *La boucle* and *Mathématique:* reveal other biographical anecdotes–such as his father's struggle against the German Occupation (*B* 74-82), or that Roubaud was near ground zero during the first French nuclear bomb tests (*M:* 221-52). Similarly, in *Poésie:* he recounts in detail his sonnet mania, and in *La bibliothèque de Warburg* he takes read-

---

[16] De Ferrari, 264.

ers on two memorable walks, the first down the Mississippi and the second through the countryside on the Isle of Skye. And, granted that the dominant narrated topics are distinctly related to all of Roubaud's work, his *Projet*, its ruin, what has taken its place, and the relations that may exist among them, readers will reconstruct his self-portrait in the shifting frames provided by the works.

Consequently, Roubaud obstinately rejects qualifying his work as pure autobiography, citing two reasons: first, out of an unapologetic distaste for autobiographical writing, he flatly condemns the genre; second, he claims the textual economy of his book, and its relation to his other writing, undermines the false transparency inevitable in conventional autobiographies. He couches his disregard for autobiography in terms of its implausibility: "Je placerai [le récit autobiographique] sur une échelle d'invraisemblance, à la même hauteur que le roman historique, et presque aussi haut que la 'science-fiction'" (*B* 17). Autobiographical writers tend to fall into two traps that Roubaud claims to avoid in '*le grand incendie de Londres*,' insincerity and dissimulation: "Je me situe, de ce point de vue, dans une position intermédiaire entre le roman de transposition et l'autobiographie, qui ne transpose, n'invente, n'imagine qu'involontairement (et je tiens compte aussi de tous les 'faux' possibles: l'insincérité d'un côté et le déguisement de l'autre)" (*GI* 363). Granted, these claims and others like them directly appeal to the reader's willing suspension of disbelief. It is this bold openness that lends rhetorical force to Roubaud's disavowal of verisimilitude. Extending this eschewal of authenticity, Roubaud foregrounds an "axiom of veracity," supported by the real time of exegesis. Accordingly, his narrative claims to recount "naively" and "sincerely" the past without privileging illusions of veracity.

This axiom of truth-telling differs rhetorically from conventional autobiographies in that here truth value is limited to the boundaries of the work itself and posits no viable relationship to empirical truth: "Ce que je viens d'écrire n'aspire à aucune pertinence physiologique, neurologique, psychologique, cognitive, ou philosophique. Les choses qui s'y disent sont dites au présent du récit, à mesure que le récit avance. Elles n'en sont pas détachables, elles ne peuvent en aucune façon prétendre au statut de vérités" (*B* 17-18). Moreover, the extent to which the rule of veridicality is obeyed in the text becomes an explicit condition in the authorial contract: "(Je désigne par 'exigence de véracité' la maxime impérieuse qui gouverne mon attitude à l'égard de mon propre récit. Mon récit affirme, lui, sa *véridicité*. La véridicité est un des axiomes de la narration. La maxime et l'axiome ne doivent pas être confondus; la déclaration de l'axiome vaut ce que valent toutes les déclarations de ce genre, autrement dit uniquement le crédit que voudra bien lui accorder le lecteur; la maxime vaut pour moi seul et, de nouveau, le lecteur qui la rencontre peut ou non me faire confiance sur ce point)" (*M:* 111). Veracity in Roubaud's récit is purely formulated in terms of the economy of a self-begetting literary text and relies, in principle, on the reader's suspension of disbelief. In themselves, these declarations of truth-telling establish the internal economy of the text, but the actual truth value of that economy–whether or not each moment is written on the stated date, or if Roubaud actually follows the rituals he describes, or whether or not he recounts events exactly as he remembers them–is not in question. The legitimacy of the text's truth quotient is discursively ratified by the very conditions put forth in its composition. The descriptions of each moment are presented *as if* the genesis of the work were infallible, but its truth-value is circumscribed by its status as fiction, as traces of memory. Consequently, any coincidence between actual writing and fictional writing (if it were verifiable) would only demonstrate an overlapping of two possible worlds, the real world and the world(s) of fiction.

In effect, this self-legitimating economy of truth cunningly reflects the strategies underlying Roubaud's "original" *Le Grand Incendie de Londres*: "Racontant le *Projet*, réel, comme s'il était fictif, donnant enfin à l'édifice du *Projet* un toit qui lui aurait assuré l'ombre nécessaire à sa protection esthétique" (*GI* 7). It is this conflation of fiction and reality that leads De Ferrari to remark that "the choice of a self-begetting novel as a frame for a *roman de mémoire* is very appropriate: the delineation of a border between fiction and reality is a dialogical, arbitrary decision that need not be made" (272). Given the independent status of the self-begetting and self-legitimating text, Roubaud suggests that the autobiographical elements provide the text with an independent identity, as if it were written about the potential life of a nonexistent work or about (a) nobody: "S'il y a autobiographie, il s'agit d'une (auto)biographie du **Projet** et de son **double, Le Grand Incendie de Londres**, et par conséquent, dans une large mesure, d'une *autobiographie de personne*" (*B* 285). This narrative play of mirrors suggests the absence of the artist whose existence or identity is figured as accessory to the history of the *Projet* and to the life of its forms.

The self-perpetuating logic of this metanarrative relegates the real *Projet* and its author to a secondary role in the work's generative process. It is not the past of the *Projet* nor the childhood memories of its writer that determine textual production–they operate instead as mnemonic effects fueling the fires of description, dissolution, and destruction. Rather, textual production is animated by the book's elided programmatic phrase, whose mystery both obscures and ensures the text's meaning: "L'aspect biographique est entièrement subordonné à un autre qui gouverne lui, chaque page et ligne et lettre du livre, est inscrit dans chacun de ses volumes comme la figure dans le tapis, choisissant chaque mot, plaçant chaque virgule, mettant le point sur chacun des *i*, et résulte d'un principe de conformité à une définition annoncée et toujours non dite: **'le grand incendie de Londres' est .. ..**" (*B* 285). Repetitively positing this thesis under erasure structures the relationship between narrator and narratee. In effect, Roubaud promises his readers that in its final pages this long, arduous narrative odyssey will (have) fulfill(ed) its raison d'être and will therewith satisfy or further engage the reader's curiosity. Hence, the silence surrounding the novel's definition casts the narrative contract in terms of a gamble.

The intrigue–and indeed the risk–of this gamble rests in that Roubaud openly solicits his reader's participation in an incomplete, constantly shifting narrative adventure. The récit establishes as its central tenet the eventual completion of this partial and self-consciously withheld thesis. Because the embodiment of this central definition is alluded to but never explained in the narrative–at least not in the text's first five branches–the contract itself is formally thematized as a *disnarrated* element of the text. The term disnarrated, in Gerald Prince's words, denotes "all the events that do not happen though they could have and are nonetheless referred to (in a negative or hypothetical mode) by the narrative text."[17] The central disnarrated event in Roubaud's self-begetting novel thus simultaneously precedes and influences, in a subterranean fashion, the text's realization. The absence of a stable narrative pledge is implied

---

[17] Prince, *Narrative as Theme*, 30.

in Roubaud's opening gesture ("je commence ici pour tenter d'expliquer (et simultanément de déterminer pour moi-même) ce que cela sera" [*GI* 8]), and it conditions the entire text's reception. That is to say, the narrative contract, which is conventionally established at the outset of a tale, is deferred until the text's completion, at which time, theoretically speaking, it will have been kept. In this respect, Roubaud invites readers to wager on silence in anticipation of narrative resolution, to accept as provisional the conditions of the text's unfolding.

I think that the originality of Roubaud's autobiographical fiction is rooted in a central and repressed narrative contract, for the imminent textual conditions constructed by this absence present the book (and its becoming) as a simulacrum of life itself. Instead of arbitrarily delineating a narrative frame in which to represent the life of the *Projet*-which would necessarily frame the life of its author-Roubaud strategically casts autobiography in a transformative structure where the temporality of narration imitates the progressive becoming of human consciousness. As in life itself, the ultimate rules and outcome of *'le grand incendie de Londres'* are indefinitely deferred, and recursively reinvented within certain predetermined limits, leaving only provisional modes and self-reflection available to the description of the work and the inscription of memories. Within the absolute present narrativity of this text, Roubaud thus records a temporal slippage between simultaneous moments of description, the explicated and attenuated past, and the potential yet deferred completion of the work and the lives it represents.

Hence, in the wager that Roubaud proposes to his readers, the book must remain imminent. It is a paradoxical contract because what *is* at stake is only determined *a posteriori*. The textual rules defer the work's completion while at the same time framing its unavoidable material end. In this respect, the narrativity of *'le grand incendie de Londres'* performs the Derridean notion of textual *différance*, for its absent (and hence hyper-present) narrative contract requires that the text continually reveal its innovative difference as *signifiant* and that, simultaneously, each moment of prose reiterate the deferral of the text's ultimate definition as *signifié*.[18]

---

[18] See Derrida, *L'écriture et la différence*, 409-28.

This *différance* is made explicit in the narrator's voice. Similar consequences can be traced in the textual role established for the narratee. One of the primary characteristics of the self-begetting novel is that the relationship between the narrator and narrated shifts as events unfold. Roubaud consciously constructs the effect of these intratextual relationships, paying particular attention to changes in each moment of description. Laying the groundwork for an understanding of these shifts, he posits that his prose moments establish an innovative relationship between narrator and narratee: "Mon intention, en me soumettant (et en vous soumettant par la même occasion) à des intervalles assez rapprochés, à de tels exercices de description, est d'établir le plus rapidement possible notre lien imaginaire d'auteur à lecteur, mais d'une manière un peu différente de celle qui est traditionnellement de mise dans les ouvrages de fiction" (*GI* 363). The nature of this "imaginary bond" between narrator and reader conforms to conventional models in that the "lecteur générique" and the "lecteur fantôme" are implied as active participants in the text's genesis. As we read each moment of the text, in each branch, we witness its coming into being, and we are challenged to discover the constraints that underlie the progression and stylistic concerns of each moment of prose.

Within these moments, however, Roubaud refuses the notion that there is a coincidence between his voice as narrator and himself as character. In this difference he sets in motion a slippage between the described, its present telling, and its future becoming (reception). "J'espère, je ne le cacherai pas, parvenir ainsi à rendre manifeste la séparation qui existe, et que je désire au sensible, aussi évidente que possible, entre celui (moi) qui vous raconte ce que je vous raconte, et ceux (parmi lesquels moi encore, très souvent) de qui ces choses sont racontées" (*GI* 363). Clearly, Roubaud's intention here is to undermine a purely autobiographical reading. This distinction between narrator and narrated also evokes the distinction between narrator and writer. Again, these differences are of a textual order, and any apparent coincidence regarding these three personae (re)presents an intended overlap between several possible worlds: the world of the past (in which Roubaud is the narrated), the world of the textual present (in which Roubaud is the narrator), and the real world (in which Roubaud is composing '*le grand incendie de Londres*'), where fiction comes into being through its reception. The narrative economy of the text thus relies on an implicit interlacing of these three textual functions, thereby constructing the persona of Roubaud as a "transworld" identity. The relationship between these worlds is not static, however. Rather, as Roubaud emphasizes above, there is a difference (at least textual) between his "narrative beings" (*FI* 87)–the character, narrator, and author–the final distinction among them deferred through the temporal mechanism of the narration.

Some narratees enjoy similarly plural textual lives. For example, Pierre Lusson, one of Roubaud's close friends, appears several times in the course of the narration. Yet he is also a potential *real* reader of the text. These are very different roles in the text's economy, for only in the latter position does Lusson exercise an agency in constructing the text. Before the publication of the first volume, Roubaud figures the reader's role as entirely analogous to those played by his own character and narrator, figuring their participation in the text as entirely hypothetical. "Je trouve d'ailleurs un autre avantage, plus immédiatement pratique, à la dichotomie, à ma '*split personality*' de narrateur et de narré: comme en l'état présent du récit (même s'il a beaucoup avancé depuis la dernière mise en garde de ce genre), l'idée même de 'lecteur' est fictive à l'extrême" (*GI* 364). By the time the third volume is published, however, Roubaud is experimenting with a limited number of highly restricted "reader interventions," whereby real readers may materially contribute to the text's genesis.[19] Even in these cases (structured by specific Oulipian constraints), the textual identity of the reader mirrors that of the writer. Both are cast in an ever-becoming textual

---

[19] Stating that he bears "quelque réticence à considérer une réelle interactivité, une intervention véritable du lecteur dans l'ouvrage," Roubaud also admits, in the following terms, that he has imagined and provided for a limited number of incursions by readers: "Je prévois cependant (il faut être de son temps, n'est-ce pas) certaines interventions limitées du lecteur sur le texte lui-même. Une première étape pourrait être le recours à ce que je nommerai des 'moules généralisés': offrir des sections de texte inachevées, n'ayant que certains points de passages obligés, à charge pour le lecteur d'achever le texte (en satisfaisant des contraintes oulipiennes, par exemple). Autre possibilité: ménager des espaces de commentaire de lecteur, posant des questions au texte, faisant des remarques, et amenant en retour à des réponses: c'est l'idée d'un livre ouvert. Un cas particulier est déjà à l'oeuvre: celui de Pierre Lusson qui figure par ailleurs comme 'personnage' dans la 'branche 3' et à qui j'ai offert de 'réagir' à ce que je raconte de lui" (*LI* 300). Further interventions were also imagined through an Internet site where Roubaud would consider publishing versions of his final branch, in Entretien avec Jacques Roubaud," *Licorne* 40 (1997): 163.

structure articulating the slippage of time in isolated moments of prose, fictively cast in an absolute present.

On one hand, the temporal slippage of the narrative economy undermines the text's status as purely autobiographical. Because the narrated differs from the narrator who also differs from the real writer, a coincidence or stable identity defining the three is indefinitely deferred. Repeating these distinctions, Roubaud encourages his readers to rely on the narrative truth of his text, for this slippage in event and time is perceived as a real textual function, implicit in "la mise en route du récit" (*GI* 49). The purpose of this function is to cast a shadow, a protective obscurity, not only over the identity of the novel that would have been but also over the *Projet* and the lives that bore it. Narrative truth, as kind of fable of the real, therefore functions as protection: "Il est vrai qu'en tout cela je ne suis pas très certain d'être cru. Les lecteurs sont méfiants (l'histoire de la lecture leur donne amplement raison). Je préférerais l'être. Je me permets néanmoins de l'affirmer explicitement, et le plus nettement possible: ce que je vous dis est vrai, dans l'ordre même où vous le découvrez. C'est ainsi, par conséquent, que je vous invite à me lire. Et, que vous le vouliez ou non, l'ombre de cette affirmation s'étendra sur votre lecture" (*GI* 50). The art of Roubaud's autobiography thus consists in establishing a continually displaced narrative subject whose moments of prose become moments of being. Its complexity lies in interweaving memories of what contributed to the conceptualization of the *Projet*, cast in a dynamic system intended alternatively to shed light on and to hide the writer's life: "Entrelacement du tout, élucidation des parties" (*GI* 222). It is the self-deferring economy of this narrativity that leads Anne Roche to remark that "même s'il n'est pas entièrement exempt des ruses narratives qu'il dénonce chez les autres biographes, notamment Sartre et Leiris, il est parvenu, tout en écrivant un texte profondément personnel et impliqué, à éviter ce piège de l'autobiographie où tout s'explique, où ne subsiste plus rien d'obscur, plus rien de ce *quelque chose noir* auquel chacun est tôt ou tard confronté."[20]

The postponed narrative contract and the imminent moments of textual becoming establish a narrative coherence in '*le grand incendie de Londres.*' The textual fragmentation, cast in terms of prose

---

[20] Roche, "Mémoire," 82.

moments deferring the different past and future temporalities, does not disperse the experience of the text. Rather, the intentional interlacing of present moments of memory tightly interweaves the simultaneous description and destruction of memory. Instead of achieving the masterwork that *Le Grand Incendie de Londres* was intended to have completed, Roubaud remembers, moment by moment, the events and revelations that led to the *Projet*'s conception. These imbricated moments become, by force of their inscription or reception, the structured ruins of a totality that was programmed to fail. And yet these fragments provide their own internal unity in their perpetual and infinite search for unrealized potential. Roubaud is explicit about this ambition when he remarks that each moment of his novel is determined by the collapse of the definition into a concrete trace of its memory: "Dans *'le grand incendie de Londres,'* la chute est ruine. Et il n'y a plus d'énigme. Il n'y a que sa mémoire" (*GI* 198).

In this sense, the fragments are apocalyptic, laying waste to the *Projet* and the novel it was to produce. Roubaud approaches this destruction without nostalgia or regret: "Je ne recherche pas les traces du temps pour, les rejouant devant mes propres yeux, rentrer, au moins le temps d'un récit, dans la jouissance d'une possession perdue, je les atteins pour les détruire, pour les abolir" (*GI* 411). Destruction by description in each moment thus further affirms the novel's coherence, for the final destructive gesture is already consciously inscribed into the novel's deferred definition. Following Jean-François Lyotard, it may be suggested that Roubaud's self-begetting novel reflects postmodern tendencies in that its coherence is formally motivated by the structure of fragmentation: "The unity of the book, the odyssey of that consciousness, even if it is deferred from chapter to chapter, is not seriously challenged: the identity of the writing with itself throughout the labyrinth of the interminable narration is enough to connote such unity."[21]

The trauma subtending the book's fragmentation and the loss of the *Projet* is hardly mentioned in the course of *'le grand incendie de Londres'* and therefore attains, like the novel's definition, prominence through understatement. The early death of Alix Cléo Roubaud underlines the motif of destruction, and in fact occasions a "*double* destruction," whereby Roubaud's projects as well as the reality of her

---

[21] Lyotard, *Postmodern Condition*, 80.

absence are attenuated: "Le présent de la prose rejoint la circonstance qui le désigne" (*GI* 208). Like the other personal losses that mark Roubaud's earlier writing, mourning Alix Cléo manifests "une forme de vie" (*GI* 188) whose practice is figured "comme alternative à la disparition volontaire" (*GI* 7). The motif of mourning through fragmented reminiscence recurs throughout Roubaud's works, and in *'le grand incendie de Londres'* he writes openly about the ethic and aesthetic of mourning, emphasizing the roles played by absence, and silence: "J'ai hérité d'une double tradition, de silence et de deuil, où les morts, après vingt ans, trente, ou cinquante, omniprésents encore, n'apparaissent pourtant que dans les creux d'un mutisme, conservant une existence violente de trous noirs contournés par les paroles, mais s'y manifestant, soulignés par quelque timbre, quelque vibration, quelque déplacement dans la trajectoire d'un récit : places absentes dans des pages d'album, images perpétuellement comme en train de brûler mais pas assez complètement pour que l'ombre, l'odeur ne se fassent encore sentir" (*GI* 108). The drama of mourning centers around silence, and in Roubaud's mourning of Alix Cléo that silence centers around her photography, "images perpétuellement comme en train de brûler."

After 1983, mourning prominently informs Roubaud's identity as a writer. When he explains the importance of his move from the apartment in the rue des Francs-Bourgeois (4e arr.) where he lived with Alix Cléo to the one he had previously inhabited, in the rue d'Amsterdam (9e arr.), he notes a progression in mourning that is also marked by completing the final typescript of *Quelque chose noir* (*GI* 227). Jean René and Alix Cléo's deaths demarcate two prominent events in the development of his collected works, most of which he situates between "deux 'bords' de mort" (*GI* 183; *QN* 132). Whereas his brother's suicide occasions Roubaud's first book (ϵ), the loss of Alix Cléo represents a double death in his work as he commingles the most consistent themes in his writing: love, memory, and poetry. Roubaud figures this double death in both *'le grand incendie de Londres'* and *Quelque chose noir* (*QN* 33), stating that "ce qui est devenu nul, pour moi, depuis janvier de l'année 1983, ce que je ne peux plus même penser, c'est la *poésie*" (*GI* 55). And yet, the absence of both Alix Cléo and poésie prominently influences *'le grand incendie de Londres.'*

Like the novel's elided definition, poetry, and its enigmas present themselves in silence: "La poésie, dans le roman, manquerait et marquerait par le manque elle prendrait sa place" (*GI* 206). Through description, Roubaud structures his mourning according to silence, placing poetry in a linguistic realm apart from, but implied in, his novel. These silences testify to his intentional talking around the more important experiences subtending creativity, as he clearly states in *La boucle*: "Il est parfois impossible de taire ce dont on ne peut parler, & quand on ne peut pas le montrer non plus, on peut essayer de parler ailleurs, par détours" (*B* 233). Roubaud mourns Alix Cléo in destroying the *Projet* to which she had contributed. As a couple, the Roubauds had invented a private language, an imbrication of photographic and verbal art. Roubaud invents a new term for his own practice of poetic love: "L'entrelacement, vital, et l'élucidation des moments du monde ont pour moi un nom, qui désigne une logique d'un univers vital possible, le *biipsisme*" (*GI* 223). Part of the trauma implied in the destruction of the *Projet* is inscribed in the lost partnership implied by that term.

The novel also represents the loss of being (in love) as a form of creativity, as a vital language: "'*Le Grand Incendie de Londres*' avait été commencé dans un état de *biipsisme*; maintenant et à défaut, son tombeau" (*GI* 209). As Elizabeth Cardonne-Arlyck has pointed out, the term *biipsisme* evokes Ludwig Wittgenstein's remarks about private languages: "Le terme manquant du syllogisme se trouve chez Wittgenstein: 'imaginer un langage signifie s'imaginer une forme de vie.' Inventant des formes, la poésie invente un langage où s'invente une forme du vivre."[22] Roubaud also conceives of biipsisme as an extension of the theory of fin'amors, for it concerns creativity (poetry and photography) and love in a formal practice of expression: "La relation biipsiste est clairement de l'ordre de l'amour. Son idée, l'être-deux au monde, je l'avais emprunté à la théorie de l'*amors* dans le 'grand chant' des troubadours" (*GI* 223). Thus, implied in the failure of the virtual *Grand Incendie de Londres* is also the absence of a long-lived romance: "Je voulais vivre un projet de poésie, et sa fiction. Mais un état d'amour n'avait pas été durablement possible" (*GI* 223). And yet, in mourning, in reinventing a literary tomb for his "relation biipsiste" (as well as for the poetry that it implies), Roubaud motivates the memory and renewed potential of that relation.

---

[22] Cardonne-Arlyck, "Poésie, forme de vie," 99.

Since Alix Cléo's death, Roubaud has worked at creating possible fictional worlds in which her shadow is inscribed: "J'ai fait de son nom le nom propre d'un personnage; qui depuis m'accompagne; c'est un personnage de prose, et un personnage temporel" (*B* 233). This process of mourning explains, in part, Roubaud's characterizing the very idea of an ideal reader as "fictive à l'extrême" (*GI* 364), for in his direct addresses to the reader he also apostrophizes Alix Cléo. Re-creating a fiction based on a potential biipsism also leads to interrogating the emotive implications of Roubaud's mourning. I have already stated that Roubaud does not cast his memories in a nostalgic tone of regret, and that re-creating moments of the past in order to preserve them contradicts his intention of destruction. His vital formalism in '*le grand incendie de Londres*' does, however, bear the mark of a studied melancholia, cast in terms of Roubaud's reading of *Lancelot en prose*.

In *La fleur inverse* Roubaud presents an analysis of the melancholia in medieval romance. The worst, incurable strain, the one that claims Galehaut's life, is *l'éros mélancolique*. Fittingly, some of the characteristics Roubaud attributes to this terminal love sickness are directly implied in his composition of '*le grand incendie de Londres*.' "Succomber à l'éros mélancolique," writes Roubaud, "c'est être *recréant*. C'est être vaincu, prisonnier de la défaite, 'chaitius,' exilé, '*en issilh*.' C'est partir on ne sait où, '*no sai on*,' en un lieu qui est sans chant, donc n'est rien" (*FI* 95). In a limited sense, this description applies to Roubaud's novel cycle, for in recreating what the virtual novel would have been he leads his readers into a suspended discourse whose primary thesis and destination are elided. But Roubaud's mourning avoids exaggerating an affinity with the éros mélancolique of Arthurian romances and the trobar by recourse to the principle of mezura. Mezura, or a balanced sense for measure in love and its expression, is served in '*le grand incendie de Londres*' by constraints and the postponed definition. This abstract and potential thesis keeps the momentum of the work directed, even if the endpoint of that direction is unknown ("partir on ne sait où").

Lyotard has remarked that modern and postmodern tendencies often coexist in the same works (80). This duplicity is aptly represented in Roubaud's novel cycle, for the goal of re-creating and remembering the past is not focused on total attainment but engenders a future becoming for both the work and the fictive beings that it implies. The residual "modérnité ténue" (*GI* 197) with which Roubaud qualifies his "roman de mémoire" is reflected in this intimation of *l'éros mélancolique*, for "cette défaite est en un sens héroïque, puisqu'elle vient de l'immensité même de l'amour" (*FI* 95). But the fact that Roubaud casts the event of the work's completion in an imminently deferred future associates its formal qualities with a postmodern work. In fact, the work's vital formalism challenges conventional notions of the novel, the autobiography and the work of memory to such an extent that accomplishment, like the central event in the novel, is deferred. This postponement associates Roubaud's writing with the aesthetic Lyotard calls postmodern:

> A postmodern artist or writer is in the position of a philosopher: the text he writes, the work he produces are not in principle governed by preestablished rules, and cannot be judged according to a determining judgment, by applying familiar categories to the text or the work. Those rules and categories are what the work of art itself is looking for. The artist and the writer, then, are working without rules in order to formulate the rules of what *will have been done*. Hence the fact that work and text have the characters of an *event*; hence also, they always come too late for their author, or, what amounts to the same thing, their being put into work, their realization (*mise en oeuvre*) always begins too soon. *Postmodern* would have to be understood according to the paradox of the future (*post*) anterior (*modo*).[23]

I believe that readers of '*le grand incendie de Londres*' who accept the conditions of imminence and deferral in Roubaud's text must necessarily also occupy "the position of a philosopher" in Lyotard's terms. They must proceed in the labyrinthine landscape constructed by Roubaud in search of what the work will have accomplished. And along the way, in exploring the writer's digressive memories, they experience the isolated events whose accumulation is intended to support the final meaning. This open-ended search is particularly important now, insofar as the novel cycle is still materially incomplete. Moreover, Roubaud's recent integration of other types of textuality into his novel cycle provides further evidence that an ultimate closure will be artfully negotiated, so as to leave the text in as constant a state of *becoming* as possible.

---

[23] Lyotard, *Postmodern Condition*, 81.

Aligning Roubaud's writing with an aesthetic of postmodernism is productive but must be tempered. If there are postmodern tendencies in Roubaldian and, more broadly, in Oulipian writing, then they are practiced in an awareness of literary tradition. That is, members of the Oulipo eschew gestures of tabula rasa. Instead, they adopt a (re)creative stance with regard to literary tradition and language. Other literary movements, like Surrealism, sought to differentiate their thought and forms of writing from those that preceded them. That avant-garde is a cry for freedom, for a liberated unconscious and for pure creative vision. Their injunctive rhetoric supported, and was supported by, the discourses of progress and emancipation that postmodern theorists call master narratives. The Oulipian stance is, paradoxically, more nihilistic and more optimistic. They claim that innovation is specifically a question of volitional experiment, particularly in literary expression. They mock the notion of their own originality, accusing their precursors of having plagiarized them in anticipation. For them, the most productive engagement with tradition is one that does not resist the past but that strategically elaborates the poetic terms already inherent in tradition.

Oulipian originality is a question of the unexpected and brilliant "find" wrought through the use of literary constraint. Within literary history, each discovery, each invention, and each deduction of its possible combinations suggests a further maturation and differentiation of the tradition, contributing additional steps toward the saturation and new invention of form. The challenge of thinking potential is that to propose new possibilities also means exhausting those that are extant. It is precisely in antiquated or exhausted literary forms that Roubaud finds his most enduring innovations, and it is in their link to the past that his works will find their greatest vitality. Destruction, in this context, represents a drive toward the maturation of a literary tradition, a drive toward change via the formal differentiation of literatures.

As I have argued, Roubaud's work sets out on this journey in a reflexive fashion—one of mourning and of memory, in guise of melancholia—so that a memory of the destroyed is conveyed in a vital form. For him, destruction encourages the virtual reconstruction of the abolished souvenir, a deferred potential for total attainment. Yet it is a re-creation that does not sustain a narrative of progress or attained freedom. Rather, his "petits récits" continually rely on the process of deconstructing and reconstructing the monuments of the past in an attempt to think differently about the present.

In *'le grand incendie de Londres,'* Roubaud imbricates the conditions of his work of mourning and work of memory, layering and overlapping each element of his lifework into an elaborate and self-conscious reflection. Part of the mystery of this modality of remembrance remains veiled in how Roubaud interweaves his personal life and his broad agenda of literary incursions, or how he entombs his private losses deep within his literary innovations. It is certain that *'le grand incendie de Londres,'* and the Roubaldian texts to which it makes reference, will support years of further imagination and elucidation. It progressively reveals and extends a vast personal and collective literary universe, both within its narrative structures and among the numerous and richly interrelated texts whose story it recollects. For, having claimed that poetic writing is difficult by nature, Roubaud has unerringly provided a formal unity complex and comprehensive enough to ensure its continued vitality, *un toit qui lui aura assuré l'ombre nécessaire à sa protection esthétique.*

A key element in Roubaud's strategy of renewal and continued vitality is incompletion. The principle of intentional incompletion appears as early as ∈ (1967) and takes a marked turn in Roubaud's novels. In *La belle Hortense,* for example, he comically addresses the problem of "Le dernier chapitre" and then displaces closure with "L'après dernier chapitre." Closure in the novel has long been considered one of the form's inherent constraints. Crucial to all novels, the question of closure is a site of potentiality. In *Poésie, etcetera: ménage,* Roubaud rehearses the wide variety of strategies novelists have used to avoid "la terrible obligation de finir, de s'achever, de résoudre les problèmes, de dévoiler les mystères" (*PM* 243). A novel's conclusion, according to Roubaud, is most interesting in respect to how it performs its own inconclusion. In this analysis of novelistic closure, Roubaud identifies an avoidance conceit he describes as the "most" postmodern (a qualification that mocks classification). Not surprisingly, his pet technique also directly describes *'le grand incendie de Londres'*: "La plus grande 'manière' de l'évitisme, la plus post-post-post-moderne de toutes, c'est le roman médiéval: les entrelacements du *Lancelot en prose.* Ce n'est pas seulement qu'il lutte contre la célèbre et bien injustement décriée linéarité par l'embranchements forestiers (au sens propre comme au figuré) de sa narration, mais parce qu'il résout le problème de l'achèvement en n'offrant jamais que des *fins provisoires*" (PM 245). Although it is too early to speculate on the ultimate outcome of *'le grand incendie de Londres'*–a horizon of reading Roubaud explicitly figured in *La bibliothèque de Warburg (version mixte)*–it is clear that he has begun and pursued his second novel series under a similar aegis of incompletion, and that he has cast closure in his work as indefinitely deferred. The drama of closure is repeated in each of the published volumes. Exemplifying the whole text's elaboration of digression, the first branch of *'le grand incendie de Londres'* avoids a definitive ending by closing with quotations from historical accounts of the Great Fire of London in 1666. This strategy is provocative not only because it subverts conventional norms of concluding, but also because the quotations are given in English. *La boucle* solves the problem by enacting a loop in the narration: at the end of this volume, the narrator turns back on what he has written and begins rereading from that text's starting point. In *Mathématique:* the material end is altogether avoided, for the text is published in an incomplete state, lacking two chapters and their respective incises and bifurcations.

Ultimately, the question of closure coincides with the question of death in *'le grand incendie de Londres.'* From the opening pages, the narrator justifies his narrative means as providing an alternative to suicide. Deferring the novel's end might therefore also be read as deferring a more personal finality. Survival, in this case, is not only a question of literary tradition (as it is in many of Roubaud's works) but also implicates the survival of the writer. In the final scene of *La vie mode d'emploi* Georges Perec interrogates novelistic closure and death in the same breath. Bartlebooth's end might be viewed as "une allégorie du drame de la forme-roman" for, as event, it stages the drama of novelistic closure, "le drame de l'achèvement, et de l'impossibilité de le surmonter" (PM 246). However, Bartlebooth's project includes a radical solution to the problem of closure, subtly inscribing at its core an element of self-destruction. His paintings were to be sent back to where they were painted and dissolved in their waters of origin, letting the colors reunite, as it were, with their birthplace. In seeking to negate his entire *Projet*, to overexpose it through description, Roubaud appears to adopt a similar strategy: "la fin par effacement, par le retour au néant d'avant le projet" (*PM* 247). Such abolition of the project reflects an impulse of fashioning one's own end; to project an effacement of the lifework is to project a literary suicide, a volitional disappearance.

The rhetoric of failure with which Roubaud's novel cycle opens announces that this literary suicide will not have taken place. Rather, *'le grand incendie de Londres'* reaffirms the coherence of the texts contributing to Roubaud's *Projet* and incites readers to retrace the intentional remembrance that each of those texts sought to effect. That is, if *'le grand incendie de Londres'* destroys the *Projet* for Roubaud, it also retraces for its readers the accomplishments that lead to this final sense of incompletion. In discussing Bartlebooth's failure, Roubaud emphasizes that his incompletion stands in contrast to the completion of the novel itself, and that this contrast underscore the accomplishment of Perec's work:

> Or l'échec de la complétion absolue du projet d'effacement de Bartlebooth et de la solution de tous les mystères (les puzzles) montre, en fait, que *La vie mode d'emploi* offre, en tant que roman, exactement le contraire d'un tel échec;
>
> montre, je pense, que *La vie mode d'emploi* est le roman d'une spirale entrelacée d'achèvements et d'inachèvements multiples (les vies, la vie), de l'achèvement et inachèvement de la mémoire, d'une réminiscence, d'une anamnèse, celle de la forme même qui le suscite et dont la poursuite (graal ou snark) fut comme le "rêve d'avant naissance" de son auteur, de son grand horloger, Georges Perec. (*PM* 247)

Roubaud demonstrates a similar sense of accomplishment, in that the formal vitality of his innovations also recollects and elucidates select sites of his tradition. This novel cycle further elaborates novelistic, autobiographic, and Oulipian writing by turning the form in upon itself to maximize the constraints already in place in the novel. And whereas Roubaud's earlier works often draw their meanings from a memory of tradition, *'le grand incendie de Londres'* meditates on Roubaud's literary *Projet*, progressively revealing details of its conception and the conditions through which they came to be, or failed to be realized. Reflecting the memories that constitute both his literary inventions and the record of his life, the evolving complexity of the work testifies to the mutability of autobiography —thereby uncannily preempting the work of chroniclers and biographers.

It is perhaps too fitting that Roubaud's works should lead to a provisional end. From an early age until the present Roubaud has led his life through literature, as a reader, an inventor, a poet-mathematician, and spokesman for the survival and transformation of literary memory. Like Percival Bartlebooth, his life resembles a long poetic performance imparting an immense wealth of poetic knowledge and an exemplary ethos of poetry.

BIBLIOGRAPHY

THIS bibliography presents an inclusive, though not exhaustive, record of Jacques Roubaud's publications from 1967 to 2004, followed by the list of secondary sources (for a more complete listing see Beaumatin, *Forme & mesure*). Roubaud's works are cross-referenced on the abbreviation page and in the endnotes by the year of their publication. The publications pertaining to each year are subdivided into two categories: works written, edited, or translated by Roubaud, followed by works completed in collaboration. In the first category, the publications are listed alphabetically by title. In the second subcategory, co-authored works are also listed alphabetically, first by authors and then by title. When available, I have listed English translations. The secondary sources are also listed in alphabetical order, first by author and then by title. Unless otherwise noted, all translations are mine and emphases in citations are present in the original.

PUBLICATIONS BY JACQUES ROUBAUD, 1967-2004

1967

"Cinq poèmes sur des toiles de Pierre Getzler." Paris: Catalogue d'une exposition chez Georges Perec, 1967.
"Le Manyoshu et la première lyrique japonaise." *Action Poétique* 36 (1967): 3-24.
"Prinsland." *Promesse* 21 (1967): 28-37.
ϵ *(signe d'appartenance)*. Paris: Gallimard, 1967.

1968

"Jacques Roubaud: 'J'ai choisi le sonnet.'" *La Quinzaine Littéraire* 42 (1968): 6-7.
"Morphismes rationels et algébriques dans les types d'algèbres à une dimension." *Publications de l'Institut de Statistique de l'Université de Paris* 17.4 (1968): 1-77.
"Sur le *Shinkokinshu*, huitième anthologie impériale japonaise." *Change* 1 (1968): 73-106.

1969

"La destruction fut ma Béatrice: essai sur la sextine de Dante et d'Arnaut Daniel." *Change* 2 (1969): 9-32.

"La disparition" (a lipogrammatic sonnet). In Georges Perec, *La Disparition*. Paris: Denoël, 1969: 9.

"Un problème de combinatoire posé par la poésie lyrique des troubadours." *Mathématiques et Sciences Humaines* 27 (1969): 5-12.

With Pierre Lusson. "Sur la sémiologie des paragrammes de Julia Kristeva (i)." *Action Poétique* 41-42 (1969): 56-61.

With Pierre Lusson and Georges Perec. *Petit traité invitant à la découverte de l'art subtil du go*. Paris: Bourgois, 1969.

1970

"B.Y.: trois ou dix-neuf poèmes." *Change* 6 (1970): 225-47.

Mono no aware: le sentiment des choses (cent quarante-trois poèmes empruntés au japonais). Paris: Gallimard, 1970.

"Quelques thèses sur la poétique." *Change* 6 (1970): 7-21.

With Jean Bénabou. "Monades et descente." *Compte-rendu de l'Académie des Sciences de Paris* 270 (1970): 96-98.

With Pierre Lusson. "Sur la sémiologie des paragrammes de Julia Kristeva (ii)." *Action Poétique* 45 (1970): 31-36.

1971

"Dix-sept poèmes." *Nouvelle Revue Française* 221 (1971): 59-62.

Trans. "Gary Snyder: sept poèmes." *Action Poétique* 47 (1971): 24-28.

"Mètre et vers: deux applications de la métrique générative de Halle-Keyser." *Poétique* 7 (1971): 336-87.

Trans. "Lettre à León Felipe," by Octavio Paz. In *Versant Est*. Paris: Gallimard, 1971. 106-13.

"Na Florensa." *Phantomas 100 (La mémoire)* (1971): 54-55.

"La notion d'associativité relative." *Mathématiques et Sciences Humaines* 34 (1971): 43-59.

With N. Boër, trans. "Salvador Espriu: Neuf poèmes de 'Cementiri de Sinera.'" *Action Poétique* 47 (1971): 12-15.

With Octavio Paz, Eduardo Sanguineti, and Charles Tomlinson. *Renga*. Trans. Jacques Roubaud. Paris: Gallimard, 1971. *Renga*. Trans. and ed. Charles Tomlinson. London: Penguin, 1980.

1972

"Entretien de Roman Jakobson avec Jean-Pierre Faye, Jean Paris et Jacques Roubaud." In *Hypothèses*. Ed. Jean-Pierre Faye, Jean Paris, Mitsou Ronat, and Jacques Roubaud. Paris: Seghers-Laffont, 1972. 161-66.

"Une rencontre de Shakespeare et de Roman Jakobson." In *Hypothèses*. Ed. Jean-Pierre Faye, Jean Paris, Mitsou Ronat, and Jacques Roubaud. Paris: Seghers-Laffont, 1972. 161-66.

1973

"Enquête sur les formules strophiques des trouvères (I)." *Cahiers de Poétique Comparée* 1.1 (1973): 62-79, 85-96.
Trans. "Poésie U.S.: présentation et traduction de Louis Zukofsky, Jack Spicer, Paul Blackburn, Jackson MacLow, Clayton Eshleman, Jerome Rothenberg, Armand Schwerner." *Action Poétique* 55 (1973): n.p.
"Sur deux lectures sémiotiques." *Action Poétique* 53 (1973): 24-27.
Trente et un au cube. Paris: Gallimard, 1973.
With Florence Delay, trans. "José Bergamín: poèmes." *Action Poétique* 54 (1973): 54-56.

1974

"Douze poèmes (objets, lieux, moments. I. Cinq poèmes. II. Sept poèmes empruntés à Cid Corman)." *Action Poétique* 57 (1974): 30-35.
Trans. "'L'estampie' de Raimbaut de Vaqueiras." *Nouvelle Critique*, spec. ed., "La Danse" (1974): 6.
Trans. and ed. "George Quasha. 'Métraduction'"; "Arnold Schwerner: 'Tablettes'"; "Jerome Rothenberg: traduction totale"; "Louis Zukofsky: 'A 22 (fragment)'"; "Quelques méthodes anciennes et nouvelles de traduction à partir du français." *Change* 19 (1974): 94-119.
"Poème de présentation composé pour une lecture de *Trente et un au cube*." *Almanach de Shakespeare and Co* 1 (1974): 167-71.
"Quatre états de poésie" (Paul Louis Rossi, Claude Royet-Journourd, Denis Roche, Michel Deguy). *Change* 19 (1974): 95-99.
With Florence Delay, trans. "Octavio Paz: 'Pétrifié pétrifiant; Saül Yurkievich: 'Poétique.'" *Change* 21 (1974): 30-36, 46-51.
With Jean-Pierre Faye. "Langage puissance *n* et totalitarisme." In *Ecrire... pourquoi? pour qui?* Grenoble: Presses Universitaires de Grenoble, 1974. 166-208.
With Pierre Lusson. "Mètre et rythme de l'alexandrin ordinaire." *Langue Française* 23 (1974): 41-53.

1975

Ed. *Colloque du change de forme. I. Biologie et prosodies*. Paris: Bourgois, 1975.
"Entretien avec Henri Deluy, Pierre Lusson et Mitsou Ronat: le rythme, le formel, le formalisme." *Action Poétique* 62 (1975): 61-75.
Etoffe. Geneva: G. K. Editions, 1975.
"Etoffe deux (trames)." *Action Poétique* 60 (1975): 146-51.
Trans. "Gertrude Stein: 'Stanzas in Meditation.'" *Action Poétique* 61 (1975): 152-58.
Mezura. Paris: Atelier, 1975.
"Mezura, spectre." *Change* 23 (1975): 5-15.
"Note sur DIRE de Danielle Collobert." *Change* 24 (1975): 169.
"Notes sur l'évolution récente de la prosodie." *Action Poétique* 62 (1975): 50-60.
"La princesse Hoppy ou le conte du Labrador, chapitre 1." *Bibliothèque Oulipienne* 2 (1975).
"Tombeaux de Pétrarque." *Solaire* 10-11 (1975).
With Florence Delay, trans. "Poèmes de Carlos Germán Belli et Saül Yurkievich." *Action Poétique* 60 (1975): 93-95, 96, 98-103.

1976

"Banque de sang." *Action Poétique* 64 (1976): 3.
Chute de langue en autre. Paris: Orange Export Ltd, 1976.
"De la branche des voyages (fragments d'*Autobiographie, chapitre dix*)." *Europe* 569 (1976): 154-57.
"Eléments de syntaxe combinatoire: I. Parenthèses binaires." Département de Mathématiques Université de Paris X, 1976. 1-44.
Trans. "Poème de Raimbaut d'Orange." *Action Poétique* 64 (1976): 52-57.
"Roman d'Alexandre III: présentation et mode d'emploi." *Cahiers de Poétique Comparée* 2.4 (1976): 6.
With Jean-Pierre Faye and Joseph Guglielmi, trans. "Le Saint Graal." In *Jack Spicer: Billy, Graal, Langage.* Paris: Seghers-Laffont, 1976. 137-68, 220-22.
With Pierre Lartigue, Gaston Planet, Lionel Ray, and Paul Louis Rossi. *Inimaginaire I-II.* Beauvoir-sur-Mer: Privately printed, 1976.

1977

"Air." In "Oulipo, A Raymond Queneau." *Bibliothèque Oulipienne* 4 (1977).
Autobiographie, chapitre dix. Paris: Gallimard, 1977.
"De l'objectivisme." *Europe* 578-79 (1977): 31-33.
"Des poètes qu'on appelait 'objectivistes': un entretien entre Serge Fauchereau, Jacques Roubaud et Charles Dobzynski." *Europe* 578-79 (1977): 7-30.
"La mathématique dans la méthode de Raymond Queneau." *Critique* 359 (1977): 392-413.
"Métrico-rythmico-linguistico-algebraico syntaxe." *Cahiers de Poétique Comparée* 3.1 (1977): 61-85.
"Notes sur l'évolution récente de la prosodie (I bis)." *Action Poétique* 69 (1977): 19, 23-25.
Trans. "Les objectivistes: Oppen, Rakosi, Reznikoff, Zukofsky." *Europe* 578-79 (1977): 55-63, 78-91, 109-21.
Trans. "Penser les choses tel qu'elles existent," by Louis Zukofsky. *Europe* 578-79 (1977): 107-8.
"Le roman d'Alexandre: un synopsis en douze branches." *Cahiers de Poétique Comparée* 3.2 (1977): 3-85.
With Florence Delay. *Graal théâtre: Gauvain et le chevalier vert; Lancelot du lac; Perceval le Gallois; L'enlèvement de Guenièvre.* Paris: Gallimard, 1977.
With Florence Delay. "La roue qui recule vers le future." *Action Poétique* 70 (1977): 64-121.
With Pierre Lartigue, Gaston Planet, Lionel Ray, and Paul Louis Rossi. "Inimaginaire III (fragments)." *Action Poétique* 70 (1977): 8-12.
With Pierre Lusson. "Indication et repères de 's'essoufler.'" *Action Poétique* 70 (1977): 13-18.

1978

"L'antéfixe poésie." *Bulletin d'Orange Export Ltd* 11 (1978): 43.
"19 mars 1978." *Action Poétique* 74bis (1978): 12.
"La double hélice." *Change* 34-35 (1978): 207-14.
"Etat: lecture un." *Action Poétique* 74 (1978): 30-32.

Trans. "Gertrude Stein: Arthur, une grammaire." *Action Poétique* 76 (1978): 59-78.
Trans. "Gertrude Stein: deux textes de 'Comment écrire.'" *Po&sie* 4 (1978): 50-64.
"Gertrude Stein, Gertrude Stein et Gertrude Stein." *Critique* 379 (1978): 1095-1106.
Graal fiction. Paris: Gallimard, 1978.
"La princesse Hoppy ou le conte du Labrador, chapitre 2: Myrtilles et Béryl." *Bibliothèque Oulipienne* 7 (1978).
"Les trobaïritz." *Action Poétique* 75 (1978): 39-41.
La viellesse d'Alexandre: essai sur quelques états récents du vers français. 1978. Rev. ed. Paris: Ramsay, 1988.
With D. Pemerle and Jean-Pierre Faye, trans. *Jerome Rothenberg: poèmes pour le jeu du silence*. Paris: Bourgois, 1978.
With Pierre Lartigue, Gaston Planet, Lionel Ray, and Paul Louis Rossi. *Inimaginaire IV*. Paris: La Ferté Macé, Privately printed, 1978.

1979

"Comme brûle jamais. Dit." *Change* 38 (1979): 43-49.
"Cri, ou comme brûle jamais dit." *Critique* 385-86 (1979): 533-36.
"De: 'paroi et dix poèmes' (cinq poèmes)." *La Rose Brunie* 1 (1979).
"Galehaut et l'éros mélancolique." *Mezura* 1 (1979): 3-37.
"'id'- chapitre quatre: poutou du soir." *Change* 38 (1979): 21-29.
"Je dis, à moins que le sel ne la roue." *La Répétition* 20 (1979).
"Mississippi haibun: description d'un projet." *In'hui* 8 (1979): 8-17.
Description du Projet. *Mezura* 9 (1979).
"Note biographique sur Jane Austen." In *Jane Austen: orgueil et préjugés*. Paris: Bourgois, 1979. 313-21.
"Obscurité et huit poèmes." *Action Poétique* 77 (1979): 112-19.
"Poèmes." *SubStance* 23-24 (1979): 37-45.
Poème commençant : "L'arbre le temps..." Paris: Orange Export Ltd., 1979.
"Préparation d'un portrait formel de Georges Perec." *L'Arc* 76 (1979): 54-60.
"La princesse Hoppy ou le conte du Labrador: chapitre trois: l'aventure de l'astronome." *Change* 38 (1979): 11-20.
"Quatre pages de poèmes: page six, neuf, onze, quatorze." *Action Poétique* 79 (1979): 84, 89, 99, 133.
"La réponse: au problème de l'amour." *Inédits* 6 (1979): n.p.
"Sept questions sur *La vieillesse d'Alexandre*" (interview with Jacques Darras). *In'hui* 8 (1979): 8-17.
"Le silence de la mathématique jusqu'au fond de la langue, poésie." *Po&sie* 10 (1979): 110-24.
With Florence Delay. *Graal théâtre: Gauvain et le chevalier vert*. Ed. Jeanne Lafitte. Approches Répertoire 5 du NTNM.
With Florence Delay. *Graal théâtre: Lancelot du lac*. Ed. Jeanne Lafitte. Approches Répertoire 6 du NTNM.
With Florence Delay. *Graal théâtre: Merlin l'enchanteur*. Ed. Jeanne Lafitte. Approches Répertoire 4 du NTNM.
With Paul Fournel. "L'hôtel de sens." *Bibliothèque Oulipienne* 10 (1979).
With Gérard Le Vot and Pierre Lusson. "La chanson de 'l'amour de loin' de Jaufre Rudel: essai de lecture rythmique." *Mezura* 3 (1979): 3-92.

1980

"La canso de noigandres." *Banana Split* 2 (1980): 81-85.
"Una carta a Jane." Trans. Andrés Sánchez Robayna. *Espiral* 8 (1980): 7-12.
"5 poèmes." Trans. William Bronk. *Comme* 108 (1980): 41-48.
"Du 'jardin de l'effort.'" Trans. Keith Waldrop. *Comme* 108 (1980): 87-96.
"Ici." *Cahiers Valentin Bru* 13-14 (1980): 10-11.
"La lampe; mur; gris; . . . partition de 13 compositions rythmiques abstraites." *Po&sie* 15 (1980): 61-75.
"N'abolira Lazare." In Stéphane Mallarmé, *Un coup de dés n'abolira le hasard*. Ed. Mitsou Ronat. Paris: D'Atelier, 1980. 10-11.
"Neuf éclat de l'âge des saints dans la vieille poésie irlandaise." *Solaire* 28 (1980).
"Onze onzains estramps en tons distincts." *Comme* 108 (1980): 37-39.
"Paysages déductifs." In *Travail de poésie*. Ed. Claude Royet-Journoud. *Revue de l'Université Libre de Bruxelles* 1-2 (1980): 63-72.
Ed. "Sonnet et sextine de Vasquin Philieul." *Po&sie* 14 (1980): 26-34.
Ed. and trans. *Les troubadours*. Paris: Seghers-Laffont, 1980.
With Michel Deguy, eds. *Vingt poètes américains*. Paris: Gallimard, 1980.
With Florence Delay. "La nuit des chants: une cérémonie navaho." *Po&sie* 13 (1980): 91-120.
With Gérard Le Vot and Pierre Lusson. "La sextine d'Arnaut Daniel: essai de lecture rythmique." *Colloque Musique, Littérature, Société au Moyen-Age. Actes Centre d'Etudes Médiévales de l'Université de Picardie* (1980): 123-57.
With Pierre Lusson. "Lectures rythmiques XI-XII: deux sonnets en vers imbriqués d'Etienne Jodelle." *Mezura* 10 (1980): 1-43.

1981

"La bête glatissant: graal fiction." *Change* 40 (1981): 157-68.
"Brouette rouge et chose vers." *In'hui* 14 (1981): 71-75.
Trans. Lewis Carroll. *La chasse au snark*. Geneva: Slatkine, 1981.
"Cinq poèmes extraits de 'Une lettre à Jane': Dix poèmes privées." In *Anthologie 80*. Paris: Le Castor Astral, 1981. 240-41.
"Dire la poésie." *Nouvelle Revue de Psychanalyse* 23 (1981): 5-21.
"Dors." *Nouvelle Revue Française* 339 (1981): 19-37.
Dors, précédé de Dire la poésie. Paris: Gallimard, 1981.
"Edward Herbert, Lord of Cherbury." *Po&sie* 19 (1981): 11-24.
"Io et le loup." *Bibliothèque Oulipienne* 15 (1981).
"Lettre à Maria Gisborne." *Po&sie* 16 (1981): 74-80.
"Notes pour le stage Oulipo de Villeneuve-les-Avignon, 3-18 juillet 1981." *Action Poétique* 85 (1981): 77-80.
"La prose invisible d'Anthony Trollope." *Critique* 405-6 (1981): 165-89.
"La sixième bucolique de Virgile. Version translatine de Jacques Roubaud (fragment)." *Faix* 5 (1981): 48-51.
Trans. Charles Reznikoff. *Témoignage*. Paris: Hachette, 1981.
With Florence Delay. *Graal théâtre: Joseph d'Arimanthie et Merlin l'enchanteur*. Paris: Gallimard, 1981.
With Paul Fournel, trans. *Italo Calvino: la forêt racine-labyrinthe*. Geneva: Slatkine-Garance, 1981.
With Pierre Lusson. "Sur la devise de noeud et de feu." *Langue Française* 49 (1981): 49-67.

With Oulipo. *Atlas de la littérature potentielle*. Paris: Gallimard, 1981.
With Alix Cléo Roubaud, trans. Gerard M. Hopkins. "La poésie et le vers." *Action Poétique* 84 (1981): 3-12.
With Alix Cléo Roubaud, trans. "Gertrude Stein: 'Lifting Belly' (fragm.)." *Action Poétique* 82-83 (1981): 87-97.

1982

Introd. Albert-Marie Schmidt. *L'amour noir*. Geneva: Slatkine, 1982. i-vii.
"Deux poèmes." *Skôria* 1 (1982): n.p.
"La fenêtre veuve." *Po&sie* 22 (1982): 29-56.
Trans. "Italo Calvino: le monde regarde le monde." *CNAC Magazine* 10 (1982): 15.
Introd. Oulipo. *La bibliothèque oulipienne*, vol. 1. Geneva: Slatkine, 1982.
"Quelques propositions pour l'étude des mètres iambiques." In *Grammaire transformationnelle: théorie et méthodologie*. Paris: Centre de Recherche de l'Université de Paris VIII, 1982. 291-312.
"Rakki tai." In *Rendez-vous à Aulnay*. Aulnay-sous-Bois: Bibliothèque Municipale, 1982. 124-27.
"Si quelque chose noir: douze poèmes." *Altaforte* 7 (1982): 29-38.
"Sur le sonnet rapporté I." In "Pierre Getzler, Pierre Lusson, Jacques Roubaud: les armes de l'amour (matériaux pour une étude du sonnet pétrarquiste européen)." *Cahiers de Poétique Comparée* 6 (1982): 85-159.
With Alix Cléo Roubaud, trans. "Vingt poèmes: Paul Blackburn, Clark Coolidge, Ron Padgett, Ted Berrigan." *Change* 41 (1982): 129-49.

1983

Les animaux de tout le monde. Illus. Marie Borel and Jean-Yves Cousseau. Paris: Ramsay, 1983. Rev. ed. Paris: Seghers, 1990.
"Gertrude Stein: Grammaticus." *In'hui* 0 (1983): 45-59.
Ed. and introd. "Guy Le Fevre de la Boderie: 22 sonnets: 'son pur cristal roule en sa pure grace.'" *Po&sie* 24 (1983): 107-17.
"Ombre, eloge inverse (I et II)." *Change International* 1 (1983): 112-13.
"Le pentamètre iambique dans mille sonnets élizabethians." *Poétique Comparée* 8 (1983): 41-112.
"Photographie; and the past performance of the sun: 6+2 1/2 poèmes pour A1.B1.C1." In Henri Deluy. *L'anthologie arbitraire d'une nouvelle poésie*. Paris: Flammarion, 1983. 299-310.
Le roi Arthur: au temps des chevaliers et des enchanteurs. Paris: Hachette, 1983.
"Shadow: Inverted Praise." Trans. Michael Bishop. *Ethos* 1.2 (1983): 90-92.
With Florence Delay, trans. "Deux poèmes d'Oskar Pastior." *Action Poétique* 89-90 (1983): 75-76.
With Pierre Lusson. "Les armes de l'amour, deuxième partie: le sonnet de Veniero et ses traductions: une lecture rythmique." *Poétique Comparée* 7 (1983): 7-32.
With Pierre Lusson. "Les armes de l'amour, quatrième partie: sur le sonnet rapporté II." *Poétique Comparée* 7 (1983): 45-59.
With Pierre Lusson. "Les armes de l'amour, troisième partie: Etienne Jodelle: noeud, feu et retz." *Poétique Comparée* 7 (1983): 33-44.

1984

Trans. "David Antin: Qu'est-ce que je fais ici?" In "David Antin: poèmes parlés." *Les Cahiers des Brisants* (1984): 63-90.
"Débris d'un projet commun maintenant sans objet." Photography by Alix Cléo Roubaud. *Change International* 2 (1984): 54-55.
"Des poètes aujourd'hui lecteurs de Rimbaud." *Textuel* 83-84.14 (1984): 71-87.
"Entiers surnaturels: première partie; entiers élémentaires." *Cahiers Mathématiques de l'Université de Paris X* (1984): 1-41.
"Instants poétiques qualifiés." *Action Poétique* 96-97 (1984): 61-74.
Introd. and ed. "Jean du Clicquet, seigneur de Flammermont: sonnets jettez en avant-propos." *Po&sie* 28 (1984): 3-27.
Ed. Alix Cléo Roubaud. *Journal, 1979-1983*. Paris: Seuil, 1984.
Trans. "Peter Riley: en suivant la veine." *In'hui* 19 (1984): 102-4.
"Possibilités étroites." In Oulipo. "A Georges Perec." *Bibliothèque Oulipienne* 23 (1984): 47.
"Sur une dynastie de programme qui aura pour nom 'Les alexandrins.'" *Action Poétique* 95 (1984): 43-44.
"Le train traverse la nuit." *Bibliothèque Oulipienne* 26 (1984).
With Gérard Le Vot and Pierre Lusson. "La conveniencia del texto y de la melodía en la canción de Los Trovadores." *Revista de Musicología* 7.1 (1984): 45-72.

1985

"Arithmétique surnaturelle et forme poétique: énoncés préparatoires à une théorie du sonnet I." *Poétique Comparée* 99 (1985): 67-136.
"Arithmétique surnaturelle et forme poétique (suite)." *Cahiers de Poétique Comparée* 12 (1985): 9-96.
La belle Hortense. Paris: Ramsay, 1985. Paris: Seghers, 1990. *Our Beautiful Heroine*. Trans. David Kornacker. Woodstock, N.Y.: Overlook Press, 1987.
Trans. "Christopher Middleton: Un autre Banquo." *Po&sie* 33 (1985): 24-29.
Lums. Paris: Manicle, 1985.
"What Have They Done to Us?: The Theory Monster and the Writer." In *Ideas from France: The Legacy of French Theory*. Ed. Lisa Appignanesi. London: ICA, 1985, 1989. 19-24.
Introd. and ed. "Zachairie de Vitré: essais de méditations poétiques." *Po&sie* 34 (1985): 117-26.
With Jean Gaudaire Thor. In *Du noir tombe*. Paris: Colorature, 1985.

1986

"La concorde des deux langages et cinq poèmes." In *Ecrire: pour Jean Levaillant*. Paris: Paris VIII, 1986. 321-28.
"Deux poésies: 'les grands paradoxes sont muets'; encre simulacre." *In Plano* 75 (1986).
"Dynastie: études sur le vers français. Sur l'alexandrin classique (première partie)." *Cahiers de Poétique Comparée* 13 (1986): 47-109.
"En." *Notes* 1 (1986): 7.
"Exercice du style." *L'Ane* 26 (1986): 46-47.

La fleur inverse: essai sur l'art formel des troubadours. Paris: Ramsay, 1986. 2nd ed. Paris: Belles Lettres, 1994.
"La maladie de l'âme V; les airs, les eaux, les lieux." *In Plano* 15 (1986). Trans. Eugene Helmle. *Passages.* Frankfurt: Institut Français de Francfort, 1986. 77-78.
"Méditation de la désolation." *Action Poétique* 102 (1986): 21-25.
Trans. "Mi-été et deux autres poèmes," by William Bronk. *In Plano* 79 (1986): n.p.
"Poèmes." *Poésie 86* 12 (1986): 32-35.
Quelque chose noir. Paris: Gallimard, 1986. *Some Thing Black.* Trans. Rosmarie Waldrop. Elmwood Park: Dalkey Archive Press, 1990.
With Laure Durien, trans. [Jim Wedderburn]. Tom Raworth. "L'arbre aux citrons." *In Plano* 69 (1986): n.p.

1987

"Au dessous du miroir." *FMR* 8 (1987): 68-74.
Introd. Oulipo. *La bibliothèque oulipienne*, vol. 2. Paris: Ramsay, 1987. Reprint Paris: Le Castor Astral, 1990.
"109 miro-gramme." In *Poésie internationale, anthologie.* Luxembourg: Guy Binsfels, 1987. 25-28.
Preface. In Micaela Henich. *Dessins.* Les Palissades Atlantides: Berggruen et Cie, 1987.
L'enlèvement d'Hortense. Paris: Ramsay, 1987. *Hortense Is Abducted.* Trans. Dominic di Bernardi. Elmwood Park: Dalkey, 1989.
"Les exercices de style de Raymond Queneau." In *Actes des Troisièmes Assises de la Traduction Littéraire–Arles 86.* Arles: Actes Sud, 1987. 99-125.
"Feuilles et lumières." *Lieux d'écrit.* Ed. Jean-Yves Cousseau and Jean-Pierre Nouhaud. Paris: Royaumont, 1987. 39.
"L'image même." In Laure Durien. *L'image même.* Paris: Limon, 1987.
"La pluralité des mondes de Lewis (vi)." *Zuk* 2 (1987): n.p.
"Poésie et l'extrême contemporain." *Po&sie* 41 (1987): 40-44.
Preface. *Poètes du Moyen Age.* Ed. Jacqueline Cerquiglini and Anne Berthelot. Paris: Hachette, 1987. 10.
Ed. "98 Sonnets françaises, 1550-1625." *Action Poétique* 109 (1987): 2-50.
With Marie Borel, trans. "Tom Raworth: Prétension." *Po&sie* 42 (1987): 33-41.
With Florence Delay, trans. *Sor Juana Inés de la Cruz: le divin Narcisse.* Paris: Gallimard, 1987. 65-115.
With Pierre Lartigue, introd. In *Vasquin Philieul.* Ed. Laure D'Avignon. Arles: Actes Sud, 1987.

1988

"Déduction de la forme (préliminaires)." *Action Poétique* 113-114 (1988): 11-18.
"Dynastie: études sur le vers français. Sur l'alexandrin classique (deuxième partie)." *Cahiers de Poétique Comparée* 16 (1988): 41-60.
"Enquête sur un cercle, une robe et un moulin." *FMR* 14 (1988): 34-42.
"Un moment interne troue l'onde d'orgence que raye d'ortie le néant d'attente sans trace." In *Transparences et opacité: hommage à Mitsou Ronat.* Ed. Pierre Pica and Tibor Papp. Paris: Cerf, 1988. 29-41.
"La pluralité des mondes de Lewis (ix)." *Zuk* 10 (1988): n.p.
"Poésie, contemporaine extrême." *La poésie française au tournant des années 80.* Ed. Philippe Delaveau. Paris: Corti, 1988. 179-85.

"Première digression sur les débuts de la photographie." In *Du visible à l'invisible. Pour Max Milner*. Paris: Corti, 1988. 205-210.
"Quelques poèmes." *Action Poétique* 112 (1988): 18-23.
Trans. "Rosmarie Waldrop: la reproduction des profils (frag)." *Zuk* 12 (1988): n.p.
With Marie Borel, trans. "Stephen Emerson: quand elle se quitte." *Zuk* 12 (1988): n.p.
With Marie Borel, trans. "Stephen Emerson: rouges." *Po&sie* 46 (1988): 122-24.
With Marie Borel. *Tom Raworth: six jours et six poèmes*. Marseille: Spectres Familiers 1988.
With Florence Delay. *Partition rouge*. Paris: Seuil, 1988.
With Pierre Getzler. "LISSON 1: Matériaux pour une base de donnés du sonnet français, 1. Une liste de sonnets composés avant 1630. Première partie, 1536-1573." *Mezura* 14 (1988).

1989

"Absence de la poésie?" *Débat* 54 (1989): 187-89.
"Deux incises." *Cahiers Pour un Temps* (1989): 133-41.
'le grand incendie de Londres.' Récit, avec incises et bifurcations. (la Destruction). Paris: Seuil, 1989.
"Jacques Roubaud lit l'article 'Jacques Roubaud' dans le volume *XXième siècle de la littérature, textes et documents* (Collection Henri Mitterand)." *Action Poétique* 115 (1989): 32-34.
Trans. "Louis Zukofsky: Roses." *Zuk* 18 (1989): n.p.
Trans. "Mina Loy: Gertrude Stein et dix poèmes des dernières années." *Action Poétique* 115 (1989): 142-53.
"La pluralité des mondes de Lewis (xviii)." *Zuk* 18 (1989): n.p.
"La pluralité des mondes de Lewis (i, ii, iii, v & xi)." *Lendemains* 52 (1989): 41-42.
"Poèmes." In *Tarascon 1988: cinquièmes rencontres internationales de poésies contemporaines*. Paris: Agrippa, 1989. 25-28.
"Quatrième déduction de la lumière." *La Photographie* 23 (1989): 17-22.
Traktat vom Licht (Traité de la lumière). Trans. Alexandre Metraux. Bremen: Neue Bremer Presse, 1989.
With Marie Borel, trans. "Tom Raworth: Sections d'éternité." *Zuk* 24 (1989): n.p.
With Marie Borel, trans. "Lyn Hejinian: From the cell." *Action Poétique* 117 (1989): 64-68.
With Marie Borel, trans. *Prétense*, by Tom Raworth. Paris: La Tuilerie Tropicale, 1989.
With Paul Braffort, Jacques Jouet, and José-Luis Reina. "Entretien avec Jacques Roubaud, Paul Braffort et Jacques Jouet, membres de l'*Oulipo*." *Lendemains* 52 (1989): 33-40.
With Laure Durien, trans. "Tom Raworth: Sections d'éternité." *Zuk* 16 (1989): n.p.
With Pierre Getzler. "LISSON 2: Matériaux pour une base de donnés du sonnet français, 1. Une liste de sonnets composés avant 1630. Deuxième partie, 1574-1585." *Mezura* 15 (1989).
With Pierre Getzler. "LISSON 3: Matériaux pour une base de donnés du sonnet français, 1. Une liste de sonnets composés avant 1630. Troisième partie, 1586-1598." *Mezura* 16 (1989).
With Pierre Getzler. "LISSON 4: Matériaux pour une base de donnés du sonnet français, 1. Une liste de sonnets composés avant 1630. Quatrième partie, 1599-1610." *Mezura* 18 (1989).

With Pierre Getzler. "LISSON 5: Matériaux pour une base de donnés du sonnet français, 1. Une liste de sonnets composés avant 1630. Cinquième partie 1611-1630." *Mezura* 19 (1989).
With Pierre Getzler. "LISSON 6: Matériaux pour une base de donnés du sonnet français, 1. Une liste de sonnets composés avant 1630. Sixième partie (sans date) & Appendice: liste d'ensembles d'au moins 10 sonnets après 1630." *Mezura* 20 (1989).

1990

Trans. *Billy the Kid*, by Jack Spicer. Paris: Fourbis, 1990.
"La disposition numérologique du *rerum vulgarium fragmenta*, précédée de Vie brève de François Pétrarque." In Oulipo. *La bibliothèque oulipienne*, vol. 3. Paris: Seghers, 1990.
Echanges de la lumière. Paris: Métailié, 1990.
L'exil d'Hortense. Paris: Seghers, 1990.
"La forme du sonnet français de Marot à Malherbe: recherche de seconde rhétorique." *Cahiers de Poétique Comparée* 17-19 (1990).
"Image et piction." *Fig* 3 (1990): 47-54.
"Je n'ai aucun souvenir de: autrement dit je ne me souviens pas." *Les Lettres Françaises* 1 (1990): 9.
"Méditation à lui-même." *Banana Split* 27 (1990): 196-97.
"La pluralité des mondes de Lewis (iv, x, xii, xiii, xv, xvi, xvii, xxi, xxii, xxviii, xxx)." *Po&sie* 52 (1990): 87-90.
La princesse Hoppy ou le conte du Labrador. Illus. Jean-Claude Castelli. Paris: Hatier, 1990. Trans. Bernard Hoepffner. Normal, Ill.: Dalkey Archive Press, 1993.
"Prose du sixième jour." *Banana Split* 26 bis (1990): 73-80.
"Récit et langue: à propos de '53 Jours' de Georges Perec." *Littérature* 80 (1990): 95-100.
Trans. "Robert Kelly: fleurs de perpetuelle coincidence." *Po&sie* 52 (1990): 26-29.
"Secondes litanies de la vierge." In Oulipo. *La bibliothèque oulipienne*, vol. 3. Paris: Seghers, 1990.
Soleil du soleil: le sonnet français de Marot à Malherbe. Paris: P.O.L., 1990.
"Vers une oulipisation conséquente de la littérature." In Oulipo. *La bibliothèque oulipienne*, vol. 3. Paris: Seghers, 1990.
With Michel Chaillou, Michel Deguy, Florence Delay, Natach Michel, and Denis Roche. *L'Hexameron.* Paris: Seuil, 1990.
With Pierre Getzler. "Matériaux pour une base de données du sonnet français. Une liste de sonnets composés avant 1630." *Mezura* 23 (1990).

1991

Les animaux de personne. Illus. Marie Borel and Jean-Yves Cousseau. Paris: Seghers, 1991.
"L'auteur oulipien." In *L'auteur et le manuscrit.* Ed. Michel Contat. Paris: Presses Universitaires de France, 1991. 77-91.
Impressions de France: incursions dans la littérature du premier seizième siècle, 1500-1550. Paris: Hatier, 1991.
"Le Pen est-il français?" *Action Poétique* 126 (1991): 2.
La pluralité des mondes de Lewis. Paris: Gallimard, 1991.
Scotland. Photography by Jean-Pierre Gilson. Paris: Editions Creaphis, 1991.

1992

[poems]. *Une autre anthologie. Biennale des poètes du Val-de-Marre.* Paris: Fourbis, 1992. 201-6.
"Autres morales élémentaires." *Bibliothèque Oulipienne* 55 (1992).
"Les entretiens d'étretat I-XV." *Le Monde de l'Education* (1992-93): 192-206.
"Grande taciturnité (1 & 2)." *Cahier du Refuge* 17 (1992): 21-22.
"N-ines, autrement dit quenines." *Bibliothèque Oulipienne* 65 (1992).
"Nuit sans date." *L'Immature* 4 (1992): 42-44.
"S + 7, le retour." *Bibliothèque Oulipienne* 54 (1992).
"Voyage d'hier." *Bibliothèque Oulipienne* 53 (1992).
Preface. *L'art à l'école.* Paris: Ministère de l'Education Nationale et de la Culture, 1992. 4-7.
With Marie Borel, trans. "Condamné à temps," by Tom Raworth. *Nioques* 4 (1992): 63-69.
With Pierre Lusson. "Materialen zu einer formalen Lekture zweier Gedichte von Reinhard Preissnitz." In *Reinhard Preissnitz symposium, Paris 1990.* Vienna: Neue Texte, 1992. 56-60.

1993

La boucle. Paris: Seuil, 1993.
"Crise de théâtre." *Bibliothèque Oulipienne* 61 (1993).
"Une critique de la poésie et quelques réponses." *Action Poétique* 131 (1993): 38-40.
Trans. "Deux satires," by Mina Loy. *If* 2 (1993): 19-26.
L'invention du fils de Leoprepes. Saulxures: Circé, 1993.
"Lieu de naissance." *Lieux Dits* 47 (1993): 14.
"Lisant les rues." *Action Poétique* 133-34 (1993-94): 114-23.
"La mémoire oubliée." In *L'art, est-il une connaissance?* Paris: Le Monde, 1993. 149-66.
"N-ines, autrement dit quenines (encore)." *Bibliothèque Oulipienne* 66 (1993).
"The Oulipo and Combinatorial Art." Trans. Harry Mathews. *New Observations* 99 (1993): 5-11.
Interview with Florence Delay. "La pluralité des proses de J. Roubaud." *Quai Voltaire* 10 (1993): 17-27.
Interview with Marie-Anne Guérin. "La prose du cinéma." *Cahiers du Cinéma* 471 (1993): 52-55.
Interview with Henri Deluy. "La question de la poésie: énumérations en vue d'un entretien." *Action Poétique* 133-34 (1993-94): 27-30.
"Rosengang." In *Typoésie.* Ed. Jérome Peignot. Paris: Imprimerie Nationale, 1993. 310-11.
Sphère de la mémoire (Pentalogue). Saulxures: Circé, 1993.
Le tout-venin d'une image irréductible, littéralement. In *L'image dans le tapis.* Paris: Association Française d'Action Artistique, 1993.
With Jacques Jouet. "[ə]." *Bibliothèque Oulipienne* 64 (1993).

1994

"Le calcul des ombres." In *BEAUX ! ART*. Le Mans: L'Ecole Régionale, 1994. 178-89.
"Cucumber Kid." *Info-matin* 156 (1994): 18-19.
"Deux poèmes pour Henri Deluy." *Java* 11 (1994): 52-55.
"L'éclair." *La Lettre Mensuelle* 133 (1994): 28.
Interview with Denise Le Dantec. "En couleur et en noir et blanc." *L'Ane* 57-58 (1994): 12-13.
"La langue des enfants." *La Main de Signe* 11-12 (1994): 15-22.
Interview with Dominique Chouchan. "La mémoire oubliée." *La Recherche* 257 (1994): 840-42.
Monsieur Goodman rêve des chats. Paris: Gallimard, 1994.
"L'Oulipo et l'art combinatoire." *Giallu* 3 (1994): 5-16.
"La parole en image de Mitsumasa Anno." *La Revue des Livres pour Enfants* 157 (1994): 60-69.
"Le poème comme théorème." *Le Monde des Débats* 17 (1994): 10.
"Un poème pour Claude Roy." In "De temps en temps." *Journal de la Fête du Livre de Bron* (1994): 3.
"La poésie américaine sous le pontificat de Helen Vendler I." *Action Poétique* 135 (1994): 52-55.
Preface. *Pour un autre soleil . . . le sonnet occitan des origines à nos jours*. Orléans: Paradigme, 1994. iii-v.
"Les quatre saisons de Mr Goodman." *FMR* 53 (1994): 114-26.
"Quelques données sur le père Gesualdo et sa Plutosofia." *Mezura* 29 (1994).
Preface. "Sans-A." In Jacques Arago. *Voyage autour du monde sans la lettre A*. Illus. Topor. Paris: Les Autodidactes, 1994. 7-12.
"Le temps de l'éclaire." *Antigone* 19 (1994): 19-28.
"Tombeau de Diogène d'Œnoanda." *La Licorne* 29 (1994): 373-77.
Interview with Serge Gavronsky. In *Toward a New Poetics*. Ed. and trans. Serge Gavronsky. Berkeley: University of California Press, 1994. 270-303.
With Oulipo. "Troll de tram (le tramway de Strasbourg)." *Bibliothèque Oulipienne* 68 (1994).

1995

Ed. *128 poèmes composés en langue française de Guillaume Apollinaire à 1968, une anthologie de poésie contemporaine*. Paris: Gallimard, 1995.
"Une couronne de laurier pour Philippe Sollers." *Passages* 68 (1995): 78.
"Cuentan, cuentan las piedras." Trans. Aurelio Asain. In *Las palabras son puentes: a Octavio Paz en sus ochenta años*. Mexico City: Vuelta, 1995.
"Denis Roche classique pour tous." *Magazine Littéraire* 330 (1995): 100.
"Hypothèse du compact." *Revue de Littérature Générale* 1 (1995): 289-99.
"Hypothèses génétiques concernant la perecquation du roman." *Le Cabinet d'Amateur* 4 (1995): 9-23.
Mille e tre, deux. 200 flèches. Illus. Micaëla Henich. Dijon: Théâtre Typographique, 1995.
"Nécessité et condition d'un hypertexte: à propos de la composition d'un ouvrage intitulé *'le grand incendie de Londres'*." In *Littérature et informatique: la littérature générée par ordinateur*. Ed. Alain Vuillemin and Michel Lenoble. Arras: Artois, 1995. 293-300.
Poésie, etcetera: ménage. Paris: Stock, 1995.

"Poésie et nombre." In *Mathématiques et art*. Ed. M. Loi. Paris: Hermann, 1995. 206-10.
"Poésie, mémoire, nombre, temps, rythme, contrainte, forme, etc.: remarques." *Mezura* 30 (1995).
"Poésie, mémoire, nombre, temps, rythme, contrainte, forme, etc.: remarques, vol. 2." *Mezura* 33 (1995).
"Poésie, mémoire, nombre, temps, rythme, contrainte, forme, etc.: remarques, vol. 3." *Mezura* 35 (1995).
Interview with Thelma Slowley. "La poésie ne fait pas partie de la littérature." *BARCA Symptome et Révolution* 5 (1995): 145-63.
"Quelques lignes." In *Mélange sur l'œuvre de Paul Bénichou*. Paris: Gallimard, 1995. 129-34.
"Rencontre d'un poète français avec la poésie japonaise." *La Revue de Hiyoshi* 20 (1995): 242-64.
"Six petites pièces logiques." *Nioques* 10 (1995): 103-20.
"Le temps de la poésie." In *Dix ans de poésie direct*. Marseille: C.I.P.M., 1995. 36.
"Trois ruminations." *Bibliothèque Oulipienne* 81 (1995).

1996

"La convenance du texte et de la mélodie dans la chanson des troubadours." *Cahiers du Centre de Recherches Musicologiques*. Ed. Anne Penesco. Lyons: Université Lumière, 1996.
"La dernière balle perdue." Festival de la Nouvelle à Saint-Quentin, 1996.
"D'un projet." In *Le projet littéraire et sa traduction*. Saint-Nazaire: Maison des Ecrivains Etrangers et des Traducteurs, 1996. 45-57.
"& (esperluette)." In *Le poète que je cherche à être; Cahiers Michel Deguy*. Paris: La Table Ronde, 1996. 17-21.
La fenêtre veuve: prose orale. Dijon: Théâtre Typographique, 1996.
"Fragment de prose parisienne." *Le Nouveau Recueil* (June-August 1996): 94-106.
"Le nombre Opalka." In *Le roman Opalka*. Paris: Di voir, 1996. 27.
"Poésie, mémoire, nombre, temps, rythme, contrainte, forme, etc.: remarques suivi des premières remarques de Monsieur Lusson sur les remarques de Monsieur Roubaud." *Mezura* 39 (1996).
"Le roman de côté." *Revue de Hiyoshi* 23 (1996): 79-99.
"Le roman du lecteur?" *Le Débat* 90 (1996): 52-61.
"Roman Photo I-II"; "Méditation du 8.5.85." *Chariton Review* 22.1 (1996): 80-85.
"RVF 1-14." *Poésie 96* 61 (1996): 67-71.
"La terre est plate: 99 dialogues dramatiques, mais brefs." *Bibliothèque Oulipienne* 83 (1996).
"What a Map!" In *What a Man!* Paris: Le Castor Astral, 1996. 49-50.
With Florence Delay, trans. "Jorge-Luis Borges: Browning se resout à être poète." In *L'épreuve des mots*. Paris: Stock, 1996.
With Florence Delay, trans. "Per el Yiyo; le choeur: diversions," by Bernard Manicet. In B. Manicet. *Le fou est dans la langue*. Annales de Littérature Occitane, William Blake & Cie., 1996. 181-88.

1997

L'abominable tisonnier de John McTaggart Ellis Mc Taggard. Paris: Seuil, 1997.
"Un certain disparate (fragments) par François Le Lionnais, suivi d'un témoignage de Jacques Roubaud et d'un rapport de commission." *Bibliothèque Oulipienne* 85 (1997).

Le chevalier silence: une aventure des temps aventureux. Paris: Gallimard, 1997.
Ciel et terre et ciel et terre, et ciel. Charenton: Flohic, 1997.
La dernière balle perdue. Paris: Fayard, 1997.
"Digt." *Banana Split* 12.13 (1997): 90-95.
"Ecrit par son support." *Formules* 1 (1997): 188.
"Fragment inédit de la branche quatre." *La Licorne* 40 (1997): 255-61.
"Jacques Roubaud on the ideal croissant." In Elisabeth Gordon. *Paris Out of Hand: A Wayward Guide.* San Francisco: Chronicle Books, 1997. 80.
"John Constable et l'histoire naturelle de l'air." *Mezura* 47 (1997).
"(Maggie: à propos du 'Concert of doors' de Franz Kamin)." *La Licorne* 40 (1997): 223-28.
"Mezura, spectre (*d'un roman moral*)." *La Licorne* 40 (1997): 211-22.
Interview with Pierre Lartigue. "Mandrin au cube." *La Licorne* 40 (1997): 159-62.
Mathématique: (récit). Paris: Seuil, 1997.
Ombres. Festival de la Nouvelle à Saint-Quentin, 1997. Ill. Benoît Jacques.
"On doit toujours penser à Staline, même quand on fait l'amour!" *Action Poétique* 148-49 (1997): 19.
"Poésie, mémoire, nombre, temps, rythme, contrainte, forme, etc.: remarques." *Mezura* 41 (1997).
Interview with Thelma Sowley. "La poésie ne fait pas partie de la littérature." *Bar!* 5 (1997): 145-63.
"Pursuing the Voice of Poetry in the Conversation of Mankind." In *Translation & Literature* 6.1 (1997): 8-22.
"Une route seule soleil." *Cahiers de la Bibliothèque Littéraire Jacques Doucet* 1 (1997): 136-44.
"S. Ramanujan et ses amis." *Mezura* 43 (1997).
"Si quelque chose noir (douze poèmes)." *La Licorne* 40 (1997): 229-34.
"Six codes du temps." In *On Kawara: Codes.* Paris: Galérie Ivan Lambert, 1997.
"Cet après-midi-là je fus rue de Bretagne." In *Cent ans passent comme un jour: 56 poètes pour Aragon.* Ed. Marie Etienne. Paris: Dumerchez, 1997.
(. . . (((*Titre provisoire (titre provisoire)) titre provisoire)) . . .) (titre provisoire).* Paris: Les Guères Epais, 1997. 139.
Interview with Pacaline Mourier-Casile and Dominique Moncond'huy. *La Licorne* 40 (1997): 163-80. Ed. and pref. Dominique Moncond'huy, Pascaline Mourier-Casile.
"Traité de la lumière." *La Licorne* 40 (1997): 235-54.
"XX et XY." In "Sexe: ce xé." *Bibliothèque Oulipienne* 90 (1997): 21-27.
With Maurice Bernard. *Quel avenir pour la mémoire?* Paris: Gallimard, 1997.
With Christian Boltanski. *Ensembles.* Paris: 9 février, 1997.
With Georges Perec. *"Le voyage d'hiver" suivi de "Le voyage d'hier."* Nantes: Le Passeur, 1997.

1998

"Langages, vérité (poétique), catégories, réponses et commentaires. " In Jaakko Hintikka. *Questions de logique et de phénoménologie.* Paris: Vrin, 1998.
L'Oulipo et les lumières, OULIPO und die Aufklärung. Tübingen: Le Divan, 1998.
"Pension Cardinal." In Jeanne Hilary. *La plume et le zinc: Writers in the cafés of Paris.* Vannes: Hazan, 1998.
[Poems]. In Pascal Boulanger. *Une "Action Poétique," de 1950 à aujourd'hui.* Paris: Flammarion, 1998.

1999

L'art de la liste: Die Kunst der Liste. Tübingen: Le Divan, 1999.
"Deductions concerning Marcel Bénabou, Oulipian Author (Notes)." Trans. Roxane Lapidus. *SubStance* 27.2 (1999): 37-40.
"Dix-neuf poèmes." In Valérie Lawitschka, Anne Longuet Marx. *Simone Boisecq: Le sculpteur et ses poètes.* Paris: Verdier, 1999. 19-30.
La forme d'une ville change plus vite, hélas, que le cœur des humains. Cent cinquante poèmes, 1991-1998. Paris: Gallimard, 1999.
"O baobab." *Bibliothèque Oulipienne* 98 (1999).
Interview. "Le poète qui se transporte." *La Vie du Rail et des Transports* 111 (December 22, 1999): 60-61.
With Michèle Grangaud and Jacques Jouet. *La Bibliothèque de Poitiers.* Poitiers: La Licorne, 1999.

2000

"Du jeu de Go comme stratégie de composition poétique." In *Échecs et Go.* Arles: Actes Sud, 2000.
"Grosstadt Paris." *Schreibheft, Zeitschrift für Literatur* 53 (2000): 91-92.
Menu, menu. Paris: Gallimard, 2000.
Poésie: (récit). Paris: Seuil, 2000.
"Quatre poèmes." In *L'anthologie 2000.* Tours: Farrago, 2000.
"Remarques sur le vers blanc dans la poésie française du second seizième siècle." In *Invisibilité du vers blanc.* Ed. Jacques Darras. Bruxelles: Le Cri, 2000. 36-45.
"Remarques sur quelques états présents de la poésie." *Poésie d'Aujourd'hui.* Tours: Farrago, 2000.
Traduire, journal. Caen: Nous, 2000.
"Sonnet-walking: New-York, and after, 29 Février – 15 Mars 2000." *Po&sie* 92 (2000): 90-103.
"Le voyage de Noël." *La Vie du Rail et du transport* (December 20, 2000): 43-49.
"Vous souvenez-vous de toutes les œuvres dont vous êtes l'auteur?" In *Voilà.* Paris: Musée d'Art moderne de la Ville de Paris (15 June-29 October), 2000.
With Marcel Bénabou, Jacques Jouet, Hervé Le Tellier. Interview with Jacques Neefs. "Oulipo, création mobile." *Genesis* 15 (2000): 121-32.
Interview with Henri Deluy. *Action Poétique* 157 (2000): 179-81.
With Denis Roche. "Portraits croisés." *Le Quotidien du Salon du Livre* 5 (March 21, 2000).

2001

Le crocodile. Illus. Zaü. Paris: Seghers, 2001.
"Déduction de Marcel Bénabou, auteur oulipien: notes." *Magazine Littéraire* 398 (2001): 55-57.
"Méditations commençantes par les sept premières *Stanzas in meditation* de Gertrude Stein." *Fin* 9 (2001): 5-13.
"Soixante-quatorze voyages pour un P.I.L.I." In Philippe Favier. *P.I.L.I. (Centenaire du Métro de Paris).* Paris: Les Fohlic, 2001.
"Traduire pour les 'idiots', Sebastien Châtellion et la Bible." *Recherches de Science Religieuse* 89.3 (2001): 353-76.
With Marcel Bénabou, Jacques Jouet, and Harry Mathews. *Un art simple et tout d'exécution, cinq leçons de l'Oulipo, cinq leçons sur l'Oulipo.* Paris: Circé, 2001.

2002

La bibliothèque de Warburg (version mixte). Paris: Seuil, 2002.
"Chaîne de remarques sur l'opération de traduction de poésie." In *Traduire, en poésie?* Paris: Farrago, 2002.
Preface. *Œuvres poétiques complètes d'Olivier Laronde.* Paris: Le Promeneur, 2002.
"Poésie et pensée: quelques remarques." In *La poésie pense-t-elle? Poésie* 92 (2002): 48-52.
Trans. *Steinzas in Médiation* by Joan Retallack. Bordeaux: Format Américain, 2002.
With Pierre Getzler and Françoise Pitras, eds. "Le sonnet en France, 1631-1800, alentour: matériaux pour une base de données du sonnet français." *Mezura* 48 (2002).

2003

"Cinq poèmes/Five Poems." *Sites* 7.2 (2003): 293-99.
"Le conte conte le conte et compte (extrait (inédit) de *La bibliothèque de Warburg, version longue).*" *Lendemain* 109 (2003): 103-16.
"Duchamp l'oulipien." *Bibliothèque Oulipienne* (2003).
Grande kyrielle du sentiment des choses. Paris: Nous, 2003.
Interview with Nadine Sautel. "Jacques Roubaud: le clinamen et l'Oulipo." *Magazine Littéraire* 425 (November 2003): 20-59.
Preface. Sylvia Townsend Warner. *Une lubie de monsieur fortune.* Trans. Denise Getzler. Paris: Gallimard, 2003.
Trans. *La reproduction des profiles,* by Rosmarie Waldrop. Paris: Melville, 2003.
Tokyo infra-ordinaire. Paris: Inventaire-Invention, 2003.
With Marie Borel and Jean L'Hour, trans. "Lévitique." In *La Bible.* Paris: Bayard, 2003.
With Marie Borel and Jean L'Hour, trans. "Nombres." In *La Bible.* Paris: Bayard, 2003.
With Marie Borel and Jean L'Hour, trans. "Qohélet." In *La Bible.* Paris: Bayard, 2003.

2004

Churchill 40, et autres sonnets de voyage (1990-1998). Paris: Gallimard, 2004.
Preface. Sylvia Townsend Warner. *Le cœur pur.* Trans. Denise Getzler. Paris: Gallimard, 2004.
"New remarks-M." *Cahier Critique de Poésie* 9 (2004): 51-87.
Preface. Jacques Bens. *De l'Oulipo et de la chandelle verte, poésie complete.* Paris: Gallimard, 2004.
"Le sonnet lichtenbergien." In Inès Oseki-Dépré. *Modes et modèles.* Aix-en-Provence: Université de Provence, 2004. 225-246.
Sous le soleil. Paris: Bayard, 2004.
"Sur la forme du sonnet mallarméen." *Cahiers de l'Association Internationale des Etudes Françaises* 56 (2004).
With Anne Garréta and Marcel Bénabou. *L'amour du Dr L.* Paris: Unebévue, 2004.

SECONDARY SOURCES

Andrews, Chris. "Constraint and Convention: The Formalism of the Oulipo." *Neophilologus* 87.2 (2003): 223-32.
Aoki, Shimpei. "Black Indebted Solely to His Handicap Stones for a Narrow Victory." *Go Review* 5.4 (1965): 24-37.
Armel, Aliette. "Jacques Roubaud: les cercles de la mémoire." *Le Magazine Littéraire* 311 (1993): 96-103.
———. "Roubaud le mathématicien." *Le Magazine Littéraire* 352 (1997): 78.
Bakhtin, Mikhail. *The Dialogic Imagination.* Ed. Michael Holquist. Trans. Caryl Emerson and Michael Holquist. Austin: University of Texas Press, 1981.
Barberger, Nathalie. "*La boucle*: du côté de Zazetski." *La Licorne* 40 (1997): 91-100.
Barth, John. "The Literature of Exhaustion." In *Metafiction.* Ed. Mark Currie. New York: Longman, 1995.
Barthes, Roland. *Essais critiques.* Paris: Seuil, 1964.
———. *Image-Music-Text.* Trans. and ed. Stephen Heath. New York: Hill and Wang, 1977.
———. *Sollers écrivain.* Paris: Seuil, 1979.
Baudart, Fabrice. *La poésie-fragments, néants, mémoire-dans "Autobiographie, chapitre dix" de Jacques Roubaud*, PhD diss., Université de Paris, 1991.
Beaudouin, Valérie. *Mètre et rythmes du vers classique: Corneille et Racine.* Paris: Champion, 2002.
Beaumatin, Eric, Pierre Getzler, Pierre Lusson, Françoise Pitras, and Léon Robel, eds. *Formes & mesure. Cercle Polivanov: pour Jacques Roubaud. Mélanges. Mezura* 49 (2001).
Bec, Pierre. *Burlesque et obscenité chez lez troubadours: pour une approche du contretexte médiéval.* Paris: Stock, 1984.
Belows, David. "The Pact of London." In *The Great Fire of London Casebook.* Ed. Peter Consenstein. Normal, Ill.: Dalkey Archive Press, 2003. http://www.center forbookculture.org/casebooks/casebook_london/belows.html (9/1/2004).
Bénabou, Marcel. "Ecrire sur Jacques Roubaud." *Lendemain* 109 (2003): 11-14.
Bens, Jacques. *Oulipo, 1960-1963.* Paris: Bourgois, 1980.
Blanchot, Maurice. *Le livre à venir.* Paris: Gallimard, 1959.
———. *L'entretien infini.* Paris: Gallimard, 1969.
———. *Faux pas.* Paris: Gallimard, 1971.
Bloom, Harold. *The Anxiety of Influence.* New York: Oxford University Press, 1973.
Bold, Steven. "Labyrynths of Invention from the New Novel to the Oulipo." *Neophilologus* 82.4 (1998): 543-57.
Bosquet, Alain. "Jacques Roubaud: *Quelque chose noir.*" *Nouvelle Revue Française* 405 (1986): 85-86.
———. "Jacques Roubaud, ou la technique ennemie du poème." *Le Monde des Livres* (February 22, 1974): 1.
———. "La poésie et ses techniques." *La Nouvelle Revue Française* (May 1974): 100-04.
Brasseur, Roland. "Relecture d'un ouvrage de poésie au moyen de l'ordinateur: *Appartient A* de Jacques Roubaud." In *Littérature et informatique: la littérature générée par ordinateur.* Ed. Alain Vuillemin and Michel Lenoble. Arras: Artois, 1995. 301-12.
Cage, John. *I-IV.* Cambridge: Harvard University Press, 1990.
Calsoyas, Aleka. "Celluloid Surgery: Poetry as Memory in Jacques Roubaud's *Autobiography, chapitre dix.*" *Lendemain* 109 (2003): 70-82.

Calvino, Italo. *The Uses of Literature*. Trans. Patrick Creagh. New York: Harcourt Brace Jovanovich, 1982.
———. *If on a Winter's Night a Traveler*. Trans. William Weaver. New York: Harcourt Brace Jovanovich, 1981.
Cardonne-Arlyck, Elizabeth. "Poésie, forme de vie (Jacques Roubaud)." *L'Esprit Créateur* 32.2 (1992): 89-101.
Cendrars, Blaise. *Du monde entier*. Paris: Denoël, 1947; rpt., Paris: Gallimard, 1967.
Chomei, Kamo-no. *Ten Foot Square Hut and Tales of the Heike*. Trans. A. L. Sadler. Westport: Greenwood Press, 1928.
Conort, Benoît. "Le chiffre de la mort." *Poesia da ciênca ciênca de poesia* (1992): 195-213.
———. "Tramer le deuil (table de lecture de *Quelque chose noir*)." *La Licorne* 40 (1997): 47-58.
Consenstein, Peter. "Asian Influence in the Poetry of Raymond Queneau and Jacques Roubaud." *West Virginia University Philological Papers* 40 (1994): 56-63.
———. "Jacques Roubaud: Life Mastered and Measured into a Masterpiece." In *The Great Fire of London Casebook*. Ed. Peter Consenstein. Normal, Ill.: Dalkey Archive Press, 2003. http://www.centerforbook culture.org/casebooks/casebook_london/consenstein.html (9/1/2004).
———. *Literary Memory, Consciousness and the Group Oulipo*. New York: Rodopi, 2002.
———. "La mémoire forgeant réversiblement des formes." *Lendemain* 109 (2003): 83-90.
———. "Memory and Oulipian Constraint." *Postmodern Culture* 6.1 (1995): 19.
———. "Rhythm and Meaning in the Poetry of Raymond Queneau and Jacques Roubaud." PhD diss., Columbia University, 1993.
———. "The Rhythm of Irony." *Cincinnati Romance Review* 20 (1996): 9.
Contat, Michel, ed. *L'auteur et le manuscrit*. Paris: P.U.F., 1991.
Cuddon, J. A. *A Dictionary of Literary Terms*. New York: Doubleday, 1977.
Dällenbach, Lucien. *Le récit spéculaire: essai sur la mise en abyme*. Paris: Seuil, 1977. Translated by Jeremy Whitley, with Emma Hughes, as *The Mirror in the Text* (Chicago: University of Chicago Press, 1989).
Davreu, Robert. *Jacques Roubaud: poète d'aujourd'hui*. Paris: Seghers, 1985.
De Ferrari, Guillermina. "Representing Absence: The Power of Metafiction in Jacques Roubaud's *Le Grand Incendie de Londres*." *Symposium* 49.4 (1996): 262-73.
Delignon, Bruno. "Jeux de pistes dans *La Belle Hortense*." *La Licorne* 40 (1997): 59-63.
Derrida, Jacques. *La dissémination*. Paris: Seuil, 1972.
———. *L'écriture et la différence*. Paris: Seuil, 1967.
———. *Feu la cendre*. Paris: Des Femmes, 1987.
Desnos, Robert. *Corps et bien*. Paris: Gallimard, 1953.
Dobzynski, Charles. "Légendes noires: André Frénaud, Jacques Roubaud." *Europe* 64.692 (1986): 190-95.
Dupriez, Bernard. *Gradus: les procédés littéraires*. Paris: UGE, 1984.
Edwards, Michael. "After a Death." *Times Literary Supplement* 4356 (September 26, 1986): 1050.
Forest, Philippe. *Histoire de Tel Quel, 1960-1982*. Paris: Seuil, 1995.
Foucault, Michel. *The Foucault Reader*. Ed. Paul Rabinow. London: Penguin, 1984.
Fournel, Paul. *Clefs pour la littérature potentielle*. Paris: Denoël, 1972.
Gavronsky, Serge, trans. and ed. *Toward a New Poetics*. Berkeley: University of California Press, 1994.

Guéron, Jacqueline. "Jacques Roubaud." *Littérature de notre temps* 5 (1974): 229-31.
———. "Jacques Roubaud: Analyse d'un discours et d'un poème." *Critique* 310 (1973): 255-84.
———. "Lecture de Jacques Roubaud." *Critique* 26 (1970): 724-740.
Hejinian, Lyn. *My Life.* Los Angeles: Sun & Moon Press, 1987.
———. *My Life in the Nineties.* New York: Shark Books, 2003.
Hutcheon, Linda. *Narcissistic Narrative: The Metafictional Paradox.* New York: Routledge, 1990.
Ireland, Susan. "The Comic World of Jacques Roubaud." *L'Esprit Créateur* 31.4 (1991): 22-31.
———. "Jacques Roubaud." In *The Contemporary Novel in France.* Ed. William Thompson. Gainesville: University Press of Florida, 1995.
Johnson, Barbara. *Défigurations du langage poétique.* Paris: Flammarion, 1979.
Jouet, Jacques. *107 Âmes.* Paris: Seghers, 1990.
———. *Fins.* Paris: P.O.L., 1999.
———. *Raymond Queneau.* Lyon: La Manufacture, 1988.
Kant, Immanuel. *Critique of Judgement.* Trans. Werner S. Pluhar. Cambridge: Hackett, 1987.
Kellman, Stephen G. *The Self-Begetting Novel.* New York: Columbia University Press, 1980.
Kendrick, Laura. *The Game of Love: Troubadour Wordplay.* Berkeley: University of California Press, 1988.
Kristeva, Julia. *La révolution du langage poétique.* Paris: Seuil, 1974.
———. *Sèméiotikè: recherche pour une sémanalyse.* Paris: Seuil, 1969.
Lartigue, Pierre. *L'hélice d'écrire: la sextine.* Paris: Les Belles Lettres, 1994.
Laskowski-Caujolle, Elvira Monika. *Die Macht der Vier – Von der pythagoreischen Zahl zum modernen mathematischen Strukturbegriff in Jacques Roubauds oulipotischer Erzählung 'La Princesse Hoppy ou le conte du Labrador.'* Frankfurt: Peter Lang Verlag, 1999.
———. "Die Macht der Vier. Literatur als angewandte Mathematik." *DMV Mitteilungen der Deutschen Mathematiker-Vereinigung* 4 (1999): 24-28.
———. "Jacques Roubaud: Literature, Mathematics and the Quest for Truth." *SubStance* 96 (2001): 71-87.
———. "Roubaud's *Destruction*: A Mathematician's Prose." In *Casebook on Jacques Roubaud's Great Fire of London.* Ed., Peter Consenstein. Normal, Ill.: Dalkey Archive, 2002. http://www.centerforbookculture.org/casebooks/casebook_london/introduction_london.html (9/1/2004).
Laskowski-Caujolle, Elvira Monika, and Jean-Jacques Poucel. "Descriptions de 'Tombeaux de Pétrarque.'" *Lendemain*, 124 (2006): 21-45.
Lavault, Elisabeth. *Jacques Roubaud: Contrainte et mémoire dans les romans d'Hortense.* Dijon: Editions Universitaires de Dijon, 2004.
Lawner, Lynne. "Notes toward an Interpretation of the *vers de dreyt nien*." *Cultura Neolatina* 28 (1968): 147-64.
Lewis, David. *On the Plurality of Worlds.* London: Blackwell, 1986.
Loewe, Siegfried. "Jacques Roubaud: le cycle labyrinthique des *Hortense*." In *Oulipo-poétiques: actes du colloque de Salzburg, 23-25 avril 1997.* Ed. Peter Kuon. Tübingen: Narr, 1999.
Lyotard, Jean-François. *The Postmodern Condition: A Report on Knowledge.* Trans. Geoff Bennington and Brian Massumi. Minneapolis: University of Minnesota Press, 1984.
Mallarmé, Stéphane. *Oeuvres.* Paris: Garnier, 1985.
Miner, Earl. *Japanese Linked Poetry.* Princeton: Princeton University Press, 1979.

Moncond'hui, Dominique. "Description d'un projet de lecture de Jacques Roubaud." *La Licorne* 40 (1997): 115-56.
———. "Qu'est-ce qu'un tombeau poétique." *La Licorne* 29 (1994): 3-16.
Montémont, Véronique. *Jacques Roubaud: l'Amour du nombre*. Lille: Presses Universitaires du Septentrion, 2004.
Motte, Warren. "Burroughs Takes a Chance." *Michigan Romance Studies* 14 (1994): 203-23.
———. *The Poetics of Experiment: A Study of the Work of Georges Perec*. Lexington: French Forum, 1984.
———. "Raymond Queneau and the Aesthetic of Formal Constraint." *Romantic Review* 82.2 (1991): 193-209.
———. *Small Worlds: Minimalism in Contemporary French Literature*. Lincoln: University of Nebraska Press, 1999.
———, trans. and ed. *Oulipo: A Primer of Potential Literature*. Lincoln: University of Nebraska Press, 1986. 2nd ed. Normal, Ill.: Dalkey Archive Press, 1998.
Oulipo. *Atlas de littérature potentielle*. Paris: Gallimard, 1981.
———. *La bibliothèque oulipienne. Vol. 1*. Paris: Seghers, 1990.
———. *La bibliothèque oulipienne. Vol. 2*. Paris: Seghers, 1990.
———. *La bibliothèque oulipienne. Vol. 3*. Paris: Seghers, 1990.
———. *La littérature potentielle*. Paris: Gallimard, 1973.
———. *Moments oulipiens*. Paris: Le Castor Astral, 2004.
Perec, Georges. *Cahiers des charges de la vie, mode d'emploi*. Ed. Hans Hartje, Bernard Magné, and Jacques Neffs. Paris: Zulma, 1993.
———. "*53 jours*." Ed. Harry Matthews and Jacques Roubaud. Paris: Gallimard, 1989.
———. *La disparition*. Paris: Denoël, 1969.
———. "Quatre figures pour *La vie mode d'emploi*." *L'Arc* 76 (1979): 50-53.
———. *La vie mode d'emploi*. Paris: Hachette, 1978.
———. *W ou souvenir d'enfance*. Paris: Denoël, 1975.
Perloff, Marjorie. *Radical Artifice*. Chicago: University of Chicago Press, 1991.
Petrarch, Francesco. *Petrarch's Lyric Poems*. Trans. and ed. Robert M. Durling. Cambridge: Harvard University Press, 1976.
Poucel, Jean-Jacques. "Jacques Roubaud's Intersections." *Sites* 7.2 (2003): 208-28.
———. "Reciting from Memory: *Destruction* in Roubaud's *The Great Fire of London*." In *The Great Fire of London Casebook*. Ed. Peter Consenstein. Normal, Ill.: Dalkey Archive Press, 2003: http://www.centerforbookculture.org/case books/casebook_london/poucel.html (9/1/2004).
———. "The Work of Mourning in Jacques Roubaud's *Quelque chose noir*." *Revista Brasileira de Sociologia da Emoção* 1.2 (2002): 206-26.
Prince, Gerald. *Narrative as Theme*. Lincoln: University of Nebraska Press, 1992.
Queneau, Raymond. *Bâtons, chiffres, et lettres*. 1950. Rev. ed. Paris: Gallimard, 1965.
———. *Cent mille milliards de poèmes*. Paris: Gallimard, 1961.
———. "Interviews with Georges Charbonnier–No. 5." Trans. Mary Campbell-Sposito. *Review of Contemporary Fiction* 17.3 (1997): 22-26.
———. *Pierrot mon ami*. Paris: Gallimard, 1943.
Rannoux, Catherine. "*La belle Hortense* de Jacques Roubaud: contes et décomptes." *La Licorne* 40 (1997): 65-75.
Roche, Anne. "Mémoire, deuil et intertexte dans *La boucle* de Jacques Roubaud." *Tangence* 45 (1994): 82.
Roche, Denis. *La poésie est inadmissible*. Paris: Seuil, 1995.
Rodd, Laurel Rasplica, trans. *Kokinshu: A Collection of Poems Ancient and Modern*. Boston: Cheng & Tsui, 1996.

Rosello, Mireille. "Jacques Roubaud: *Quelque chose noir.*" *French Review* 60 (1986): 914-15.
Roubaud, Alix Cléo. *Journal, 1979-1983.* Paris: Seuil, 1984.
Ruppert, S. "La quadrature du cercle: etude de *Renga*, d'Octavio Paz, Jacques Roubaud, Charles Tomlinson et Edouardo Sanguineti: d'une langue l'autre." *Textuel* 32 (1997): 97-111.
Sacks, Peter M. *The English Elegy: Studies in the Genre from Spenser to Yeats.* Baltimore: Johns Hopkins University Press, 1985.
Samoyault, Tiphaine. "Autobiographie, chapitre trois: archétypes de la totalité et formes de la totalisation dans *Mathématique.*" *La Licorne* 40 (1997): 101-14.
Savigneau, Josyane. "*Quelque chose noir*: la mort, la poésie." *Le Monde* 1970 (31 July-6 August 1986): 11.
Scheypen, Uwe. "Six petites pièces logiques." *Lendemain* 109 (2003): 59-69.
Smock, Ann. "Cloudy Roubaud." *Representations* 86 (2004): 141-74.
Taylor, John. "Reading Jacques Roubaud." *Context, A Forum for Literary Arts and Culture* 2 (2000): 4-5.
Thomas, Jean-Jacques. "Amstramtram, pic et pic et hypogrammes." *Lendemain* 109 (2003): 15-58.
———. "Chances Aren't: Roubaud's Numerical Poe-tricks." *SubStance* 23-24 (1979): 177-91.
———. "Lecture/montage/espace." *Stanford French Review* 6.1 (1982): 87-100.
———. "README.DOC: On Oulipo." *SubStance* 56 (1988): 18-28.
———. "Swing Troubadour: Roubaud's Self-portrait." In *The Great Fire of London Casebook.* Ed. Peter Consenstein. Normal, Ill.: Dalkey Archive Press, 2003. <http://www.centerforbookculture.org/casebooks/casebook_london/thomas.html> (9/1/2004).
Tzara, Tristan. *L'homme approximatif.* Paris: Foucard, 1931.
Vuillemin, Alain, and Michel Lenoble, eds. *Littérature et informatique: la littérature générée par ordinateur.* Arras: Presses Universitaires d'Artois, 1995.
Wagneur, Jean-Didier. "Roubaud entre texte et hypertexte." *Nouvelle Revue Française* 537 (1997): 107-14.
Warren, F. M. "The Troubadour *Canso* and Latin Poetry." *Modern Philology* 9 (1912): 469-87.
Watt, Ian. *The Rise of the Novel.* London: Chatto and Windus, 1957.
Wilson, Edmund, "Who Cares Who Killed Roger Ackroyd?" In *Detective Fiction: A Collection of Critical Essays.* Ed. Robin W. Winks. Englewood Cliffs: Prentice-Hall, 1980.
Wimmer, Manfred. "Go." In *Discover Japan: Words, Customs and Concepts.* New York: Kodansha International, 1987.
Wittgenstein, Ludwig. *Philosophical Investigations.* Trans. G. E. M. Anscombe. Oxford: Blackwell, 1953, 1958.
Yates, Frances. *The Art of Memory.* Chicago: University of Chicago Press, 1966.
Zukofsky, Louis. *"A" 1-12.* London: Lowe and Brydone, 1966.
———. *Complete Short Poetry.* Baltimore: Johns Hopkins University Press, 1991.
Zumthor, Paul. *Essai de poétique médiévale.* Paris: Seuil, 1972.

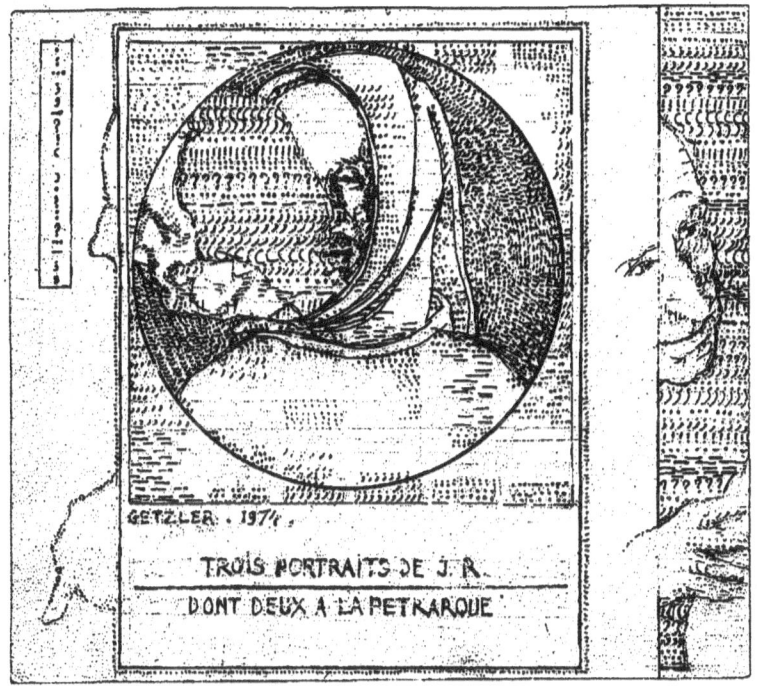

Pierre Getzler, "Trois portraits de J. R. dont deux à la Pétrarque," 1974. Variant of frontispiece published in / Tombeaux de Pétrarque / (Solaire, 1975). Reproduced with permission of the artist.

TOMBEAUX DE PÉTRARQUE

by Jacques Roubaud

cobla I

Ou le soleil mange les étoiles dans l'aube
ou dans la neige tes cheveux prendront rive
comme les vents aux fleuves liés de glace
si des écueils   but amer de ma voile
une lumière   de collines   entre branches
m'écarte neuf   j'aborde au cours d'un bois
contre la lune   dans tes bois c'est le soir
pas une fleur   que la trame   de ces notes
poisse les nuits comme rimes   à la mort

cobla II

Poisse des fleurs   ou dans le style joyeux
si la forêt   d'un seul jour sur la terre
s'éveille force   de ces vers qui voient l'air
vibrer des yeux   s'emplir d'années-laurier
qu'ainsi la pente   (la nuit jette les eaux
à ces vallées   soit de pluie soit de brume)
partout légère   (c'est le prix de ce lieu
nommé le port mais sans navires) : la vie
la nôtre Temps du ciel gavé de feuilles

cobla III

Dans ces collines   montre le temps aux feuilles
qui sont ses rimes   ses pleurs   je suis joyeux
d'avoir son but   le port   car toute vie
aussi d'étoiles   en forêts de la terre
espère un cours   et légère où son lieu
lavé de flamme   prend sa force   depuis l'air
criant les fleuves   toutes vallées sont brume
où tes cheveux   ont les yeux du laurier
il sert les bois   par la pente   de ses eaux

cobla IV

Découpe la nuit   là des soirs de la lune
devant le ciel   là branches dans sa lumière
durant des années   une rive sous la neige
si c'est ton style   mais de mort liées nuits
balaie de pluie   ou glaces sifflant de vents
ou de navires   crevées voiles sur écueils
dépêtre tes vers   notes sonnant soient fleurs
vautrées au jour   depuis l'aube couvre terre
qui seule a prix telle entre en bois neuf

cobla V

Partout légère   c'est le prix qu'ici neuf
paya la pente   une nuit sous la lune
quand la forêt   d'un vrai jour fit soleil
le notre temps   borde ciel   toi lumière
asservie force   qui va vers   gommés fleurs
compte tes yeux   pour d'autres années la neige
l'évide port   en navires où d'écueils
s'effrite pleurs   est-ce un style st les nuits
cédées vallées   qui disent pluie les vents

cobla VI

Car la glace la broie   brume en maint fleuve
que précoce bois sans lieu qui n'a plus cours
bâilleuse mort   d'un poing joyeux sans rimes
retire au soir   et les eaux restent bois
outrés de voile   ma vie presque le but
interne l'aube   fait que terre fait qu'étoiles
vues de la rive   au laurier sans cheveux
ensablent branches   feuilles de ces collines
ferrées de notes   et l'air où elle rame

cobla VII

Entends mes vers   ils ont note mais pas âme
comment la pluie   gratte glace sur les fleuves
ou bien le ciel   paît branches en des collines
et fait le prix   d'un bois où n'a plus cours
après année   la rive des verts cheveux
j'en fais mon style   mort à moitié de rimes
je happe jour   freine aube jusqu'en étoiles
frappant la nuit   arrime soir des bois
de tes navires   la voile qui n'a de but

cobla VIII

Brillons la vie   et sans écueils au port
cumulons l'air et les fleurs dans la force
des longues eaux   une lune suit la pente
pliant la brume   ni les vents aux vallées
pas plus la terre   qu'un soleil prés forêt
signe de feuilles   ni la lumière sans temps
ni moins joyeux   pour ces nuits de cent fleurs
ton rare lieu   rouvert neuf pour légère
t'entrer laurier   frottée de neige sans yeux

cobla IX

Jamais la rive   ni le laurier n'a d'yeux
que pour la voile   reprenant vie au port
n'aura de bois   en ce lieu que légère
table de notes   en tuyaux d'air à force
d'être la mort   la mort aux joyeux pleurs
coudra de soir   muet d'eaux nues en pente
et si branches plongent feuilles de temps
sortent glace   si la brume des vallées
tranche l'aube   si la terre tremble forets

X *tornada*

Si la terre   bouclier d'étoiles de neige
mange tes yeux   que la pluie que la glace
arme ma vie   il y aura ce but
épais joyeux   peut-être nuits tes rimes
d'ici la mort.

INDEX

absence, 178, 193, 194, 195, 197-98, 244
Abstract Rhythm Theory (ART), 13-14, 34-36, 34n6, 37, 39, 42, 62
alexandrine, 34n6, 134n11, 152, 153-54, 202
amors. See fin'amors
anthologies, Japanese imperial, 110, 111n17, 121, 125-27, 125n6, 129. *See also* Japanese poetry; *Les troubadours; Manyoshu; Shinkokinshu*
Apollinaire, Guillaume, 156
apostrophe, 191-94, 196-98, 246
Aragon, Louis, and *Feu de joie,* 167
arborescent images, 127n7, 227
Aristotle, 162
Arthurian romance, 37, 127n7, 227, 231, 246
"Aujourd'hui est blanc" (Roubaud), 138
Autobiographie, chapitre dix (Roubaud), 15, 148-51, 153, 155, 157-66, 170-73
autobiography, 235-37, 239, 240, 242, 247, 251
avant-garde, 153, 155, 172, 248
axiom, 12, 36-39, 41, 45-46, 51, 55, 57, 63, 85, 105, 109, 114, 116, 201, 227, 237-38

"B.Y. Trois ou dix-neuf poèmes" (Roubaud), 113
Bakhtin, Mikhail, 203
Barth, John, 202, 203
Barthes, Roland, 118, 203, 214; and *Essais critiques,* 201

Bartlebooth, Percival, 219-20, 250-52. *See also* Perec, Georges, and *La vie mode d'emploi*
Baudelaire, Charles, 79, 95n7, 152, 213; and *Spleen de Paris,* 151
Bec, Pierre, 24
Bens, Jacques, 166n20
Berrigan, Ted, 95n7
Blanchot, Maurice, and *L'entretien infini,* 139-40
Blognard, 206, 207, 208, 212, 215
Bloom, Harold, 156n9
Bosquet, Alain, 136, 174n3; and "La poésie et ses techniques," 124, 135
Bourbaki, Nicolas, 12, 38, 114, 130n8
Breton, André, 155, 156; and *Revolver aux cheveaux blancs,* 166
Burroughs, William, 168

caesura, 130n8, 151, 169
Cage, John, 168, 168n24
Calvino, Italo, 199
canso, 24, 28, 30, 31, 33, 34, 36, 39, 40, 42, 43, 44, 47, 48, 49, 50-51, 53, 56, 57, 58, 74, 84, 87, 128, 131, 146, 207; and *canzone,* 31, 56
Carcasonne, 28
Cardenal, Peire, 56
Cardonne-Arlyck, Elizabeth, 234, 245
Carroll, Lewis, 105
Cavalcanti, Guido, 24, 31, 95n7
Cendrars, Blaise, 95n7, 156, 163, 171; and *Dix-neuf poèmes élastiques,* 168
cento, 148, 158
Cervantes, Miguel de, and *Don Quixote,* 204

Change, 168n22
Churchill 40 (Roubaud), 25
clinamen, 74, 74n14, 83n20, 134n11, 234n14
closure, 249-50
cobla, 56, 57, 82, 89
cobla capcaudée, 77, 85, 128
Conort, Benoît, 177n6
Conrad, Joseph, 216
Consenstein, Peter, 119, 128, 133-35, 134n11; and "The Rhythm of Irony," 103
constraints, in writing, 51, 59, 62, 63, 71, 73, 74n14, 75, 78-79, 81n18, 90, 92, 95, 97, 101-3, 111, 111n17, 127n7, 149-50, 156n9, 219, 223, 224n4, 225, 234, 240, 246, 248, 249, 251; numerical, 133, 135, 200; and Oulipian theory, 14-15, 22, 65, 69-70, 94, 116-17, 154-55, 241; and *Trente et un au cube,* 118-22, 123, 131, 134n11, 136, 143-44, 146
"Construction" (Roubaud), 170
counting. *See* number
Crusades, Albigensian, 56
crystal du trobar, 56, 58, 59, 233
crystallization, image of, 86, 90
Cuddon, J., and *A Dictionary of Literary Terms,* 79
cummings, e.e., 95n7

Dada, 58, 148, 152, 154, 163-64, 170, 172
Dällenbach, Lucien, 202
Daniel, Arnaut, 48-50, 55, 56, 59n2, 63, 72, 74, 76; and "Lo ferm voler q'el cor m'intra," 41, 43, 49-52, 54, 65, 208
"Dans cet arbre" (Roubaud), 198
"Dans une pause abstraite" (Roubaud), 138
Dante Alighieri, 95n7, 24, 31, 48, 59n2, 88n21; and *Inferno,* 179, 210; and *Pexa et hirsuta,* 192
De Ferrari, Guillermina, 223n3, 234, 234n14, 237
"De mes oiseaux" (Roubaud), 165
de Montanhagol, Guilhem, 57
de Peguilhan, Aimeric, 42; and "tenzos de non res," 52
de Sisteron, Alberet, and "tenzos de non res," 52
de Ventadour, Bernart, and "Non es mervalha s'eu chan," 44-45

death, as theme, 88, 175, 180, 184, 186, 197, 250
Derrida, Jacques, 239
Description du Projet. See Mezura 9: Description du projet
Desnos, Robert, and "Rrose Sélavy," 166
Destruction (Roubaud), 224. *See also 'le grand incendie de Londres'*
Diderot, Denis, and *Jacques le fataliste,* 204
"Dire la poésie" (Roubaud), 65
dona, 37-38, 44, 53
Dors (book) (Roubaud), 65-67, 66n8; "Dors" (poem) (Roubaud), 65-66, 66n8
Duchamp, Marcel, 166
Dumas, Alexandre, 167, 216
Dupriez, Bernard, and *Gradus,* 79

$\in$ *(signe d'appartenance)* (Roubaud), 15, 25, 92-98, 100-103, 105-6, 109, 109n16, 111, 113, 114, 116-17, 156, 175, 244, 249
elegy, 178-79, 181-84, 187, 190, 197, 198. *See also Quelque chose noir*
Eluard, Paul, and *Les nécessités de la vie et les conséquences des rêves,* 165
engo. See Japanese poetry
entrebescar, 46-48, 54, 79; as aesthetic, 47, 51, 59, 65, 84-85, 127n7; and *entrelacement,* 85, 227, 245
envoi, 64, 71, 179, 190; and *tornada,* 86
estramp. *See* poetry, rimes estramps
estribot poetry, 42, 52-53, 61, 82, 84
Etoffe (Roubaud), 148n1
Eusèbe, 212-13
Evêque d'Angoulème, 29

failure, rhetoric of, 220, 222, 251
Faye, Jean-Pierre, 168n22
fin'amors, 23-24, 30, 34, 37, 41, 45-47, 46n7, 52-54, 56, 57, 59n2, 63, 83n20, 87, 217, 245
Foucault, Michel, 203, 217
Frank, Istvan, and *Répertoire métrique des troubadours,* 39
free verse. *See* poetry, *vers libre*

games, chess, 105, 110; Go (Japanese board game), 104-12, 106n15, 115-17; language, 14-16, 36, 51-53, 84, 85, 93, 96, 102, 108, 114, 120, 141, 145, 146-47, 162, 182, 187, 190, 202, 213, 233
Gleize, Jean-Marie, 58

INDEX 283

Góngora, Luis de, 95n7
Graal fiction (Roubaud), 227
Graal théâtre (Roubaud), 227
grand chant, the. *See le grand chant*
Great Fire of London. *See 'le grand incendie de Londres'*
Guéron, Jacqueline, 99; and "Lecture de Jacques Roubaud," 103-4
Guillaume IX, 25, 29, 43; and "Faray un vers de dreit nien," 52, 84

haiku. See Japanese poetry
Hejinian, Lyn, and *My Life*, 160
Homer, and *Iliad*, 202; and *Odyssey*, 202
Hopkins, Gerard Manley, 95n7
Hortense (character), 199, 210, 212n19, 216, 217
Hortense novels, 25, 59, 150n4, 205-6, 208, 210, 211, 214, 214n20, 224. *See also La belle Hortense, L'enlèvement d'Hortense, L'exil d'Hortense*
Hugo, Victor, 152, 216
Hutcheon, Linda, and *Narcissistic Narrative*, 203

improvisation, 163
incompletion, 113, 117, 224n6
innovation, in writing, 38, 40, 201, 248, 251
interruption, use of in poetry, 139-40
intertextuality, 24, 32, 46, 47, 51, 124, 128, 129, 130n8, 205, 210, 227
intratextuality, 103, 134n11, 240
Ireland, Susan, 204
irony, 192n10, 204, 216. *See also* parody

J'arrange le blanc (Roubaud), 138
Jacques le fataliste, 163
Jakobson, Roman, 13
Japanese poetry, 22; and *engo*, 127-29; and *haiku*, 69-70, 72, 79, 86, 121, 124-25, 127; and *kake kotoba*, 127-28; and *ko*, 106-9, 116; and *kokoro* (heart), 123-24; and *kotoba* (words), 123-24; and *makura kotoba*, 127-29; and *renga*, 121, 127; and *tanka*, 118, 120, 123, 124-27, 130, 130n8, 131, 132, 138, 146. *See also* anthologies, Japanese imperial
Je vais me détourner (Roubaud), 191
Jouet, Jacques, 156n9, 199
jouissance, 85, 87, 88, 89

Jouve, Pierre Jean, 95n7
Joyce, James, and *Ulysses*, 201; and *Finnegans Wake*, 201

Kafka, Franz, and *Amerika*, 103
Kamo no Chomei, 230n12; and *Ten Foot Square Hut and Tales of the Heike*, 157n10
Kant, Immanuel, 111
Kellman, Stephen G., and *The Self-Begetting Novel*, 223n3
ko. See Japanese poetry
kokoro. See Japanese poetry
kotoba. See Japanese poetry

L'enlèvement d'Hortense (Roubaud), 199, 208, 214
L'exil d'Hortense (Roubaud), 199
"L'histoire n'a pas de souvenirs" (Roubaud), 186
L'invention du fils de Leprepes (Roubaud), 22
La belle Hortense (Roubaud), 15, 199, 200, 204-8, 105n12, 210-12, 217, 249
La bibliothèque de Warburg (Roubaud), 101n10, 127n7, 224, 229n11, 235, 250
"La bouche est double" (Roubaud), 145-46
La boucle (Roubaud), 50, 90, 127n7, 224, 232, 235, 245, 250
La fleur inverse (Roubaud), 17, 21, 24, 25-26, 28, 29-31, 33, 34, 36, 41, 42, 58-59, 61, 66, 84, 89, 90, 232, 246
"La menthe poussait" (Roubaud), 125
"La piste du vent" (Roubaud), 65
La pluralité des mondes de Lewis (Roubaud), 189n9
La vieillesse d'Alexandre (Roubaud), 17, 22, 34n6, 57n1, 153, 153n7, 155, 158, 170
Lancelot en prose (Roubaud), 246
Lartigue, Pierre, 69; and *L'hélice d'écrire*, 68
Lautréamont, Comte de, and *Chants de Maldoror*, 151
Lawner, Lynne, 45, 52
le grand chant (the grand chant), 24, 27, 28, 30, 32-33, 36-37, 41-44, 46, 47, 48, 53, 56, 65, 68, 80, 87, 245
'le grand incendie de Londres' (Roubaud), 15, 16, 25, 59, 127n7, 150n4, 157, 173, 178, 220-24, 223n3, 226, 228, 229n11, 231, 232n13, 233, 234-

235-36, 239-40, 242-44, 246-47, 249, 250-51; and *Le Grand Incendie de Londres* (Roubaud), 221-22, 225, 228, 229n12, 231, 233, 235, 237, 243, 245
Le Lionnais, François, 12, 35, 91, 92, 131, 131n9, 155
Le "Manyoshu" et la première poésie lyrique japonaise (Roubaud), 122
Leiris, Michel, 155
Lentino, Giacomo da, 95n7
"Les mois: un poème de douze vers" (Roubaud), 171
Les troubadours (Roubaud), 21, 26
Lewis, David, 189n9
linking techniques, 40, 98, 127-28, 131, 146. *See also* Japanese poetry, and *engo*
ludics, poetic, 15, 24, 53, 70, 79, 114, 146, 155, 200
Lusson, Pierre, 13, 34n6, 110-11, 241
Lyotard, Jean-François, 246-47

Mallarmé, Stéphane, 11, 70, 79, 81, 152, 153, 201, 226; and "Crise de vers," 53-54; and *Divagations,* 151; and "Le vierge, le vivace, le bel aujourd'hui," 69
Manyoshu, 111n17, 125
Marcabru, 46, 46n7, 48; and *Vita breve*, 162
Marti, Bernart, and "Bel m'es lai latz fontana," 46-47, 145
mathematics, 22, 90, 103-5, 114-15, 119, 149n3, 156, 199, 200, 206; and Oulipian theory, 35, 69; and poetry, 11-13, 35, 44, 67, 81n18, 98, 131-32, 135, 175, 210
Mathématique: (récit) (Roubaud), 127n7, 224, 235, 250
Mathews, Harry, 199
"Méditation de l'indistinction, de l'hérésie" (Roubaud), 188
"Méditation du 12/5/85" (Roubaud), 180, 182
memory, 29, 40, 54, 57n1, 94, 143-44, 172-73, 175, 227-28, 229n11, 231-35, 232n13, 237, 243-45, 247, 248, 249, 251, 252; and language, 12-17, 22, 94, 99, 119, 127n7, 128-29, 227; and nostalgia, 26, 30; and poetry, 25-27, 29-31, 38, 41, 48-49, 51, 56-63, 65-66, 85, 108, 118, 122, 128, 152, 156, 164-65, 184, 190, 221, 224n6

metanarrative, 162, 203, 214, 216, 217, 229, 238
mezura. *See* poetry
Mezura 9: Description du projet (Roubaud), 11, 12, 14-15, 17, 25, 67, 92, 97, 99, 113, 117, 118, 127, 150, 173, 221, 226, 228, 232n13, 233-36, 238-39, 242, 251; and conception of, 93, 94, 101, 131, 221-22, 231; and failure of, 17, 59, 220, 230, 236, 243, 245, 250-51; and gaming, 16, 17, 116
Milton, John, and *Lycidas,* 179
Miner, Earl, and *An Introduction to Japanese Court Poetry*, 122-27
mode d'emploi (user's manual), 16, 65, 92, 98, 99, 104, 116, 136
modernism, 23, 25
Mono no aware: Le sentiment des choses (cent quarante-trois poèmes empruntés au japonais) (Roubaud), 122
Mornacier, 207, 208, 214-15
Morphismes rationnels et algébriques dans les types d'A-algèbres discrètes à une dimension (Roubaud), 114
Motte, Warren, 105, 154
mourning, 101n10, 182, 183, 189, 196, 198, 244, 245-46, 248-49

Narcissus, 203
"Nécessités et conséquences" (Roubaud), 165
"Neuf éclats d'âge des saints" (Roubaud), 65
Nicolas of Cusa (Cardinal), 52
ninetina, 55, 64, 68, 70, 71, 72, 74, 77, 80, 82, 88. *See also* quenine
"Nonvie, I-IV" (Roubaud), 193
nothingness, 32, 42-44, 51, 53, 100, 117, 189, 190
novel, self-begetting, 223n3, 238, 240, 243
"Noyade" (Roubaud), 103
numbers, and counting, 12, 35, 119-20, 134, 137, 140, 141, 144, 157, 235; and pet numbers, 131; and prime numbers, 131-32, 146, 171; and Queneau, 63n5, 132n9, 149, 206n14; and series, 12, 131, 224

Occitan language. *See* Provencal language
Occitan poetry. *See* Provencal poetry
octine, 81n18. *See also* quenine

"Or dans ce jardin" (Roubaud), 125
Orwells, Philibert, 212
"Où vivions nous?" (Roubaud), 138, 141, 144, 146
Oulipo, 11-12, 19, 55, 63, 91-92, 94, 149, 199-200, 204, 212, 214n20, 218, 226, 248, 251; Oulipian theory, 14-17, 22, 24, 35-36, 55, 60, 63n5, 65, 69, 70, 92-94, 103, 115-17, 119, 121, 134n11, 154-56, 156n9, 158, 165, 165n18, 167, 204, 227, 234, 241
Ovid, 203

palindrome, 222, 222n2,
parataxis. *See* poetry
parody, 164, 166, 166n20, 172, 203, 204, 206, 208, 212, 213, 217
Paz, Octavio, 12
Perec, Georges, 92, 94, 103, 110-11, 199, 210, 251; and *La disparition*, 200; and *La vie mode d'emploi*, 211, 219-20, 250; and *W ou le souvenir d'enfance*, 165
permutations, in rhyme series, 73, 75-78, 85
Petrarch, Francesco, 24, 31, 55, 56, 68, 70, 70n13, 80, 89, 90, 128; and *Canzoniere*, 60, 63, 65, 67, 68, 69, 70n13, 72, 73-75, 79-80, 86, 89, 97, 97n8; and "In morte di M. Laura," 88, and *Rime sparse*, 67, 71, 74, 75-76, 76n15, 78, 80, 84, 88, 172
"Pexa et hirsuta" (Roubaud), 192
plagiarism, 151, 154, 158, 215, 248
Plato, 162
"Poème de présentation composé pour une lecture de *Trente et un au cube* à Shakespeare et C" (Roubaud), 136
Poésie, contemporaine extrême (Roubaud), 60, 159
Poésie, etcetera: ménage (Roubaud), 17, 22, 29, 61, 249
Poésie: (récit) (Roubaud), 92, 127n7, 224, 229n11, 232, 235
poetry, fixed-form, 92, 93, 199, 207; memorization of, 59, 65; *mezura*, 43, 52; mnemonic aspects of, 13, 32, 41, 48, 85, 211, 238; parataxis, 83; *repos* (rest), 151, 152; rhyme, use of, 32, 39, 41, 49, 71, 74, 75, 76, 77, 78, 80, 85, 87, 89, 94, 101, 108, 152, 210, 229; rhythm, use of, 13-14, 34-36, 41, 48, 66, 69n12, 79, 85, 103, 109n16, 118, 122, 130n8, 136-39, 144, 146, 150, 152-53, 197-98, 229, 230n12; rimes estramps, 49, 69; scansion, 152; spaces in, 136-39, 141, 153, 183, 187, 227; tercets, 94; *vers libre* (free verse), 57n1, 100, 101, 152, 153-55, 153n7, 160, 162, 169, 170; wordplay, 166-68. *See also estribot* poetry, Japanese poetry, prose poetry, Provencal poetry
"Portrait en méditation, III" (Roubaud), 184
postmodernism, 62, 243, 246-49
Pound, Ezra, 23
pretz, 55; axiom of, 38-39
Prince, Gerald, 238
"Prinsland" (Roubaud), 113
Projet. See Mezura 9: Description du projet. See also 'le grand incendie de Londres'
prose poetry, 95, 150-52
Provençal language, 27-31, 56; and Occitan language, 28, 31, 56
Provençal poetry, 21, 23, 26, 33, 38, 41, 122, 123, 128; and Occitan poetry, 21; and troubadour poetry, 21, 22-34, 36-39, 41, 43, 46, 48, 55-57, 79, 131, 156, 227, 245. *See also canso, fin'amors*

"Que voir? l'immobile" (Roubaud), 138
Quelque chose noir (Roubaud), 90, 174-79, 174n3, 182-83, 187-98, 189n9, 192n10, 244
Queneau, Raymond, 12, 35, 55, 63, 63n5, 67, 69-70, 72, 79, 80-81, 81n18, 86, 92-93, 131n9, 149n3, 154-56, 156n9, 200, 202-3, 205, 210-11; and *Bâtons, chiffres et lettres*, 81n18; and *Cent mille milliards de poèmes*, 91-92, 95, 97n8; and *Gueule de Pierre*, 199; and "Littérature potentielle," 35, 69; and *Le chiendent*, 199; and *Les derniers jours*, 199, 212; and *Morale élémentaire*, 162; and *Pierrot mon ami*, 205; and "Technique du roman," 149, 199; and *Un cadavre*, 155. *See also* numbers, and Queneau
quenine, 63-66, 63n5, 71-72, 74, 76, 77, 78, 81n18, 210, 211

Raimbaut d'Orange, 48, 50, 55, 61, 81; and "Ar resplan la flors enversa," 49, 51-52, 54, 65, 85, 89, 232
reader, and relationship to author's work, 38, 93, 98-99, 101, 112, 120, 136-37, 139-41, 145-46, 161, 194-95, 207, 212, 215, 229, 234, 235, 238, 239, 241, 251
"Récit du sureaux" (Roubaud), 125
Renaissance, 62
renga. See Japanese poetry
repos. See poetry
Reverdy, Pierre, 157
rhyme. *See* poetry
rhythm. *See* poetry
"Rien" (Roubaud), 179
Rilke, Rainer Maria, and *Duino Elegien*, 179
Rimbaud, Arthur, 95n7, 213; and *Les Illuminations*, 151; and *Une saison en enfer*, 151
rimes estramps. *See* poetry
Riquier, Guiraut, 57
Robinson Crusoe, 103
Roche, Anne, 242
Roche, Denis, 58, 155
Romanticism, 152, 154
"Rome hebdos" (Roubaud), 171
Roubaud, Alix Cléo, 174-78, 180-81, 183, 184-93, 192n10, 195-96, 222n2, 226, 243-46; and "Si quelque chose noir," 175, 177
Roubaud, Jacques. *See*
(Articles): Le *"Manyoshu" et la première poésie lyrique japonaise; Poésie, contemporaine extrême; Sur le Shin-kokinshu, huitième anthologie japonaise*
(Books): *Autobiographie, chapitre dix; Churchill 40; Destruction; Dors, précédé de Dire la poésie;* ∈ *(signe d'appartenance); Etoffe; Graal fiction; Graal théâtre; L'invention du fils de Leoprepes; L'enlèvement d'Hortense; L'exil d'Hortense; La belle Hortense; La bibliothèque de Warburg; La boucle; La fleur inverse; La pluralité des mondes de Lewis; La vieillesse d'Alexandre; Lancelot en prose; 'le grand incendie de Londres'; Les troubadours; Mathématique: (récit); Mezura 9: Description du projet; Mono no aware: Le sentiment des choses; Morphismes rationnels et algébriques dans les types d'A-algèbres discrètes à une dimension; Poésie, etcetera: ménage; Poésie: (récit); Quelque chose noir; Tombeaux de Pétrarque; Trente et un au cube*
(Poems): "Aujourd'hui est blanc" (in *Trente et un au cube*); "B.Y. Trois ou dix-neuf poèmes"; "Construction" (in *Autobiographie, chapitre dix*); "Dans cet arbre"; "Dans une pause abstraite" (in *Autobiographie, chapitre dix*); "De mes oiseaux" (in *Autobiographie, chapitre dix*); "Dire la poésie" (in *Dors, précédé de Dire la poésie*); "Dors"; "J'arrange le blanc" (in *Trente et un au cube*); "L'histoire n'a pas de souvenirs" (in *Quelque chose noir*); "La bouche est double" (in *Trente et un au cube*); "La menthe poussait"; "La piste du vent"; "Les mois: un poème de douze vers" (in *Autobiographie, chapitre dix*); "Méditation de l'indistinction, de l'hérésie" (in *Quelque chose noir*); "Méditation du 12/5/85" (in *Quelque chose noir*); "Nécessités et conséquences" (in *Autobiographie, chapitre dix*); "Neuf éclats d'âge des saints" (in *Dors*); "Nonvie, I-IV" (in *Quelque chose noir*); "Noya-de" (in ∈ *(signe d'appartenance)*); "Or dans ce jardin"; "Ou vivions nous?" (in *Trente et un au cube*); "Pexa et hirsuta" (in *Quelque chose noir*); "Poème de présentation composé pour une lecture de *Trente et un au cube* à Shakespeare et Cie"; "Portrait en méditation, III" (in *Quelque chose noir*); "Prinsland"; "Que voir? l'immobile" (in *Autobiographie, chapitre dix*); "Récit du sureaux" (in *Autobiographie, chapitre dix*); "Rien" (in *Quelque chose noir*); "Rome hebdos" (in *Autobiographie, chapitre dix*); "RVF 1-14"; "Sallèles"; "Une

année finit" (in *Trente et un au cube*); "Vient le repos tout" (in *Trente et un au cube*)
Roubaud, Jean René, 99, 101, 101n10, 244
Rudel, Jaufre, 43; and "Lanquand li jorn son lonc enmai," 52
"RVF 1-14" (Roubaud), 69n12

Sacks, Peter, and *The English Elegy*, 184
"Sallèles" (Roubaud), 113
Saussure, Ferdinand de, 12
scansion. *See* poetry
Scève, Maurice, and *Délie*, 97n8
sestina, 15, 31, 43, 49, 51, 55, 59, 59n2, 60, 62-64, 67, 69, 70, 72, 74-77, 79, 80, 88-89, 93, 207-8, 210, 212, 217, 233; and *sextine*, 66; and *sextine retrograde*, 71-72, 74-76, 78; and structure of, 25, 41, 50, 54, 71, 74, 211; and trobar, 56, 58, 59. *See also* quenine
set theory, 114, 115, 116. *See also* axiom; Bourbaki, Nicolas
Shinkokinshu, 111n17, 125, 127
Sicilian poets, 57
Sisteron, Albert, 42
Socrates, 17
song. *See* canso
sonnet, 15, 25, 31, 34, 34n6, 56, 57, 58, 59, 91-97, 99, 100, 102, 103, 106, 108, 112-17, 172, 230, 232, 236
spiral, 207-8, 210
Sterne, Laurence, and *Tristram Shandy*, 163, 204
Sur le Shinkokinshu, huitième anthologie japonaise (Roubaud), 122
Surrealism, 15, 34, 58, 100, 148, 149, 152, 154-55, 163, 165n18, 167, 170, 172, 248
syntagma, 138-39

tanka. *See* Japanese poetry
Tel Quel, 168, 168n22
tercets. *See* poetry
Thomas, Jean-Jacques, 103, 132-35, 145; and "Chances Aren't: Roubaud's Numerical Poe-tricks," 132
Thomson, John, 13, 118

Tombeaux de Pétrarque (Roubaud), 21, 25, 55, 59-60, 62-63, 65-71, 73, 74-81, 84-86, 88
tombeaux poétique, 178
tombeaux, 67, 79
tornada. *See* envoi
Trente et un au cube (Roubaud), 118-47, 131n9, 134n11
trobar clus, 41-44, 45-48, 46n7, 50-51, 53-55, 56, 60, 65, 76, 84, 85, 87, 90; and *motz clus*, 69
trobar leu, 41-44, 46, 51, 52, 53-54, 65, 76; and clarity, 44-45
trobar, 21, 23-30, 32-34, 36-44, 48, 49, 50, 52, 54-55, 57-59, 68, 80, 86, 123, 227, 231, 246. *See also trobar clus; trobar leu*
troubadour poetry. *See* Provencal poetry
troubadours, 23, 28, 33, 46, 79, 227
trouvères, 32, 41
Troyes, Chrétien de, and *Lancelot en prose*, 226
Tzara, Tristan, and *De nois oiseaux*, 165; and *L'homme approximatif*, 164

"Une année finit" (Roubaud), 126
unicity, 116, 170, 193; axiom of, 38
unity, 97, 98, 103, 130n8, 136, 230, 249; of poetic tradition, 22, 30
user's manual. *See mode d'emploi*

vers libre. *See* poetry
Vidal, Piere, 31
"Vient le repos tout" (Roubaud), 130n8
von Clausewitz, Carl, 150

Waddington, Conrad, 116
Watt, Ian, 202
Williams, William Carlos, 66n8
Winckler, Gaspard, 219. *See also* Perec, Georges, and *La vie mode d'emploi*
Wittgenstein, Ludwig, 60, 177n6, 245
World War II, 28, 29

Zola, Emile, 216
Zukofsky, Louis, 59n2, 66n8, 159, 160 n13, 161
Zumthor, Paul, 23, 33; and *mouvance*, 32

NORTH CAROLINA STUDIES IN THE ROMANCE LANGUAGES AND LITERATURES

I.S.B.N. Prefix 0-8078-

Recent Titles

THE CHARM OF CATASTROPHE: A STUDY OF RABELAIS'S *QUART LIVRE*, by Alice Fiola Berry. 2000. (No. 267). *-9271-8.*
PUERTO RICAN CULTURAL IDENTITY AND THE WORK OF LUIS RAFAEL SÁNCHEZ, by John Dimitri Perivolaris. 2000. (No. 268). *-9272-6.*
MANNERISM AND BAROQUE IN SEVENTEENTH-CENTURY FRENCH POETRY: THE EXAMPLE OF TRISTAN L'HERMITE, by James Crenshaw Shepard. 2001. (No. 269). *-9273-4.*
RECLAIMING THE BODY: MARÍA DE ZAYA'S EARLY MODERN FEMINISM, by Lisa Vollendorf. 2001. (No. 270). *-9274-2.*
FORGED GENEALOGIES: SAINT-JOHN PERSE'S CONVERSATIONS WITH CULTURE, by Carol Rigolot. 2001. (No. 271). *-9275-0.*
VISIONES DE ESTEREOSCOPIO (PARADIGMA DE HIBRIDACIÓN EN EL ARTE Y LA NARRATIVA DE LA VANGUARDIA ESPAÑOLA), por María Soledad Fernández Utrera. 2001. (No. 272). *-9276-9.*
TRANSPOSING ART INTO TEXTS IN FRENCH ROMANTIC LITERATURE, by Henry F. Majewski. 2002. (No. 273). *-9277-7.*
IMAGES IN MIND: LOVESICKNESS, SPANISH SENTIMENTAL FICTION AND *DON QUIJOTE*, by Robert Folger. 2002. (No. 274). *-9278-5.*
INDISCERNIBLE COUNTERPARTS: THE INVENTION OF THE TEXT IN FRENCH CLASSICAL DRAMA, by Christopher Braider. 2002. (No. 275). *-9279-3.*
SAVAGE SIGHT/CONSTRUCTED NOISE. POETIC ADAPTATIONS OF PAINTERLY TECHNIQUES IN THE FRENCH AND AMERICAN AVANT-GARDES, by David LeHardy Sweet. 2003. (No. 276). *-9281-5.*
AN EARLY BOURGEOIS LITERATURE IN GOLDEN AGE SPAIN. *LAZARILLO DE TORMES, GUZMÁN DE ALFARACHE* AND BALTASAR GRACIÁN, by Francisco J. Sánchez. 2003. (No. 277). *-9280-7.*
METAFACT: ESSAYISTIC SCIENCE IN EIGHTEENTH-CENTURY FRANCE, by Lars O. Erickson. 2004. (No. 278). *-9282-3.*
THE INVENTION OF THE EYEWITNESS. A HISTORY OF TESTIMONY IN FRANCE, by Andrea Frisch. 2004. (No. 279). *-9283-1.*
SUBJECT TO CHANGE: THE LESSONS OF LATIN AMERICAN WOMEN'S *TESTIMONIO* FOR TRUTH, FICTION, AND THEORY, by Joanna R. Bartow. 2005. (No. 280). *-9284-X.*
QUESTIONING RACINIAN TRAGEDY, by John Campbell. 2005. (No. 281). *-9285-8.*
THE POLITICS OF FARCE IN CONTEMPORARY SPANISH AMERICAN THEATRE, by Priscilla Meléndez. 2006. (No. 282). *-9286-6.*
MODERATING MASCULINITY IN EARLY MODERN CULTURE, by Todd W. Reeser. 2006. (No. 283). *-9287-4.*
PORNOBOSCODIDASCALUS LATINUS (1624). KASPAR BARTH'S NEO-LATIN TRANSLATION OF *CELESTINA*, by Enrique Fernández. 2006. (No. 284). *-9288-2.*
JACQUES ROUBAUD AND THE INVENTION OF MEMORY, by Jean-Jacques F. Poucel. 2006. (No. 285). *-9289-0.*
THE "I" OF HISTORY. SELF-FASHIONING AND NATIONAL CONSCIOUSNESS IN JULES MICHELET, by Vivian Kogan. 2006. (No. 286). *-9290-4.*

When ordering please cite the *ISBN Prefix* plus the last four digits for each title.

Send orders to: University of North Carolina Press
P.O. Box 2288
Chapel Hill, NC 27515-2288
U.S.A.
www.uncpress.unc.edu
FAX: 919 966-3829

www.ingramcontent.com/pod-product-compliance
Lightning Source LLC
Chambersburg PA
CBHW030338240426
43661CB00052B/1666